A History of Early Childhood Education in Canada, Australia, and New Zealand

A History of Early Childhood Education in Canada, Australia, and New Zealand

Larry Prochner

UBCPress · Vancouver · Toronto

© UBC Press 2009

All rights reserved. No part of this publication may be reproduced, stored in a retrieval system, or transmitted, in any form or by any means, without prior written permission of the publisher, or, in Canada, in the case of photocopying or other reprographic copying, a licence from Access Copyright (Canadian Copyright Licensing Agency), www.accesscopyright.ca.

19 18 17 16 15 14 13 12 11 10 09   5 4 3 2 1

Printed in Canada with vegetable-based inks on paper that is processed chlorine- and acid-free.

Library and Archives Canada Cataloguing in Publication

Prochner, Laurence Wayne, 1956-
  History of early childhood education in Canada, Australia and New Zealand / Larry Prochner.

Includes bibliographical references and index.
ISBN 978-0-7748-1659-5 (bound)
ISBN 978-0-7748-1660-1 (pbk.)
ISBN 978-0-7748-1661-8 (e-book)

  1. Early childhood education—History. 2. Early childhood education—Canada—History. 3. Early childhood education—Australia—History. 4. Early childhood education—New Zealand—History. I. Title.

LB1139.23.P76 2009   372.21'09   C2009-901347-9

Canadä

UBC Press gratefully acknowledges the financial support for our publishing program of the Government of Canada through the Book Publishing Industry Development Program (BPIDP), and of the Canada Council for the Arts, and the British Columbia Arts Council.

This book has been published with the help of a grant from the Canadian Federation for the Humanities and Social Sciences, through the Aid to Scholarly Publications Programme, using funds provided by the Social Sciences and Humanities Research Council of Canada.

Printed and bound in Canada by Friesens
Set in Bembo and Meta by Artegraphica Design Co. Ltd.
Copy editor: Deborah Kerr
Indexer: Patricia Buchanan

UBC Press
The University of British Columbia
2029 West Mall
Vancouver, BC V6T 1Z2
604-822-5959 / Fax: 604-822-6083
www.ubcpress.ca

I dedicate this book to the pioneer directors of the kindergarten associations in Winnipeg, Sydney, and Wellington.

Contents

List of Illustrations / ix

Acknowledgments / xi

List of Abbreviations / xii

1 Childhood and Education / 1
2 Infant Schools in Britain / 12
3 Infant Schools in the Case-Study Countries / 42
4 Childcare and Daycare / 86
5 Kindergarten from Germany to England and America / 102
6 Kindergarten in the Case-Study Countries / 132
7 Winnipeg Free Kindergarten Association / 172
8 Kindergarten Union of New South Wales / 200
9 Wellington Free Kindergarten Association / 219
10 Conclusion: Change and Continuity / 235

Notes / 252

Selected Bibliography / 311

Index / 317

Illustrations

Figures

30 / Infant school classroom, 1825

33 / Infant school playground, 1825

63 / John Neagle, *An Indian Boy: Shahwahnekzhih,* 1829

72 / *Interior of New Infants' School,* Waimate, by William Bambridge, 1844

108 / Froebel Gift four

108 / A winding staircase, Gift four

108 / Froebel Gift six

140 / A prospective student at St. Michael's residential school, Saskatchewan, 1909

145 / Demonstration kindergarten at the Philadelphia Centennial Exhibition, 1876

147 / Student teachers at the Toronto Normal School demonstration kindergarten, c. 1898

178 / All People's Mission Kindergarten class, Winnipeg, 1904

214 / Children at play in a KUNSW kindergarten, Sydney, 1928

227 / Children using Montessori materials, Perth, 1920

239 / Circle time in a KUNSW kindergarten, Sydney, 1928

245 / Children at play, selling fruit at the Beretainia Kindergarten, Honolulu, 1928

245 / Children at play, doing laundry at the Beretainia Kindergarten, Honolulu, 1928

250 / Student teachers at the Wellington FKA, c. 1930

Tables

1 Kindergarten courses at Western State Normal School, 1909 / 185

2 Kindergarten courses at Oberlin Kindergarten Training School, 1924-25 / 193

3 Student schedule, Wellington FKA, 1920 / 223

4 Student duties, Wellington FKA, 1926 / 224

5 KUWA Training College program of study, 1915-16 / 227

Acknowledgments

THIS BOOK WOULD NOT have been possible without help and support from many friends, colleagues, archivists, and librarians. Thanks to my colleagues in New Zealand and Australia, and in particular to Dr. Helen May at Otago University. Her encouragement over the past ten years of research and writing has been invaluable. Thanks also to Dr. Kerry Bethell at Massey University for reading and commenting on Chapter 9. I am indebted to Margaret White at Macquarie University for helping me track down the Sydney story and for providing me with a copy of Mary Walker's excellent thesis. Thanks to the patient and knowledgeable staff at the Archives of Manitoba, the Alexander Turnbull Library in Wellington, and the Mitchell Library in Sydney. Thanks to Isabel Prochner for the photographs of Froebel's gifts in Chapter 5. I appreciated the editorial support at UBC Press. Thanks to the anonymous reviewers for their helpful comments.

Portions of Chapter 3, previously published in *Paedagogica Historica* (Larry Prochner, Helen May, and Baljit Kaur, "'The Blessings of Civilisation': Nineteenth-Century Missionary Infant Schools for Young Native Children in Three Colonial Settings – India, Canada and New Zealand 1820s-1840s," *Paedagogica Historica* 45, 1-2 [2009]: 83-102) and the *Australian Journal of Early Childhood,* and of Chapter 4, previously published in *Contemporary Issues in Early Childhood,* are reprinted here with kind permission. Research for this book was supported by grants from the Social Science and Humanities Research Council of Canada.

Abbreviations

CMS	Anglican Church Missionary Society
CPR	Canadian Pacific Railway
CWM	Church World Mission
FKCAA	Free Kindergarten and Children's Aid Association of the Hawaiian Islands
GGKA	Golden Gate Kindergarten Association
IKU	International Kindergarten Union
JSFKA	Jackson Street Free Kindergarten Association
KSAW	Kindergarten Settlement Association of Winnipeg
KUNSW	Kindergarten Union of New South Wales
KUSA	Kindergarten Union of South Australia
KUWA	Kindergarten Union of Western Australia
LMS	London Missionary Society
NSW	New South Wales
NZC	New Zealand Company
OEA	Ontario Educational Association
OKTS	Oberlin Kindergarten Training School
SFI	Sydney Foundling Institution
SKTC	Sydney Kindergarten Teachers College
Wellington FKA	Wellington Free Kindergarten Association
Winnipeg FKA	Winnipeg Free Kindergarten Association

chapter 1   Childhood and Education

ON JUNE 6, 1825, the Infant School Society held its second annual meeting at the Freemasons' Tavern in London. The meeting was filled with long-winded speeches, leading the exasperated journalist for the *Times* to write of speaker the Reverend Edward Irving, "Owing to the impossibility of extracting any meaning from many parts of the metaphysical poetical prose with which the rev. orator's address abounded, we were unable to follow him, except so far as he detailed the progress of an infant school established under his eye in Billingsgate, by two sisters, who confined themselves to certain limits, and whose efforts were crowned with complete success."[1] Other contributions were more to the point, and some even inspired applause. They described the schools as having both "negative" and "positive" benefits: preventing crime and increasing human potential. They claimed that reaching children early on was a matter of some urgency: though mouldable at birth, their abilities, temperament, and morals were fixed soon after. Although family-based care was preferred, it was believed that the parental care of poor families "at best was only negligence."[2] Most poor children, the *Times* journalist reported, "did not receive the slightest particle of education."[3] It was argued that the poor children targeted by infant schools were not actually taken from families, but from the streets, "corrupted neighbourhoods," or inept child minders to whom they were sent while their parents were at work.[4] The children saved from this situation, being too young for parents to send them out to work, would barely be missed. In place of parental care, infant schools offered poor youngsters a sound moral education using teaching methods that acknowledged their propensity to learn by playing, a remarkable innovation at the time. Henry Brougham, social reformer and parliamentarian, described the infant school system as marked by the "total absence of all restraint upon the children" and estimated that 90 percent of instruction came through amusements.[5] However, to understand Brougham's view of play, it is best to leave behind our own.

The twentieth-century notion of "free play," with its emphasis on individuals making free choices among available activities, is different from the infant school idea of learning by amusements. Amusements in this case were generally singing, marching, or movement exercises performed by groups of up to three hundred children. The "five objects" of the infant school designated by the teacher and vicar William Wilson were order, attention, obedience, instruction, and amusement. He explained that "amusement is mentioned last ... not because it is of the least importance, but because it is intimately interwoven in all other parts of the system, which is eminently a system of *instruction by amusement.*"[6] Even outdoor play was quite controlled. Play materials were found to cause injuries or arguments and were gradually withdrawn. For older children, learning was also meant to be an effortful process — a lesson in persistence in the face of difficulties — and play did not fit this idea. Educationists did not immediately shift their thinking in consideration of the young age of their pupils.

In 1825, infant schools were a modest experiment, with a scattering of schools established in Britain. By 1835, there were several hundred.[7] In the same period, missionary societies established infant schools for Ojibway children in Upper Canada, Maori in New Zealand, and for poor European children in urban centres from Quebec City to Sydney to Wellington. The schools were an important component of mission work with indigenous children, though most had closed by the 1850s. Infant schools for European children continued as an infants' class in public schools. This book documents the history of infant schools and the later development of kindergartens as they moved from their European origins to Canada, Australia, and New Zealand, where they were shaped by colonial politics and policies and by shifting social, educational, and scientific ideas.

One motivation in writing this book about the past is to gain a better understanding of the important place given to early childhood education in the present. As a strategy for long-term economic social development, most nations around the globe list early childhood services providing childcare, health, and educational benefits for young children as a top priority.[8] Governments and non-governmental organizations have produced report after report on the benefits of investing in children's health and education, as well as policies directing the delivery of services. These policies have only sometimes been translated into meaningful programs.

Cross-national research on early childhood services focusing on the current scene has added to our understanding of developments in a number of national systems, particularly in the area of policy.[9] Nonetheless, there are gaps in the overall approach to cross-national research, as identified by Peter Moss in his review of the Organisation for Economic Co-operation and Development's Thematic Review of Early Childhood Education and Care. Moss stresses the need to engage a wider range of perspectives to avoid viewing children and services for children through a single lens: "We need to be aware that the cross-national researcher is partial and is involved in a meaning making process, using his or her favoured collection of theories and perspectives. We also need to consider what disciplinary perspectives are *not* being brought to the work and what the consequences might be."[10]

One approach to comparative education is to consider schooling within a given nation as a variation on a theme, subject to changes directed by local policy, priorities, and other circumstances. I began my research believing that early childhood education, which, for the most part, developed outside state-sanctioned schooling systems, would be more nuanced and would have greater space for variation than that offered by the state system. What I found was that early education models such as the infant school and the kindergarten were reproduced quite faithfully in the corners of the globe, with classrooms having a similar look across diverse settings. There was also remarkable congruence in the meanings attached to the programs and to poor children and their families. What distinguished the colonial experience was the application of ideas to new populations of children: those of slaves, of British and European settlers, of indigenous parents, and of mixed unions. Examining early education in these contexts sheds light not only on colonial schooling, but also on the pedagogies in their original forms. Writing about the Belgian experience in the Congo, Marc Depaepe observes, "Because Western civilizing took place in the colonies under pressure, the study of the colonial educational past, even more than that of Western history in general, reveals the systemic faults and pedagogical paradoxes of the 'modern' educational project."[11]

The nature of early childhood education was greatly shaped by the contribution of individuals such as Robert Owen and Friedrich Froebel, along with their philosophies and the appurtenances of their programs. The standard genealogy of the kindergarten, for example, charts links among individuals leading outward from Froebel, credited as the father of kindergarten, rather than looking to other sources of influence.[12] As an attempt at critical history, this book charts the polygenesis of ideas contributing to early childhood education.[13]

An example of the way in which ideas concerning preschool education crossed boundaries was the interchange between England and France in the nineteenth century. In 1802, visitors from England, including Richard Edgeworth and his daughter Mary Edgeworth, toured the infant daycare centres in Paris established by Adelaide de Pastoret.[14] Their observations were shared with educationists in the United Kingdom, influencing the ideas of the Welsh industrialist and social reformer Robert Owen. In 1816, Owen established what is considered to be the first infant school, at his mills at New Lanark, Scotland, for the children of his employees. The meeting of the Infant School Society in London recounted at the start of this chapter was inspired by his effort. In 1827, Eugénie Millet visited England on behalf of a committee set up in Paris, to learn about the infant school system. Although none of the committee understood English, they were nevertheless impressed with the spirit of the schools. Upon her return, Millet worked with Jean Denys Cochin to establish the first *salle d'asile* (refuge) in Paris. A few years later, a book attributed to teacher James Buchanan was brought from London to serve as a guide.[15]

Savage

Ideas crossed from other disciplines as well as other nations. A prevalent view of child development in the nineteenth century was that,[16] by virtue of their place in the life course, children were savage by nature. A theory of racial recapitulation was prominent in psychology when kindergarten ideas gained entry into public schools and the educational childcare services called free kindergartens. It was also a core idea in Froebel's concept of child development and was contained in Maria Montessori's vision. In an address to members of the International Kindergarten Union in 1915, Montessori explained, "All forms of imperfect development which we find in the child, bear some resemblance to like characteristics in the savage." At Clark University in the United States, psychologist G. Stanley Hall set out to discover the true nature of childhood by studying children in situ. Though children were everywhere, the content of their minds was unknown to scientists. The development of the mind, however, was believed to occur in a particular fashion in line with cultural epoch theory. As explained by Perry Le Fevre, "For Hall, it became one of the organizing images of his system of thought, both for understanding human development and for educational psychology."[17]

In the popular Herbartian theory to which many kindergarten theorists subscribed, child development repeated the cultural evolution of the human race, and the school curriculum should take this into account. This was only the natural outcome of Froebel's call to study children and their interests, explains Le Fevre. What was seen via observation was filtered through the lens of evolutionary theory, which was at the forefront of scientific thinking in education and psychology. Kindergarten was the appropriate beginning of formal education, and children should be taught about savage peoples through a naturalistic curriculum including gardening and animal husbandry, reduced in the school to working a small plot or to the care and feeding of a class rabbit or goldfish. Beading and weaving, handicrafts taught as part of manual education, were traced to their primitive origins. This was described in Mary Ledyard and Bertha Breckenfeld's 1912 *Guide to Primary Manual Work,* in their lessons titled "Primitive Indian Life." Children were "shown the value of beads to the Child-Race" — indigenous peoples — "and the child of today finds equal delight in them."[18]

It was believed that, due to their age and genetic origins, adult Europeans had reached the apex of civilization and that a teacher brought her "race experience" to the kindergarten classroom. According to Grace Fulmer, a prominent trainer of kindergarten teachers in New York and Los Angeles, "'Race experience' we have seen represented in the teacher — in her knowledge, skill, appreciation, and wisdom, and in her standards of value, which are an inheritance of the ages used by her to lift the acts of her children to ever-higher levels of consciousness and give them ever-increasing power."[19]

Florence Thompson, while a student at the Ottawa Normal School in 1910, faithfully recorded course lectures on how, "in the development of the individual man, the history of the spiritual development of the human race is repeated and the race in its totality may be viewed as one human being, in whom there will be found the necessary steps in the development of the individual man."[20] Her notes detailed the necessary steps before going on to outline some applications of the ideas for instruction in music and crafts:

> Develop from savage state (gratification of physical appetites and passions) — leave wandering lifestyle to settle, learn ethical conduct. When rightly understood, each child is seen to pass through these stages of development.
>
> The young infant, loving and cared for as he is, is a savage crying when he is physically uncomfortable, peaceful and happy when his creative wants are satisfied. Learns to recognize people and respond to mother with smile — begins tribal life.
>
> Nomadic period, wandering and exploring. Increasing sense of possession — need to develop idea of ethical rights and sense of justice.
>
> The music of barbarous and semi-barbarous nations is crude, and we find that the child is attracted to rhythm before he shows a liking for melody. A love of harmony comes at a later stage.
>
> Again, the delight of the savage in ornamentations shows the childishness of his pleasures, and a child's delight in a string of beads and the wearing of [illegible] glittering ornaments, shows the savage state of his development.[21]

Young children took baby steps to maturity, a civilized state. On the frontier, far from the influence of European culture, it was necessary to re-create civilization, and infant schools and kindergartens in the colonies had a special role in teaching respect for teachers, punctuality, and work skills. In some cases, they also separated settler children from indigenous children or slave children. In Southwest Africa (Namibia), under the German colonial administration during the years prior to the First World War, kindergartens functioned to remove settler children from the influence of their African caregivers. Kindergartens were reserved for the children of German colonists and, in some instances, for "coloured" children until they were barred in about 1905.[22] The Woman's League of the German Colonial Society believed that kindergartens would provide employment for "surplus" German women and would help settlers by "removing their children from the 'danger' that African nannies and servants supposedly posed."[23]

Civilized

Evolutionary theory had a long-lived influence on kindergarten ideas via educational psychology and the popularity of habit training in the 1920s. Educational play civilized children by developing their internal controls. If this was to occur, historian Marc Depaepe observes, children "had to play and be happy on the pedagogical island that adults had reserved for them."[24] Infant schools and kindergartens separated out the youngest children, treating them to unique and sometimes odd-sounding methods with far-reaching aims. For Montessori, a long-term goal of early education was the "perfection of the human race," which would be accomplished via one child at a time and through children to their parents.[25]

Early education also had the more prosaic purpose of child socialization. Colonial administrators, the social elite, educationists, and in some cases, parents, were uneasy about children growing up on the frontier. The pull of nature on an immature child might prove too strong. Some nature experience was desired for urban children and made available by organizations such as Boy Scouts, Girl Guides, and summer camps, but this was contained, controlled, and under the supervision of adults. Peter Pierce describes the theme of the "lost child" in Australian literature and folklore as an expression of a fear of the bush as well as a metaphor for isolation from the home country.[26] Children could be lost in the bush and to the bush. Regardless, it held an attraction for them that they were unprepared or unable to resist.

Infant schools and kindergartens were mainly urban institutions offering protection from moral dangers lurking in the urban "jungle" — unsupervised play on the street. Kindergarten was eventually seen as a good fit for colonial children, part of an evolutionary approach to schooling with kindergarten at the base. Kindergarten was a sanctuary from academic work, permitting freedom of growth within careful limits — a commonwealth of childhood governed by adults. Literacy distinguished children from adults and the savage from the civilized.[27] Whereas, in the infant school, reading was a key part of the curriculum, kindergarten children were protected from books and the pressure of the mental activity brought on by reading. The move from children's supposed union with nature to dominion over children's nature was a significant conceptual shift.[28] Had it not occurred, the kindergarten could not have endured as long as it did or have assumed a place in systems of mass education. Other metaphysical approaches to early education, such as the Waldorf Schools, have continued as alternative approaches to schooling.[29]

The pedagogical island described by Depaepe was an important site for assimilation and citizenship education. Reporting on her US kindergarten for Indian children in the 1890s, teacher Lucie Calista Maley highlighted, "One important thing we teach is patriotism. They never knew before that they had any share in the flag, but now they say proudly, 'it is our flag.'"[30] At Florence Thompson's kindergarten in Ottawa, children constructed models of the Parliament buildings using educational blocks called Gift number five, which had been devised by Froebel. Presumably, this activity was intended to provide a local flavour to the kindergarten work, as much as to raise awareness of Canadian government.

In Australia at the end of the nineteenth century, the social and intellectual elite were concerned that the country's convict history had resulted in lasting damage to family and human development. The growth of the middle class following an economic upturn in the 1880s made the poor and their children more visible.[31] The allegiance of the poor to king and colony was reinforced through their children's kindergarten education. A British visitor to a Sydney kindergarten about 1909 described a typical flag ceremony: "The children went through the ceremony of saluting the Union Jack. One child held the flag, and we all sang 'God save the King.' Then they gave three cheers for the flag, and touched their heads and their hearts, and held out their hands as a sign of service to it, and we all saluted it."[32]

In daily flag ceremonies and on special occasions such as Empire Day, the bond between Britain and the former colonies and among the colonies themselves was reinforced. Relationships between settlers and indigenous people were also clearly established. This occurred at teachers' colleges as well as in children's programs. At the Sydney Kindergarten Teachers College, student teachers celebrated Empire Day with a "pageant representing the different possessions of the British Empire": "Each of the eight free Kindergartens represent one, by dressing in the characteristic costume of each country, and by the gifts it lays at Britannia's feet. Most picturesque was Canada portraying the incident of Wolf's mission to the Red Indians, the girls being disguised as a Red Indian squaw and brave, and the red-coated military men of the period. Africa was represented by miners, and an excellently got-up kaffir man and woman, and Australia by shearers, miners, and an aboriginal man and woman."[33] The qualities of England and some its possessions were set out:

England — rose laden and womanly
Scotland — kilted and strong
Ireland — whimsical, petulant but wholly dear
India — with her subtle, Oriental witchery
Africa — with a rushing, whirlwind of patriotic fervour
Mäoriland — with "supple wrist" beating a rhythm of loyalty
Australia — happy, human Australia.[34]

Bent

"As the twig is bent" was painted on a sign above the entrance to the Woolloomooloo kindergarten in Sydney, Australia, during the 1890s. The kindergarten administrators had ambitious aims for the children who attended. The proverb reflected their belief that children's development was malleable only to a point, after which the impression set.[35] Thus, their program offered more than a safe place or a play space for children — it was to be a conversion experience for poor youngsters, permanently altering their development. The fact that the activities themselves were banal and seemingly unconnected with child life was not a great contradiction for kindergarteners. Historian Barbara Beatty notes that kindergarteners were relentlessly optimistic and future oriented, unmindful of possible limitations of the system and defensive regarding its peculiarities.[36] Dorothy Hewes describes their thinking as a kind of "phantasy when they visualized families reformed and communities restructured through the music and games of their young children."[37] Part of the story told in this book is how the fantasy was constructed. There were, however, skeptics, including Henriette Schrader-Breymann, who was a student at Froebel's school in the village of Keilhau in Germany. From Keilhau she wrote to her parents, "I must confess, I could not believe that these interminable games could really be the chief expression of Froebel's idea. Yes, I must say, there was much that struck me as laughable, it seems so narrow, so limiting, so small, that so much playing to order should ennoble mankind!"[38]

Mission

In kindergarten, as well as in infant schools, children were believed to gain negative and positive benefits. A rallying call for supporters of charity kindergartens was that they were the "surest preventatives to lives of crime."[39]

Leaders in the child welfare movement chimed in. To his calls for children's refuges, industrial homes, and other institutions, John Joseph Kelso, founder of the Children's Aid Society of Toronto, added "kindergarten mission schools, established in different parts of the city, to take care of young children before they become hardened juvenile criminals."[40]

This dual orientation of social welfare and education was reflected in what can be distinguished as the missionary and the academic traditions of schools for young children. In the missionary tradition, religious groups sought to civilize and convert indigenous children, as well as to rescue European children living in urban slums. The aims of civilization and Christianization were intertwined in what Thomas Popkewitz and Marianne Bloch call the "salvation narrative."[41] The salvation narrative connected the child, the parents, and the school: the school was the site of redemption, the child the object of redemption, and the parents a secondary object rescued indirectly through the child. Infant schools and the private charity kindergartens called "free" kindergartens were founded in this missionary tradition. Many free kindergartens were part of initiatives called settlement houses, which aimed to bring middle-class standards of sanitation and cultural and social life to poor children and their families. Martha Vicinus describes settlement work as an outgrowth of mission work in the empire: "The settlers in the slums would colonize the 'natives,' teaching them not only cleanliness, but also new standards of speech, deportment, and manners."[42]

The aim was clearly assimilation, and some educational leaders were overwhelmed by the task, recognizing the limits of a part-time and short-term kindergarten education. At the Memorial Kindergarten in Hawaii, where Japanese children made up the majority of enrolment by the 1920s, Katherine Murdoch from Columbia University lamented the continued influence of parents, whom she called a "foreign influence": "Although these children had had the inestimable advantage of two years of kindergarten, the twelve hundred hours in this happy environment inevitably had not been able entirely to counterbalance the one-hundred-and-sixty-three hundred hours of foreign influence exerted during these same two years, much less entirely to supplant the effect of all the hours of their previous four or five years of life."[43] Whatever the actual impact on the children, it was believed that preschool programs would eventually encourage parents to participate in settlement house programs or other activities. Kindergartens were a gateway program to the larger target community.[44] The same principle applied to mission work among indigenous peoples, where infant schools attracted entire families to the mission community. If this did not occur, the mostly mission-run infant schools and kindergartens could at least attempt to alienate children from their families, or in some cases forcibly remove them.

chapter 2 Infant Schools in Britain

THE SCHOOLS FOR YOUNG children popularly known as infant schools were an experiment in early intervention targeting young poor children, tying a social reform agenda to an experimental pedagogy. First developed in Scotland in the early nineteenth century by the industrialist and humanist Robert Owen, the schools enrolled pupils from eighteen months to age six — that is, the children to whom they catered ranged from those who were old enough to walk to those who were too young for the newly formed or forming elementary schools. The schools' intended emphasis was on learning through structured "amusements" such as songs and games, in a setting free from rote learning. Children needed to be free from what Owen called the annoyance of books in order to form their knowledge through sense impressions of the natural world. It was important for children to get along with their fellows. Teachers were instructed never to beat them and to use instead a rational system of rewards and punishments. The notion that children learn best via amusements suggested an understanding of early childhood as a distinct period of development. As expressed by Jean-Jacques Rousseau about a half century earlier, "Childhood has its ways of seeing, thinking, and feeling that are proper to it."[1] However, amusements or educational play were highly regimented in infant schools, involving action games and frequent changes in activity performed en masse.

In their idealized form, the schools integrated childcare and instruction. In contrast, the infants' nurseries or asylums that sprung up in the large

European cities during the same period had mainly a custodial function. Infant schools were not initially conceived as preschools. During the early nineteenth century, only a minority of poor children attended school in Great Britain. The infant school was meant to provide a basic education, enough to set children on a proper course. For some, it was a first and a last chance at schooling. In the words of James Brown, the "teacher of babes" at the famed Spitalfields Infant School in London, *"It is highly probable that if they do not learn here they will be dunces for life."*[2]

The schools also had a strong moral agenda. As explained by Samuel Wilderspin, infant school promoter and author, "It is the inside of the Platter that we desire to be cleansed."[3] The schools were seen as a brief one-time opportunity to turn children toward goodness and away from evil, the positive and negative benefits described in Chapter 1. Goodness meant following the Christian path and knowing one's place in the social order. Evil was rooted in the immorality associated with poverty: drunkenness, debauchery, and crime.[4] The schools rescued poor children from the streets and set them on a righteous path toward a moral life. "If you can train a child to steal," wrote Wilderspin, you can "train them to be moral."[5] Subscribing to the view that a child's parents were a corrupting force, Wilderspin concluded, "I consider it to be of public importance ... to take children out of harm's way as soon as they can walk."[6] Robert Owen claimed this as a motivation for his school at New Lanark, where he portrayed the villagers, his employees, as composing a mob living "in idleness, in poverty, in almost every kind of crime." He added, "In ninety-nine cases out of a hundred, parents are altogether ignorant of the right method of treating children, and their own children especially. These considerations created in me the first thoughts respecting the necessity of an infant school to be based on the true principle of forming character from the earliest period at which the infants could leave their parents."[7]

The many metaphors associated with infant schools captured the idea that early moral treatment could effectively safeguard children against later problems. Wilderspin looked to a proverb for inspiration. *"Bend the twig while it is young,"* he wrote, and the tree will grow straight and tall.[8] A report of a Boston infant school included an image from the laboratory: "If the colouring mixture be poured upon ice it may readily be removed, but imparted to the water at the moment of freezing, becomes part and parcel thereof, and cannot be removed."[9] Child education was a preventative measure; schools for adults were remedial efforts with uncertain results. Yet, as Owen's son, Robert Dale, wrote in 1824, children's education was limited so long as they "lodge with their parents." Since they "remain in school during five hours only, each day, the counteracting influence of an association with persons who have not received a similar education, must be very great."[10]

Infant schools were not the first experiment in schooling for young poor children. Starting in the late eighteenth century, schools for the very young were established independently in several locations on the Continent. The best known were the so-called knitting schools organized by Lutheran minister Jean-Frédéric Oberlin in France in 1770 for the poor children of his parish. Oberlin also developed a set of pedagogical materials. The children learned useful crafts, such as knitting, and had time for games, songs, and stories, activities initially under the direction of Oberlin's wife and her fifteen-year-old maid, Louise Scheppler.[11] Oberlin's school for poor children set out the basic format for infant schools over the next eighty years or so, with supervised play for the youngest children, instruction suitable to their age for the older ones, and a combination of academics and crafts under the direction of a male teacher with female assistants who were commonly his wife or daughter.

New Lanark

In 1816, Owen was inspired by the Continental examples to start a school for the young children of workers employed in his knitting mills at New Lanark, Scotland, about twenty-five miles southeast of Glasgow. The mill town already had separate nursery buildings for children under age two, from around 1810. Owen's infant school was initially established in 1816 in the community social centre built by Owen called the Institute for the Formation of Character. The institute also housed a library and education and recreation facilities for youth and adults. A school for older children and a hall used for dance instruction and lectures occupied the top floor of the institute, and classrooms for younger children were on the ground floor. The infants' class moved into its own building in 1819.

In Owen's original plan, children under age ten were grouped into three schools "according to age and progress."[12] The infant school included children "from the time they can walk alone until they enter school" at about age five.[13] They had as "their chief occupation ... to play and amuse themselves" indoors or in the attached play yard.[14] Children aged five to about age ten were divided into two classes where they were "instructed in the rudiments of common learning."[15] The oldest children were instructed using the methods of Joseph Lancaster, which included the use of older pupils as monitors. At age ten, most children went to work in the mills.

As Owen's idea of having a special infant school for young children spread and was applied elsewhere, it often included all children from age two to seven or eight. At Owen's school at New Lanark in the 1820s, the upper age of the infants' class was six.[16] In Henry Macnab's report on the New Lanark school, which was based on the 1819 account of its headmaster, the infants' class was split into a playgroup for the youngest children and a preparatory class for children aged four to six.[17] A focus on early reading was evident, reportedly brought about under pressure from parents:[18]

> The centre room on the ground floor is set apart for the exercise and amusement of children from two to four years of age. In fine weather they generally prefer the large area which is in front of the building, and regularly walled in, and kept shut during the hours of teaching. The children of this class, as soon as they have acquired habits of speaking, are taken in rotation in classes of ten or twelve, into the room on the left hand, where they are taught the letters of the alphabet, monosyllables, etc. They have a teacher and three female attendants, who train them up in the paths of virtue and watch over their growing infancy. This class is called the infant school.
>
> The room on the left is occupied by children from four to six years of age. They are taught to read short and easy lessons, adapted to their capacities; they are permitted to amuse themselves, and to receive lessons alternately during the day.
>
> The room to the right hand is occupied by children from six to eight years of age. They begin the business of the day with arithmetic. The girls are employed in making figures on their slates or in simple accounts of addition; whilst the boys, who are classed by themselves, are learning arithmetic, attended by the master. After the boys have been employed three quarters of an hour, the girls are called upon in rotation, and the boys are seated and exercised in the same manner as the girls were, whilst seated. In the forenoon they are all employed in reading, writing, and spelling, and also nearly in the same manner in the afternoon. They attend alternately the singing and dancing master. They form the second class.[19]

In establishing his school, Owen built on initiatives instigated by his father-in-law, mill owner David Dale, who sold his factory to Owen after Owen married his daughter, Ann Caroline Dale. In Dale's time, pauper children from the workhouses in Edinburgh and Glasgow comprised about a quarter of the factory workforce of two thousand, with about two hundred of them under the age of ten. Owen phased out this practice, employing his own workers' children, but only those over ten. His school provided a way to manage the younger children, keeping them safe and preparing them for factory employment. A large percentage of villagers came to New Lanark from the Highlands, and it is probable that Gaelic was spoken in many homes. The school would serve to teach the children English, though Owen never discussed this.[20] Schools in factory colonies, including at New Lanark under Dale's management, were not new, but earlier initiatives were evening or Sunday schools for working children from age six and schools led by dominies, or village teachers, for the youngest. Owen's scheme differed in its approach to education and the status of the children enrolled.[21] In other factory schools, except for the youngest, "pupils were not the workers' children, but the 'hands' themselves," whereas at New Lanark they were future workers.[22] Dale's school, in a factory with its pauper pupils/workers, was similar to industrial schools formed in Scotland in the seventeenth century; these followed the English model in which basic academic instruction was combined with work training.

Owen's association with New Lanark ended in 1825, and after this time, the school continued as an unremarkable village school, though with traces of earlier practices. A visitor in 1839 commented upon the discarded equipment from the schools of Owen's time: globes and other materials in a storeroom at the Institute for the Formation of Character.[23] Of the infant school, he observed children "under the charge of an amiable and pretty young woman and a kindly-looking elderly man; the youngsters, under the care of the latter, were receiving a lesson in geography when we entered, which they were taught, not verbally, but from a large painted map without any names."[24]

During Owen's association with New Lanark, the mills, village, and schools were a popular tourist destination.[25] The mills combined a picturesque natural setting with industry, and many paintings of New Lanark capture these two views. The proximity of the mills to Glasgow and an increase in local tourism due to war in Europe were additional reasons to come to New Lanark.[26] Its visitors had diverse interests. According to historian Ian Donnachie, the mill's visiting books list industrialists, clergy, military officers, doctors, and educational reformers. The largest numbers of visitors, however, were women and children who had a high interest in seeing the school. Most visitors did not see much of the mills, and the typical tour focused on institute, town, villagers, and Owen himself, who had become "an attraction in his own right."[27]

For the first few years after the school opened, visitors could have observed infants' class teacher James Buchanan at work. Owen selected Buchanan for the post from among the factory operatives as one of a dozen or so teachers employed at the school. Seventeen-year-old Mary Young assisted him.[28] Buchanan and Young taught the children aged two to about six.

Buchanan was born in Edinburgh in 1784, where he worked as a weaver and served as a lay preacher of Primitive Methodism.[29] During the general depression of the 1810s, he moved with his second wife, Isabella, and their children to work at the New Lanark mills. According to a family history compiled by his granddaughter Barbara Buchanan, when they arrived in 1814, he was appalled to see very young children left without proper supervision while their mothers were employed in the mills. He proposed a school, and because "Mr. Owen was anxious to retain the women's services ... he finally agreed to Grandpa's plan to devote himself to the children."[30] According to Barbara Buchanan, Owen provided a room as a nursery, which opened in June 1815.[31] In her version of events, Owen initially had no thought of a school: "Years afterwards Mr. Owen seems to have claimed (or, perhaps, someone made the claim for him) that he originated the school and trained Grandpa, but he did neither. He simply supplied a bare room without even seats, much less toys, pictures, or anything else to occupy, instruct or amuse the children."[32] Her claim that there was no thought of a school is incorrect. Owen detailed his plans for education as early as 1813, in *A New View of Society*.[33] Although there were no toys, this was part of Owen's understanding of child education in which social relations was the key. "Thirty to fifty infants," he claimed, "when left to themselves, will always amuse each other without useless childish toys."[34] In the preparatory class for four- to five-year-olds, there were the wall maps, and Buchanan was instructed in their use. Lessons in geography and reading were planned for children's amusement, along with more active pursuits of singing, dancing, and military exercises, which included the very youngest children.

Because a gap existed between Owen's philosophical ideas and the vagaries of teaching large numbers of very young children, educational devices and teaching strategies were incorporated from Lancaster's method.

The common view at the time was that Buchanan "did not thoroughly enter into the views of his enthusiastic master."[35] It is perhaps significant that James and Isabella Buchanan named one of their sons David Dale, but none after Owen. The New Lanark experience was important to the Buchanan family, however, as is evident in the fact that David Dale Buchanan named his Natal farm after the factory town.[36]

London

When a group of social reformers, including Henry Brougham, formed the Westminster Infant School Committee and decided to establish an infant school in London according to the New Lanark plan, "Owen kindly furnished them with a master, James Buchanan."[37] Although this is regarded as the first infant school in England, the term was not widely known at the time, and it was first named the Westminster Free Day Infant Asylum when it opened in 1819.[38] The institution retained roughly the same divisions of classes by age as at New Lanark, but with the upper age raised to about seven. Buchanan taught the older children, and his wife, Isabella, later helped by their daughter Annie looked after the youngest.

Brougham did not visit the New Lanark school himself until 1822, though he discussed it with Owen and was thoroughly familiar with its operation. New Lanark was not the only influence on the Westminster Infant School Committee. Brougham was impressed by Phillip Emanuel de Fellenberg's agricultural school in Switzerland, reporting on his visit to the Select Committee on Education of the Lower Orders of the Metropolis in 1818. He recounted that, "happening to be in Switzerland" in 1816, he took a brief side trip to Berne to tour the institution, finding it "situated in pleasant country, about four miles from the town."[39]

De Fellenberg started his experiment as a free school for poor children in 1799. When Brougham visited, he observed thirty or forty children at the school, who had been rescued by de Fellenberg from "degraded" circumstances. "With hardly any exception," Brougham remarked, "they were sunk in the vicious and idle habits of their parents, a class of dissolute vagrants, resembling the worst kind of gipsies."[40] There was, in addition, an Agricultural Institution for youth; patterned after the free school model, it provided practical training in farming with some scholarly instruction. Attached to it was a "Manufactory of agricultural implements" designed by de Fellenberg and made by students. The children lived at the school and worked on the farm, making it self-sufficient. Their studies included geography, history, mineralogy, botany, reading, writing, and "cyphering," all of which were linked to nature and their work. They apparently enjoyed conversations about botany and other such topics while working in the fields.

De Fellenberg believed that the rich and the poor should understand their connection, the essence of which was the useful labour of the latter. This reasoning informed his academy for wealthy children, called the Scientific Educational Institution for the Higher Social Classes. Its pupils, too, worked in the fields, and their payments helped support the school for the poor. What most impressed Brougham was de Fellenberg's ability to accomplish so much "with such slender means" at his school for the poor. Brougham noted that the children who attended the private academy, including "seven or eight German princes," came from aristocratic families. Whereas poor students were educated in the vernacular, pupils at the academy learned Latin and Greek under the direction of "20 eminent professors." This was an interesting aspect of the school. The predominance of the study of Latin and Greek grammar was one reason for including manual labour in the curriculum of schools such as de Fellenberg's. Robert Owen was so inspired that, after visiting de Fellenberg's institutions in 1817, he sent his two sons to study at the academy where they stayed from 1818 to 1821.

The school had a strong moral and religious dimension. Children were treated kindly "so as to win their affections" and teach them the value of work and its relation to their happiness.[41] This was made easier by their isolation on the farm and their training by older, more experienced boys under the supervision of a teacher. This comprised their "treatment." As Brougham noted, "A constant and even minute superintendence, at every instant of the lives, forms of course a part of the system."[42]

De Fellenberg's institution and others like it inspired reform schools as well as industrial schools for indigenous children (discussed in Chapter 3). Infant schools similarly aimed to train children in work skills in a situation apart from their parents and under the scrutiny of their teachers. At New Lanark, the Institute for the Formation of Character was centrally located, the youngest children playing much of the day in a yard at the front. Because the children were so young, they did not actually work but acquired a disposition to work in industrial situations — punctuality and attendance (infant teacher Samuel Wilderspin's most severe punishments were saved for truants), docility, and following instructions en masse. It is also possible to see the influence of Jeremy Bentham, who was a financial partner with Owen at New Lanark at the time of his reforms from 1813. Bentham explained his "inspection principle" in relation to pupils at school, the object being "to make them not only suspect, but be assured, that whatever they do is known, even though that should not be the case."[43] With their fellow pupils as monitors — no monitor was older than seven at the Spitalfields school — the sense of being watched was perhaps more real than imagined.

The Westminster school was situated near Buckingham Palace at 23 Brewer's Green in premises formerly used by a coach-spring and axletree maker.[44] Purpose-built infant schools were unnecessary at this point; the important features were a large open room with adjacent space for a play yard. Little is known about the school at Brewer's Green, and it is not known if a gallery was added. Galleries were tiered seating arrangements as in a theatre, accommodating large numbers of pupils for whole class instruction. Westminster was home to some of London's poorest citizens, and one commentator observed that the location of the school was greatly inferior to that of New Lanark, in the "beautiful and healthful vicinity of the Clyde."[45] Though this was a romanticized impression of life in factory colonies, the observation was accurate. An investigation into the education of the "lower orders" of the Metropolis, chaired by Brougham in 1816, recorded families living in desperate circumstances and homeless children sleeping under crates outside markets. A select committee of the same year investigated the "State of Police in the Metropolis," with respondents linking crime with children's lack of education rather than poverty.[46] The Westminster school was intended as a remedy to these problems.

Parents were apparently uninterested in sending their children to the Westminster school, and the original patrons withdrew support. The Westminster Infant School Committee regrouped with some new members, still wishing to promote mass education as a remedy for the "distressing crime rate," and established Buchanan in a two-story building on Carey Street at Vincent Square, a short distance from the first school at Brewer's Green.[47] This school, established in 1822, was popularly called the Vincent Square Infant School, but both it and the first school were also known as the Westminster Infant School. In order to distinguish between the two, subsequent references will be to the Brewer's Green school and the Vincent Square school. Joseph Wilson, a friend of Henry Brougham and member of the committee, sponsored a second school on Quaker Street in Spitalfields in 1820 that was also organized by Buchanan, who trained its director, Samuel Wilderspin. From these halting beginnings, infant schools were established in various locations in Britain and around the world over the next two decades.

At the start, the schools were little understood by local residents and highly unpopular. In Spitalfields, Wilderspin explained that, unlike at New Lanark, where parents felt an obligation to send their children, parents worked for various employers and could "assume an air of independence; therefore, unless the mode of teaching meets their approbation, they will not send their children at all to school."[48] He reported suffering considerable abuse from the populace, being "pelted with filth" as he walked down the street.[49] Spitalfields was much poorer than Westminster, with large numbers of unattended children playing on the streets or locked in their apartments while their mothers were at work. For many years, an area near the school had been used as a hiring fair for child weavers, but young prostitutes and their clients also frequented it.

"The problem of their education," according to infant school historian Phillip McCann, was seen in "terms of their socialization."[50] In this situation, members of the upper classes considered the infant school to be "a very great benefit" to the "young population" as a means of crime reduction.[51] Claims were made that this was in fact achieved. A review of education in 1836 reported that there was "no instance of a former scholar of Quaker Street appearing before a magistrate."[52] Writer and publisher Mathew Carey highlighted this aspect of the schools in an essay calling for their support in Philadelphia. He estimated that one dollar spent saved three dollars "in the expense of criminal trials, and the support of paupers in alms-houses, and criminals in houses of refuge and penitentiaries."[53] Nurseries, it was argued, were cheaper than jails. Wilderspin estimated that "800 babes might be instructed for a year, for what it costs the country to transport every individual," referring to convict transportation to Australia.[54] As we will see in subsequent chapters, claims for crime reduction and cost savings were also made on behalf of kindergarten education for lower-class children.

For some months when Wilderspin was starting out at the Spitalfields school, Buchanan went every morning to help him prepare his lessons. According to his granddaughter, Barbara Buchanan, James brought his son David Dale Buchanan along with him to calm the children and demonstrate proper behaviour.[55] Infant school teachers made extensive use of "emulation" — a Lancasterian idea in which a pupil carefully observed other pupils and then strove to outdo them.[56] Its effect would seem to have been limited in this case, as David was less than a year old when the

Spitalfields school opened in 1820. For the first while, Wilderspin used shaming and other punishments that would have been familiar to him from Lancasterian schools, as well as corporal punishment when all else failed — a decision that made him unpopular with parents and, we might assume, his pupils.

Except for a brief period when he left to establish other schools owing to a disagreement with the Infant School Society concerning his religious beliefs, Buchanan spent the years from 1819 to 1839 teaching at the Brewer's Green and Vincent Square schools.[57] Accounts of his teaching generally describe him as having a natural gift for music, delighting in children and their play. At the same time, they note that he was an odd man, "impractical, childlike, thriftless," in the description of Barbara Leigh Smith, daughter of the school's patron, Benjamin Leigh Smith.[58] She continued: "He was queer, but he knew his trade — infants — and he was adored by them."[59] He taught by example, patterning his pedagogy on the way in which children learned and serving as a model for aspiring teachers. At the heart of his approach were simple songs and stories, as well as marching and movement games, which involved and amused the children. His flute was always close at hand.

His contribution to the infant school system probably featured little that was unique. The strongest claims for his particular inventions come mostly from his granddaughter in her oft-cited and privately published family history. Barbara Buchanan attributed a set of children's rhymes to James Buchanan, including one concerning sheep, which goes in part,

> The sheep are taken once a year,
> And plunged in water cool and clear;
> And there they swim and never bite
> While men do wash them clean and white.[60]

Wilderspin included the same rhyme in a collection titled "Practical Lessons for Infant Schools," which he noted were "original and select."[61] The origin may be a much older Irish folk song.

We can learn something of Buchanan's approach by considering the systems used by teachers known to have been influenced by him. One was David Goyder, who, while preparing to take charge of the Bristol Infant School, observed Buchanan and Wilderspin in 1821, finding no difference between the two.[62] Goyder was acquainted with Buchanan through the New Jerusalem Church on Waterloo Road. He wrote in his memoir that

Buchanan received a request to find a teacher for an infant school opening in Bristol and invited him to apply. Buchanan offered to train him one day per week and encouraged him to study the ideas of Johann Pestalozzi.[63] Goyder was appointed master, and the Bristol Infant School opened in 1821. We might assume that at least some of his approach was learned from Buchanan and that Buchanan had some knowledge of and admired Pestalozzi. Pestalozzian James Pierrepont Greaves is known to have visited Buchanan's school at Brewer's Green after returning from four years at Yverdon, Switzerland.[64] David Goyder wrote his own book on infant education after three years of teaching in Bristol.[65]

Class lessons at Goyder's school were organized according to the Lancasterian system; pupils were slotted into lower and higher divisions, the former subdivided into smaller groups. In the first level of the "alphabet class," the task was to identify all the letters that had been cut out and "placed promiscuously on a board."[66] Children were then promoted to the "two-letter" and then the "three-letter class," where they spelt three-letter words. Higher classes learned words of more than one syllable. Transitions were signalled by the ringing of a bell, and pupils marched from their lessons to the playground or to and from the gallery. Reading was mainly from the Bible, and according to a visitor to the school, the instruction overall was "chiefly of a religious character." This aspect of the Bristol school, with its catechistical or interrogatory instruction and the school rules sung to the tune of hymns, was closer to the approach of Church of England teachers Thomas Bilby and R.B. Ridgway than to that of Wilderspin. Buchanan too trained Bilby.[67]

Buchanan and Wilderspin admired the teachings of the eighteenth-century Swedish mystic Emanuel Swedenborg and were members of the New Jerusalem Church on Waterloo Road, London, where they may have met.[68] Buchanan made his beliefs well known through his teaching, whereas Wilderspin was not forthright about their influence. The thirty-six-year-old Buchanan was baptized at the New Church in 1820; his wife, Isabella, and seven of their children were baptized after this date. Swedenborgians believed that a correspondence existed between the things on earth and in heaven; for example, "the rays of [the] spiritual Sun are love and truth corresponding to the heat and light of natural suns."[69] Children were seen as innocent, being angels in earthly bodies.[70]

Details concerning Buchanan's informal and playful approach to teaching and its Swedenborgian influence are mainly attributed to the recollections of Barbara Leigh Smith. Her father, Benjamin Leigh Smith, owned the Vincent Square school, building it for the purpose in 1822, and subsidized Buchanan's salary over the years. Barbara Leigh Smith and her four younger siblings played at the school when they were in London, starting when she was about seven. Buchanan spent the holidays at the country home of the family, where he tutored the children. This continued until Barbara Leigh Smith was twelve, and Buchanan left London for New Zealand.

She remembered Buchanan as greatly influenced by Swedenborgian teachings, though the spiritual meaning of the lessons was not always clear to her. She recalled,

> He would arrange the children in a circle and make us all dance round joining hands with them.
> "There!" said he, "when the round is made, is truth" (or harmony, I forget which).
> "Yes," said I, not attending, but taking for granted he was explaining something that could not be explained.
> "Yes," replied he in a rather scornful tone. "Yes, says you, but you don't know what I mean."
> "Well, what do you mean?" I asked.
> "I mean that the circle corresponds with harmony (or truth), and then the angels come and join us."[71]

Barbara Leigh Smith's aunt recollected that the children also acquired basic academic skills, and it may be that the more playful and spiritual aspect of Buchanan's teaching has been overdrawn, or at least interpreted in relation to later understandings of play. Barbara Leigh Smith may also have been describing only a part of the day's schedule. Edward Baines, writing in the *Leeds Mercury* in 1824, observed the Vincent Square school during the dinner break, finding the children at play. When the class commenced, the 140 pupils were divided by gender, with Buchanan teaching the older boys and Isabella the girls and the younger children. Baines observed that the approach "resembles the Lancasterian plan, but has more variety."[72] Buchanan started the afternoon with all of the children marching about the room. They then recited the Ten Commandments and prayed. Small groups gathered around alphabet frames attached to the wall to recite their letters, after which Buchanan took the oldest boys to another room for instruction in arithmetic, writing, and object lessons using pictures.

Isabella remained with the girls and the youngest children, teaching a few of the older girls sewing while the youngest children played with toys. Older girls working as monitors instructed some of the children in the alphabet, but most did "nothing except talk to each other, and play with their toys."[73]

The sole influence that Wilderspin acknowledged from his training with Buchanan was in relation to the lessons, rather than his playful approach. While children take turns reading, Wilderspin advised, "The teacher walks behind them, so that if any child is inattentive, he is sure of being detected." He noted, "This part of the plan is not my own, but was taught me by the Master of the Westminster Infant School."[74]

The situation looked much the same almost fifteen years later, as described in a report on schools in Westminster. Of the six infant schools operating in the district in 1838, the Vincent Square school was unique as having the largest enrolment. However, what occurred there was not unusual: "The instruction comprises reading, writing on slates, mental arithmetic, sewing to a few, grammar in conversation, and moral and religious duties. Monitors and classes according to the Infant system, and individual instruction, are adopted, and lecturing occasionally. The room is well ventilated: the children are questioned on what they learn, and are tolerably clean and orderly. The teachers consist of a man and wife, with a young female assistant."[75] The latter was probably Buchanan's daughter.

A further source of information on Buchanan's teaching and the original Brewer's Green school is Wilderspin's 1835 letter to the editor of the *Educational Magazine* in which he defended his claim to have originated the infant school system. He was not one to back down from criticism, writing, "Though I have been so much *amongst babies,* I am not a baby myself."[76] He described the Brewer's Green school in 1820 as having only a few materials, "some little *penny books*" and "some *inch cubes.*" Children ranged in age from two to eleven, and Buchanan "picked them up in the streets wherever he could find them." Because Buchanan had no system at his "asylum," Wilderspin claimed he had nothing to teach him. When Buchanan left the Vincent Square school temporarily around 1827, Wilderspin apparently reorganized it according to his own infant system. We know at least some of this account is incorrect from Baines' 1824 report, which describes the school schedule, lessons, and classes divided by age and ability in a manner similar to Wilderspin's system. However, in 1820, as Buchanan worked to establish the first infant school in England, the Westminster Free

Day Infant Asylum at Brewer's Green may have been more of a daycare facility than a school.

Transfer

In the period 1825 to 1835, infant schools with similar features were established across Europe and around the world. Wilderspin estimated that, by 1835, approximately 2,000 had started up in Britain serving about sixty-four thousand children.[77] Though this was wildly exaggerated — an 1837 review estimated that there were 270 schools in Britain — they had gained acceptance across a wide spectrum of school promoters as good places for poor children.[78]

Robert Owen never fleshed out infant school pedagogies, and Wilderspin and others filled this gap by outlining the materials and methods that became the "infant system." The reference to a "system" was used repeatedly by infant school promoters to describe their approaches. This was also the case with the monitorial schools, which invited industrial metaphors. Samuel Taylor Coleridge called Andrew Bell's system "an incomparable machine — a vast moral steam engine."[79] As explained by Carl Kaestle, "The developing technological ideology of the nineteenth century applied not only to material production but to social organization and reform institutions as well."[80] This reflected faith that a single system of education could be applied in the same manner in diverse circumstances with the same results. For Owen, this suggested a set of rational ideas for forming human character and intelligence, much like a production system in a manufactory. For Wilderspin, Goyder, Wilson, and other infant teachers, it was a set of techniques, which, based on their sometimes quite brief experience, was set down in manuals of instruction.

The infant school guide books are valuable historical sources, giving us a sense of their authors' search for an efficient system for teaching large numbers of very young children and their rationale for wanting to do so. The various teaching guides, springing from the same source, the New Lanark school, diverged mainly on their treatment of religion; the mechanics and core principles were similar. D.A. Turner observes that, in histories of infant schooling, much is made of the disparity between the New Lanark school and the system that developed later.[81] As if to prove this point, Denison Deasey, writing six years after Turner, summarizes events of the nineteenth century, lamenting, "After Robert Owen departed for Indiana and the Lancaster gallery method took over in Britain, infants' education ... went through a slough of despond."[82] The schools, however, retained elements that set them apart from schools for older children: they included playgrounds, discouraged corporal punishment, and adapted gallery instruction and other monitorial methods to the age of their pupils. Turner argues that "such characteristics did not survive by accident."[83] The demands on the schools, such as community pressure to teach reading, remained constant as well. This was perhaps the greatest incursion on Owen's plan. As Bilby and Ridgway remarked, "The parent's constant cry is (and we think justly so too), the book — the book."[84]

At least in theory, the schools were gentle places, as much home as school. According to the 1834 annual report of a school in the small colonial city of Montreal, "Inasmuch as the fundamental principle of the Infant School system is love, it should be the constant endeavour of the Teacher to win the affection of the children, and then cause them to feel pleasure in submission to his will."[85] Lawrence Cremin's characterization of infant schools, in his history of education in the United States, focuses on this attribute. In the schools, children entered a "quasi-domestic environment under the supervision of a quasi-maternal female teacher" — a situation that foreshadowed the kindergarten.[86]

A main difference between the monitorial and infant systems was the place afforded play and self-activity. Infant school supporters recognized the need for efficiency but in the context of a somewhat more child-oriented pedagogy. In the monitorial system, a single teacher managed the instruction of up to several hundred young scholars with the help of monitors. Its aim was to be efficient. Because many children attended school for only a few years before leaving to watch over younger siblings or for paid employment, their time in school could not be idly spent. This was the view of a mother interviewed by the Select Committee on the Education of the Poorer Classes in Great Britain in 1838. She stated, "I don't like the infant school ... because they learn nothing ... They do nothing but play."[87] This was hardly the case, and her knowledge of infant schools may have been quite limited. Nevertheless, many working-class parents favoured community-based programs that promised quick results. The private preschools called dame schools, where children learned by rote and did not play at all, were far more popular with working-class parents and would remain so even after the passage of the Education Act in 1870.[88] *A Dame's School,* painted by Thomas Webster in 1845, shows a group of young scholars engaged in serious study under the close supervision of their elderly teacher. Although she grips a switch in her hand, children's memories of their time at dame schools were generally quite positive, and we know that corporal punishment was also used in infant schools.[89]

System

Samuel Wilderspin made it his mission to tout the benefits of the infant school.[90] For a time, he was employed by the Infant School Society to conduct this work, and the Spitalfields school was used for training teachers in "the mechanical parts of the system."[91] He first laid out his approach in *On the Importance of Educating the Infant Children of the Poor*, available for sale in 1822.[92] Numerous subsequent editions and other publications followed over the next twenty years, and infants' teaching was frequently equated with "Wilderspin's System."[93] William Russell, describing it for American readers in 1826, warned that it contained "some startling novelties" concerning infant education, but many of these were adapted from systems for older pupils or already in use at the Brewer's Green and New Lanark schools.[94]

Wilderspin was ungenerous in giving credit to others for these ideas, claiming in later years to have trained Buchanan and superseded the ideas of Oberlin, de Fellenberg, and Owen.[95] On smaller points as well, he was an active collector of others' ideas. In 1829, he published Buchanan's verses without credit, in his fourth edition of *Infant Education*.[96] In *A System of Education for the Young*, published in 1840, he cribbed passages from Brougham.[97] At least some of his contemporaries resented his claim to have invented the system of infant teaching. Thomas Bilby and R.B. Ridgway, teachers at schools organized by the London Infant School Society, remarked that he "appears to doubt even the existence of such a being as Louise Scheppler," pioneer teacher at Oberlin's school.[98] They offered a different version of the events that led to Wilderspin's teaching career, claiming that he was originally hired as the assistant at Spitalfields. Buchanan's own assistant at the Vincent Square school was expected to take charge at Spitalfields, but her frail health caused the organizing committee to seek someone to work alongside her. David Goyder recommended Samuel Wilderspin. Wilderspin was then trained by Buchanan, taking full charge of the school with his wife only after the original teacher became ill.[99]

Bilby and Ridgway, adherents of the Church of England who described their "field of labour ... [as] the tender and ductile soil of infancy," infused their own schools with religious instruction.[100] This may have caused them to challenge Wilderspin, whose approach was influenced by the religious teachings of Swedenborg. Bilby may also have felt a need to defend his mentor, James Buchanan.

Owen's twenty-three-year-old son, Robert Dale, published *An Outline of the System of Education at New Lanark* in 1824. Although it was mainly a defence against attacks that the school ignored religious instruction, Robert Dale described the curriculum for older students in some detail. He was, however, vague concerning the infant classes, noting only that the two- to five-year-olds attended for a half-day and then played under the supervision of a young woman who managed them "without harshness or punishment."[101] We know from the reports cited above that, grouped in "classes" within the large classroom, the older children were taught lessons in reading, writing, and other subjects, but this was not detailed by Robert Dale. He described a gallery in the lecture room on the upper floor but made no suggestion that it was used for the infants' class. When teacher David Goyder visited New Lanark in 1825, Robert Dale told him that he had met Pestalozzi at Yverdon before returning from de Fellenberg's academy in Switzerland and that the New Lanark system followed Pestalozzi's methods.[102]

A flurry of books on infant schools was published about the same time as Robert Dale's, all presenting similar ideas on such matters as punishment, the importance of happy children, and infant school versions of monitorial methods. Wilderspin's *Infant Education* preceded Robert Dale's book and is known to be the first publication on the English infant school. Wilderspin prefaced his description of the method with an extensive rationale for the need for the schools, and he emphasized the importance of the early formation of good habits.[103] He did not call his method a system until 1832, when "Infant System" was incorporated into the guide's title.

A review in the *Christian Observer* called Wilderspin's book "chiefly a book of details" related in a straightforward style.[104] Teaching was structured around a strict timetable, with two half-day sessions starting at 9:30 a.m. and 1:00 p.m. After a prayer and a hymn with the entire assembly of pupils, children dispersed to lessons. Up to fourteen classes of five or six children were grouped around lesson posts, which displayed their reading assignment and were fixed to the floor or on a stand. Several monitors circulated about the room, attending to the groups. Younger children identified pictures instead of words. This worked well, according to Wilderspin, who explained that "I have had children whom one would think were complete blockheads" because they did not know their alphabet, for whom

An infant school classroom with two ranks of lesson posts, a selection of large wall maps, and a gallery at the back. Samuel Wilderspin, *Infant Education: Remarks on the Importance of Educating the Infant Poor from the Age of Eighteen Months to Seven Years,* 3rd ed. (London: J.S. Hodson, 1825).

the picture lessons were highly effective.[105] To maintain order, children were grouped according to age or ability, "for order is essential in an Infant school as in any other, and you cannot have order without being classed."[106]

Wilderspin used a number of other devices as learning aids for mathematics and geometry, some of which he claimed to have invented, though many were adapted from Lancasterian schools for older children or already in use by Buchanan. His pupils did not learn to write by tracing letters in sand, as was the case in Lancaster's schools. Instead, starting at about age five, they used slates to which engravings of letters were attached. As Wilderspin explained, "The children then put the pencil into the engraving and work it round into the shape of a letter."[107] Because he believed that "all our ideas are admitted through the medium of the senses," children used objects they could touch, such as wooden cubes, for adding and subtracting.[108] A version of the abacus, called an arithmeticon, was employed for more complex operations.[109]

Methods for instruction in geometry were elaborated in great detail. Following patterns printed on paper, children constructed geometrical forms from brick-shaped blocks, learning "the principle of brick-building" as applied to houses, walls, and bridges.[110] Wilderspin used a "many jointed rod" to create one-dimensional shapes, "like a counting house candlestick, from which I borrowed the idea."[111] Other devices were designed for whole-class teaching, with children seated in a gallery under the direction of the teacher. These included lesson stands on seven-foot posts and wall-sized maps as shown in the image above.

The system of mutual instruction was modified when it was used with younger or older students. Thomas Pole, who wrote in support of both infant and adult education, quoted an experienced teacher who observed, "We have found it very difficult to get the learners, especially persons far advanced in years, to stand for an hour in semicircles round a card suspended upon a wall."[112] A greater reliance on simultaneous instruction was a characteristic of infant schools in this period. Using child monitors to teach other children — a five-year-old teaching a four-year-old — was found to be ineffective and impractical. The monitors were often unhappy with their role, asking, "Please, sir, may I sit down, I do not like to be a monitor?"[113] Wilderspin solved this problem, which he attributed to lack of motivation, by paying them a penny. This was a significant amount; many schools charged parents a penny a week. However, other elements from monitorial schools — the lesson posts, the alphabet wheel, and instructional principles such as breaking learning into small components — were used in the infant school system.

Infant school teachers adapted gallery instruction from monitorial schools, where the floors of the vast schoolrooms were sloped. A report described the floor at the Sheffield school for seven hundred students, which, "paved with brick, gradually rises from the lowest part in front of the master's platform to the extreme end, like the pit of a place of public entertainment; so as to give the master a *bird's eye-view* of all the boys."[114] As the technology developed, students sat on benches arranged in a gallery for whole-class lessons, as in a lecture theatre, an arrangement already in use in medical training. Because monitorial schools served a wide age range, the youngest children were separated out, placed near the teacher at the front of the class, and occupied with lessons such as tracing letters in sand. They were dubbed the "sand class" and in later generations, the "alphabet class" or the "babies class." Sand was contained in a specially constructed table, spread in a thin layer across its surface. Children used small sticks to create letters, which were wiped clean by smoothing the sand. Individual sand trays were later introduced, along with elaborate teaching devices such as the alphabet wheel.

Wilderspin described a gallery as a set of stairs running the width of a room. As in Lancasterian schools, the youngest children were placed at the bottom, and the gallery had the same aim — "to place them in one mass immediately under the eye of the master."[115] Wilderspin estimated that, for a class of three hundred, each scholar could be allotted twelve inches of bench-space in a room with a total area of twenty-five hundred square feet. To save space and to make the room multi-functional, he proposed a system of ropes and pulleys to lower the benches from the ceiling as required, an idea Thomas Pole criticized as exceedingly dangerous.[116] Infant schools, lacking older monitors, could never reach the size of monitorial schools that boasted up to ten thousand pupils. However, it was likely that children who continued their schooling would go on to attend a monitorial school. After graduating from the Spitalfields Infant School, most children went on to the National School across the road, which also owed its origins to Joseph Wilson.[117]

Wilderspin believed that children were active and amused in the gallery. He wrote that they would come up to him and say, "Please Sir, may we say the picture alphabet up in the gallery?"[118] Galleries fitted his understanding that ideas were formed from sensory information. A "child receives a great deal of knowledge from the eye," he explained, and the eye required training.[119]

Later writers such as educationist James Kay-Shuttleworth theorized gallery instruction in a similar way. Effective gallery lessons were short, about ten to fifteen minutes, and would engage the children. One way of achieving this was via the "elliptical method" in which "the teacher, while instructing the children in the gallery, seldom uses many words in a series without dropping one or two, which the children have to supply, and that the subsequent train of the teacher's conversation with the children depends upon the word being correctly supplied by them." In this way, the "activity of the children's minds" was constantly stimulated.[120]

Playgrounds, such as the one in the image below, were a draw for children, motivating them to come to school. They were permitted to use the playground after school hours as a means to "keep them out of the streets."[121] Wilderspin believed that much could be learned about children by observing them on the playground. He described the purpose of playgrounds in

An idealized image of children playing with blocks and on swings in an infant school playground. Samuel Wilderspin, *Infant Education: Remarks on the Importance of Educating the Infant Poor from the Age of Eighteen Months to Seven Years,* 3rd ed. (London: J.S. Hodson, 1825).

terms of social and moral education, as well as an alternative setting for lessons in arithmetic and other subjects. Trees were strategically planted as gathering points for classes, much like the lesson posts indoors. In the larger space, children formed circles or joined hands, snaking around the play area while reciting the alphabet or multiplication tables. Fruit trees and flowerpots were placed to beautify the grounds and to teach children to respect the school property. Swings were located outside and also within the schoolroom for physical activity during inclement weather. While swinging, children chanted rhymes or the "pence-table."[122] Swings were the main permanent apparatus on the playground, and Wilderspin paid significant attention to their use in developing his pupils' social, intellectual, and physical abilities. He was firm that children should not be helped to get on the swing and claimed that no serious accidents had occurred. He cited Buchanan's use of a similar rule at Brewer's Green and New Lanark as further proof. Separate swings were designated for younger children, and one was reserved "for the little girls."[123]

Other guides offered minor variations on the methods described by Wilderspin. The Bristol physician Dr. Thomas Pole was an early supporter of infant schools, publishing his *Observations Relative to Infant Schools* in 1823. He was aware of the Spitalfields school and had read Wilderspin's book, but, for his description of methods, he relied on his observations of the Bristol Infant School run by David Goyder. He especially recommended the Bristol school's military-like exercises, in which pupils were commanded to march double time at the sound of the whistle and the "sharp stamp of the Master's foot."[124] The lessons following these exercises were undertaken with monitors in classes "similar to those used in the Lancasterian Schools."[125]

Pole was critical of Wilderspin's use of corporal punishment, claiming it was never employed at the Bristol Infant School or by Buchanan at the Brewer's Green or Vincent Square schools. He also disagreed with punishments such as cages, shaming children, or encouraging them to tease or taunt a misbehaving pupil. Wilderspin responded to Pole's criticism in the next edition of his guide, charging that Goyder used handcuffs and stocks at Bristol, which were also Lancasterian punishments, and that corporal punishment rationally applied was a better option.[126] In these publications, we can see that debates on select topics were giving shape to a system. Interestingly, Wilderspin never gave up his point on corporal punishment, though it was better explained in later editions. However, there were significant inconsistencies in his approach to punishment, which he claimed to employ as a last resort and mainly to cure truancy. In his evidence provided before the 1835 Select Committee on Education, he described using it with very young children, in one instance whipping a fifteen-month-old who had not wanted to come down from his caregiver's back. He recalled, "I had to whip it twice."[127]

The Spitalfields school was the initiative of Joseph Wilson, a member of the committee that sponsored the school at Brewer's Green. Wilson's brother, the vicar William Wilson, trained with Wilderspin and opened St. Mary's Infant School in a barn at Walthamstow near London, in 1824. A year later he published a manual titled *The System of Infants' Schools*. Superior in its organization and writing style to Wilderspin's guide, and with a far greater focus on religious education, it was widely used, including in the United States where it formed the basis for William Russell's account of infant schools in the inaugural issue of the *American Journal of Education* in 1826. Although there was no American edition of Wilderspin's guide, Wilson's book, "adapted for use in the United States," was published in

1830. Wilson differed with Wilderspin on the point of corporal punishment, even for truants, believing that the order of lessons, scheduling, and the physical environment should make punishment unnecessary. When it was warranted, the teacher should not act in haste, but observe the child to understand his or her behaviour. Teachers were advised to "use the mildest punishment possible to effect your purposes" and to resort to corporal punishment only after consulting with the school managers.[128]

Wilson separated out the children who did not know their letters — mostly the youngest — and placed them in what he called a "fold," which was located behind the rostrum. "Fold" referred to the enclosure that contained a shepherd's flock. Typically attended to by monitors or an assistant, these children were treated much like those in the sand classes of monitorial schools. Folds were also similar to fenced play areas in children's institutions, which were designed for safety and ease of management. These structures — like modern playpens but intended for many children — were called *pouponnières* in France, where the term also referred to infant nurseries. The one-time lieutenant governor of Upper Canada, Francis Bond Head, observed one at a crèche (charity-sponsored daycare) in Paris, describing it as a "pound, in which those little errant infants that can stand are allowed to scramble round a small circular enclosure, composed of a rail, just high enough for them to hold."[129] Wilderspin was highly critical of Wilson's folds, which he called cages, believing they conflicted with the idea behind gallery instruction — that younger children would learn by hearing the lessons directed to the older.[130] Wilderspin agreed with the idea of separating children according to ability or age for instruction in class work, but not for gallery lessons.

Wilson favoured a low semi-circular gallery, claiming it to have "superior advantages" to one rising as a simple staircase.[131] In a low gallery, all the children sat at about the same distance from the teacher, making it easier for them to see and hear. In this type of gallery, the pupils were arranged according to age: the senior students, positioned along the outer edge of the semi-circle, sat farthest from the teachers' rostrum; the intermediate students, who occupied the inner edge of the semi-circle, sat nearest the teacher; the babies, sandwiched between the senior and intermediate students, were placed so that they could be "more exactly and constantly under the observation of the teacher, and may be learners by the repeated examinations of those below."[132] This mode of gallery instruction was put into place at the demonstration school operated by the London Infant School Society. Wilson stressed that gallery lessons required "silence, order, and attention" but that the children were nevertheless active and amused through the use of verse, clapping, and short lessons that changed from day to day.[133] His understanding of the infant school as a preparatory school and its greater religious focus meant that it seemed less playful than Wilderspin's. The playground was used for exercise and lessons, but time was limited to thirty minutes each day including organized gymnastics.

Overall, guides published in the 1820s and 1830s were in fair agreement on the methods and materials of an infant school, revealing a developing collective understanding of the meaning of an "infant system" despite occasional bickering among authors. The main division focused on the role played by religious education: Wilderspin advocated moral education through more indirect means, whereas Wilson, Bilby, and Ridgway represented a Bible-based approach. Among the "Suitable Texts of Scriptures for the Walls of an Infants' School," Wilson included "DRUNKARDS SHALL NOT INHERIT THE KINGDOM" along with "THE EYES OF THE LORD ARE IN EVERY PLACE."[134]

"Prayers, graces, catechisms and creeds" dominated the curriculum in schools operated by the City of London Infant School Society.[135] Bilby included the Bishopsgate's schedule — the "Plan of a Day's Employment" — in his *Course of Lessons* for infant schools.[136] It was notable for its attention to Bible reading, aspects of instruction for young children discouraged by Wilderspin. Bilby, who was a hymn writer, advocated teaching via music, and much of the curriculum was sung. Even school rules were set to music, such as the following ditty sung after playtime:

> We'll go to our places, and make no wry faces,
> And say all our lessons distinctly and slow;
> For if we don't do it, our Mistress will know it,
> And into the corner we surely shall go.[137]

In the main, the manuals published in the 1820s and 1830s were written by people who had some experience with teaching young children. Initial editions described the system in relation to an individual school, as a kind of case study. None of the authors was a theorist or a philosopher, and their training in most cases was informal and brief. Most were familiar with Pestalozzi, at least in terms of the notion of "picture lessons." All seemed knowledgeable regarding the Lancasterian system. Their approaches represented the best thinking of individuals faced with teaching 150 to 200 children aged two to six or seven and charged with showing rapid results to their sponsors and to parents. As described in the guides, the schools were mostly orderly — the watchword of the teacher/authors — but sometimes riotous. Wilson admitted that, on some occasions, "the attention of the whole school is lost."[138] In such cases, he recommended that a teacher break into song or play a tune, gaining the children's attention and proceeding. "If this may fail," he added, "he may next entirely change the lesson for another more pleasant to the children."[139] This was not to create an impression of the schools as child-centred in the sense that would be used by later educationists, but Wilderspin, too, admitted to losing control — during his first day of teaching, he rounded up his pupils by clowning, holding a woman's hat on a pole — and stressed the importance for children to enjoy school.

The publications were less explicit in their descriptions of the teaching activities for the youngest children. Wilderspin believed that babies as young as twelve months of age learned by watching the older pupils, though it could be imagined they spent considerable time sleeping, fussing, or crawling about. Wilson's use of folds was one solution, keeping them separate from the older pupils and instructed by female teachers. This pattern was common, even without the folds. Buchanan, Goyder, and Wilderspin all worked with their wives and, in some cases, their daughters. For class work, pupils were separated according to gender, and the older girls learned sewing and weaving from the female teachers, while the youngest children played. As we will see in Chapter 3, missionary teachers repeated this arrangement.

Because the guides provided such a high level of detail and accompanying illustrations, a school could be organized solely on the basis of the information they supplied. In Italy, the Catholic priest Ferrante Aporti opened an infant school in Cremona in 1827 after reading the German version of Wilderspin's manual, which was translated by Joseph Wertheimer and published in 1826.[140] His school gave rise to the Italian preschool movement. It was more often the case that knowledge of the system was acquired through observation, as with Eugénie Millet, who spent a few months visiting schools in London in 1827 on behalf of an infant school committee in Paris. In the United Kingdom, Wilderspin promoted the system in person on behalf of the Infant School Society. Infant schools in Scotland and Ireland were among the first outside London. Though he did not visit Ireland until much later, he trained a teacher for a school opening in 1824 at Enniskerry, the first established in Ireland on the English plan.[141] His 1832 *Early Discipline Illustrated* is a record of his work as a "travelling

37

missionary" for the Infant School Society from 1824 to 1829.[142] His observations of "peasants," "slightly clad children," and "fine Highland girls" echoed missionary observations of foreign peoples. He visited a family in their "hut," remarking, "The whole reminded me of what I had read of the dwellings of the Esquimaux."[143]

He also used the missionary strategy of training local teachers to continue the work. Training was conducted mainly via observation and could be obtained by attending student exhibitions of the children in action, which were also open to the public. The Glasgow Infant School Society used touring exhibitions where there were no schools. Teachers went from town to town with a few young pupils to demonstrate the system and collect donations.[144] Wilderspin tried travelling with students, but he found them troublesome or easily led astray. At least one fell into debt from gambling. He eventually toured with a few trusted students and his eldest daughter. In this way, he aimed "to train many for the work, and, at a comparatively small expense, diffuse the advantages of the system throughout the empire."[145] As another aspect of his work, he established a home business called the Infant School Depot, which marketed kits of materials for use in setting up a school for several hundred children at minimum cost.[146]

To any community wishing to start an infant school, he offered a guarantee that, for a fee, he would exert his control of up to two hundred children in a period of two weeks. At a school in an Edinburgh slum, he accomplished the beginnings of this in only a few minutes. Faced with a "fresh band of little barbarians" — all crying inconsolably in the gallery — Wilderspin cued the adults in attendance to clap loudly. This diversion caused the children to stop crying, and the "mourners were reduced to three, while the mouths and eyes of the rest opened, and remained for what might next befall. A song was sung and time beat, and one voice only was heard weeping."[147] "Now," said Wilderspin, "I shall have no more trouble with the new children; imitation and their trained playfellows will do the rest."[148]

Demonstrations helped standardize the system in these few cases, though any actual training of teachers and children was necessarily short. When the wealthy Scottish industrialist David Stow planned to establish a model infant school in Glasgow, he invited Wilderspin to present a series of lectures.[149] Stow's school was successful, and the local teachers soon "impressed on the public the fact that Wilderspin is not essential to its continuance."[150] Neither Stow nor Wilderspin were great theorists, and the schools started in this way did not have a strong intellectual foundation, relying instead on tricks to gain children's attention and teaching devices from the monitorial system.

The results were nonetheless impressive, but it was the performance of the children that visitors remembered. In a report of his visit during the 1830s, the Philadelphian Alexander Dallas Bache described the model school operated by the Glasgow Education Society as among the best in Europe. He observed the school under invitation by Stow. His detailed description included all aspects of the school day, with a focus on the teaching strategies developed to manage large groups. This management was achieved through whole-class instruction in the gallery, small-group instruction with monitors at lesson posts, and various drills and movement exercises performed while singing. These simple exercises in the gallery — "raising and lowering hands, rising and sitting down" — ensured order and helped the teacher manage transitions between activities. As Bache noted, "The passage from the gallery to the lesson posts is performed while singing, and always in regular order."[151]

By midcentury, the methods and materials were standard in infants' classes in public schools. Henry Barnard included illustrations of an arithmeticon and gonigraph — the jointed rod — in his 1848 *School Architecture*.[152] John George Hodgins compiled a similar book for the Department of Public Instruction for Upper Canada in 1857, describing the use of blocks in a manner reminiscent of Wilderspin: "Building Blocks: for the purpose of illustrating the principle of gravitation, about one hundred blocks, each one inch thick, one inch wide, and two inches long, would be provided. Many practical arithmetical difficulties might be explained by reference to a construction by the blocks; but the chief excellence of such a set would consist in the amusement and employment it would afford the 'little ones.' While the teacher was busy teaching a class, they would be no less busy in quietly building those little houses."[153]

"Babies classes" for children as young as two — they needed only to walk and talk — became part of elementary schools, and in the infants' classes for older children, learning was no longer by means of "amusements." After the British Education Act of 1870 set compulsory schooling at age five, the first two years of elementary schooling were designated the infants' stage. The babies class had a definite social-welfare purpose, namely, to care for the children in the daytime hours while their mothers were at work. At these times, teachers of the youngest children were required to offer substitute care as well as some preparatory work for the infants' class proper. The largest part of preparatory work involved teaching social skills necessary for school success in overcrowded conditions. Children did learn in these situations, and Wilderspin reported examples in which they displayed their knowledge in the community. He related the case of one of his students, who demonstrated her grasp of geometry while attending the local market with her mother and contemplating the sheep hanging at the butcher's stall. Having puzzled her mother by remarking that the sheep were "suspended, perpendicular, and parallels," she elaborated: "don't you see they hang up, that's suspended; they are straight up, that's perpendicular; and they are at equal distances, tha, [sic] that's parallel."[154]

THE PRESCHOOL MODELS imported from England derived in circumstances not re-created in the colonies until the close of the nineteenth century. This was also true of the schools in the United States. According to Caroline Winterer, the Boston infant schools under the influence of Bronson Alcott and William Russell "were, first and foremost, a form of innovative pedagogy and only second, an attempt to forestall urban decay."[155] Leading thinkers in the colonies saw potential in infant schools as a pedagogical reform. However, they also recognized their further positive and negative purpose: spiritual uplift and the prevention of moral decay.

In England, interest in the system as an innovative pedagogy was overtaken by its efficiency in training children. Following on Owen's scheme, the schools were widely established in factory towns in England. Manufacturers recognized their value in providing basic training and discipline for children during the few years prior to their employment. Schooling the young gained popularity in the midst of a rise in child labour and pressures to reduce their workday. Its popularity was directly related to the history of industrial child labour in Britain. Factory towns were full of children who had a high economic value for families and were required as industrial workers by factory owners. For example, when adults who worked in the pin-making industry applied for employment in pointing and cutting pins, their letters often referred to "their quiverful of children ready for service" as pin-headers.[156]

Historian Michael Sanderson observes that the factory infant schools were "an ideal way of exerting the social control of the firm over its workers and of raising up young labourers in obedience if not in scientific skill."[157] Infant school graduates were sought out as docile workers — happy workers, in Owen's terminology. In 1833, when the Royal Commission on Employment of Children in Factories asked mill owner Henry Ashworth about the "practical effects" of the infant schools, he responded that his workmen "always prefer a child who has been educated at an infant school, as those children are most obedient and docile."[158] Another mill owner, who had started a school under the direction of Wilderspin, noted that it was specifically used for recruiting child labourers. Children attending the school were promised "preference of employment when fresh children are taken on."[159]

For Henry Ashworth, who modelled his school on Owen's example, the schools were an "economic investment."[160] His infant school at the New Eagley cotton mill was attended by any child of his adult workers who was between the ages of two and nine. Their time in class decreased in stages as they shifted status from scholars to workers. At age nine, they went to work at the mill for reduced hours, dividing their days between eight-hour work shifts and two hours of study at the mill school for older children. This was called the short-time system. From age thirteen to eighteen, they worked a full shift of twelve hours and, with adult workers as their teachers, undertook forty-five minutes of schooling.[161]

A version of the short-time system was replicated in plantation settlements in the Caribbean and elsewhere in the colonies, where schooling was organized to fit work routines.[162] This suited schooling for slaves by providing basic education and care for very young children prior to their use as full-time labourers. Appearing before the Select Committee on the Extinction of Slavery in 1831, James Beckford Wildman described the system on his Jamaica estate, which was designed to provide basic schooling while maintaining profits. For younger children, early schooling held appeal due to their low value as workers in the present, but high value in the future. "I established an infant school," Wildman explained, "and I kept the little children all day; the gang or class above them I took for a couple of hours in the morning and a couple of hours in the afternoon; the second gang I took for one hour a day out of my time, and endeavoured to induce them to stay one hour out of their time; as they did not work for themselves, it was rest to them being in the school; then the adults were under no regular system of instruction."[163]

chapter 3 **Infant Schools in the Case-Study Countries**

THE SPREAD OF INFANT schools to the British colonies was helped by organizations such as the Home and Colonial Infant School Society and by numerous evangelical missionary groups. Of the thirty modern nations in which children generally start school at age five, many were once British colonies.[1] In New South Wales, Australia, and in New Zealand, where compulsory schooling was initially set at age six and seven respectively, the infants' stage was made available for children from age five as part of the public system.[2] In Canada, the compulsory school age differed from province to province.[3] In Quebec, public schooling was available from the 1870s to all children from age five but was not compulsory until 1942. A kindergarten or transition year was available in only a few jurisdictions until the 1960s.

In Canada and Australia, as in Britain, specialized pre-primary classes within some public and denominational schools replaced infant schools as educational systems developed. The more rigid aspects of the infant system seeped into these "infants' classes," including whole-class teaching, rote learning, and galleries, which endured into the twentieth century.[4] A typical infant school in Victorian London occupied the lower level of a primary school and consisted of a large open space with sliding partitions.[5] It could accommodate four hundred children aged from three to seven within sections of the large room. In a school described by Deborah Weiner in her study of school architecture, 215 children could be contained in the largest gallery, 80 in a smaller section that could be further divided into two classrooms of 40, and 80 in the "babies gallery" youngest children, those aged three to five. There was space for 350 children in the boys' and girls' school in the upstairs classroom arrangement contrasted with the Prussian system, in which smaller classrooms opened off a long hallway, with each class directed by an individual teacher.[6] At first, few schools were built on the Prussian system, with administrators arguing that it was too expensive and that the barrack-like arrangement was not in keeping with the British idea of freedom of development.[7]

Describing school architecture in mid-nineteenth-century Upper Canada (Ontario) in a publication for the Department of Public Instruction, John George Hodgins mentioned that, in the 1850s, the design of a school in Simcoe, Ontario, was selected from thirteen submissions.[8] The exterior reflected an "Old English style," and the interior followed many of the guidelines described in the December 1851 issue of the *American Journal of Education*. The school included separate classrooms for older boys and girls, and an infants' classroom built as a "gallery room" with a capacity for 120 pupils. A door opened from the gallery room to an outdoor covered playroom. Hodgins noted that "the gallery-room is an important feature in the construction of school houses, and its adoption has been strongly urged by the school authorities of Upper Canada."[9]

Before infant schools became part of public schools, they were established by private charities. Several dozen infant schools were founded in Canada between 1825 and 1860, with lesser numbers in Australia and New Zealand. In 1820, Canada consisted of two provinces known as Upper and Lower Canada, having a combined European population of about 500,000. The nineteenth-century Aboriginal population in the area was approximately a hundred thousand, less than one-fifth of what it had been before European contact in the sixteenth century.[10] Most Europeans lived along the St. Lawrence River in the former French colonial settlement of Quebec. Immigration from Britain and Europe was minor, and most of the population was born in North America. Apart from that devoted to the fur trade, there was little or no European settlement in the regions north of the St. Lawrence River and the Great Lakes, or in the West. The situation was very different in the United States, where expansion across the West had occurred at a great rate since the war of the American Revolution.

The European population of Australia in 1825 was approximately fifty thousand, including convicts, free settlers, and soldiers and their families. The Aboriginal population, numbering around 200,000, was vastly larger

43

than the European, with the majority residing in present-day Queensland.[11] During the early period, little contact occurred between Europeans and Aboriginal Australians. Most Europeans resided in the mainland colony, which had Sydney as its centre, and in Van Diemen's Land (Tasmania). Convicts outnumbered the free European population by about three to one, and men outnumbered women by four to one. Convicts would remain in the majority until the 1840s, when assisted immigration schemes and gold discoveries attracted free settlers to Australia.

New Zealand did not become a British colony until 1840, after the signing of the Treaty of Waitangi. In the 1820s, no more than several hundred Europeans lived in New Zealand and approximately 200,000 Maori. Most Europeans lived around the Bay of Islands in the North Island, although there were coastal settlements on both islands. The economic interest in New Zealand centred on whaling, sealing, timber for boatbuilding, and flax. Missionaries followed the whalers and began to establish mission stations in 1816. The timing of colonization and European settlement in New Zealand meant that, between 1825 and 1840, separate infant schools for European children did not exist; as a result, missionary and Maori children attended the same infant schools.[12]

Schools for Settler Children

Canada

Canadian infant schools were never numerous, with the largest number operating from 1848 to 1854, when nine schools received aid through provincial legislatures. Most of these predated 1848. One of the first, established in Halifax, Nova Scotia, dated from 1824. Following the Halifax Infant School and several in Montreal, four more schools in various locations opened in the 1830s and four in the 1840s, with the last in 1848. Other schools did not receive aid, but the general development is noteworthy. Infant schools in Canada enjoyed early popularity, and some of the initial schools remained open for decades. However, few new ones opened after 1850.

The schools were generally managed by local infant school societies. As in England, they provided education, childcare, and religious training for poor children. The York Infant School (Toronto) was established in 1832 and was reported in a local newspaper as the first in Upper Canada. This claim was not accurate, however, as infant schools for indigenous children had formed during the 1820s. The newspaper described the York school children demonstrating their lessons under the direction of their teacher, Sarah Bliss, who had been recruited from the United States. Their curriculum included reading, geography, astronomy, geometry, botany, natural history, and the history of the Bible. The curriculum and exhibitions by pupils resembled those of British infant schools, though there were comparatively fewer children in the Canadian example: "12 boys and 12 girls — between the ages of 7 and 2 years — all very neatly dressed, and formed in a double file — the boys to the right and the girls to the left — regularly sized — the tallest in front and hand in hand. In this order and headed by their teacher, they marched along the aisle of the church, singing a hymn and keeping step with each other, and to the tune, with the precision of a platoon of light infantry."[13]

The Halifax Infant School was more rough and ready. It accepted children from two to six years, sheltering them while their parents were at work. It followed the example of the English workhouse infant school. The annual report for 1834 listed its aims and objectives. Many aspects seem drawn from Wilderspin or inspired by Brougham:

> The object of the Institution is wholly for the purpose of receiving, instructing and when necessary clothing, the children of the poor, endeavouring to counteract any bad habits they may have imbibed at home, by drawing them to the love and practice of virtue, blending amusement, with instruction in the useful branches of knowledge. The children are taken from two to six years of age — an age most troublesome to mothers in indigent circumstances, who gladly avail themselves of an institution, where their infant offspring may be carefully attended, and their young minds trained to heaven, when otherwise vice must unavoidably be engendered in the child, by the careless — or even industrious parent, who leaves her home for the labours of the day, and her children to be guided by their own caprices. During this period, a foundation is laid for moral and religious character, the other public schools are then required to carry on the work — strengthening the assurance that those early labours will not be lost.[14]

The Halifax school had a difficult start. Keen to demonstrate the wider application of infant schools and wanting the public to gain a favourable impression, the local society hired a teacher from Philadelphia to organize the school and stay on for three months. The first schoolroom proved too small — a common story — and the society rented a stable that "after much trouble and expense [was] converted into an eligible school room" with a gallery and benches.[15] The teacher's stay was extended when she could not recruit a replacement, and a year passed before another was hired from the United States.

The ambitious organizers of a Quebec City school initially planned for three hundred children, in accordance with the "system of Wilderspin."[16] Two teachers were hired from England and were asked to bring instructional materials with them. The opening was delayed due to an outbreak of cholera in the city, but within six months of its eventual opening in 1832, ninety-seven children were enrolled in a classroom with a capacity for seventy. More would have come, but overcrowding of the small room discouraged some parents from sending their children. Nonetheless, the teachers claimed that the low numbers limited the impact of the instruction and that full benefits could be seen only with a full complement of three hundred scholars.

The Halifax and Quebec City schools illustrate some of the common problems experienced in Canada in recruiting staff and finding sufficient materials and suitable classrooms. The Charlottetown school opened in 1840 under the direction of a husband and wife recruited from England. Remaining in charge for many years, they were still in place when the school eventually became a kindergarten.[17] In 1843, the organizers of a school in Fredericton were relieved to hire what they believed was the only trained infant teacher in New Brunswick.[18] The problem for the Fredericton Infant School Society was the expense of materials. Supplies from England took six months to arrive. Apparently feeling some urgency to get started, the society ordered materials from Boston, electing to pay an extravagant import duty.[19]

The lack of trained teachers continued to be a problem as infant schools were incorporated into public school systems. In 1859, the Toronto board was fortunate to hire Elizabeth Mitchell, who had been "trained in the Infant School System of Wilderspin" in England, as teacher at the Louisa Street Public School.[20] With the start-up of Normal Schools in this period, training became available locally. The McGill Normal School opened in 1857, and in the same year, it started a model infant school.[21] It was hoped that the mostly female student teachers would raise the standards of "teaching the very young."[22]

Most schools charged parents a small fee for their children's tuition, but this was discretional on their ability to pay. Funds also came from benefactors and the annual fundraising efforts of ladies' committees or church groups. In Charlottetown, a school was specially constructed using funds collected from the congregation of St. Paul's Church (Church of England). An important source of financial support for some schools came from government. The Halifax Infant School enjoyed regular government grants from the 1830s to the 1860s. In many cases, aid was claimed for a portion of the teacher's salary, a sum that remained stable at around twenty pounds per year over the period 1830 to 1860, being about 25 percent of the total salary of seventy-five pounds.[23] There was little debate in Parliament over paying the grant to the schools, although members of the Nova Scotia House of Assembly were initially reluctant to support an infant school at Pictou, fearing that it would take monies away from other schools.[24] The Pictou school enrolled about seventy-five children, two-thirds of whom paid fees. The remainders were "children of the poor who had been clothed and taught in all the branches of infant training."[25] The school demonstrated its worth and received grants from both the county and the province. In 1851, a visitor enthused that it "is in very superior condition, and is diffusing the blessings of the Infant School Training to a very large number of the poor."[26]

The need for the charity infant schools waned in the late 1860s when young children in large cities joined their older brothers and sisters, entering schools at the initial primary grade level. Infant schools opening after 1860 were short-lived affairs. The Montreal Infant School Association, a new body unconnected with the Montreal Infant School Society of the 1820s, opened the Mountain Street Infant School in 1868. There was also a private fee-charging infant school in the same neighbourhood, which had been started two years earlier "under the pious care of Miss Morison."[27]

The association hired a teacher at twelve dollars a month. Students were grouped into three classes according to age, and some paid fees. The directors stressed that they were to be treated kindly and fairly, with both rewards and punishments avoided.[28] Over the first year, student numbers grew too large for the building, and the directors decided to lower the maximum age from eight to seven.[29] They also sought a government grant for the school on the basis of its success, describing its plans in a letter to the school commission:

> The Montreal Infant School Association has acquired [illegible] with an old building [illegible] being no. 114 Mountain Street and is

conducting therein an infant school for children under 8 years of age as nearly as possible on the most approved infant School System now in use in the Old World. The intention of the Association is to build a school house 60 (by 30 feet) feet long in this place and to develop the school as fast as the means at their disposal may permit so to be a useful rival to the large Catholic institutions of a similar kind [salles d'asile] which are flourishing in the City ... [We ask] for assistance in carrying on these operations from the school taxes and what would be the terms of such assistance.[30]

The City denied funds, pointing out that school commissioners were responsible for the provision of schooling, including for five-year-olds. The association was nonetheless concerned regarding the quality and accessibility of available schooling, and it obtained a written agreement from the school commission that it would proceed to introduce the "most approved and advanced methods in a short time, and that the youngest children who can go to school would be provided for."[31] It may have been too soon for graduates of the McGill Normal School to make a difference in the quality of teaching in infants' classes. In 1870, the association abruptly shifted focus: abandoning the infant school, it turned its attention to the welfare of working-class boys and opened a boys' home.[32] The time for infant schools as a charity had passed.

Australia

In 1824, the Reverend Richard Hill established an infant school for poor children in the schoolhouse next to St. James' Anglican Church in Sydney.[33] St. James' was newly opened in that year and served a cross-section of the colony including colonial administrators, the lower classes, and convicts and former convicts. Encouraged to start an infant school by a colleague in London who had one in his parish, Hill waited until he had read Wilderspin's 1823 book on the subject before doing so.[34] A female teacher was hired, and she set to work assembling her materials, mainly a set of boards to which lessons were pasted and Isaac Watts' *Divine and Moral Songs for Children*. The latter, a standard in English infant schools, "functioned as both a hymn book and as a textbook for the religious and moral instruction of infants and children."[35] St. James' was a parish school, so its emphasis was on the inculcation of religious values.

Hill's enthusiasm led him to write to the editor of the *Sydney Gazette* extolling the benefits of the infant system: "The efficiency of this method, for affording the very important assistance, to the labouring classes, of relieving mothers during a considerable part of the day, from the care and anxiety of their infants when beginning to lisp; as well as, during that time, relieving the little ones from the danger of drowning in wells, which too often happens."[36]

He drew directly from Wilderspin, using his gardening metaphor to compare children's minds to a "garden where he would plant desirable values to 'pre-occupy' the soil, preventing 'the growth of noxious weeds.'"[37] Nonetheless, though he was impressed by the children's "facility to learn by imitation" the hymns and catechism, he found that progress in the alphabet was slow, "as it is found difficult to fix the eye of very young children."[38] The school was well attended from the start, indicating both a need for the service and acceptance by parents. In its first months, it had an enrolment of between twenty and thirty children each day, ranging from "the lispers," who were aged eighteen months, to four-year-olds. Hill's description did not mention teaching young children through amusements or the need for play or playgrounds.

The Male Orphan School in Sydney used Andrew Bell's monitorial system. Introduced on a large scale in 1820 by the Reverend Thomas Reddall, this, too, was an innovation in Australia.[39] Reddall arrived in the colony as a schoolmaster and rose to become director-general of the government public schools of New South Wales in 1824. However, his efforts did not seem to have improved the quality of education, as revealed in his report to the secretary of state to the colonies: "I have also reported on the lamentable want of plain and practical education, arising from the deficiency of parochial Schools. I found but 17 which were very ill conducted, and very thinly attended. These have now been extended to 36, including 5 Infant Schools in the Town of Sydney, Parramatta, and Windsor."[40]

He drew attention to the infant schools as a bright spot in an otherwise dreary educational landscape: "These Infant Schools, which are daily attended by about 80 to 100 children under six years of age, have succeeded beyond my most sanguine expectation. I trust and hope they are more placed on such a footing so at least to lay the foundation, one which may raise a better generation than exists at present."[41]

Within the space of a few years, what was initially a little-understood charity became a common feature of denominational schools. By 1830, there were four additional infant schools in Sydney and nearby towns, each with an enrolment of approximately one hundred pupils.[42] From 1848, which saw the instigation of government public schools, all schools with more than two hundred pupils had infants' departments.[43] Praise for their exemplary quality did not persist. One historian regards their success at teaching academic skills as minimal, calling these early infant schools "Australia's first childminding centres."[44]

As described by William Burton in his 1840 survey of education in New South Wales, the two Church of England infant schools in Sydney seemed to have lost their way. He remarked that, "although denominated an Infant School," the institution at St. Phillip's "is not conducted upon the system pursued in Schools properly so called: The same mode of teaching is pursued as in the Primary School: the monitor of a class instructing aloud, and the whole class repeating after the child; the school-room is small and inconvenient; and both the room and system of teaching require to be formed anew."[45] Burton's terse description of the St. James' Infant School was that it was "conducted ... upon the same principles as that of St. Phillip."[46] His review of the infant school at the Presbyterian church was more favourable, describing it as operating according to the training system at David Stow's Glasgow Normal School under graduate Joseph Andrews.[47]

In 1828, a group of private citizens in Sydney proposed creating a school founded more clearly on Pestalozzi's ideas as a remedy for what they considered to be the lax approach of infant schools.[48] Although they admitted to knowing little about Pestalozzi, they were convinced that his ideas were superior in their greater attention to formal instruction. They charged that, at infant schools, children spent too much time in "idleness or play."[49]

In their understanding of Pestalozzi, children were constantly kept under the direction of the teacher, whose only method was whole-group instruction. They would recite their lessons en masse, play games, march, and clap, never spending much time on one activity. Children remained in a "perpetual and almost endless variety of exercises."[50] Through this treatment, they would achieve deep learning and an awakening of the imagination. The use of a questioning technique in the form of a dialogue between the teacher and the group of students, and starting with what was familiar to the children, meant that "every branch of knowledge ... [can be] brought down to a level with the capacity of children, may be introduced, as it were, into the nursery."[51] Because children were drawn naturally to learn, the teacher did not need to be a disciplinarian. Instead, she could be "the mild and even playful leader of the little circle, uniting with the antics of a governess the tenderness and care of a mother and a nurse."⁵² The children themselves, however, did not play. When a teacher called on a child to demonstrate its skills by reciting a verse, it was helped to "repress its natural inclination for amusement and play."⁵³

New Zealand

In 1839, infant teacher James Buchanan left London for Wellington, New Zealand, with the intent of establishing a school for European children under the sponsorship of the New Zealand Company (NZC).⁵⁴ A detailed account of this venture is found in Helen May's book on New Zealand infant schools.⁵⁵ The Buchanan family's influence on infant schools in foreign missions was significant and will be detailed later in the chapter. Two of Buchanan's sons, William and David, had set out ten years earlier to seek a better life in the Cape Colony and had organized infant schools for the London Missionary Society (LMS). A third, Ebenezer, lived in Cape Town from 1833, leaving in 1838 to establish infant schools in Samoa, also for the LMS.

As James Buchanan was fifty-five years old when he left England, we might expect that his career as an infant school teacher was nearing its end. Times may have been difficult for Buchanan, as they were for Wilderspin, who had returned from Dublin in 1838 after the quick termination of his appointment as principal of the Dublin Model Infant and Training School. Phillip McCann writes of this time, "The great days of his missionary work were over and a few years later he retired, penniless and affected in health."⁵⁶ More than two decades of teaching upwards of 150 young children may have been enough for James and Isabella Buchanan. But this was not the reason for his emigration, according to son William, who wrote in 1847 that his father "became impressed with a desire to extend [the infant system's] usefulness to the promising sphere which, according to the accounts then published, appeared to be opening so favorably to the settlement projected by the New Zealand Company."⁵⁷

Buchanan travelled on the *Adelaide,* the first ship sent out by the company to New Zealand.⁵⁸ Accompanying him was Wilmott Huxtable Tilke, aged thirty, who was to be his assistant. George Samuel Evans, chairman of the NZC, had previously employed her, presumably as a teacher.⁵⁹ Buchanan's wife, Isabella, and daughter Ann remained in London, waiting for him to prepare a situation for them in New Zealand.

The New Zealand infant school was an initiative of the New Zealand Company Ladies Committee led by the chairman's wife, Harriet Evans.[60] It was planned as the company's main educational initiative as a school for Maori and settler children.[61] The company brought prefabricated buildings, including those for the school.[62] Other institutions were planned to replicate those in England. A collection of books was brought for a public library. As explained by historian Gilbert Herbert, the replicas of English villages were not intended solely to make the settlers feel at home, but were part of the "technology of colonial expansion"; "the concept of prefabrication had become linked in official thought and imagination with the idea of colonization and emigration."[63]

As it happened, Buchanan never reached New Zealand. The *Adelaide* was troubled by unruly passengers, causing the captain to stop in Cape Town to settle the disputes, where Buchanan's sons David and William convinced their father to stay.[64] Isabella and Ann joined him in Cape Town, where Isabella died within a few years. Ann established a school in Cape Town, and in 1857, she moved with her father to Pietermaritzburg where David and Ebenezer had settled. James Buchanan died in Pietermaritzburg in the same year.[65]

Tilke continued to New Zealand, opening an infant school in Wellington shortly after her arrival. The school, known as one of the first in Wellington, served the children of settlers. In 1841, Tilke married a fellow passenger on the *Adelaide* and moved to Australia. The prefabricated school was given to Richard Barrett, an influential trader who was living in New Zealand, for his help in purchasing land from Maori.[66] It was operated as Barrett's Hotel until 1855 when it was damaged in an earthquake.

Mary Ann Buxton, who also arrived on the *Adelaide,* operated a Wellington school from January 1, 1843, in the mode of a dame school. Accounts of the school emphasize her humane approach and the esteem in which the community held her.[67] For Buxton, the school was a means of livelihood. Her husband, who had been a gardener in England, had difficulty finding steady employment in Wellington. He taught with her in the school for a time and worked as a part-time gravedigger, before his death in 1847. She continued the school with the assistance of her daughter, Sophia, who taught the older girls in a second room in their home while she herself managed the younger ones. The school continued in this manner until 1878 and Mary Ann Buxton's retirement. She died in 1886 at age ninety-three.

Helen May has documented a scattering of other schools for young European children, which operated in larger settlements from the 1840s.[68] Many encountered difficulties with staffing, similar to those experienced in Canada and Australia twenty years earlier. The Lyttelton Infant School was established in 1851 under the direction of the Reverend Thomas Jackson, who for seven years was principal of the Church of England's Battersea Training School. The school was well supplied, though its equipment list did not include playground items. It suffered over the years from want of a trained teacher. May notes another school, which was operated by the British and Foreign School Society in Nelson, and an Irish Catholic infant school in Auckland, established respectively in 1847 and 1850.

Infant Schools for Indigenous Children

The ten years from 1825 to 1835 saw tremendous missionary activity among indigenous people around the world. Thousands of European men and women took up the call to "preach the Gospel in the regions beyond," in association with organizations such as the Anglican Church Missionary Society (CMS) and the evangelical London Missionary Society.[69] Education was an evangelizing strategy, and infant schools for indigenous children developed concurrently with those for settlers. In Canada and New Zealand, relations between settlers and indigenous people had developed to make such endeavours possible. Indigenous parents were keen to have their children learn to read and write in English, whereas missionaries sought their conversion and assimilation.

The Royal Proclamation of 1763 recognized Aboriginal land rights in Canada by ensuring the Crown's protection of hunting lands from purchase or settlement. The Crown's motivation lay partly in fear of Aboriginal rebellions and partly in a desire to establish boundaries for Crown colonies. The proclamation provided the basis for subsequent treaties in which large tracts of First Nations land were transferred to settlers during the nineteenth century.[70] After the War of 1812, and the increased security of the British hold on the colony, the need for a military alliance with the First Nations diminished. The Crown Lands Protection Act of 1839 declared Indian lands to be Crown lands and thus made the Crown the guardian of Aboriginal territories.

Starting in the 1830s, the more paternalistic policy reflected the priorities of protection and assimilation rather than partnership, culminating in the Gradual Assimilation Act of 1857. The act aimed to remove special status from Aboriginal peoples through enfranchisement.⁷¹ For a practical-minded mission teacher, assimilation meant conversion to Christianity and the adoption of Euro-Canadian values, morality, and lifestyle. Missionaries were keen to employ new methods with Aboriginal children, including the infant school system of education.

In New Zealand, the Treaty of Waitangi was signed in 1840 by representatives of the British Crown and Maori leaders with the aim of protecting the rights of Maori people and ensuring the "orderly" settlement of New Zealand by Europeans. Maori interest in literacy was already well established by this time. During the period of early contact, mission schools were well attended by Maori adults and children. As in Canada, infant schools were established in mission settlements during the 1830s and 1840s.⁷²

The military and economic interdependence that defined the early relationship between Europeans and Aboriginal peoples in Canada did not exist in Australia. The major trade commodity in Australia was wool, which depended on pastoral farming and the displacement of those Aboriginal Australians who were not employed as stockmen or domestic workers. No treaties were ever negotiated to provide schools for Aboriginal Australian children, leaving education in the hands of voluntary religious organizations.

Conversion and civilization were closely tied, and the question of which came first was hotly debated. The Select Committee on Aborigines, a British parliamentary committee, asked the New Zealand missionary William Yate, "From the experience you have had in missionary exertions, would you begin by attempting to civilise or by attempting to Christianise?" He answered that conversion must necessarily come first but that civilization "commences at the moment Christ is established."⁷³ John Beecham, who had experience in the Friendly Islands (Tonga), agreed, believing that a direct cause and effect existed between conversion and civilization: "No sooner does the Gospel begin to operate on the mind of the heathen than it leads to the first step in civilisation."⁷⁴ In accordance with missionary thinking, civilization triggered by conversion meant giving up traditional ways of life in exchange for European-style farming, housing, clothing, gender relations, and child rearing. It was further marked by the use of the English language, regular attendance at church, and respecting the Sabbath.

Other missionaries believed that a European worldview, in which, for example, the rights of the individual took precedence over those of the group, must precede conversion. According to James Axtell, there was a "widespread colonial belief that 'civility must precede Christianity,' that is, the Indians must adopt an English lifestyle before they can be trusted with the Christian sacraments. For the English this was not just an ideological statement but a statement of fact because the English Protestant version of Christianity was bound up with a version of English cultural style ... It was therefore not possible to accept their brand of Christianity without the accompanying cultural baggage."[75]

Samuel Marsden, director of the CMS in the Pacific, was of the view that civilization preceded conversion, a belief that was partly responsible for his founding of schools in New Zealand mission stations. Yet, whichever came first, the other was a close second, and missionary assimilation strategies included the immersion of Aboriginal peoples in a European way of life.

At the same time, Aboriginal parents who sought benefits for their children and community through the acquisition of English and literacy skills were greatly interested in schooling. At the Methodist mission station at St. Clair in Upper Canada, the Reverend James Evans reported, "The school has been well attended during the winter, averaging about thirty scholars; and as a proof that the Indians are not, as heretofore, careless in this respect, I may add that some of the families being now about four miles back in the wood making sugar, (this being the season), frequently come in a morning and bring the children from five to six years of age, and fetch them home again at night; so anxious are they that their children should learn."[76]

Canada

In Canada and the United States, infant schools for Aboriginal children began to be established during the late 1820s as an element of missionary work undertaken by a number of Protestant groups, including Methodists, Presbyterians, and Baptists. There is little evidence of formal education for young indigenous children prior to this time. In New France, schools for indigenous people were organized by Catholic religious orders from 1620. Their aim — evangelism and francization — employed a variety of means, including experiments with a reserve system of mission schooling developed by Jesuits in Brazil and Paraguay during the sixteenth century.[77] In this system, converts lived in a segregated settlement administered by European missionaries. Reserves were planned to be self-sufficient, and residents were taught European trades and agricultural techniques. In New

55

France, mission schools had little success, with teachers lamenting that parents were too attached to their children to release them to schools for long. Parents were also unwilling to permit European teachers to use force to discipline their children, as was the custom in schools. During the eighteenth century, the missionary strategy changed its focus from children to adults and largely abandoned formal schooling for young children.

A mission community managed by the Jesuits at Ancienne Lorette, near Quebec City, demonstrated the success of this shift in focus. During the seventeenth century, the Huron-Wendat had settled in the area as refugees from war with the Iroquois. The land they occupied had been given to "Christian savage neophytes" by the king of France and was managed by the Jesuits. In 1699, the Jesuits appropriated the land from the Huron-Wendat, sparking a land claim that brought Huron-Wendat grand chief Abarathaha Tsawenhohi and three others to London more than a century later. They aimed to petition King George IV to settle the land dispute.[78] After meeting the king at Windsor Castle in April, they remained in London for a few months longer, taking part in events such as the June 1825 meeting of the Infant School Society. There, they sat on the platform as special guests alongside Henry Brougham and other leaders in the society.

Europeans perceived Ancienne Lorette as a "model village of the potential of native Christianity."[79] Success was marked by loss of indigenous culture and assimilation of its European counterpart. This included a change in child-rearing practices that the French considered too indulgent, to a punishment regime in which no fault was overlooked. According to the Jesuit managers of the mission, Huron parents nominated their children for punishment, which was carried out by the teachers, making "the little savages so well-behaved that one can now do with them whatever he wishes."[80]

By the mid-nineteenth century, the Huron-Wendat were judged to be fully integrated and virtually without their language. There were reportedly no regular speakers of Huron. In his 1890 annual report, Superintendent General of Indian Affairs Edgar Dewdney described what he believed to be the Huron-Wendat success story:

> The Hurons, whose reserve is situated at Lorette in the County of Quebec, have probably less trace, physically, of the aboriginal inhabitants of this Continent than any other Indian Band in Canada, and intellectually they are on a par with the white husbandman of the vicinity; indeed many of them are very shrewd men of business, and are quite well off, the articles manufactured by them being generally

in good demand: though last year sales appear not to have been so profitable as usual. The school at this point continued its operations during the year. Order and decorum characterised the conduct of the greater number of the members of the Band.[81]

The "articles" to which Dewdney referred were traditional handcrafts sold as curios to tourists as well as practical items such as snowshoes and moccasins.

Dewdney described "three tests which especially mark the advance of Indians towards civilisation, viz, the adoption of the dress of the white man, engaging in agriculture, and the education of their children."[82] It was under Dewdney's administration that starving First Nations people in Western Canada were forced to work for food rations on inadequate agricultural settlements, and residential schools were established in collaboration with religious groups. Only by removing children from community influence could the desired transformation of the mind occur. Dewdney continued in his report: "The work ... of transforming an Indian into a whiteman in sentiment, is necessarily a slow one, and we have to be satisfied with gradual results, and to persevere in the hope of accomplishing, if not in the present, then in the next, and if not in that, in the succeeding generation, his emancipation from the delusions with which his inherent proclivities and early association trammel his mind and obscure his intellect."[83]

In Upper Canada, the Methodists established the Grape Island Mission to the Mississauga in 1826, which was later memorialized as the "Nursery of Indian Missions."[84] Regarded at the time as a model settlement, the mission contained an infant school. Its proximity to the town of Belleville made it a popular destination for visitors, who came to admire the scenery and view the village and its residents, much as factory tourists did at New Lanark. A visitor in 1834 remarked that "the view of Grape Island, on sailing up the Bay of Quinte about sunrise, is very beautiful" but expressed disappointment after seeing the settlement: "The houses looming away in the distance seem much larger and more numerous than they really are, and give the idea of a well built, regularly planned town. On our arrival at it, therefore, we are something disappointed."[85] In 1834, the mission was already in decline. Three years later, its members relocated to Alderville, a village on Rice Lake, the Grape Island buildings sold to finance the new community.

In the three decades following the war of the American Revolution, the numbers of settlers in the St. Lawrence River region in Upper Canada increased dramatically, and First Nations people were pressured by the colonial government to make room. As one example, the Mississauga (Ojibway) First Nations forfeited 3 million acres in a series of "land surrenders" to the Crown over a period of fifty years.[86] In 1805, the Crown purchased 250,000 acres from the Mississauga at Credit River for a pence per acre or the equivalent amount in gifts.[87] The Crown's strategy was to then resell the land to settlers at a profit, in a process described by historian Alan Taylor as "building state power from a web of private-properties."[88] The Mississauga sold land as a strategy to retain control over their future, expecting it to result in long-term rewards. Instead, the British perceived the sale as a "one-shot commercial purchase that extinguished native title."[89]

In the midst of these developments, some Mississauga converted to Christianity. They were motivated by spiritual and pragmatic reasons, including the promise of schools for their children. The region around the Bay of Quinte was a site of intense mission activity led by American Methodists such as the Reverend William Case, known as the Big Black Coat Man by the Mississauga.[90] Case worked alongside First Nations preachers, most notably the Reverend Peter Jones. Their strategy followed a proven scheme, starting with camp meetings that could last for several days in which preachers such as Jones sermonized in Ojibway, and converts prayed and sang. This was followed by gathering converts into a settlement designed to resemble a settler village. In this way, believers were isolated from unbelievers and provided with a full cultural immersion. The final stage was to train local leaders in the mission schools who would then move to other regions as preachers and teachers.

The Grape Island Mission was organized by Jones under invitation from Case. In 1826, the Society of Methodist Indians paid the Mississauga people five shillings to lease Grape Island and another nearby island for 999 years.[91] As historian Ruth Clarke notes, the Society of Methodist Indians were in effect leasing land they owned.[92] The residents, initially numbering about 150, lived in tents during the first winter. In the spring, with the assistance of artisan missionaries, they built log residences and public buildings — a chapel, a schoolhouse with a separate room for the infant school, a hospital, a general store, a smithy, and a mechanic shop.[93] While their children were at school, women manufactured handicrafts to sell to tourists, as well as baskets and brooms to exchange for provisions such as flour. At the height of its success, the ten-acre island had a population of about three hundred living in thirty-three log residences. The Mississauga were not obligated to remain on the island, and the population shifted as residents came and went. For long periods, there was no resident missionary, and near the end of the mission, Chief John Sunday assumed this role, but he was often away preaching at other Indian communities, including Sault Ste. Marie.

Although life on the Island, as it was often simply called, was meant to imitate that of an English village, it was regulated to a far greater extent, much like that of an English factory village. Time was marked by the sound of a cow horn, blown by Case himself when he was present, which could be heard across the small island. Nuclear families lived in individual cottages, with the male taking position as head of the household. On occasion, there were home inspections. In 1830, Peter Jones went unannounced into every home as well as the school, taking brief notes on the state of housekeeping and the women's activities: at Joseph Skunk's, "a woman was making light bread like a white woman"; at Jacob Snowstorm's, "one woman making baskets — one sewing — one idle"; at John Pigeon's (the home of a model convert) "everything looked like industry, and improvement in the house."[94] William Case visited the home of John Pigeon in 1833, remarking on "the Britannia cups and spoons as bright as silver."[95] Some households also had chinaware donated to the mission by Methodists in Britain. For both Jones and Case, "the neatness of their houses, the luxuriant growth of their crops, and everything else showed that our Grape Island brethren had made great proficiency in the arts of civilized life."[96] The daily routine revolved around the fields and workshops, except on Sunday when no work was permitted.

The infant school at the Grape Island Mission commenced on June 2, 1829, though the school for older children had been established from the very start of the mission. The overall enrolment was about sixty children and youth in a building measuring thirty feet by twenty-five feet and divided into separate "apartments" for male and female students. A gallery was built into one end. Gifted students were identified for special treatment and trained as preachers, but the school was open to all.

The mission infant school admitted pupils across a wide age range. Teacher John B. Benham explained this in reporting that they had "adopted it in connection with the common school system, for all at school."[97] Perhaps there were too few children or too few teachers to warrant separate schools for younger and older pupils. However, it was also believed that, with its use of picture cards as a starting point for lessons and recitation, the infant system was well suited in a "Native school" for teaching non-English speakers. On the basis of the pupils' six-month experience, Benham wrote, "We are of opinion that the knowledge they gain, will leave a more lasting impression on the mind, from the plan on which they are taught; being by representation or familiar comparisons." The teacher at the Credit River infant school agreed that the simplicity of the system was "particularly suited to the tastes and dispositions of Indian children."[98]

Male and female students began their school day in their separate classes for about ninety minutes of lessons, which were structured according to the Lancasterian system. After a recess break, all students gathered in the gallery, "where they are taught on the infant plan, the elements of arithmetic, geography, astronomy, geometry, English grammar, and natural and sacred history."[99] The school was well equipped with number frames, a world map, a globe, a blackboard, and forms to teach geometry. Some of the material, such as the number frames, was built in the shop.[100]

William Case, describing the school at Credit River, referred to the efficiency of the Pestalozzian system and to the maps and "lessons on cards" donated by ladies in Philadelphia and New York.[101] The Credit River school comprised a single room with a gallery at one end, which was divided for male and female pupils. It was equipped in the same manner as at Grape Island. William Lyon Mackenzie, visiting the school, noted "the figure of a clock, in pasteboard, by which to explain the principles of the time-piece." He added that "the walls of the school are adorned with good moral maxims; and I perceived that one of the rules was rather novel, though doubtless in place here. — It was, 'No blankets to be worn in school.'"[102]

The schools were one aspect of a conversion and assimilation strategy. A visitor in 1829 observed that children were taught to read, write, and worship God.[103] But their schooling involved more than this. Indian children needed to be remade. Otherwise, as Benham believed, "it would have been putting *new wine* into *old bottles*."[104] Creating "new bottles" required re-socialization. Initially, the schools taught basic literacy skills, often in both English and indigenous languages. At the Rice Lake mission, the teacher reported, "In the infant school the children repeat the answer both in English and in Indian. This plan I have adopted, lest they should be found not to understand the meaning."[105] This gave way to a curriculum of cultural replacement. The Methodist preacher John Carroll, writing about the infant school at Grape Island, noted, "We hope the plan of the Infant School system will do well for teaching the Indian children English, and that we shall be able to extend the influence of religion and education more generally."[106]

Assimilation through these means was slow, and attention turned to children alone and their more efficient assimilation and education through enforced school attendance.¹⁰⁷ It was expected that this would lead to conversion, both to Christianity and to the English lifestyle and culture. The shift in attitude was evident in changes in the Methodist mission schools referred to above; bilingual instruction was dropped in favour of English immersion. In 1830, instruction at the Rice Lake school was in "Indian" and English. In 1858, the teacher at the New Credit school wanted to "burn or destroy all Indian books, and put an end to talking Indian in school."¹⁰⁸ Another teacher at the school observed, "The English language is used almost exclusively in the play as well as the studies of the children, which is in itself a great advantage to the Indian children, and is becoming more and more appreciated by the Indian parents."¹⁰⁹ This was considered to be the ideal, that the children's training would have an impact on their parents and community. How First Nations parents responded to the infant schools is unknown, but the schools seemed to have been well attended and the methods accepted.

Grape Island included a number of institutions that required staffing, though there seemed to be no shortage of teachers.¹¹⁰ There was a boarding school for girls, Sunday and evening schools for adults, and a vocational school for instruction in agriculture and trades. At the day school, male and female teachers led separate classes for the boys and girls. Teachers came to the mission from a number of circumstances. John B. Benham was a student at the Methodist seminary at Cazenovia when he was recruited by Case.¹¹¹ John Carroll described Benham as "heavenly-minded and angelic-looking." He later served as superintendent of Methodist missions in Liberia. However, the organization of the infant school may have been the work of Betsey Stockton, who taught at the mission in 1829.

Stockton was a freed slave from New England and a Presbyterian missionary.¹¹² Part of a mission to Hawaii, she had formed and led a school for missionary children and adult Hawaiians on Maui from 1824 to 1825, reputed to be the first school for commoners in the Sandwich (Hawaiian) Islands.¹¹³ In 1840, it was still known as Betsey Stockton's school. A visitor at this later date commented on its evangelical focus: "I wish I knew of a white school where religion was so faithfully inculcated."¹¹⁴ The mission schools were organized with the co-operation of Hawaiian chiefs, and it is estimated that, by 1830, almost all adults on the islands attended school, but few children.¹¹⁵ After Stockton returned to the United States, she led an infant school for African American children in Philadelphia in 1827, probably her first exposure to the system, and then taught briefly at Grape Island in 1829.

While still in Philadelphia, she was drawn to the mission by Case, who had visited the city accompanied by Peter Jones and several boys from the mission, including the ten-year-old Shahwahnekzhih, later named Henry Bird Steinhauer.[116] In Philadelphia, John Neagle painted a portrait of Shahwahnekzhih in traditional dress. Case made a number of trips to the United States to solicit volunteers and raise funds. Model students such as Shahwahnekzhih sang hymns in Ojibway and displayed craftwork before an audience.[117] In this way, Case also recruited Hester (Hetty) Ann Hubbard and her friend Eliza Barnes. Both taught the girls at Grape Island, and Barnes worked for a time at Rice Lake, teaching the girls domestic arts. One account notes that the two friends became rivals for Case's attention, and Case married each in turn: first Hubbard in 1829, and after her death, Barnes in 1833.

Plans to leave Grape Island began in the early 1830s. It was recognized almost from the start that the ten-acre island could not sustain the population; firewood, cattle, and crops were situated on three separate islands, and the converts lived on a fourth. Under Case's direction, the residents resettled at Alderville in 1837. Here, the first school was a boarding school for girls, opened in 1838.[118] As at Grape Island, Case designed Alderville as an industrial village. Residents were offered larger farms, and there was a day school as well as a boarding school. These eventually combined to become the Alderville Manual Labour School, regarded as Canada's first residential school.[119] As described in a report of the British Wesleyan Missionary Society, which administered the school, children could thus be separated from their families "until they are made emphatically new creatures."[120] Although the infant system continued to be used at other missions, such as the New Credit River Mission, there is no record of it at Alderville.

There are few traces of infant schools for indigenous children after this time. As late as 1842, Moses Henry Perley proposed opening infant schools for Indian children in New Brunswick. In his report on Indian reserves, written for the government, he pointed out the value of isolated settlements at Burnt Church and elsewhere, though without reference to mission work. "The first step towards the real improvement of the Indians is to gain them over from a wandering to a settled life, and to form them into compact settlements" having agricultural schools for youth and infant schools for the very young.[121] He suggested, "If attended with a reasonable degree of success, it may not be too much to anticipate that [infant schools] would lead to the perfect civilization of the rising generation of Indians."[122]

John Neagle, *An Indian Boy: Shahwahnekzhih* (Henry Steinhauer), 1829, oil on canvas. 79.1.1, Collection of Glenbow Museum, Calgary.

Perley stated that First Nations and settler children should be educated together in English, as the proximity to white children was believed beneficial as a means of assimilation of "the habits, thoughts and feelings of the other inhabitants of the Province."[123] Recognizing that First Nations parents might be reluctant to send their young children, Perley proposed that benefits received by parents be contingent on their children's attendance. Nonetheless, he believed that parents, "upon finding themselves relieved from the trouble of looking after them for a considerable portion of each day, would insist upon the attendance of the children as a relief to themselves."[124]

From the 1840s, the residential school model was the favoured approach to Indian education in the context of assimilationist policies, which culminated in the passing of the Indian Act in 1876. The act defined who held Indian status, and it legislated control over many aspects of the lives of First Nations peoples, ranging from outlawing certain traditional practices to controlling movement and enforcing school attendance. Regulations governing education became more restrictive over time, following the pattern of compulsory school laws enacted in provincial school systems. An 1894 amendment to the Indian Act permitted the government to forcibly commit children to the school. In the twentieth century, children not attending school were classed as delinquent, and their parents were fined.[125]

Residential schools provided instruction for a half-day only; for the remaining time, students worked on farms, school maintenance, or in learning trades.[126] At the time, school administrators and the government were aware of the problems in some residential schools — poorly trained teachers, high staff turnover, teaching by rote, disease and death among students, poor buildings, enforced labour by students, and a high dropout rate — but little was done to improve the overall situation for more than a century.[127] William Hailmann, US superintendent of Indian schools in the 1890s, reflected, "It is interesting to note that, in spite of practically total external failure, the spirit and even much of the form of these early enterprises persisted."[128] In the United States, and to an extent in Canada, kindergarten and object teaching influenced methods in day schools in the early twentieth century, though little academic work was accomplished. An academic focus was not the aim, as Hailmann observed: "The school as such serves as a concrete illustration of a civilized Christian home which the Indians learn to respect and in an appreciable degree to emulate."[129]

In Hailmann's description, some day school teachers had a missionary zeal for their work, if not pedagogical expertise. He remarked, "It is not rare ... to find among them sanctified men and women whose very presence is an inspiration."[130] In the main, however, teachers in Indian schools were poorly trained. This was due in part to the dual-track system of education in which schooling for Indian children was racialized and church-based. Bernard Schissel and Terry Wotherspoon describe this as "one of the great ironies" of residential schooling: "Ambiguous attitudes about the capabilities of Aboriginal children resulted in schools that were largely dysfunctional pedagogically. This was the result of institutionalized bigotry that had, at its core, a system of education based on curricula that were ineffective and intentionally dismissive, a system that was staffed by teachers who were poorly trained, incompetent, and in some respects morally bankrupt, and a system based on several degrees of reward and punishment that violated the human dignity of the schools' charges."[131]

Australia

The first missionary school for Aboriginal children in Australia — the Native Institution at Parramatta — opened in 1816. It was supported by Governor Macquarie as a means of easing tensions between settlers and Aborigines through the introduction of Aborigines to European civilization and Christianity. This approach was a poor match for the problems caused by European settlement. The arrival of Europeans had been devastating for Aborigines: large numbers had perished from disease and others through government-sanctioned extermination. In 1801, Governor King issued a government order to "drive back" Aborigines from settlements "by firing on them."[132]

The Native Institution was undertaken as a small-scale experiment in Aboriginal education. Governor Macquarie set about securing its students by ordering their kidnapping. He instructed soldiers to take as prisoners "twelve Aboriginal boys and six girls between four and six years of age for the Native Institution at Parramatta" and specified that they should be "only fine, healthy and good-looking children."[133] Only four children were "rescued" from their wandering lives to become the first inmates of the Native Institution.[134] The institution's rules and regulations stipulated the conditions of their confinement: "No Child after having been admitted into the Institution, shall be permitted to leave it, or be taken away by any Person whatever, (whatever parents or other relatives) until such time as the Boys shall have attained the age of sixteen years, and the Girls fourteen years, at which ages they shall be respectively discharged."[135]

London Missionary Society teacher William Shelley and his wife, Elizabeth, provided the educational foundation of the institution. Shelley was an artisan missionary who had apprenticed as a cabinetmaker in England.[136] It was Shelley's idea to form a boarding school for boys and girls under the age of seven to teach them skills such as carpentry and sewing and to provide them with religious training. On graduation, they were expected to take up positions as servants or labourers. Shelley was appointed teacher but died soon after, and Elizabeth took over his responsibilities. Although the school is an important historical example, being similar in many respects to future mission schools set apart from community and parents, it floundered until closing in 1822.

A second school with a similar purpose was opened in 1826. The Blacktown Native Institution was meant to be the first of several established for Aboriginal children by order of King George IV to Governor Darling. By this time, the Infant School Society had formed in London, and the first infant schools had opened in Sydney for European children. An infant school for Aboriginal children was part of Darling's plan. The teacher at the Blacktown Native Institution was the Church Missionary Society missionary William Hall, who had worked at mission stations in New Zealand before ill health led him to Sydney.

The Blacktown Native Institution functioned as an industrial school on Lancasterian principles; providing basic literacy and skill training, it used a token system of rewards for "good behaviour, good work, and Religious knowledge."[137] It was a sad place for the few children unlucky enough to attend, all of whom were "half-caste" (of part Aboriginal descent). They included children from the orphanage, a two-year-old girl from Port Macquarie, and a young Maori girl sent by the Reverend Richard Hill from his St. James' Infant School in Sydney.[138] About half were Maori European and half were Aborigine European. Enrolment decreased when some were removed from the school by their parents. Others became so ill that the school resembled a "hospice for the dying."[139] The children's security was also at risk. In 1829, escaped convicts attacked the school, resulting in a gunfight and the death of one of the convict gang. With no support from parents, largely ignored by the colonial administration, and given limited financial support, the school closed in 1829. The Parramatta Native Institution and the Blacktown Native Institution never restricted their enrolment to children under the age of seven, despite their original intent. In most cases, parents refused to give over their young children to schools for which they could see no purpose.

In 1834, William Watson formed an infant school for children of the Wiradjuri people as part of the CMS mission in Wellington Valley, northwest of Sydney. On his way to Australia, Watson visited the Buchanan brothers' infant school in Cape Town and was apparently impressed by what he saw. Having no teaching materials at the Wellington Valley Mission, he fabricated a lesson post with features to display and hide the alphabet and words in the manner recommended by Wilderspin. The display measured about two square feet and was attached to a seven-and-a-half-foot upright. His enthusiasm for the infant system was recorded in the *Church Missionary Record,* a CMS publication distributed in England for fundraising purposes: "Surely never were human means better adapted to the design, than the Infant System is adapted to teach the Aborigines of New Holland! The pleasing and amusing manner in which instruction is presented to them, makes it rather desirable a task. The clapping of hands, marching, etc., falls in so much with their native habits of corrobborroing (dancing), that the Black children are quite delighted with it."[140] *Corrobborree* was a dance ritual enacted by the Wiradjuri people in response to the smallpox epidemic. Although Watson and the Wellington Valley missionaries provided descriptions of the ritual, they were dismissive of it and appeared not to understand its significance.[141]

In the actual situation, instruction was never so systematic or sustained, and it involved only a few children at a time. There was certainly no need for his lesson post, which was intended for teaching large numbers of pupils efficiently without the aid of books. In his journal from the same period, Watson described a much simpler scene: "I taught them letters by marking them out with pipe clay on a board, let them have a slate and a piece of pipe clay to make letters themselves. They were much entertained by looking at my pictures."[142]

The Wiradjuri people were living in a time of crisis, under pressure from pastoral farmers for their land and devastated by smallpox. Historian Jan Kociumbas calls mission efforts like the one at Wellington Valley "schools for survivors."[143] Watson and his wife, Anne, travelled through the region among the "wild natives," seeking their children to take back to the mission station. Anne Watson was particularly good at convincing the women to give over their girls.

The children were understandably anxious in their new circumstances: sick, away from family, and locked in mission buildings that had once been part of a convict farm, the former use of the site. Some had been blinded by smallpox. Watson related the scene at the mission in 1834:

> We have had all the girls sleeping in my study for seven nights in order to prevent their escaping. But they are so dirty and bring in so many things as fish bones, etc, etc., that the smell and dirt they make has become almost intolerable. Today I made a shutter and put it on the window in the hut for them to sleep there. But they had not

been in it half an hour before the blind girl had climbed up through a small hole which had been left to admit light into the hut. She, however, was brought in again. It is not to be understood that we keep them as prisoners night and day. During the day they have sufficient liberty but at night we are anxious to have them where there is neither ingress nor egress for several reasons.[144]

The next afternoon, the children absconded, making their escape by swimming across a river.[145] Watson brooded, "We have no claim on the children."[146]

From the 1830s, a series of Aborigine protection acts at the level of state governments sought to regulate the lives of Aboriginal Australian people in favour of the rights of settlers. Colonial Aboriginal policies related to education were aimed at conversion and assimilation until the 1860s.[147] After this time, policies were directed toward protection and segregation, supported by the common scientific and popular belief that Aborigines were a dying race. From the 1870s to the 1920s, state governments lost interest in education, favouring segregation until the population expired. A renewed emphasis on assimilation in the 1930s prompted state officials to accord more importance and resources to education.[148]

From 1912 until the early 1960s, thousands of "half-caste" children were permanently removed from their families to government or mission schools.[149] The aim was assimilation, and the focus was on children with light skin, who were considered able to leave the reserves and make their own way in European Australian society. The children were provided with basic education and work-skills training for employment as servants and labourers. The object of techniques resembling those used in Canadian residential schools, the children were compelled to speak English and were provided with new, mainly Biblical, names.

New Zealand

The first infant schools in New Zealand were organized by the CMS, which was the most active Protestant mission group in New Zealand during the nineteenth century.[150] Under the direction of the Reverend Samuel Marsden, who over the years was appointed chaplain of the penal colony at New South Wales and LMS director in the Pacific, and who founded the CMS in New Zealand, the CMS established a number of mission stations in New Zealand. These included a church, residences, workshops, and, invariably, a school. Schools were considered such an essential part of mission work in New Zealand that they often preceded the construction of a church.[151] Attendance grew slowly, but those children who did attend were observed by mission teachers to be "very quick in learning."[152] The schools enrolled a mix of ages in a setting intended to replicate an idealized vision of the European way of life. As described by the teacher at Kerikeri, the key CMS mission station, "Our School now begins to put on the appearance of a Country Day School in England."[153] This was an exaggeration, but missionary families went to great lengths to replicate life in England. Maori girls were taught skills such as sewing, which were useful to the missionaries and which enabled the girls to work as servants. For acquiring these skills, they were rewarded with small presents.[154] Domestic and manual education was also considered essential for the civilization and Christianization of Maori.

Missionaries of all denominations agreed that Maori children and adults were keen to learn how to read and that, once literate, they had a great desire to possess books. The representative of the Wesleyan Missionary Society in New Zealand observed, "It has become fashionable for the young people to try to learn to read; and such is the manner in which they teach one another, that very many of them who have never lived in any of the Mission Stations, can read the translated portions of the Scriptures well."[155] The arrival of a printing press in New Zealand in 1835 was a significant event for missionaries and Maori, further stimulating demand for books.[156] According to William Colenso, who operated the printing press for the CMS, "Throughout the island there appears to be a universal movement, a mighty stirring of the people. The Chiefs of distant tribes come down to Waimate and this place, for books and Missionaries. These seem to be the *ne plus ultra* of their ambition. I have seen them myself, gladly bring their store of potatoes for a book."[157]

In the Maori tradition of family-based education, the schools were attended by all ages, "from the youth just entering upon life even to decrepit old age."[158] Some infant schools, as was the case at Paihia, were conducted by the wives of missionaries. At the CMS mission station at Puriri, one of the teachers was a Maori woman named Tini, who was the wife of a chief.[159] The Reverend Henry Williams described the Puriri school's operation in detail:

> In the afternoon, I attended Mr. Fairburn's Infant School: 28 were present. It was exceedingly interesting, as being early in this quarter.

Most of the children were boys from seven years downwards. Each put on a blue frock upon entering the house, which gave a clean, uniform, and pleasing appearance. The children manifested much pleasure, and desire to learn, and went through their various evolutions with considerable precision. At the conclusion, some of the old ladies, among the visitors, made a special request that the children might be marched round the flag-staff, in order that they might see them. Their wishes were complied with, to their great admiration. But one of the most important characters of this school was Tini, a lady of considerable note, and the wife of one of the principal Chiefs here. She came in a clean blue gown; and took the lead, under Mrs. Fairburn, in pointing to the letters, and keeping order. She appeared very quick and intelligent, and is, I understand, a very well-behaved person. This is a highly important feature in this early Mission.[160]

The infant school at the Waikato Mission had six Maori teachers, including Mary Ngataru, who, along with her husband, an important chief, had been converted. Mary Ngataru was described at the time as a teacher who "labours with considerable diligence."[161] Training such "Native teachers" was itself a missionary strategy for converting the local population, but it required acceptance by the community and the interest and commitment of individual women.

The school at Waimate was established in 1832. William Yate recorded that, in about 1835, it enrolled twenty-two students, "English and Native," with the "general system of instruction used in England" in English as well as Maori, "together with Watts' Catechisms." He judged the system "to succeed equally well with native children as with European."[162] He remarked, "The children of the Infant School are brought up in habits of industry. They are taught to prepare flax, to be used for weaving themselves garments and other purposes; by which they are not only occupied in some beneficial employment, but they learn to what good account the resources of their own country may be turned."[163]

In 1844, William Bambridge, who was a teacher at St. John's College for older Maori and European students at the Waimate Mission, sketched the new infant school building at Waimate. The image, reproduced below, offers a rare glimpse into the interior of a mission infant school, depicting a gallery constructed at one end of what had initially been a church and later a dining hall before its conversion to an infant school.[164] The school was planned by Bishop George Selwyn as a key educational initiative complementing his plan to conduct boarding schools for youth as a means of converting and assimilating local peoples. Bambridge considered it a success, and on his visit in November, 1843, three months after its opening, he remarked on the pleasing manner in which the children sang "God Save the King," though Queen Victoria ruled from 1837.[165] Prior to sending their children to the school, parents took great care to inquire about its operation and methods. Bambridge's account is worth relating in full:

> Children were brought to the number of 57 whom the Bishop arranged in the church and then told them to follow him in a single file to the building which he has lately had fitted up for the purpose. After I had registered the Adult Natives in the Church, I went to the Infant School and entered the names. The Bishop had had a high day if I may so think and seemed to be filled with delight at the prospect of establishing an institution for the neglected but interesting children of New Zealanders. The parents required very minute explanation as to the treatment which the Child would receive, and very closely inspected the Dormitories which His Lordship had had nicely arranged under the Gallery. Thus having been satisfied, the children were left at 12 o'clock and were in a short time in full exercise upon the English Alphabet, clapping hands and various other amusements.[166]

The school appears to have been regularly attended by about twenty-seven children, though attendance records exist for only a brief period, and the date of its closure is unknown.[167]

The popularity and efficiency of the infant schools, as well as of other educational endeavours for both adults and children, are underscored by the Maori literacy rate, which surpassed that of the New Zealand settlers at midcentury.[168] Fifty percent of Maori adults were literate in the Maori language, and many also spoke English. In the mission schools of the period, instruction was mainly in the Maori language. Judith Simon and Linda Tuhiwai Smith suggest that, though this made teaching easier and reflected a valuing of the culture and language, it also served to control access to English texts.[169]

Interior of New Infants' School. Sketch by William Bambridge, November 1844, Waimate (North). MS-0130-208, Alexander Turnbull Library, Wellington.

From 1860 to 1867, during the period of the Land Wars, mission schools were abandoned. One outcome of the eventual defeat of the Maori "rebels" was the confiscation of 3 million acres for European settlement. At this time, colonial authorities embarked on a policy of assimilation of Maori, and a bureaucracy and legislation were put into place to achieve this goal: a Native Department was formed in 1861, the Maori Land Act was passed in 1862, and the Native School Act was generated in 1867. Unlike those in Canada and Australia, most primary schools established under the Native School Act were village-based day schools. Children attending them continued to live in their community.

Following the pattern established by missionaries, instruction in the initial levels of primary school was in Maori. In later classes, English was used and Maori was actively discouraged. This policy was included in the Education Ordinance of 1847 and subsequently outlined in the Native Schools Code (1880), which stated, "In the junior classes the Maori language may be used for the purpose of making the children acquainted with the meanings of English words and sentences. The aim of the teacher, however, should be to dispense with the use of Maori as soon as possible."[170] Maori language in this case was used as a means to learn English.[171]

Cape Town

A final story of infant schools relates the continuing involvement of the Buchanans, as a family of teachers, in demonstrating the institution's value — in this case, in foreign missions. In 1829, ten-year-old David Dale Buchanan and his older half-brother William set off from London for the new settlement at Swan River in Western Australia, but they settled instead in Cape Town after hearing reports of a poor future for the Swan River Colony.[172] Their emigration followed their father's ouster from the Vincent Square infant school in 1827. David had accompanied his parents to Derbyshire where his father taught school, while two of his brothers were apprenticed and living in London. Though James was reinstated at the Vincent Square school, the conflict may have caused him to be uncertain about his future.

David and William had been pupils at their father's London school and had probably performed duties as monitors. As an infant, David had been taken by his father to the school in Spitalfields during Wilderspin's training. When the brothers arrived in Cape Town in December 1829, they approached Dr. John Philip, LMS superintendent for the region, and offered their services as teachers. They were enlisted by the Infant School Society to take charge of a school for poor European children and children of slaves.[173] By 1831, David, aged twelve, was directing a school of his own at Graham's Town in Albany. The Cape Town school had been set up and briefly directed by Elizabeth Lyndall, whose half-sister was married to an LMS missionary in South Africa.[174] The school was organized by Dr. Philip and his wife, Jane, who had recruited Lyndall while they were on leave in England.[175]

Lyndall's preparation for teaching is unknown, but her approach was strongly based on the monitorial system. Shortly after setting up the Cape Town school, she turned her attention to opening a private school for children of upper-class Europeans, which was known as the Upper School; the Cape Town school for slave and poor European children was left in the charge of older students whom she had trained as monitors and became known as the Lower School.[176] From about 1830 William Buchanan directed the Lower School, and under an invitation from Dr. Philip, he set up other schools in rural LMS missions starting in 1833.[177] Throughout the 1830s, the Cape Town Infant Schools were used as a training ground for teachers who went on to establish other schools in the Cape Colony.[178]

Ebenezer Buchanan, another of James Buchanan's sons, arrived in Cape Town in 1833, taking charge of a newly organized class for European boys.[179] Born in 1812, Ebenezer was two when his family moved to New Lanark, where he attended his father's infant school. From age seven to fourteen, he attended a Lancasterian school in London. This was followed by seven years as an apprentice armourer and brazier. It is unlikely that he had worked as a teacher prior to coming to Cape Town. Accounts of his Cape Town teaching describe it as adhering to Lancasterian principles, consistent with later descriptions of his work in the South Seas.[180]

Dr. Philip was a defender of the rights of coloured persons and slaves, and the infant schools were multiracial. In 1831, the 153 pupils enrolled in the Lower School consisted of 24 "free blacks," 37 English, 17 Dutch, and 75 "slaves sent by owners."[181] As a result of this, the novice missionaries who stopped in Cape Town en route to India, Madagascar, or Australia found the schools influential in demonstrating how the infant system functioned with a multiracial group of children.[182] Among the first of these was the independent Quaker missionary George Washington Walker, en route to Van Diemen's Land in 1832. A threatened rebellion by his ship's drunken crew over alcohol rations had forced the captain to stop at Cape Town. Walker spent his time meeting with local mission workers, paying a visit to the London Missionary Society office where he met Dr. Philip. As Walker recorded in his journal, "Dr. Philip took us to see the Infant Schools. The first we visited was for the children of the poor, many of the slave mothers having some of their progeny there. It was gratifying to observe white and black, and all the intermediate grades of colour indiscriminately seated together. The other Infant School consists of children of the upper class; the distinction resulting from a higher payment."[183]

Other visiting missionaries also focused their observations on the multiracial enrolment of the Lower School. In the 1830s, American missionary George Champion reported seeing "70 or 80 children of every cast of complexion from jet black to perfect white."[184] A few months after Walker's visit, CMS missionary William Watson toured the Lower School on his way to New South Wales. He observed the pupils undergoing an examination: "Nearly 150 Black infants go through the various departments of Spelling reading singing praying etc. which they perform'd in an excellent manner."[185] Also in 1832, Daniel Wilson, bishop of Calcutta, and his daughter Ann toured the school.[186] Daniel Wilson would later initiate a school in

Calcutta.[187]

The infant system was believed to be as effective for Africans and European settlers as it was in England with working-class children, with basic academic and subject knowledge offered along with religious instruction.[188] For Africans, the missionaries worked toward their conversion and acquisition of English. On the basis of what he had seen at the Cape Town Lower School, George Champion believed that "in the course of 2 or 3 generations the native language may be extirpated."[189] Philip recognized that the promise of the schools in Cape Town and the surrounding missions mirrored that of their counterparts in the slums of London: "The children of barbarous tribes start with the advantages of those of civilized man, and instead of being retarded in their progress by the ignorance and imbecility of a people only rising above the savage state, they raise up to cultivate and humanize their parents, and become the elements of a society that will soon be able to supply its own wants, advocate their own rights, and diffuse the blessings of civilization among the tribes in the interior of Africa."[190]

South Seas

In 1838, the Reverend John Williams, who worked under the banner of the London Missionary Society, stopped in Cape Town on his way to Samoa. He was returning from London, where he had raised funds for the LMS in the Pacific. He had first visited the Society Islands (modern Tahiti) in 1817. Over the next fifteen years, he claimed to have converted almost the entire population of some islands.[191] He had established schools during his years in the Pacific, mainly for adults, with the objective of teaching them to read the Bible. According to his 1836 testimony given in London before the Select Committee on Aborigines, youth aged fifteen to twenty were uninterested in the current schools, but he anticipated greater success with younger children via use of the infant system. He reported, "We did not know much about it till I came to England, but we intend to introduce it immediately I go back [sic]." His plan was to train Pacific Islanders as teachers.[192]

Oddly, after four years of leave in England, and two years after making his statements before the committee, he left without engaging a teacher to carry out this plan. According to Williams himself, he intended to spend time in Cape Town, where he would attempt "to procure a nice youth of about 14 years of age who has just been received by the Infant School Committee as a master."[193] Ebenezer Buchanan related the story differently. In his report to the LMS, he wrote that Williams' first choice was the daughter of LMS missionary Aaron Buzacott. When she declined, Buchanan himself offered to take her place.[194] Ebenezer was evidently unsure of his prospects in Cape Town. He had married Jane Cowan several months earlier and had written to his sister in London that, though he was content to remain in Cape Town, he would return to England if he could be assured of a well-paying position there.[195] A few months later, in an unexplained turn of events, he signed a five-year contract to establish infant schools in the South Seas for the LMS.

Williams expressed tremendous enthusiasm for the future of infant schools in Pacific missions: "Every Missionary [should have] a thorough knowledge of the Infant School System. And if a College education or the Infant System must give way I would certainly say that a thorough knowledge of the Infant School System, with the heart delighting in it, is to be preferred to any education you can give them in any College in the Kingdom. It is the training that will fit them for usefulness in the spheres of labour to which they are destined."[196] At this point, Williams' enthusiasm for infant schools was not matched by any great planning. Only after Buchanan volunteered, and during a meeting organized for another purpose, did Williams make an effort to raise funds for the schools.[197]

Ebenezer and Jane arrived in Samoa in November 1838. Williams wrote that, though he had "determined that our invaluable young friend, Mr. Buchanan, should commence his infant school labours at Rarotonga, so urgent were the solicitations of the Samoan brethren that I felt compelled to yield to their wishes. Mr. Buchanan, therefore, is located on the east side of Upolu, at a large station called Falealili."[198] Williams remained in Samoa for two months, leaving for Tahiti in January 1839. Later in 1839, he and a companion were killed in the New Hebrides (modern Vanuatu) on the island of Erromanga.[199]

From the journal of LMS missionary George Pritchard, we learn that Buchanan quickly organized a school. As Pritchard described the scene, the missionaries and members of the community met at the Manono *malae* (gathering place) for a presentation by the children — the "little creatures," as he called them — which was reminiscent in some ways of teaching demonstrations in England: "Mr. Buchanan, the Infant School teacher, set them all to work in such a way as greatly to interest the spectators. The little creatures themselves seemed exceedingly delighted while shouting, clapping hands, and going through the various manoeuvres peculiar to infant-schools."[200] Pritchard commented on Samoan clothing, adding an exotic element for the benefit of readers in the home missions. Providing European clothing for local peoples was a "conversion strategy" not yet undertaken on the island.[201] A common practice was to use articles of clothing as a form of payment for indigenous mission-trained teachers.[202] Pritchard continued: "Had an artist been present, he might have taken a sketch of a very novel and interesting character. In the centre a company of little boys and girls, partially dressed in a very singular manner, unconsciously receiving instruction, by imitating the sounds and gestures of their teacher; in the front, a band of Missionaries; in the rear and on each side, a crowd, presenting a most remarkable appearance from the strange dresses of the people."[203]

Despite the suggestion that the schools constituted an important part of mission work, they were poorly supported by the LMS. Buchanan often complained of a lack of supplies, writing in 1839 that he had one incomplete set of "infant school apparatus" for a network of schools with a potential enrolment of twenty thousand children.[204] Eight months after his arrival, Buchanan had established five infant schools, with 110 to 150 children attending at each, though the schools were "very imperfect" as the scholars had no materials.[205] He eventually directed older students to make equipment — counting frames and slates — but even this was limited by a lack of woodworking tools.[206] Nevertheless, within six months he had set up a two-month teacher-training program for twenty-six local students. By 1848, near the end of Buchanan's time in Samoa, teacher training was organized within a Normal School as a seventeen-month program.[207] For part of their preparation, students taught lessons in a demonstration infant school under Buchanan's supervision.

Jane Buchanan taught in the infant schools and organized both sewing lessons and classes in which girls learned to read and write. The Buchanans initially conducted all schools themselves, those for children and adults — an exhausting task to which was added the labour of learning the Samoan language. Buchanan related his schedule in a report to the LMS governors:

8:00–9:30	Infant school (with youth and student teachers attending)
9:30–11:00	School for youth and student teachers alone
2:00–4:00	School for student teachers alone
4:30–sunset	Church service or school for adults

The schools appear to have had strong support from Samoans. In a village of seven hundred, 150 children attended the infant school.[208] In another village, two hundred children attended, along with a hundred youths and a hundred young men and women. Younger pupils were taught reading, counting, and spelling, and the older ones were taught writing as well. Buchanan believed the schools were a success: "Many of the children formerly in the senior class have left during the last half year, being able to assist their parents and too big to attend an infant school. They are able to read the word of God, to write on slate and paper correctly, to understand the elementary rules of arithmetic and are familiar with the histories of many of the Old and New Testament characters, and I believe most of them have a correct knowledge of the Gospel scheme of salvation."[209]

From 1841 to 1844, Buchanan left Samoa to establish schools on Tahiti, as part of his original contract with the LMS. His work there was a great challenge to him, particularly after the colonial government made schooling compulsory. Dismayed by "the vice that has been introduced into the school with it [compulsory education]," he wrote,

> Many of the obscene gestures and much of the filthy conversation which old and young are in the constant habit of using had been banished from the school and playground and had every reason to praise God for his goodness ... I have three times within the last month detected (what a person unacquainted with Tahiti would hardly credit) boys pretending to copulate. Two of them were [illegible] boys and the third one a girl. These are the deeds of those brought to me by the new law.
>
> Disgusting conduct of older children just brought in from the bush. I must also hold out the pleasing prospect of the younger scholars repaying our labours on their behalf ... Could we but prevent them from hearing the polluting conversations that is carried on in their families and from seeing the demoralising scenes so shamelessly exhibited by their seniors our labours would be greatly facilitated. While I am endeavoring to plough and weed the ground to sow the wheat how many are scattering the [chaff?] over the same.[210]

This situation caused him concern regarding the education of his two oldest children, Jane (born in 1839) and James (born in 1842), though they were not sent to a school in England until 1848. (When no school for foreigners existed at a mission, missionary families were commonly obliged to send their children home to be educated in England.) Buchanan's report to the LMS governors highlighted his continuing discomfort with indigenous approaches to child rearing:

> Being surrounded from about 8 in the morning till seven in the evening by such a number of active children, it requires the greatest vigilance on our part, to prevent her [Jane] from hearing and seeing that which it is almost at the present time impossible to prevent among them.
>
> Again the shamelessness of the natives bathing naked in water only a few inches deep over which we have to pass in going to chapel, and the filthy habits of the children who may be seen sitting and standing about the beach quite naked, playing with their own and each others privates for want of other toys, compel us to keep her much more within the house than is beneficial for her health and make us frequently tremble at the thought of bringing up a family here.[211]

When the Buchanan family returned to Upolu, Samoa, in 1844, Ebenezer wrote to the LMS that, after having "fulfilled my engagement with Mr. Williams by visiting all the islands mentioned by him," he considered himself permanently settled.[212] He and Jane again organized an infant school and girls' school in Samoa. Older children were sometimes absent when ships arrived in the harbour, working to replenish their provisions. Otherwise, large numbers of scholars, up to 180 including many very young children, attended the school. In good weather, the class for the older children was held outdoors. The school was highly regarded, and in 1848, when Bishop George Selwyn travelled from New Zealand to Samoa, he asked Buchanan to return with him to set up additional schools there, an invitation he declined.

Buchanan resigned as an LMS teacher in 1849, citing a disagreement with the society over his housing arrangements.[213] The circumstances were unusual, however, and the LMS at Samoa had also conducted a secretive investigation of unidentified aspects of Ebenezer and Jane's "moral character." In a letter detailing his meeting with the local LMS committee, Buchanan wrote that he had "denied the truth of most of the charges and attempted to explain others, but what and how they had heard of I cannot tell, my refutation procured but little effect."[214] Buchanan resigned. The secretary of the local committee wrote that he regretted "the circumstances which have led to the conviction in his [Buchanan's] mind of the necessity for the present step" but that he had accepted his resignation.[215] The LMS paid for the Buchanan family's return to England on the *John Williams*.[216] They stayed briefly in England before settling in Pietermaritzburg, Natal, near Ebenezer's brother, where he was eventually employed as the town clerk.[217]

Buchanan proved himself to be an effective teacher and administrator, fulfilling his contract by establishing infant schools at LMS missions throughout the South Seas. The mission schools in Samoa were ultimately successful in their aim to convert the people of the islands through education. They achieved this by grafting methods of Western schooling onto traditional patterns of family-based education, creating the system of schooling that continues to the present.[218]

After Infant Schools

Education for European children in the colonies, which developed in tandem with the system of mass elementary schooling in nineteenth-century Britain and Europe, largely followed the British pattern. Pre-primary education, including that offered in infant schools, was part of this movement. The nineteenth-century drive to provide schooling for the masses had the stated humanitarian aim of improving the lives of the poor. However, it was also believed that schools were properly a means of social control and assimilation. "Foreign" parents were considered to be poor role models for their children. It was thought that schools could achieve social and economic stability by serving as a melting pot, blending together children of various backgrounds to create new Canadians, Australians, and New Zealanders.

Schooling for indigenous children shared the aims of public education to promote social and economic stability and social amelioration. However, the colonial relationship between indigenous peoples and Europeans steered indigenous education along a separate and segregated course. In the period of early contact, missionaries directed schools, generally with the support or at least the approval of the colonial administration. The curriculum was dominated by religious instruction and basic academic skills, and students included indigenous children and adults who were often eager to acquire European ideas and to learn to read and write. Mis-

Pestalozza [handwritten annotation]

sion teachers generally were optimistic in their evaluation of infant schools. In 1830, the Credit River school teacher reported, "Lately the Infant School system has been introduced, with good results of being useful. The children are much pleased with this mode of instruction, and are rapidly acquiring knowledge of the different branches taught by the Pestalozzian system."[219] The teacher also believed that this version of early education could be systematized and that it had general appeal: "I think the children are making greater improvement than the community of white children in any of the Common Schools with which I am acquainted ... and think it would be well if the [system] were established generally throughout the country."[220] On the other hand, many mission teachers criticized the playful way in which children behaved in the schools and what they considered to be the lax discipline exercised by parents. The infant school ideal of children learning via amusements was tightly defined within a Western view of children's play in institutional settings: playing with blocks or educational toys for younger children, marching and singing for the older. There is, in any case, no evidence of educational play in mission infant schools or the presence of these kinds of materials.

Missionaries and indigenous parents felt little appreciation of each other's approach to child rearing. For European parents, using physical force to punish children was a parent's responsibility and an important part of a child's socialization. In many cases, indigenous parents employed alternative means for socializing their offspring. Some missionaries took matters into their own hands. On Erromanga, Canadian Presbyterian missionary James Gordon recorded his observations of an Erromangan boy who lived at the mission, probably as a servant. Gordon remarked that "he was an only child of his parents, and they used to indulge him in every way, till at last he paid no heed to his mother." One day, Gordon found him lying on the floor of the cookhouse "screeching lustily just for the fun of it." He continued: "I approached him unobserved, saying to myself, 'Now, my little lad, I'll give you something worth crying about,' and with a flat stick I gave him a few hard stripes."[221]

Later developments in Canada, Australia, and New Zealand were organized to assimilate indigenous children into mainstream colonial society while providing basic vocational training and academic instruction. In some cases, mission teachers used the latest pedagogical innovations in their classrooms. In others, indigenous schools were rigid, authoritarian institutions in which punishments were a matter of course. From the 1840s onward, despite some national variations, the aim and form of colonial education for indigenous children was fairly similar across the British Empire, a situation that did not arise through the chance migration of ideas. Colonial governments held common principles concerning both education and the management of relationships with Aboriginal peoples. The British House of Commons Select Committee on Aborigines aimed to guide the colonies regarding the treatment and management of Aboriginal peoples: "To secure to them the due observance of Justice and the protection of their Rights; to promote the spread of Civilization among them, and to lead them to the peaceful and voluntary reception of the Christian religion."[222]

In hindsight, it is clear that the aims were not achieved and that education for indigenous children was almost entirely in the political and economic interest of colonial governments. In all three nations, developments in indigenous education were limited by shifting colonial policies that promoted the aims of protection, assimilation, and segregation in differing proportions. In Canada and New Zealand, an early focus on protection and conversion ended in the mid-nineteenth century, replaced by policies aimed at assimilating Aboriginal Canadians and Maori into the dominant society. In Australia, legislation to protect Aboriginal Australians was overtaken by policies that segregated them from Euro-Australian life. Interest in assimilation was not rekindled until the 1930s, stimulated by an increase in the part-descent population.

A focus on young indigenous children was evident from the early nineteenth century. Mission teachers and colonial administrators used the rhetoric of infant school supporters, reflecting the extreme environmentalist position that indigenous children merely needed proper instruction in order to be remade as Europeans. In 1818, the Reverend Robert Cartwright explained to New South Wales governor Macquarie that Aboriginal Australian children, like their working-class British counterparts, were intelligent and could be trained under the right conditions: "I think it will now be admitted by every candid person, that the materials we have to work upon, although extremely rude, are nevertheless good. Buried as is the intellect of these savages in Augean filth, we may yet find gems of the first magnitude and brilliance."[223]

This optimism was less frequently applied to indigenous parents, who were viewed as impediments to progress. An 1837 evaluation of the work of the Indian Department in Quebec City reflected a growing frustration with parents and hinted at the more punitive measures to come: "It may … be necessary to make it a Condition of their continuing to receive Presents either for themselves or their Families, that they should send their Children to such Schools; and it may be hoped that the Clergy will lend their Aid in recommending and enforcing the Measure, as a necessary Part of any Plan for assimilating the Indians as much and as soon as possible to the rest of the Inhabitants of the Province."[224]

By the 1880s, indigenous parents were seen as a definite obstacle to the efficient assimilation of their children. Were it not for interference from parents, it was believed, complete assimilation could be achieved within three or four generations. The faith in assimilation as a progressive solution to the "Indian problem," and the necessity of having full control of children in order for it to take hold, was partly responsible for the growth of residential schools in Canada from the 1860s. In contrast, the day-school model was used in most of Eastern Canada and New Zealand, where, by the late nineteenth century, governments believed that assimilation had generally succeeded. In New Zealand, measures such as bans on cultural practices or the removal of children from their families were considered unnecessary. Nevertheless, an ideology of assimilation in schools and the dominance of the English language contributed to cultural change in Maori communities.

The residential school combined features of industrial schools with those of the mission schools of earlier periods. The former offered a basic general education but stressed the acquisition of manual skills. The latter developed as a model of education to serve educational and humanitarian purposes in a colonial context; initially, it taught adults, provided education in local languages, and employed modern approaches (such as the pedagogical ideas of Pestalozzi) that, at first, were supported by some indigenous leaders and parents. Education in residential schools retained their mission focus and included two strands — saving souls and training labourers — both of which aimed at the assimilation of indigenous children. In Australia, families were generally not permitted to visit their children at the residential schools. Internment at the school was meant to be a permanent separation.[225]

Historians writing about the North American experience have viewed the persistence of the residential school model as tinged with irony: although it was based on an ideology of assimilation, it set out to achieve this by segregating children, not only from their parents and communities, but also from European society. In some cases, administrators and teachers managed schools with humanitarian aims, talent, and considerable goodwill; but as educational efforts directed at assimilation, they were a failure.

Upon leaving the schools, children returned to their home communities, having had their relationship with their parents disrupted and often severed by the blunt intrusion of institutional life during a critical stage in their development. In addition, the generally poor quality of their vocational and academic education meant that they were ill-prepared to take a place in European society. James Axtell suggests that, in any case, assimilation was never really possible: "The acute English sense of cultural superiority ... helped the Indians to maintain the crucial ethnic core at the heart of their newly acquired Christian personae. In colonial eyes, they were still Indians and always would be, no matter how 'civilized' or 'Christian' they became."[226] Finally, David Adams notes that, by bringing together Aboriginal children from many different nations and treating them all according to a colonial definition of "Indian," "the very institution designed to extinguish Indian identity altogether may have in fact contributed to its very persistence in the form of twentieth-century pan-Indian consciousness."[227]

The schools certainly met resistance from poor and indigenous parents, who correctly identified the patronizing and manipulative aspects of the system, as was the case with poor parents and the infant schools in Britain.[228] Aboriginal families in Australia rejected the first school established for their children in Parramatta after it "became apparent that its purpose was to distance the children from their families and communities."[229] A different situation existed in New Zealand, where Maori parents supported the mission schools and actively sought opportunities for education. The mission teachers may have "had their own ideas of what Maori should be taught in the schools ... in accordance with their own agendas," but Maori were determined to become literate and saw benefits for themselves as well.[230]

THE INFANT SCHOOLS STRESSING academics closed because their rigid approach was out of step with the new maternalist thinking in education. Very young children were sent home to be with their mothers, and education for children aged five and six was incorporated into public schools in the form of infant or kindergarten classes. In the 1840s, opinion began to turn against formal instruction for very young children, at least for children from privileged classes.[231] A popular advice book warned that "children at the present day are too highly educated — their brains are over-taxed, and thus weakened. Children are now taught what formerly youths were taught."[232] Others argued that pupils merely parroted lists and definitions, and that no *real* learning ever occurred. However, if middle-class children stayed home to avoid such pressures, very young children from the poorer classes flocked to free elementary schools. In both Australia and Canada, large numbers of underage pupils attended the initial grade level of public schools. In the 1850s, almost half of the students in New South Wales elementary schools were aged seven or under, with some as young as two and a half. Like those in Britain, colonial infant schools in public and denominational school systems were "stubbornly resistant to innovation."[233] The time was ripe for a revitalized approach, one more suited to the needs of very young children.

The kindergarten was a possible alternative, but it was not yet well developed outside Germany. Furthermore, in the 1880s, even after kindergartens had gained some ground in Britain and the United States, the New South Wales minister for public instruction argued, "The results of [the kindergarten] method are not immediately apparent, and for that reason would not recommend themselves to the approval of the working classes and others who are anxious that their children should reach the standard of education prescribed by the [Education] Act as soon as possible."[234]

In the metropolitan areas of New South Wales, a few of the youngest pupils were segregated in infant or kindergarten departments within a primary school or in separate infant schools. The fate of these programs depended to a large extent on financial considerations. However, the youngest children — particularly those of poor settlers and Aboriginals — were left without an educational program aimed specifically at their needs.

chapter 4   **Childcare and Daycare**

IN 1835, WHEN THE chairman of the Select Committee on the Education of People in England and Wales asked Samuel Wilderspin to explain the history of infant schools, he responded, "Lord Brougham considers the first Infant school [in England] was founded in 1818 [1819]. A mere assembling of young children is not an Infant school. I consider the first systematised school was commenced in the beginning of 1820."[1] Wilderspin insisted on calling Buchanan's school an asylum, by which he meant to draw attention to its central purpose as temporary childcare and what he considered to be its lack of an educational system. Infant schools — including those set up by Wilderspin himself — did provide childcare as a support for mothers engaged in wage-labour outside the home. Brougham considered this a selling point of the schools. Parents could send their children to the school to ensure their physical well-being whether or not they had an interest in their education. This dual mission was described in the plan for the schools at Newcastle-upon-Tyne in 1825: "The children of the labouring classes, from the age of two to six years, may, for a small weekly payment by the parents, be not only kept from the danger of accidents, to which at this tender age they are liable without the most watchful care, but, by a judicious and pleasing interchange of exercise and instruction, may experience a gradual development at once of their bodily and mental powers, and may be prepared for a more beneficial improvement of the means of education provided for children of a more advanced age."[2]

However, because most schools enrolled children from about eighteen months to two years of age, there was a gap in daily care services for younger children, with the exception of private community-based arrangements. Married working mothers requiring daytime-only care for their infants often employed neighbourhood women. Poor single mothers had few options in the early nineteenth century, driving some to leave their babies alone at home or in parish workhouses. Institutions arose, mainly through private and church-run charities, to serve working or impoverished mothers and their children. These followed two main models: The first and more common approach was long-term care — orphan homes for older children and, for infants, boarding homes under the direction of a foundling institution. The second was daytime-only care in a crèche, or day nursery, sometimes combined with basic education for slightly older youngsters. These two models are reviewed below.

Long-Term Care

Hospital

A key example of hospital care is the service provided by the London Foundling Hospital, which was established in 1741. The aim of the hospital — meaning a shelter or asylum in this case — was to rescue infants of single mothers from abandonment and death. It also served as home for infants "whom their Parents are not able to maintain" and who did not qualify for parish care.[3] Initially, the hospital received infants in a rented house staffed by two wet nurses and two dry nurses.[4] The results were poor: half of the 136 children admitted in the first year died of gastro-intestinal illness from contaminated food or dirty feeding devices. The governors wisely concluded that more wet nurses were required. In time, infants were sent to the country to live with wet nurses in a foster-family situation until they were about four, at which point they returned to the institution. A similar system was popularly used on the Continent. From age four to five, children were given basic reading lessons as well as minor tasks and responsibilities. From six to twelve, they were trained in basic work skills and then apprenticed in the community until they were twenty-one or older. There were many exceptions to this pattern, and some children remained with their nurses for a longer period; others were apprenticed at a much earlier age.

The hospital's daily schedule included play for the younger children as a way to keep fit and acquire skills. The hospital administrators experimented with new approaches. Kindergarten methods, as a means of training for younger children, were demonstrated by Bertha Ronge in 1854 but not continued.[5] At one juncture, the hospital governors proposed that the older boys be provided with javelins as training for "throwing a Harpoon in the Greenland Fishery."[6] Schooling for older children followed the monitorial system used by Andrew Bell at the Madras Military Male Orphan Asylum, the aim of which was to "prevent the waste of time in school; to render the condition of pupils pleasant to themselves; and to lead the attention to proper pursuits."[7] This included training in work skills under highly regimented conditions.

The hospital governors anticipated that, through their education, the children would "become useful members of the Common-Wealth."[8] They were not expected to rise above their lot in life. Instead, as stated in a hospital regulation, their training would instill gratitude and contentment with their situation: "They ought to submit to the lowest stations, and should not be educated in such a manner as to put them upon a level with the children of parents who have the humanity and virtue to preserve them, and industry to support them."[9]

The London Foundling Hospital served as a model for long-term childcare institutions throughout the Commonwealth in two ways. First, it had been established and financed through the efforts of individual citizens imbued with philanthropic and humanitarian desires. The hospital was formed as a corporation, and its governors paid annual subscription fees and participated in its management. This system differed from that of institutions on the Continent, which were rejected as models because they were financed and managed by church or state.[10] The hospital's second influential feature was a restriction on admissions: only those children whose mothers met certain moral and economic criteria would be accepted. In the beginning, however, this was not the case; the hospital had an open-door policy, accepting infants according to a shifting quota and using a ballot system, under circumstances that, at least in principle, ensured anonymity. Staff members were forbidden to ask any questions of mothers that would reveal their identity or that of their child.[11]

The hospital was popular with poor women and well used: from 1741 to 1760, fifteen thousand infants were admitted. Their numbers strained the institution financially and led to charges that it encouraged moral laxness. Mortality rates also increased, caused in part by a shortage of wet nurses. The spike in admissions was due to parish officials who sought to transfer responsibility for children of unmarried mothers to the foundling hospital.

The numbers surprised the governors, who had imagined taking in only those children who were abandoned on the street or at the workhouse and who had no other options for their care. The result was a policy change in 1760 that drastically reduced admissions through the introduction of a moral and economic means test, whereby only the children of poor unmarried mothers were admitted. In 1756, in the period of hospital history known as the General Reception, 117 infants had been admitted in a single day; from 1760 to 1767, 116 were admitted. The admission tests contributed to a bias toward the hospital as an institution that assisted mothers in the easy disposal of babies born out of wedlock, and during the nineteenth century, the hospital went into a long period of decline.

Workhouse

Another venue for long-term childcare was the workhouse, known for providing low-quality care and education for poor children. It was the preferred model in Scotland, for example, where foundling homes were never established. As described in Chapter 2, David Dale and other industrialists employed large numbers of children from workhouses. As a cost-saving measure, workhouses relied on mothers and wet nurses as caregivers for infants. For older children, there was a mix of play and some basic instruction, often under the direction of a pauper teacher. Although whole families resided in workhouses, testimony at the 1861 Education Commission expressed concern over "the evil of the children mixing with their parents," who were also resident, as well as with other "improper persons."[12] These facilities were sometimes wholly inadequate, as at London's Marylebone Workhouse, which exhibited a high rate of sickness, mortality, and corruption. An 1843 report on conditions at Marylebone offered a detailed account of the operation of both the infant school and the nursery, where most deaths occurred. One of the events sparking the inquiry was the death of a six-year-old girl in the infant school after her teacher apparently failed to seek medical attention for her.[13]

The Marylebone Workhouse nursery accommodated children aged one month to two years. At the time of the report, thirty-three children lived there as did twenty-three women, some of whom were nursing a baby in addition to their own. The nursery had one nurse on staff. Orphan children slept in a separate room with their nurse. The main room, in which mothers and babies slept, was used for all other activities. According to a workhouse order, children were to be weaned at nine months, and their mothers were "kept to work" but not allowed in the nursery without permission.[14] The timing of weaning was one focus of the investigation. Administrators forced weaning much earlier than nine months, with some babies separated from their mothers at age six weeks. Some mothers were threatened with separation if they did not agree to nurse another baby. Single mothers were particularly vulnerable to this kind of manipulation.

The infant school at Marylebone Workhouse housed an average of sixty children aged two to seven. The teacher, working under the supervision of the matron, had charge of them during their waking hours, from 6:30 a.m. to 8:00 p.m. This included bathing them, repairing their clothing, and supervising them at their meals in addition to instructing them in "spelling, reading, tables, use of clock-dial and catechism." A nurse, two "pauper helpers," and a monitor selected from among the older girls assisted the teacher in her tasks.[15] Schoolwork occupied two hours in the morning and another two in the afternoon, though this included outdoor playtime in the morning when the weather was suitable.

Neither the teacher's mode of instruction nor her materials were described, though it was noted that the children sat on the floor in small circles for teaching purposes.[16] A number of factors limited the potential impact of whatever formal instruction did occur. A large constraint was the physical set-up of the schoolroom, which was also used for sleeping at night. Half the space was allocated to beds. In addition, an eight-foot wooden trough ran along one wall. A partition at its centre divided it into two sections, with one side "appropriated for washing the children, and the other for washing dishes, socks, linen, etc."[17] Laundry was hung to dry about the room. The water closet, a source of considerable odour, stood "in a kind of sentry-box" in the centre of the room.[18]

Short-Term Care

Crèche

A childcare model distinct from the foundling hospital or the workhouse was the French crèche, established in Paris in 1844 as a charity-sponsored daycare service for children under the age of two. The crèche provided the model for daycare centres established in the mid-nineteenth century in Europe, the United States, and the colonies.[19] The earliest recorded crèche-style institution in an English-speaking country was a Marylebone nursery opened in 1850. Located on Nassau Street bordering Middlesex Hospital, it was not far from the Marylebone Workhouse. Marylebone was an area of wealthy residences, with small pockets of poverty.[20] A group of upper-class women financed the nursery. Although they called their institution a public nursery, they acknowledged their debt to the crèche. Their aim was to stem infant deaths by providing a higher quality of care than was otherwise available to mothers employed as factory workers. In particular, they offered it as an alternative to use of neighbourhood child minders, some of whom had reputations for drugging their young charges with laudanum.

The nursery venture was short-lived, perhaps due to its high fees.[21] One commentator speculated that the location was ill-suited to heavier use and that an industrial city such as Manchester would have been a better choice.[22] In fact, a public nursery was opened in Manchester in the same year, although it too appears to have soon closed.[23] Nevertheless, the public was made more aware of this novel charity. An article in a popular periodical explained the institution to readers, noting in particular that the care was on a daily basis, of high quality, and available as a charity service for families unable to pay:

> The French crèche is a sort of public nursery, combining for the elder children the features of an infant school. It is under the superintendence of mistresses and a nurse paid by public charity, or by the municipality. The children are brought every morning by the parents, and taken away every night. They have all sorts of household accommodation, and a playground; and their wants and appetites are attended to as well as if they were at home — often very much better. The parents of course provide the food, and some pay a small fee, but the crèche is open to all the world; and if the mother be too poor to contribute to the common stock of bread and milk, and soup, public benevolence makes up the deficiency.[24]

Public nurseries developed slowly in England, with only three or four in London by 1855. The features of one — the Public Nursery, Infant Ragged School, and Laundry — are worth noting in relation to later developments in the colonies.[25] It combined on-site employment for mothers in the laundry with separate facilities for infants and older children. The oldest girls from the school, which operated as a charity for poor children, were sent upstairs to help an elderly woman look after the babies. It and other nurseries bore little resemblance to the crèche, yet the name endured. Alfred Sennett's 1905 survey of crèches found crèches in London and most British industrial cities, all of them intended to decrease "industrial infant mortality." Of the thirteen that responded to his survey, only one had opened after 1891.[26] All were small-scale institutions admitting from twenty to seventy children aged two weeks to seven years, with the majority reporting a capacity of thirty or less.[27]

Diffusion

Similar types of long- and short-term childcare were propagated in the case-study countries, with the crèche dominating by the end of the nineteenth century. In Australia, workhouse-type nurseries began to be part of Female Factories (prisons for women) in the 1820s. While their mothers worked outside the prison, generally as domestics, infants living with them were placed in nurseries and older children in infant schools. At the Female Factory at Parramatta in 1840, the Governor reported: "All the children above one year old in the factory are made to attend an infant school within the establishment, an arrangement which is producing good effects."[28] At age three or four, they were sent to orphanages; when they were old enough, they worked as labourers. As was the case at workhouse nurseries in England, it was argued that children should be separated from their mothers so as to remove them from bad influences. Also like the English nurseries, but worsened by malaria and contaminated water, the nurseries at the Female Factories had exceptionally high rates of infant mortality.

In small colonial cities, a combination infant school and childcare centre, where it was available, met the needs of poor parents who were in dire circumstances due to the lack of any integrated or public system of social welfare. One example of these was the Halifax Infant School, where parents "at their work [had] the comfort of knowing their children were comfortably lodged and protected from harm and also receiving all the instruction suitable to their tender years in a manner that amuses while it instructs the child."[29] When infant schools declined in popularity at mid-century, the childcare service was not dropped: it merely shifted to other settings, such as hospitals and orphanages, until the rise of the crèche model in the colonies in the 1880s.

Long-term childcare was initially more popular than the short-term alternatives. Protestant foundling homes opened in rapid succession in Australia and Canada during the 1870s: in Sydney in 1874 and in Toronto and Halifax in 1875.[30] In New Zealand, a foundling home organized by Marie Aubert was opened in 1890 at the Jerusalem Mission, north of

Wellington. Aubert established another in Auckland as late as 1910.[31] The Sydney Foundling Institution (SFI), which opened in 1874, was patterned on the London Foundling Hospital, its founders believing that the British solution to the problems of infanticide and baby farming (discussed below) was also appropriate for the colony.[32] Although some children were left anonymously at the doors of the SFI, others were admitted with their mothers, who were seen to be in need of assistance themselves. In an important departure from the practice at the London Foundling Hospital, infants were not sent out to wet nurses but remained at the institution until they were taken out by their mothers or were boarded out. Mothers living with their children at the SFI repaid the institution with their labour; others were employed internally as wet nurses or were engaged in day work elsewhere. SFI administrators sought wet nurses at other women's shelters such as the Benevolent Asylum, perpetuating a cycle encouraging mothers to leave their own children to work as wet nurses at the SFI.

In choosing the London Foundling Hospital as its template, the SFI was outmoded from the start — in 1874, the year in which it opened its doors, a report of the commissioners of public charities recommended boarding children with wet nurses.[33] In 1876, the SFI moved to suburban Ashfield and subsequently became the Infants' Home, a name change that at least recognized its true nature as a long-term residence. Living at the home was dangerous to its inmates' health: in 1876, sixteen children died of outbreaks of cholera and typhoid fever. At the time, no provision was made for isolating infected infants.[34] Administrators attributed the deaths to the children's poor state of health at the time of their admission. They also claimed that their charges received the same food as they had prior to their admission, believing that, in many cases, they were already weaned.[35] However, this was impossible to determine for children who had been abandoned.

The Infants' Home operated in much the same fashion for decades, offering primarily custodial care. Educational provisions in the form of kindergarten and nursery school were introduced, mostly as volunteer efforts or staffed by student teachers from local colleges. A shift to modern methods of child welfare and boarding out was never made. The introduction of social-work practices came with the hiring of a social worker in 1949, but residential care continued until 1972. At this time, the Infants' Home shifted to daycare for children of sole parents and to foster care.

The Toronto Infants' Home was established in 1875. Its founders made no reference to the London Foundling Hospital as a model or inspiration. Boundaries between permanent and daily care at the Toronto Infants'

Home were blurred. Its ambitious mission was to operate simultaneously as a daycare, children's infirmary, and foundling home. Its mandate included "the care of children of wet nurses; the Daily Charge of infants whose parents labour away from home, the care or charge of destitute children under 2 years of age, entrusted to its care by any municipality in Ontario, the care, medical attention, and nursing of sickly and dying infants."[36]

At the time of its founding, the Toronto Infants' Home was the only charity in Toronto to admit children under the age of two. It was designed expressly to prevent baby farming. It cared for two categories of children: those abandoned or orphaned whose custody was granted to the home by parents or authorities, and children of wage-earning mothers who remained in their parent's custody but who were boarded at the infants' home or cared for on a daily basis. In practice, however, the Toronto Infants' Home functioned as a foundling home and a maternity home for single mothers in a manner similar to the Ashfield Infants' Home. There is no record of any child having been admitted on a daily-care basis; instead, expectant mothers lived at the home during the period of their confinement. They were required to petition for their admission or for the admission of their infant according to moral criteria: unwed mothers were obliged to demonstrate that the birth was their first. Following it, they were offered work outside the infants' home while the baby remained in residence there. However, the infants' home saw itself as the true custodian of the children. Mothers who left to work outside it were not permitted to "re-enter without special permission of the Board, except to visit [their] child on visiting day."[37]

Because the home took in so many infants in poor health, it established a hospital as a component of its work and changed its name to the Infants' Home and Infirmary in 1877. Initially, the institution occupied a house but moved into a newly constructed building in 1881. In the year before the move, it admitted a total of 112 children ranging in age from two months to two years.[38] Most were the male offspring of Protestant mothers and were under twelve months old. Three children were sent to the Girls' Home for adoption, indicating co-operation between Protestant children's charities in the city. At the Infants' Home and Infirmary, the 1881 mortality rate was 22 percent, a situation blamed on the children's weakened state upon admission, being "enfeebled through privations and neglect before coming into care and by constitutional ailments."[39] The mortality rate remained high throughout the time that the home offered residential care.

The home's original aim was to employ new mothers as wet nurses for the foundlings in its care.[40] However, many mothers were not willing to be so employed, and this requirement was eventually withdrawn. The home's operation remained largely unchanged until 1919, when a nurse was appointed as director; this move introduced a progressive approach to child welfare in which foster care, known as boarding out, was favoured. The residence for mothers eventually closed in 1926, and in 1951 the infants' home merged with the Children's Aid Society of Toronto.

Foundling homes generally housed children under age two. Orphanages provided long-term institutional care for older children. As free public education became more readily available over the course of the nineteenth century, daytime care for older children became available in schools. However, for poor families in desperate circumstances, the main institutional childcare service for this age group was the orphanage. Orphanages arose out of the new understanding that the various categories of dependent poor should be cared for in separate facilities.[41] Few children were actually committed to orphanages because of the death of both parents or even the loss of one. Instead, most were brought to orphanages by a parent in times of extreme need. With reference to Canada, Patricia Rooke and R.L. Schnell note that the "'ins and outs' (non-orphans in temporary custodial care) ... were always in the majority."[42] In terms of the range of services they offered, orphanages in the colonies were very flexible child-welfare institutions.

In Lower Canada (Quebec), the term "crèche" was sometimes used to mean foundling asylum but never referred to care on a daily basis. An example is the Montreal Crèche d'Youville, founded by Marguerite d'Youville in 1754. Children over the age of two who needed daytime care were provided for in salles d'asile founded by Catholic orders in the 1850s. The asiles were modelled on those in France that were inspired by the English infant school. They mainly served the children of working mothers and were an important part of child-welfare work in Montreal for more than fifty years. In 1900, five asiles existed in Montreal, with a total enrolment of one thousand. They offered an educational program consisting of the rote study of the alphabet and numbers. In the early twentieth century, their focus changed, and they were reorganized as orphanages or schools.[43]

In 1857, during the decade in which the Quebec asiles were being founded, the Public Nursery in Toronto was established as one of the first day nurseries in North America.[44] In 1863, it succumbed to the greater influence of the orphanage by becoming a permanent-care facility called the Girls' Home, the institution that co-operated with the Toronto Infants' Home described earlier. It adopted the management structure, staffing practices, and general rules of operation of a public nursery but not its social mission. From the beginning, it functioned as combination employment bureau and training centre for wet nurses and domestics. The fact that it also provided daily care created a tension between the objectives of child saving and the growing need for readily available domestic workers.[45] Because the nursery was designed to care for the babies of wet nurses, not for those of factory workers, most of its charges were not admitted on a daily basis but were boarded there for periods ranging from a few weeks to several months while their mothers worked for the social elite. If mothers failed to pay the monthly boarding fee, they forfeited custody of the child to the institution.

Wet-nursing was a class-bound enterprise in which the social position of the nurse was always lower than that of her employer.[46] Although nursing-out — nursing and childcare that took place in the home of a wet nurse — was common in Europe, in the colonies wet nurses were more likely to live in their employer's home. Such nursing-in offered substantial benefits to the employer: the nurse could be used for non-childcare household tasks, and her behaviour and physical condition could be monitored.[47] It also ensured that she would be more likely to stay with the family, as she was dependent on her employer for food and lodging as well as her wage.

Some wet nurses were single mothers with few other options for employment. Like the day nurseries, lying-in hospitals and maternity homes helped link new mothers with employers by offering an employment service or registry. The managing committee of the Toronto Lying-In Hospital considered this to be part of the rehabilitation of "fallen" women. The hospital's 1857 report noted that "a large number of patients who have been admitted into respectable families as wet nurses, have invariably been reformed, and in many instances have become respectable and orderly, many of them having married, to wit, six within the past year."[48] The fate of the nurse's own child, however, was then in the hands of a benevolent agency or private establishment. This was seen as a natural series of events, with "control over the erring young mother's child ... an appropriate responsibility for her social betters."[49]

The use of wet nurses for the feeding and upbringing of bourgeois children posed a social and moral dilemma. First, the nursing child's intimate contact with a member of the lower classes was viewed as a threat to its normal development. By the mid-nineteenth century, medical knowledge had integrated new ideas on heredity with the earlier belief that breast milk was a diluted form of blood. The "disposition" of the nurse or mother could then be passed on to the child through the milk. The nursing child was placed at risk of inheriting what were thought to be the lax morals of its nurse. During the 1850s, the London-based medical journal the *Lancet* contained a series of articles in which the use of "wet nurses from the fallen" was condemned for this reason.[50] C.H.F. Routh noted that "I myself have known two [such] cases: one of a lady suckled by a bad woman, who in youth was full of like bad passions, ... and another of a gentleman suckled by a nurse of strong sexual passions, who has inherited all her propensities."[51]

Physicians cautioned that wet nurses disrupted the natural relationship between mother and child.[52] Nursing a child was to a large part the same as rearing a child. Indeed, many children who were "sent out to nurse" did not return until the age of seven or eight. A mother who permitted a stranger to suckle her infant was neglecting her maternal duty. In the colonies, European women requiring a wet nurse frequently hired Aboriginal women.[53] The greater concern for Europeans was the Aboriginal nurse's influence on a child's upbringing. This class- or race-based bias was expressed repeatedly, in different periods and in diverse settings, and was an impetus for developing kindergarten nurses' training later in the century.

Baby Farms

In Ontario, infants were occasionally left at the House of Industry, the local workhouse. Three infants, one of them a "coloured girl" only two hours old, were abandoned at the "gate of the poorhouse" in Toronto early in 1862.[54] These children were then sent to wet nurses employed by the House of Industry. This process was not unlike that practised in Britain, where a 1767 act of Parliament required that infants left at parish workhouses be farmed out, or fostered out, to wet nurses.[55] Women who cared for a number of infants in this way were said to have established a baby farm. When the allowance was sufficient, children on the parish baby farms appear to have been adequately maintained at a basic standard of care.[56] When it was not, or when baby farmers were unscrupulous or cruel, the mortality rate was shockingly high.

This class of baby farms was a desperate option for poor families or single mothers. The term came into popular use in 1869, coinciding with famous murder trials of private baby farmers in London and New York.[57]

Social and moral reformers represented baby farms as a means of disposing of unwanted, primarily illegitimate children.[58] The operators received a small fee, sometimes as a lump sum and sometimes as a weekly payment, supposedly for the care of the infant, after which the child was neglected and frequently left to die from malnutrition or was murdered outright.[59]

In the 1870s, shutting down baby farms became a popular cause in Britain and the colonies, particularly for physicians who had defined infanticide as a curable disease.[60] Later in the century, baby farms were targeted by children's aid societies as examples of extreme child neglect.[61] Mothers who used such facilities were luridly described in a pamphlet distributed by the London Society for the Prevention of Cruelty to Children in 1890: "While cannibal mothers, when an unwanted child is born, are said 'to put it back again' in a meal, English mothers put their unwanted children back by a process of which the cannibal would be ashamed, but which, happily for the comparison, her eye does not actually see."[62]

In the language of British imperialism, infanticide was associated with savagery and uncivilized peoples. Great effort had been exerted in the colonies to reform the child-rearing practices of so-called cannibal mothers. David Stannard describes the idea of the cannibal mother as a "fable of savagery" that provided a contrast to the civilization of the white colonials.[63] Efforts to change modes of indigenous child rearing included coercion, conversion, or the removal of the child to a mission school. The rhetoric also served the interests of the late nineteenth-century Child Rescue Movement in its pursuit of legislation and conviction of baby farmers. Paying someone to kill your baby — a premeditated act — was a worse crime than doing it yourself in a moment of insanity. Although baby farmers sometimes killed their charges through strangulation, drug overdose, or exposure, the same techniques sometimes used by mothers themselves, children were more often left to die through passive neglect. As a result, the death of the child would be more difficult to attribute directly to the caregiver.

In the nineteenth century, the courts did not deal harshly with individual mothers who murdered their own infant children. Sympathy was generally felt for such women, who were seen as victims of cruel circumstances.[64] In London, England, 276 dead babies were found on the streets in 1870.[65] In Halifax, 124 dead infants were found on the streets between 1850 and 1875.[66] In Toronto, between 1850 and 1860, 256 dead infants were brought to the attention of the coroner, having been found abandoned in the streets and alleys.[67] Foundling homes were established to offer mothers an alternative.

Humanitarian interest was slow to be translated into legislation. As Ivy Pinchbeck and Margaret Hewitt describe, "Concerted action was impossible in the absence of convincing information, and even when such information had been collected, some particularly sensational piece of evidence was often needed to rally a wavering public to the cause of the reformers."[68] In England, the murder trial of baby farmer Margaret Waters served this purpose, leading to the Infant Life Protection Act (1872), which required boarding homes with more than two children under one year of age to be inspected and registered with the authorities. The act was inadequately enforced, and another murder case in 1896 resulted in a tightening up of the act the next year. As explained by Pinchbeck and Hewitt, legislation developed from a focus on child survival to the more general improvement of the care provided, including measures to improve overall health and nutrition.[69]

A similar pattern evolved in the colonies, from recognition of the baby-farming problem to the passage of legislation to regulate the fostering or boarding of infants. In Australia, two baby farmers were executed for separate crimes in 1893 and 1894 — one for murdering nine babies. In nineteenth-century New Zealand, the problem was widespread.[70] Baby farmer Minnie Dean was hanged in New Zealand in 1895, the only woman ever to receive the death penalty in that country.[71] In the Australian state of Victoria, baby farming had "developed as a cottage industry" in urban settings, providing a semi-permanent form of childcare for mothers with few options.[72] Baby farming was also widespread in New South Wales, often involving a number of individuals, including midwives or others implicated in the actual murder, and in many cases, an undertaker who buried the dead infants.[73] More often, infants were left on the streets.

In twentieth-century Canada, following the trial of Quebec baby farmer Jeanne Dequire, the Quebec government passed the Children's Protection Act in 1944.[74] Dequire operated a nursery that cared for up to fifty children. Two of her infant charges had died in shocking circumstances. One was a ten-week-old who had starved to death. As he weighed only three pounds at death, his mother did not recognize him. Dequire blamed the government's inadequate financial support for infant boarding homes, and she was eventually acquitted of the charges.

Sherri Broder suggests there might be other facets to the baby-farming issue.[75] Her study of the situation in Philadelphia concludes that, in the majority of cases, "baby farming was a legitimate occupation that merely formalised the informal child-care networks of single mothers and other labouring women."[76] Although, in some instances, baby farmers clearly intended to kill their charges, the term "baby farmer" became a generic reference to neighbourhood childcare providers. The term fit the already lively social reformer critique of working and single mothers. Mothers who resorted to daycare were therefore seen as abandoning their infants to the neglect, or worse, of paid caregivers. Group infant care was seen as immoral and dangerous, associated with single mothers and linked with criminals bent on profiting from infant lives. It was within this climate that, in the 1890s, the first day nurseries were established in the colonies, and the care of infants in groups was stigmatized as a poverty-track service.

NEITHER OF THE FIRST two nurseries known to have opened in the US and Canada during the 1850s — the New York Nursery for the Children of Poor Women (1854) and the Toronto Public Nursery (1856) — was called a crèche. However, their founders were aware that the crèche was of French derivation. A letter to a Toronto newspaper in support of the nursery cited a German history of the crèche that traced its origins to France.[77] As was the case in London, these experiments with the daily childcare idea did not catch hold. Other services, such as medical care and permanent child placement, met the more immediate needs of destitute mothers.[78] However, during the brief time that they functioned as childcare facilities, their practices resembled those of the London nurseries described above. In this way, the English day nursery, as a variation of the French crèche, established its first shallow roots in the colonies. In the case of the Toronto Public Nursery, mothers were hired as wet nurses by wealthy women or in the nursery itself. Moreover, the institution accepted children from birth to age six.

As the daycare idea continued to develop in this early period, services were established to meet particular needs but not according to any one system or under the direction of a leader. During the nineteenth century, nothing in the case-study countries could be described as a daycare movement. This non-system prevented easy identification, and daycare was often twinned with other services that were considered complementary. In Australia and Canada, day nurseries following similar patterns of development were opened by women-led philanthropic organizations in Melbourne (1885), Montreal (1887), Toronto (1890), and somewhat later in Sydney (1905). In New Zealand, nurseries operated briefly in Dunedin and Auckland but took hold in the early twentieth century in Wellington with the

1903 start-up of a crèche operated by the Sisters of Compassion under the leadership of Marie Aubert. A unique aspect of developments in Australia and New Zealand was the association in some instances of crèche and free-kindergarten societies to provide care across a wider age range.[79]

In the United States also, the growth of day nurseries in the late 1870s coincided with the development of free kindergartens. Both types of children's institutions grew in relation to phenomenal population increases, including large numbers of immigrants, in cities such as New York, Chicago, and San Francisco. The rise of day nurseries and free kindergartens closely followed patterns of industrial expansion.[80] Private kindergartens had existed in the United States since at least 1856, and despite sporadic developments in the intervening decades, they did not establish themselves on a wider scale until the end of the century when there were three thousand in 1898.[81] In 1892, there were ninety nurseries and a nascent day nursery movement, but on a limited scale compared with educational programs for preschool-aged children.

Spearheaded by the Federation of Day Nurseries, which was based in New York City, attempts were made to incorporate scientific ideas focused on health and hygiene into group daycare. However, day nurseries in the Progressive era were not progressive, resisting, for example, social-work practice and later, nursery education, and retaining their earlier charity orientation. However, they did understand that older children at least needed a more stimulating environment during their long days at the nursery. Where nurseries were located near a school kindergarten, the children were sometimes sent for the half-day. In the 1890s, some day nurseries introduced their own kindergarten classes, hiring part-time teachers. A similar development occurred in the 1920s, with the introduction of nursery schools in day nurseries.

The operation of day nurseries was generally not governed by municipal or state laws and regulations until the 1910s. Few mandatory regulations applied to programs and materials, length of day, numbers of children and caregivers, or training for caregivers, and day nurseries persisted as a Victorian-era charity well into the twentieth century. With few exceptions, they were financed through private subscriptions and donations, and managed by philanthropic women. Across the three nations, new ideas from the field of social welfare or education were rare until the renewal of day nurseries stimulated by conditions in the Depression and government initiatives during the Second World War.

chapter 5   **Kindergarten from Germany
               to England and America**

AMONG EDUCATIONISTS, SUPPORT FOR infant school pedagogy faded by the 1860s. There was a growing opposition to what was seen as stuffing children with facts and teaching them en masse. The new child study indicated that this was inappropriate developmentally, endangering a young child's fragile mind and sensitive disposition. It was also inconsistent with the increasing sentimentality attached to childhood. Large infant schools with up to two hundred pupils operated as a factory system, a connection so obvious that factories were compared to schools as in the following description of young children working at pin heading in England in 1833: "A large room is filled with small tables, at each of which sit four children; about thirty or forty altogether in a room, and certainly of ages lower than I should suppose it possible could be employed in any other gainful occupation. The majority of those I saw did not appear to be above seven or eight, and in fact the scene, as far as respects the ages of the children, reminded me more of an infant school than of anything else I had ever witnessed."[1]

Changes in religious thinking also played a role; particularly relevant here was the idea that conversion of children was not required, because they were born innocent. For a Methodist mother in Canada at mid-century, the "main concern was not conversion but Christian nurture to keep children in their initial condition of innocence."[2] Retaining this innocence was helped by keeping children under the protection of mother's love within the family or, where this was not possible, in a sympathetic educational setting such as a kindergarten. Friedrich Froebel (1782-1852) established mothers as the central figure in their children's development. He conceived the kindergarten system as a structured, non-academic approach to early education. Historian Marguerite Van Die suggests that, in the "new" Methodist family, "the exhortations of a godly mother" replaced the popular revival meetings of earlier in the nineteenth century: "A mother, unlike a preacher, had the advantage of ubiquity and even omniscience in the eyes of her young children."[3] Kindergarteners had similar advantages, and some even shared the Methodist mother's evangelistic spirit, as in the free kindergartens in Winnipeg described in chapter 7.

Froebel

In 1839, Froebel organized a kind of infant school called the Play and Activity Institute (Spiel- und Beschäftigungsanstalt) in Bad Blankenburg, Germany.[4] In the same year, infant teacher James Buchanan arrived in Cape Town from London. Buchanan and Froebel were contemporaries, born two years apart. Buchanan's own education is unknown, whereas Froebel's studies were varied although sometimes brief and informal. Buchanan's pedagogy probably changed over the course of his career, but there is no evidence that it moved much beyond the style he adopted at New Lanark. In contrast, Froebel evolved his approach, living for two years with his students at Pestalozzi's Institute of Education in Switzerland; in 1816, he became the director of a small school at Keilhau where he developed his materials and wrote *The Education of Man*. Unlike Buchanan, Froebel surrounded himself with gifted and innovative teachers and students, leaving a group of dedicated women who identified as his disciples to more fully articulate his ideas after his death.

His philosophy of education was strongly influenced by his religious beliefs, his studies in mathematics, physics, and architecture, and his observations at Pestalozzi's school at Yverdon. Like Rousseau, he believed in the innocence of childhood, though, for Froebel, its nature required ordering. Like Pestalozzi, he understood the importance of connecting learning to real-life experiences, but he used materials with a more symbolic and spiritual purpose. Central to this was his religious belief in the unity of all things. Kindergarten activities were planned to enable children to make these essential connections. The credo of the movement, "come let us live for our children," did not mean that children took the lead in their own education, but that teachers should show the way based on their understanding of the nature of childhood.[5] Froebel believed that children's minds were fully formed at birth and capable of reason but were unfocused and disordered. The sensitive guidance of a female teacher — the ideal candidate being a sensitive mother or mother surrogate — could bring children's reason to full flower by providing materials known as play-gifts and crafts, and by engaging children in activities called occupations. The materials could mediate these big ideas, helping children achieve an integrated understanding of their relation to the world and facilitating their natural development, or "unfoldment." The materials mediated children's development but could not change it.

Froebel's materials were not entirely unique. Jean-Frédéric Oberlin had devised various educational playthings for his schools, and a number of materials were familiar from the English infant school. The cubes and bricks used by Wilderspin were basic forms in Froebel's building Gifts. In the kindergarten, Wilderspin's jointed slats, later marketed by others as the gonigraph, were known as the sixteenth Gift. Wilderspin's first book — *On the Importance of Educating the Infant Children of the Poor* — was published in 1823; Joseph Wertheimer's German translation of it appeared in 1826. Froebel's *The Education of Man* was privately published in the same year. There is no evidence that Froebel had any direct knowledge of the English infant school, but certainly infant schools were known on the Continent. In 1828, employing a system resembling Wilderspin's and using Wertheimer's translation as a guide, an infant school called an Engelsgarten (Angel Garden) — perhaps a Swedenborgian reference — was established in Vienna for the children of the poor.[6]

Interpreters of the kindergarten, such as the German American Edward Wiebé, incorporated the common infant school drills along with Froebel's materials. As Wiebé described,

> The children are made to stand in one or two rows, with heads erect, and feet upon a given line, or spots marked on the floor. The teacher then gives directions like the following:
> "Lift up your right hands as high as you can raise them."
> "Take them down."
> "Lift up your left hands." "Down."
> "Lift up both your hands." "Down."

Once given a ball to hold, the children were quizzed on its properties, much as in the popularized Pestalozzian method:

"Who can tell me the name of what you have received?" Questions may follow about the color, material, shape, and other qualities of the ball ...The children are then required to repeat sentences pronounced by the teacher, as — "The ball is round." "My ball is green." "All these balls are made of rubber," etc.[7]

A great difference between the infant school and kindergarten systems lay in the correspondence between philosophy and pedagogy: in the kindergarten, teaching and learning were considered a spiritual activity. Although this was also true of Buchanan's approach, it did not typify the system as described by Wilderspin. Certainly, no infant school philosophers wrote about their system as Froebel did about the kindergarten. In typically cryptic terms, Froebel explained the meaning of play with sticks in this way: "In a similar manner [to magnetism] a constantly invisible and not less attractive outwardly acting inner power abides in Nature as a whole, as well as in the parts of Nature. An example of this is given in our little simple and yet tangible stick, not only by the middle line which is indented by its visible ends, and is hence, as it were visibly invisible, but also by the middle of this line which is purely invisible, merely perceptible to the intellect, though never to be made visible."[8] Kindergarten activity such as this checked the passions of children, as they engaged in the prayerful and silent manipulation of their playthings. In this situation, the greatest punishment was to deny them access to the materials and their companions. Johannes Ronge explained the use of punishment in the kindergarten that he had established with his wife, Bertha, who had trained with Froebel in Hamburg: "We punish children who have not attended their lessons by depriving them of the pleasure which nature produces, and which for children is playing with their companions; children who disturb the class are simply separated for one or more hours."[9]

Froebel's obtuse writing style was a factor limiting the propagation of the kindergarten outside Germany until after his death and the publication of numerous more readily understandable interpretations. Learning through play and activity had also been described by educators such as Oberlin and J.H. Campe on the Continent, and of course, by Owen in Britain. Historian Mary Hilton argues that women educators had expressed the essential aspects of the kindergarten idea for one hundred years before Froebel came on the scene. She suggests that women intellectuals in England, the United States, and the British colonies accepted it because the "feminine tissue onto which it was grafted was ready, receptive and related."[10] The kindergarten fitted a need at the end of the nineteenth century, a situation that very probably saved it from remaining a marginal educational experiment, as it was in Germany.[11] Indeed, sixty years passed before Froebel's *Die Menschenerziehung* was published in English as *The Education of Man* in 1886.[12]

The System

A dominant feature of the kindergarten was Froebel's educational appliances. Froebel worked out his system by enlisting families to try out his materials under his direction. In this way, he developed and modified the toys called gifts in English, so named as to emphasize their symbolic nature. Experiments with materials continued in the first "sixteen genuine and real kindergartens" opened in Germany in the 1840s, where children's other activities included gardening, nature study, songs, and games.[13] Hermann Poesche, who published a selection of Froebel's letters on the kindergarten in 1887, believed the propagation of Froebel's system in Germany was partly accomplished through the distribution of his educational materials. The playthings carried the ideas: "The games and occupations which he had created in the silence of solitude, often with locked doors, living the life of a hermit, now had to be carefully illustrated and made plain by lithographs and directions, to be packed up by the work-people at his Kindergarten Factory, and pushed in a mercantile way. The gifts thus made their way through the toyshops to the children in the bosoms of their families; and this purely mercantile method was the first form of Froebel's propaganda."[14]

Historian W.E. Marsden calls the Gifts "surrogate toys, designed for learning."[15] In Froebel's plan, they were to be used sequentially, with one preparing the way for the next. They were numbered, although Froebel's numbering was added to in the various guides written by others at a later date.[16] The first Gift was a set of six brightly coloured knitted balls, each attached to a string. Gifts two through nine were manipulative materials.[17] The second to the sixth Gifts were sets of small blocks, each set contained in a wooden box with a sliding cover so the child could gain an "impression of the whole, of the self-contained."[18] The seventh Gift was a collection of paper or wooden shapes, Gift eight consisted of sticks, and Gift nine of rings. These were used for "laying figures" on a flat surface. Gift ten was drawing, and eleven to twenty were constructive or occupational materials, used mainly for crafts such as weaving or folding paper, sewing, or modelling with clay. As described by Kate Douglas Wiggin and Nora Archibald Smith, American interpreters of Froebel's system, "In the gifts there is investigation, combination, rearrangement of certain definite material, but no change in its form; in the occupations the material is modified, reshaped, and transformed."[19]

For Froebel, the materials had both practical play value and metaphysical properties. Mothers used the first two Gifts with their babies, the balls being objects that mediated play as well as suggesting the big idea of unity. Balls were also a familiar play item, though the string was meant to unite the child to the object. Gift two was introduced at around eighteen months of age. Play with the sphere and the cubes extended from the first Gift, giving the child experience with objects that were "externally opposite ... yet alike." According to Froebel, "The sphere can be considered as the material expression of pure movement; the cube as the material expression of complete rest."[20] A mother's songs accompanied play "to indicate by movement and word this connection of life and things, the reciprocal life between child and plaything; and this so much the more as by using the gift in this way the hearing capacity of the child is generally wholly developed, and his speaking capacity begins to develop."[21] The blocks could be suspended by string and spun, twirled as tops, rolled, and stacked. Children's play in this manner momentarily focused their attention, developing their concentration and perception, thus enabling them to recognize the inherent order in the world and their place within it, an idea that differed from Wilderspin's notion of training the eye.

In Gifts three to six, older children manipulated the blocks as well as observed their properties. The blocks were cubes that were divided or left whole and organized into sets of increasing complexity. Gifts three and four consisted of eight one-inch blocks and eight tiles respectively which, when properly stacked together, formed a two-inch cube. Each tile (or parallelepiped, as they were termed in the formal language used in kindergarten guidebooks) measured two inches by one inch by one-half inch. Gift five comprised twenty-one one-inch blocks and six that had been created by cutting one-inch pieces diagonally into halves or quarters. When properly assembled, Gift five formed a three-inch cube, as did Gift six. This consisted of twenty-seven parallelepipeds; eighteen of these had been left whole, six had been cut in half crosswise, and three lengthwise.

These "building Gifts" developed children's constructive powers as they used them to represent forms of life, beauty, and knowledge. Forms of life were familiar objects in a child's physical world, the examples given by

Clockwise from top:

Froebel's Gift four, manufactured by J.W. Schermerhorn and Co. Author's collection.

A winding staircase constructed from Gift four. Author's collection.

Gift six assembled as a cube. Manufactured by the Milton Bradley Company. Author's collection.

Froebel highlighting the middle-class origins of his preschools: a writing table, a chair, and a wastepaper basket.[22] Children started by building representations of their home environment, including their house, and moved outward to the immediate community: the market place, monuments, and the city gates. All blocks in a set were used to instill the idea of unity in nature. Forms of beauty were patterns resulting from arrangements of blocks into triangular and other geometrical forms, whereas forms of knowledge illustrated mathematical and scientific principles.

Children used the materials while seated at a long, low table inscribed with a one-inch grid across its surface. Following a teacher's instructions or a printed plan, they placed the cubes and bricks in a pattern on the grid. This constraint was necessary for them to understand the order revealed by the materials. They worked individually, each with his or her own Gift. This task may have been followed by a game or movement activity before they returned to the tables to complete a craft. Though the occupations or handicrafts were numbered, they were meant to supplement the manipulative Gifts and did not need to be presented in strict sequence. The occupations supported manual training as well as artistic development, but their true aim was "full and free development for creative self-activity, for the expression of the inner life of the child."[23] In the kindergarten system, a child's unfoldment needed guided instruction in an ordered environment. This required "the early training of children in general" and "the training of healthy-minded and brave-hearted maidens" as the children's "first real nurses."[24]

Although the kindergarten system included group games, nature study, gardening, songs, and stories, the kindergarten appliances were its most visible element. Froebel's philosophy of education, which underlay the development of the materials, was often neglected in descriptions of the system. In reviewing the writings of early kindergarten interpreters such as Bertha Ronge, Kevin Brehony notes the supremacy they accorded to Gift work technique rather than to an exposition of Froebel's ideas.[25] The philosophy lacked staying power, and even as the kindergarten gained in popularity, its exponents distanced themselves from its intellectual base. In their introduction to the English edition of Froebel's letters, published to mark the fiftieth anniversary of the kindergarten, British kindergarteners Emilie Michaelis and H. Keatley Moore revealed the following, which reads as a strange tribute: "We have ... left unaltered the peculiarities of our Socrates, even such as are most unattractive; that is, we have not abbreviated Froebel's diffuseness, nor omitted his repetitions, nor cleared his mysticism, nor modernised his antique philosophy, nor corrected his absurd symbolic etymology."[26] As enthusiasm for Froebel's philosophy dissolved, the materials remained. These were not immediately discarded.

The growth of kindergartens in the case-study countries occurred as Froebelism was challenged by new ideas in education. Evelyn Weber suggests that Froebelism was itself a provocation for reform-minded educators to devise an alternative: "In the Froebelian program, content had been built around the symbolic meanings of gifts and occupations, which acted as organizing centres for the program; if this content were to be abandoned, some tangible substitute for both content and organizing centres had to be developed."[27] The story of kindergarten in the colonies includes efforts to fill this space with a social and moral curriculum, and with education for citizenship in a secular and New World interpretation of Froebel's "antique philosophy."

Free Kindergartens

Only about fifty kindergartens were established in Germany between 1840 and 1851, when they were closed by government order. Regardless of this edict, the idea of early education outside the family had very limited support in Germany. Froebel died in 1852, shortly after marrying his much younger second wife, kindergarten teacher Luise Levin. Before his death, he had established a training school for kindergarten teachers, and the commitment of his former students, including Luise Levin-Froebel, as well as the emigration of some during the Franco-Prussian War, helped spread the approach beyond the borders of Germany, where it gained new life.[28]

A central figure in its propagation was Bertha von Marenholtz-Bülow, who, from the 1860s, had advocated the start-up of *Volkskindergärten* (people's kindergartens) for poor children in Germany.[29] Her conception of these programs differed from Froebel's vision for a universal system by stressing manual or vocational training over holistic development for poor children.[30] A free kindergarten of this kind was opened in Berlin in 1874 by the Society for Family and Popular Education, an organization founded by von Marenholtz-Bülow. This kindergarten was the forerunner of the Pestalozzi-Froebel House in Berlin, which was established by Henriette Schrader-Breymann and was similar to settlement houses in England, the United States, and the colonies. Thus, a two-tier system of kindergarten education was initiated: private kindergartens for wealthy children, which had an educational purpose, and free kindergartens for the poor, which operated as full-day childcare and provided skill-based training.[31] The latter were distinct from both Wilderspin's infant schools and the German *Bewahranstalt* — daycare centres for poor children — by aiming to replicate home life in the school, with children participating in chores such as laundry, cleaning, and cooking.[32] Von Marenholtz-Bülow's ideas were influential in the United States. In the late 1880s, the directors of the newly created Chicago Kindergarten Training School went to Germany so as to learn about kindergarten work directly from her, and a separate Pestalozzi-Froebel Kindergarten Training School opened in Chicago in 1896. At Berlin's Pestalozzi-Froebel House, Froebel's Gifts and occupations were set aside in favour of real-life work. This represented another important division in the kindergarten movement, between conservative "Froebelians" and the more liberal interpreters of the kindergarten idea.

Few free kindergartens existed in Britain, where education for working-class children was established within infant schools. However, private kindergartens for bourgeois children were more common than the free variant, starting with the London school organized by Bertha and Johannes Ronge in 1851. Their school for children and an associated school for training kindergarteners, established in 1854, were important for the demonstration of kindergarten methods and as a training ground for other German émigré teachers in using the method in an English setting. Of significance for her influence on American and Canadian developments, Maria Kraus-Boelte studied in Hamburg with Luise Levin-Froebel before coming to London to teach at the Ronges' school.[33] In the 1860s, she organized her own kindergarten, where Lord Brougham's grandchildren were her students. In 1872, she immigrated to the United States, where she established a training school in New York with her husband John Kraus. Kristen Nawrotzki characterizes this crossing over of experience and influences as an Anglo-American Kindergarten Movement.[34] British kindergarten-teacher education through the private National Froebel Union (1887) and the Froebel Educational Institute (1892) was also influential in developments in New Zealand and Australian free kindergartens.

Free kindergartens were fitted to the colonial experience and thrived there; the first free kindergarten in England did not open until 1900, almost a quarter-century after their start in America. They first developed in the United States in the late 1870s for "neglected waifs and strays," mostly children of recent immigrants living in urban slums.[35] They combined a social service — childcare, food, and shelter — with moral lessons underpinned to varying degrees by a Froebelian educational program that placed more emphasis on what was called hand culture (arts and crafts) than on mind culture (intellectual exercises). In America, free kindergartens came of age during the period of late Victorian-era social reform that saw the rise of the day nursery movement discussed in Chapter 4. The two services were often established as combined day nursery–kindergartens to serve the entire age range from birth to school age. Even in cases where a day nursery was not part of the service, free kindergartens included what, by current standards, were very young children. In Australia, they catered to children aged eighteen months to four years. This continued until the 1950s, when, due to pressure from child development experts who warned of negative effects of early separation of mother and baby, the minimum age was raised to three.

The development of elementary school systems in the colonies, and the accompanying legislation that governed who could attend and who could not, also stimulated the growth of free kindergartens. However, the kindergartens were only one of several initiatives designed to catch children who could not or did not want to attend the available common schools. These were mainly the offspring of the poor. Free kindergartens built upon the ideas of the infant schools, as well as the later development of the ragged schools that dominated education for the poor from the 1820s. Whereas infant schools and kindergartens aimed to prevent problems, ragged schools were organized as a remedial measure.

Industrialization pushed poor mothers of young children into employment in factories and service jobs; their small children were gathered together into infant schools and provided with lessons, food, and shelter. Ragged schools offered a similar service for somewhat older children. During the 1850s and 1860s, a small number of poor children in the larger Australian and Canadian cities received a nominal education at ragged schools.[36] In her history of Australian kindergartens, Mary Walker observes that the Sydney ragged schools of the 1860s to the 1880s were the "forerunners of the Free Kindergartens, using very similar methods and serving [children in] the same areas."[37] Ragged schools were not formed in any number in New Zealand.

The schools took their name from the tattered clothing of their pupils.[38] Designed for older working children and held at night so as not to interfere with their daytime labour, they provided free basic schooling with a heavy dose of Christian training. Charles Dickens wrote about the London ragged schools in the 1840s: "I have no desire to praise the system pursued in the Ragged Schools; which is necessarily very imperfect, if indeed there be one. So far as I have any means of judging of what is taught there, I should individually object to it, as not being sufficiently secular, and as presenting too many religious mysteries and difficulties, to minds not sufficiently prepared for their reception."[39]

Ragged schools and kindergartens were contemporaneous institutions in London, though the latter remained experimental. A decade after Dickens wrote his ragged-schools article, he published "Child-Gardens," by Henry Morley in *Household Words*.[40] Morley described Bertha and Johannes Ronges' school, which catered to children from age three to seven. The pupils played indoors with the special materials and outside in the sunshine with individual garden plots for them to attend. There were no books, although children could form letters out of shapes cut from coloured pasteboard, placing them on the gridlines of a slate, an infant school material that the Ronges renamed the Kinder Garten Alphabet, claiming its invention.[41] Charles Dickens himself was not overly impressed. In his correspondence, he wrote that he had been alerted to the start-up of London kindergartens by "a certain Baroness here the other day, who was strongly interested in some such system. She was a German Baroness and lived (I suppose) in a Castle somewhere — to which stronghold she has returned."[42]

The first ragged school operating under that name opened in London in 1843. A Ragged School Union was formed in 1844 to draw attention to the cause and to help groups who desired to start a school. The union oversaw an increasing number of schools to 1870, when education was made compulsory and even the poorest children gained entry to free elementary schools.[43] Because the needs of their pupils went beyond education, the ragged schools offered food and clothing in addition to lessons. Humane and community based, they provided general support for poor parents. In some schools, teachers conducted home visits, led mothers' classes, and organized nurseries for the youngest children of working mothers.[44]

As Dickens suggested, ragged schools were not based on a particular system of education. As in infant schools, learning for the youngest children was through amusements, and corporal punishment was not permitted. The ragged schools also shared the humanitarian orientation of infant schools in the context of a general fear regarding the criminal potential of the underclass. Like infant school advocates, their supporters asserted their practical value as a prophylaxis, using statistics to demonstrate their impact in a manner that would later be exploited by proponents of free kindergartens. The Edinburgh Ragged School claimed that, in the first five years of its existence, the percentage of children under the age of fourteen who were in prison had dropped from 5.6 to 0.9. Had the school not existed, Ragged school advocate and philanthropist Thomas Guthrie postulated, "at least two-thirds" of its pupils would have "developed into full-blown criminals."[45] The school was thus represented as a substantial saving in terms of prison expenditure. Since it was observed that a criminal life started early, separate "infant ragged schools" were proposed, but few were established.[46] The Reverend John Garwood, clerical secretary for the London City Mission, repeated the mantra of infant school supporters from thirty years before, writing, "Children of this class are extremely precocious, and an immense amount of misery and crime might be prevented by *early* instruction."[47]

Some children were sent from English workhouses for settlement in the colonies and to work as labourers.[48] Mission workers in Britain such as Garwood were critical of this general approach: "In these eddies of civilized society are gathered all the filth, the crime, the savage recklessness, which is subsequently carried to the Antipodes, and causes the sad and melancholy statement from New Zealand, that the white settlers have more to fear from the white man, their countryman, a member once of a refined state of society, than they have to dread from the savage and the cannibal!"[49]

Some emigrants may have found their way to ragged schools in the colonies. In Hobart, Australia, a ragged school opened in 1854, with more following in Melbourne and Sydney after the 1859 report of the Select Committee Investigating the Social Conditions of the Working Class. The Halifax Ragged School, established in 1864, survived until shortly after the Second World War. It was aligned with child-welfare bodies in the city, including the Children's Aid Society and the Juvenile Court.[50] Although the schools were city-based institutions, the central image of cleansing and civilizing children, and thus halting their fall into vice and immorality, was also applied to Aboriginal children. Both groups comprised a "wild lawless tribe."[51] The Reverend Joseph Kingsmill compared the teachers working with First Nations children on Manitoulin Island to ragged-school teachers. Each served "barbarous or half-civilised people."[52] Before the children could be taught, Kingsmill wrote, they needed to be washed, barbered, and dressed in European clothing.

Pupils attended ragged schools because their labour was needed to bring home a wage during the day or because their family could not afford the fees for books or clothing for school. Some were homeless and living on the street. The passing of compulsory education laws in the three colonies in the period 1870 to 1885 meant that even these children were included in school. Ragged schools mutated into vocational schools for older children.

THE DEVELOPMENT OF FREE kindergartens was stimulated by a dramatic increase in immigration to America and the colonies. Cities experienced a period of rapid expansion that characterized New World urbanization in the nineteenth century. Rising numbers of immigrants and migration in the years following the American Civil War strained the resources of cities such as New York, Chicago, and San Francisco. Slums grew up as landlords capitalized on severe housing shortages by building cheap tenements. The tenements became immigrant ghettos that facilitated the exploitation of home workers by contractors in the garment industry and other trades. Access to potable water was difficult or not available. Antiquated sewage systems were insufficient. The spread of disease in these circumstances, including typhoid and cholera, meant that high infant mortality was a "fact of life" for poor urban parents in the last half of the nineteenth century.

These problems gave rise to a number of solutions directed at health and education for the masses, in a period of social reform dominated by the Progressive Movement. The movement blended a Victorian spirit of benevolence, in which the rich had a duty to help the poor, with discoveries and innovations in the fields of medicine, public health, education, and social service. Of particular importance to poor families were the construction of sewage systems, the opening of community centres called settlement houses, and the visits of nurses who gave practical assistance to mothers on matters of child health, clean milk campaigns, and vaccination programs. Free kindergartens were only one of many child-welfare services associated with the Progressive Movement. They existed along with older Victorian-era charities, such as ragged schools, that continued in Sydney and Halifax into the twentieth century.[53] In Tasmania, the first free kindergarten shared a building with the Hobart Ragged School.[54] As late as 1909, a Melbourne free kindergarten operated in a building owned by a ragged-school society.[55] A single family was sometimes associated with the old and new charities. For example, Mary Windeyer was involved with establishing the Sydney Foundling Institution in 1874; two decades later, her daughter Margaret helped organize the Kindergarten Union of New South Wales.

Well-intentioned men and women who came forward to do their part founded all sorts of groups dedicated to poor relief. Giving aid to people in need was a Christian duty. In my own copy of *Children of the Tenements*, written by crime reporter Jacob Riis, the original owner inscribed a verse from Philippians, perhaps for inspiration: "Look not every man on his own things, but every man also on the things of others."[56] This was followed by a paraphrase — "In other words, try to see how the other fellow is getting on." Journalists such as Riis in New York, John Joseph Kelso in Toronto, and Mark Cohen in Dunedin brought the struggles of the poor for subsistence into the drawing rooms of the middle and upper classes. An exchange between a small boy and a policeman, related by Riis in *How the Other Half Lives*, was typical of this genre:

"Where do you go to church, my boy?"
"We don't have no clothes to go to church," And indeed his appearance, as he was, in the door of any New York church would have caused a sensation.
"Well, where do you go to school, then?"
"I don't go to school," with a snort of contempt.
"Where do you buy your bread?"
"We don't buy no bread; we buy beer," said the boy, and it was eventually the saloon that led the police as a landmark to his "home." It was worthy of the boy. As he had said, his only bed was a heap of dirty straw on the floor, his daily diet a crust in the morning, nothing else.[57]

Explorers and missionaries had earlier established a tradition of recording their contact with exotic tribes as well as their observations of their customs in popular books. Back in England, social explorers such as Friedrich Engels, Henry Mayhew, John Thomson, and Adolphe Smith focused their studies on the range of human experience that existed in the London slums.[58] They mapped poverty in a way that was by turns voyeuristic, sympathetic, and indicative of a fear of and fascination with the underclass. Whatever their motivation, they made the lives of the poor more visible through their writings, photography, and lectures.

Riis believed that the solution to the problem of poverty and to getting ahead in America was education. If the lad he described in the preceding dialogue grew up unchurched and unschooled, he would take his place in the "tramps' army."[59] The little fellow would have been a perfect candidate for an infant ragged school. Charles Loring Brace, founder of the New York Children's Aid Society, published his own warning concerning the "dangerous classes": "The class of a large city most dangerous to its property, its morals, and its political life are the ignorant, destitute, untrained, and abandoned youth; the outcast street-children grown up to be voters, to be the implements of demagogues, the 'feeders' of the criminals, and the sources of domestic outbreaks and violations of the law."[60]

Brace also advocated for education as a solution to poverty. However, for Brace, the morally polluted city environment and uncaring or absent parents reduced the effect of education. His plan to correct this, carried out in the spirit of what was called child saving or child rescue, centred on the mass relocation of poor children from cities to the countryside. From 1853 to 1929, thousands of children were transported on "orphan trains" from New York children's institutions to work on farms in the American Midwest.

A smaller number, 566 by 1910, were sent to Canada.[61] The internal transport of children in the US resembled similar schemes for the removal of poor British children to the colonies that had been in operation since the seventeen hundreds.[62] During Australia's Transportation Era, the children were convicts themselves or were the offspring of convicts. Others were rescued from the streets by men such as Thomas John Barnardo in London, whose work paralleled that of Brace in New York. Both Brace and Barnardo initially had an interest in foreign mission work. As urban missionaries, they directed their attention to the "heathen in their midst."[63] A hundred thousand children were transported on "orphan boats" from Great Britain to Canada under child migration schemes such as Barnardo's. In 1903, the secretary of the State Children's Aid Association in England reasoned that, "as the mother of nations," England had a duty "to do a mother's part — send those [children] able to contend with the world out in it, and keep those in need of care and protection within the shelter of the home."[64] Once in the colonies, children were transported from city to country through schemes in which they were indentured as labourers or boarded out with foster families. Many were successful; others lived in abusive situations. Child migration from Britain to Canada ended in 1939 but continued to Australia and South Africa until 1967.

Thus, for children who were deemed to be at risk due to poverty, the dominant nineteenth-century trend in child welfare was to remove them from their family and local community. At the same time, a very small number of children were served by community-based services, such as day nurseries and free kindergartens, that supported them within their families. The rhetoric of child rescue underpinning child migration and orphan care was also part of the free-kindergarten movement. Classing children as "strays" implied that they were lost or separated from their families. As small children played on the street, away for a time from the crowded quarters of their tenement homes, they came to the attention of upper-class reformers, who considered their unsupervised play to be dangerous for both them and society at large. In the metaphor of the time, the street was a "nursery for crime," a dangerous and uncontrolled space in which young children could be inducted into gang life. A variety of local solutions were devised to contain children's play, among them playgrounds and kindergartens. Both public and free kindergartens shared similar objectives: to protect children from unsavoury influences and to assimilate them into the mainstream of society through Bible lessons and education in citizenship.[65] Public school kindergartens also included preparation for the first compulsory grade level, but whether they achieved this goal was a source of debate.

In the main, assimilation was viewed as a positive thing. An outward sign of successful integration was the ability to speak and understand English. The view of writers such as Riis, himself an immigrant, was that fluency in English was a ticket to prosperity. Riis' "goal was to see the slum-dweller assimilated by the process of Americanisation," which could best be achieved by starting fresh with the children.[66] As he remarked, "Nothing is now better understood than that the rescue of the children is the key to the problem of city poverty, as presented for our solution today; that character may be formed where to reform it would be a hopeless task ...The young are naturally neither vicious nor hardened, simply weak and undeveloped, except by the bad influences of the street."[67] This theme was repeated over and over again by supporters of popular education. Early education, if it was well executed, could erase differences and create a homogeneous and docile population supporting a single idea of what it meant to be a Canadian, an Australian, or a New Zealander. In the colonies, however, where immigration came overwhelmingly from the United Kingdom, assimilation was class-based and directed toward giving poor children a head start on primary school.

What were the characteristics of children that made them the obvious access point for this type of citizenship education? Shurlee Swain, writing about the history of child welfare in Australia, identifies a shift that occurred around the mid-nineteenth century, in which children, no longer seen as vagrants, became identified as victims.[68] As vagrants, they were threats to the social order, and their removal to an orphanage, a children's home, or the outback was the most efficient solution. Perceiving poor children as victims of circumstances beyond their control concentrated attention on the cause of poverty. Social surveys, such as those mentioned above, described the industrialized city as foul and inhumane in its treatment of its weakest citizens. The change to a focus on environment as the culprit was reflected in criticism of large-scale children's institutions. Children needed love, care, and affection, which could be offered only within a home or home-like environment. Complicated schemes, such as those of Barnardo and Brace, were one outcome of this thinking. However, kindergartens also fit the bill, with their maternalist philosophy and emphasis on family support through parent education and as a by-product of child education. In addition, they were popular with working-class parents, filling a real need for support in trying times and reflecting their valuing of education for their children.

The benefits ensuing from kindergartens, for philanthropists as well as poor parents and children, were depicted in a promotional film titled *At the Threshold of Life,* created for the New York-based National Kindergarten Association in 1911.[69] The film begins in the well-appointed drawing room of a young kindergarten teacher who has just received a package containing a set of Froebel's Gifts. A male friend enters and asks her to join him for a ride in his new automobile. She declines, indicating that she has a higher calling: her kindergarten work. In the next scene, the friend receives a letter from the National Kindergarten Association soliciting donations for its work. Enraged by the request in light of the kindergartener's preference for her work rather than spending time with him, he rips the letter into pieces.

A second storyline, one linking the lives of these privileged characters with those of the poor, is set in a tenement. Annoyed by their children's exuberance, an overworked mother and father chase them out of their crowded apartment to play on the street, where they fight over an unlucky kitten. The young son happens upon the free kindergarten where the teacher is at work. He stands outside the gate, gazing longingly at the happy children playing safely within. He returns to the street to play, and there he meets his cruel fate: a car driven by the kindergartener's male friend runs him down. The distraught friend and the kindergartener, who chanced to be nearby, rush the boy to the hospital, where he recovers. The friend redeems himself by writing a generous cheque to the National Kindergarten Association.

The film contains the major themes at work in the free-kindergarten movement from the late 1870s. First, kindergarten teaching afforded employment for single women from wealthy families. Their privileged backgrounds enabled them to pursue the calling either as volunteers or for minimal pay. Accepting the call and making the commitment to kindergarten work could mean forgoing courtship and marriage. Second, poor families, by dint of their unfortunate circumstances, were powerless to protect their children from all the dangers of the street. Physical harm would inevitably befall them, as in the case of the car accident, even if they somehow managed to avoid collateral social and moral damage.

A central concept in Froebel's vision of the kindergarten was that it was meant for all children without consideration for social class. Children qualified for kindergarten simply because they were children. Leaders within the kindergarten movement took this to mean that kindergarten could be advantageously applied to both rich and poor children as a balm for bad parenting. In this view, privileged children's problems were more clearly located within the family — a centre of "sloth, gluttony, and covetousness" according to kindergarten teacher Susan Blow — whereas poor children, whose parents set them loose on the street, were more susceptible to peer group or other outside influences.[70] Blow's former associate William Torrey Harris worried about the problem of poor children as well as those of the newly rich, the latter the result of a too-rapid creation of a capitalist class.[71] He shared this view in an essay published while he served as the United States commissioner of education:

> The kindergarten provides for two classes of weaklings that develop in a city community. First, the children of the very poor who lack the virtue of thrift, and do what they can to educate their children in the same weakness. The kindergarten takes these from the street at an early stage, and gives them a humane introduction to neatness, cleanliness, and social union with their fellows, thus initiating them into civilisation … The second class of weaklings which develop are the moral weaklings; for example, those furnished by the class of spoiled children. The many chances for wealth in this country combine to create a class of people newly become wealthy. The time for the father has been absorbed in gaining the wealth, that of the mother in

adjusting to the new social caste into which she has entered ... In the absence of parental restraint, they develop selfishness, indulge all their appetites, and often die of excess in early manhood. The kindergarten, through its mild discipline, and its facilities for employing these precocious children in work, by means of gifts, occupations, and games, succeeds in saving most of them.[72]

It might be wondered if Harris was a friend of the movement, yet he is a principal figure in the history of the kindergarten in the United States. In 1871, while he was superintendent of schools for St. Louis, Missouri, he hired Susan Blow to establish a kindergarten there, the first in a US public school. By the 1890s, Harris' educational ideas mixed Herbartian theory with Froebel's child-centred idealism.

We have seen how colonial infant schools served various purposes, for childcare, instruction, and evangelism. The three functions were bundled into the entity of the free kindergarten. In the United States, Felix Adler, a strong advocate of free kindergartens, expressed the educational function as preparation for living in a democracy. He encouraged education for the people as a means, not for control, but for ensuring the greater "co-operation of the masses."[73] "Society," wrote Adler, "is an organism; a part cannot flourish at the expense of the whole. Each function attains its maximum excellence in the perfect action of the others."[74] However, kindergarten was not narrowly construed as a preschool experience. It was a class in citizenship, complete in itself, that laid the groundwork for living in a democracy.

Other writers on the educational value of kindergarten took the view that, if childhood were left to its natural course, humanity would not rise above the savage state. This view focused on the civilizing value of the kindergarten as an influence on childhood as a life phase. For example, in his 1893 essay on kindergarten education, Talcott Williams described the unrestrained child as fearsome. Drawing on race-recapitulation theory, evident in the field of child study as exemplified by such men as G. Stanley Hall, he wrote: "The young savage needs to be humanised. What are more brutal than the self-invented games of blameless children? Do we not all know the infant who has sought to kill or maim his pet? Have we not all met the child who, when taken to the sorrowing home where his playmate lies dead, at once asks, with the blunt avarice of a four years old, 'Now that Peter is dead, you will give me his horse and his drum, won't you?'"[75]

In colonial settings, where some European parents felt anxiety regarding their new environment, taming the savage child was especially urgent. The new settlements in the southern hemisphere were oceans away from the civilizing influence of England. Helen May suggests that the kindergarten movement in New Zealand was sparked by this anxiety. It was one of several institutions that aimed to tame what she calls the "wild colonial child."[76] Others included playgrounds, boys' and girls' clubs, and Sunday schools. This theme was not unique to its time: Robert Owen and others in the infant school movement expressed concern regarding the underclass, as did the founders of ragged schools and, in the early twentieth century, the Italian educator Maria Montessori. In a speech given at the opening of a crèche in a Roman slum, Montessori painted a picture of poor children as subhuman. Relating the story "of a wretched woman thrown, by the drunken men who have preyed upon her, forth into the gutter," she added that, "there, when day has come, the children of the neighbourhood crowd about her like scavengers about their dead prey, shouting and laughing at the sight of this wreck of womanhood, kicking her bruised and filthy body as it lies in the mud of the gutter!"[77] Montessori praised the teacher who dared to enter this dark world as a "true missionary, a moral queen."[78] She continued: "Among these almost savage people, into these houses where at night no one dared to go about unarmed, there has come not only to teach, but to live the very life they live, a gentlewoman of culture, an educator by profession, who dedicates her time and her life to helping those about her!"[79]

The role of educated adults, for writers like Talcott Williams, was to civilize children according to a series of apparently benign but necessary social, moral, and educational interventions. Although Williams and others believed that kindergarten could meet this need, Froebel's kindergarten was founded on a philosophy that was at odds with the idea of the unformed child and the civilized adult. Nevertheless, the two ideas were often set beside one another, as if they were complementary and not conflicting. Cultural theorist Neil Postman explains that both understandings of childhood were active in the minds of Americans in the late nineteenth century.[80] The kindergarten was a container for these differing ideas of childhood, development, and education. Some stressed that the greatest threat to childhood's natural order was ill-conceived instruction or parenting that would contort development. Others assumed an evolutionary view of child development; focusing on the moral and social spheres, they regarded the natural order as an object of fear and repulsion. The natural child was primitive, savage. The poor child in particular, isolated in the slum from positive role models, lacked the good "breeding" necessary for participation in a civilized society. This last view was a foundation for the mission function of the free kindergarten, where the aim was to rehabilitate children whose upbringing or general environment was inadequate because of poverty or the failure to fit with the dominant view of citizenship as the new nations undertook to colonize themselves. The kindergarten idea stretched to accommodate the agendas of educators and thinkers of various kinds, and was refashioned according to New World conditions in the late nineteenth and early twentieth centuries.

Kindergarten and Indigenous Children

The mission function of the infant school for indigenous children, which aimed at their assimilation and conversion, continued in kindergartens to the limited extent that they were available. The term "savage" was first used to refer to indigenous people. The new sciences of anthropology and ethnology were given a boost at this time by the common belief that Indians, Australian Aborigines, and Maori were dying out and that their cultures should be documented before they disappeared. Various race theories were postulated that organized the human population in hierarchical terms based on physical and cultural features. Here, too, conflicting ideas were at work. One view held that the "noble savage" was corrupted through contact with Euro-civilization. The term "forest children" appeared in descriptions of Indian children and adults in Canada during the late nineteenth century. Although these children could be dressed in European clothing, this could not bring about a fundamental change in their nature. When a European traveller in Labrador met an indigenous family, he observed that "the little children had also new suits of clothes, which, with their hair close-cropped, quite changed their appearance, and gave them a dirty half-civilised look, much less agreeable than the wild air of forest children which they possessed when we saw them on the Moisie [River]."[81]

Following on this idea, it was suggested that kindergarten was suitable for indigenous children because of their supposed lack of concern for academics and distrust of books. In an essay titled "Wild Babies," Henry W. Elliott explained that, in infancy, all babies were similar. The difference between European and Aboriginal children "does not commence to show itself until they have reached that age where the mind begins to feed and reason upon what it sees, hears, feels, and tastes; then the gulf yawns between our baby and the Indian's; the latter stands still, while the former is ever moving onward and upward."[82]

Referring to the situation in Arizona, US Infantry lieutenant George S. Wilson asserted that "there would be no good purpose served in expending all energies in giving the mass of Indian children a good education, as we understand the term." Instead, he believed that separation from families and placement in kindergarten "will habituate them to the customs and advantages of a civilised life, and put them in a way of leading it, and at the same time cause them to look with feelings of repugnance on their native state."[83] Wilson's description of a racialized kindergarten for indigenous children had parallels with the poverty discourse and free kindergartens for immigrant children. It drew on a similar vocabulary — the "savage" and the "civilized" — and set of concepts: that preschool could supplant the family and that racial and class differences could be softened through the absorption of kindergarten culture. This was very different from the extreme environmentalist position of the infant school, which saw limitless human potential.

Another view held that racial recapitulation was more amenable to environmental interventions and that Indian education was a vehicle for racial progress. As described by historian David Adams, it was thought, "by means of the common school, Indians could, in effect, be catapulted directly from savagism to civilisation, skipping all the intervening stages of social evolution."[84] There are also many accounts of indigenous parents seeking out opportunities for European education for their children. However, in the residential school system, many Indian children were forcibly removed from their parents and communities.[85] This form of education aimed at cultural extinction, as David Adams argues in his study of American boarding schools.[86] From 1880, the United States Bureau of Indian Affairs made English instruction mandatory in mission and government schools. Failing to follow this edict meant loss of funding. This policy represented a change from the approach to Indian education in the pre-Civil War period, when education in the vernacular was accepted as best practice by mission teachers.[87] By the 1880s, education was viewed as a means of solving the "Indian problem" by assimilating Native American children into the white world: "If there were a sufficient number of reservation boarding-school buildings to accommodate all the Indian children of school age, and these buildings could be filled and kept filled with Indian pupils, the Indian problem would be solved within the school age of the Indian children now six years old."[88]

Transfer

From the mid-1850s, private fee-charging kindergartens had been available in the United States to very few children from privileged families, and it could be imagined that a handful of charity kindergartens, now hidden to history, were also opened during this period. The years 1850 to 1880 saw a transition from the infant school system to that of the kindergarten. Charity organizations that had once operated infant schools turned to kindergartens as modern alternatives. In San Francisco, the Young Women's Christian Association replaced its infant school with a kindergarten in the 1880s.[89] Some key historical personalities, such as Elizabeth Peabody, advocated each in turn. Peabody and Bronson Alcott had established the Temple School in Boston in 1834, which aimed to educate the hearts and minds of children by way of meaningful activities, chiefly conversations related to the spiritual, imaginative, and rational faculties.[90] In 1860, Peabody opened the first English-language kindergarten in the United States, also in Boston.[91] In both ventures, Peabody was an active teacher. Shortly after her own kindergarten had opened, she compared the value of the kindergarten with that of the infant school, with which her readers would have been familiar: "What is a Kindergarten? ... It is not the old-fashioned infant-school. That was a narrow institution, comparatively; the object being ... to take the children of poor labourers, and keep them out of the fire and the streets, while their mothers went to necessary labour ... Their principle of discipline was to circumvent the wills of children, in every way that would enable their teachers to keep them within bounds, and quiet."[92]

In the kindergarten, children descended from the galleries to take their place around child-sized tables and on chairs in the ubiquitous circle, a symbol of the unity of humankind. Peabody believed the object of play to be the development of internal controls rather than free expression: "Order is the child of reason, and in turn cultivates the intellectual principle. To bring out order on the physical plane, the Kindergarten makes it a serious purpose to organise *romping,* and set it to music, which cultivates the physical nature also. Romping is the ecstasy of the body, and we shall find that in proportion as children tend to be violent they are vigorous in body."[93] Organized romping was standardized in such activities as marching in time to music and ritualized movement derived from Froebel's scripts for songs and games.

Kindergartens in public schools required alterations to make them efficient for large numbers of pupils and comparatively few teachers; one of these innovations was the double shift of morning and afternoon classes. Many classrooms blended infant school management techniques with kindergarten activities. The objective of self-discipline was paramount, though achieved via external controls. This was evident in the first free kindergarten in New York City, established in 1878 under the sponsorship of the Society for Ethical Culture and described in an article written and illustrated for *Harper's New Monthly Magazine* by F.E. Fryatt shortly after it opened.[94] The scene she observed had similarities with infant schools, particularly the focus on militaristic drill: "My little friends — for so I have learned to call them — are moving in couples to the sound of a lively air played on a piano by the principal of the school; several assistant teachers, walking before, instruct the 'little men and women' in the figures of the marching exercise, two hundred tiny feet keeping time with vigorous tread, two hundred chubby hands clapping in unison, and all their baby voices piping merrily."[95] However, whereas children in the infant school sat in a gallery and parroted their lessons, those in the kindergarten played with Froebel's materials and went on excursions to Central Park.

The kindergarten itself was a single large room, dominated in one corner by a piano. Equipment and furnishings included a few books, large amounts of kindergarten blocks and occupational materials, six low tables with benches for seating, a blackboard, pegs for children's coats with symbols above them, and a food cupboard. There was no corporal punishment; teachers were to "govern them by love and kindness" in a maternal fashion.[96] Teacher Fanny Schwedler established a training class from the outset. The student teachers, all female, were from the upper class and worked as volunteers. The teachers went door to door and requested or convinced parents to send their children to the novel institution. Their encounters with poor families encouraged them to extend their social program to include general relief: giving them food and clothing or helping parents find employment.

Other free kindergartens had opened earlier, but they were less influential than that established by the Society for Ethical Culture in New York City. A free kindergarten was part of the educational and community program of the Poppenhusen Institute, which was established in 1870 at College Point, Long Island. Conrad Poppenhusen was a reform-minded industrialist who had established the company town of College Point in 1854. The institute, dedicated to improving the conditions of the working class, included a trade school as well as a kindergarten. A newspaper report noted that "as near as possible the system of the German Kindergarten will be adhered to."[97]

Kindergartens did not catch on as quickly as infant schools. In Boston, almost seventeen years elapsed between the opening of Elizabeth Peabody's private kindergarten and that of the first free equivalent. Kindergartens in the public schools of St. Louis, Missouri, established from 1871, were anomalies, and public school kindergartens were not at all common until the mid-1880s. One reason for the slower take-up was that the infant school movement coincided with the development of free elementary school systems in Australia, Canada, the United States, and Great Britain. School bureaucracies transformed the former common schools, leaving little room for innovation. Since underage children were typically accommodated in primary school, there was also less need for a separate service for four- or five-year-olds.

The kindergarten's moment in American education history came in the late 1870s, with increased immigration and the perceived need to assimilate the children of newcomers into New World life. After the rise of the infant school, the growth of free and public school kindergartens represented the second popular wave of early education in the nineteenth century. The free-kindergarten movement — at its peak in the 1880s — spread outward from the epicentres of what was termed the "crusade" in Boston, New York, Chicago, and San Francisco. Free kindergartens were established in Minneapolis (1880), Chicago (1881), Indianapolis (1884), and the then independent kingdom of Hawaii (1895). From the United States, the movement spread west across the Pacific as well as north, reaching New Zealand in 1889, Canada in 1892, and Australia in 1895. In the US, the centres of kindergarten activity were cities with a high percentage of foreign-born residents, affirming its place in social settlement work. In 1890, more than 40 percent of the populations of New York, Chicago, and San Francisco were foreign-born.[98] Other cities approaching the 40 percent mark also had active free-kindergarten associations: Detroit (39.7 percent), Milwaukee (38.9 percent), and Minneapolis (36.8 percent) and St. Paul (39.9 percent).

The rapid spread of the free kindergarten after its slow start was due to a number of factors: its appeal as an acceptable charity for upper-class women; the plethora of written accounts circulated in newspapers, books, and pamphlets; and the quick introduction of training for teachers in the voluntary sector, along with programs for children. "The kindergarten requires trained hands," wrote Talcott Williams. "With trivial teachers its methods may easily degenerate into mere amusement."[99] Newly trained teachers helped expand the reach of free kindergartens beyond the larger cities, as teachers migrated across America. In large urban centres, city-wide associations underwritten by philanthropists most often administered free kindergartens: in Boston, Pauline Agassiz Shaw took up the cause; in San Francisco, it was Phoebe Apperson Hearst and Jane Stanford. In other cases, kindergartens were a part of social settlement work, as at Hull House in Chicago. Free kindergartens were also associated with child-welfare services; examples include the Indianapolis Free Kindergarten and Children's Aid Society, and the Free Kindergarten and Children's Aid Association of the Hawaiian Islands. A similar connection developed in some colonial initiatives, as in Christchurch, New Zealand.

San Francisco

The free kindergartens in California were particularly relevant to developments in the Pacific and, to a lesser degree, in Canada. Kindergartener and teacher trainer Emma Marwedel was encouraged by Felix Adler to establish the Public Kindergarten Society of San Francisco in 1878. The circle of influence in the movement at this early stage was very small. Marwedel was a German emigrant who had trained with Luise Levin-Froebel.[100] Elizabeth Peabody met Marwedel in Germany during her study tour of kindergartens in 1867 and suggested that she come to the United States. Marwedel appointed her student Kate Douglas Wiggin as first teacher of the Public Kindergarten Society's Silver Street Kindergarten, which was located in a San Francisco slum called Tar Flats.

The Silver Street Kindergarten attracted many visitors, including Sarah Brown Cooper, who was inspired to start her own program as an extension of her Bible schoolwork. Cooper opened the Jackson Street Kindergarten in 1879 and several others in the early 1880s with the support of the Hearst family. In 1884, she reorganized the kindergartens as the Golden Gate Kindergarten Association. This received substantial assistance from Jane and Leyland Stanford, who established a $100,000 endowment for the kindergartens in 1890, in honour of their son Leyland Jr., who had died in 1889. Cooper went so far as to claim that the proposed Leyland Stanford Jr. University, established in Palo Alto in 1891, was influenced by the kindergarten philosophy that linked theory with practice.[101] The Golden Gate Kindergarten Free Normal Training School was established in the same year to train teachers for the expanding program. On the basis of this work and her profuse writing, Cooper rose to prominence as a founder and first president of the American-based International Kindergarten Union, in 1892.

Cooper did not train as a kindergartener herself. She placed Anna M. Stovall, another of Emma Marwedel's students, in charge of the Normal School. Curiously, she asked educational psychologist Charles McGrew, principal of San Jose's California School of Methods for Teachers and Kindergarteners, to develop the training-school curriculum and an outline for the children's program in the demonstration kindergarten.[102] The program was later revised for application in all Golden Gate kindergartens in 1893. It included extensive use of kindergarten Gifts and occupations, with the emphasis entirely on geometry, numbers, and art. References to religious study were absent. Moral education was mainly through games, conversations, and stories "showing why dirty, unkind and rude children are not loved."[103]

The Golden Gate Association underwent phenomenal growth over a period of fifteen years. When Cooper died in 1896, it managed forty kindergartens serving thirty-six hundred children. The San Francisco Produce Exchange supported thirty-two of these kindergartens, a mark of Cooper's success in bridging the philanthropic and business communities. Moreover, Cooper's work helped spread the idea of similar kindergartens for poor children at home and abroad. There was nothing original about Cooper's approach to kindergarten work, and as she was untrained, it is unlikely that she had a strong understanding of its underlying philosophy.[104] Her strength lay in attracting the interest of "persons of large wealth" and her promotion of the movement on the national and even international scale.[105] Both Cooper and Hearst knew the importance of pageantry and propaganda in advancing the cause. As one example, Cooper hosted a reception for Hearst on her return from a trip to Europe, which was then reported in the local newspapers.[106] The seven hundred guests who attended watched as two hundred kindergarten children marched past the stage, each giving Hearst a flower as they went.

Awareness of the Golden Gate's success was aided by Cooper's widespread distribution of the association's annual reports: sixty thousand copies had been disseminated by 1892. From the start, she recognized the report's potential to promote the kindergarten cause on a large scale. According to Cooper, Elizabeth Peabody had described an early report as a "pattern pamphlet for propaganda" for the movement and had encouraged her to continue to write in detail about the kindergartens.[107] Cooper seemed to take this to heart; the reports, with their vivid red covers, were manuals on starting a kindergarten. They included reprints of press reports and magazine articles touting its moral, social, and economic benefits. Fundraising was given prominence, and later reports included articles such as "How to Interest Businessmen." The reports bloated to the size of a book: the "World's Fair Edition" in 1892 was 261 pages and included an index. The 1890 report reprinted a series of articles on the kindergarten movement written by Cooper twelve years earlier for the *San Francisco Evening Bulletin*. The articles, with titles such as "Education of the Young: The Best Remedy for Hoodlumism," were extensively reproduced.[108] A community leader in Sydney, Dunedin, or Winnipeg, reading a Golden Gate annual report, could find inspiration within its covers and would perhaps be moved to establish a kindergarten.

Absent from the reports was an examination of Froebel's philosophy. Instead, Cooper emphasized the social advantage of kindergarten as a moral uplift for poor children.[109] She agreed with British mental health pioneer Henry Maudsley's view that environment directed development, or, in a phrase she borrowed from Maudsley, that "drunkards [are] as much manufactured articles as are steam engines and printing presses."[110] However, she also subscribed to the dominant thinking in criminology that slum children were "freighted down with evil inheritances."[111] These two ideas co-existed in a manner that apparently was not intellectually troubling. The future of young children could be redirected despite their genetic burden, whereas their parents were beyond hope. The view from the new sciences of sociology and psychology was that criminal behaviour was a heritable trait. Without kindergarten, poor children would quickly become an encumbrance, if not a threat, to society. Cooper frequently used a cost-benefit argument to make her case, referring to Richard Dugdale's 1877 study of the "Jukes" family, in which twelve hundred children were traced to "one perverted and depraved woman."[112] The implication was that, had their ancestor attended kindergarten, the children would have been industrious citizens instead of loafers, drunks, thieves, and prostitutes.

The Golden Gate reports mixed this imagery with sentimental stories of children whose lives were touched by the kindergarten. Brave but fragile, many suddenly died, their time at kindergarten being an "earthly paradise."[113] These stories resembled those written by Kate Douglas Wiggin to raise funds for the Silver Street Kindergarten.

The sentimental images contrasted with the reality of human tragedy that befell the San Francisco kindergartens. In 1893, a woman working as the night cleaner at the Felix Adler Kindergarten was murdered by her husband in the cloakroom.[114] The morning after the murder, the kindergarten opened as usual, the teachers washing the blood from walls and floor before the children arrived.[115] Cooper met a tragic end in 1896, murdered in her bed by her daughter, who then committed suicide. The Golden Gate kindergartens continued without Cooper's leadership but suffered in the 1906 earthquake, which destroyed several of them, as well as the training college and the homes of the students. Also lost were historical records of the early years of the association.

The development of the kindergarten varied in differing regions of the United States as well as within regions. The free kindergartens in San Francisco were distinct in several ways from similar associations in the East and elsewhere in California. With their roots in philanthropy and their focus on poverty prevention through early intervention, they were removed from eastern developments where kindergartens entered public schools on the merits of their educational purpose.[116] The deep pockets and generosity of sponsors such as Phoebe Hearst and Jane Stanford were a further barrier to public support for kindergartens in San Francisco. Cooper's success in fundraising proved too great.

Nevertheless, support for kindergartens in public schools was often tenuous, waning in times of economic shortfall. In situations where kindergartens were an add-on to existing schools, space for the worktables and movement activities essential for the program was frequently insufficient. Large numbers of children and small budgets forced changes in the system. William Torrey Harris believed that kindergarten would never be widespread in schools without reducing its cost. Explaining in 1879 that classes needed to be larger and teachers needed the assistance of monitors, Harris recalled a solution to the problem of mass education that had been presented eighty years before: "The Lancasterian system or the 'monitorial' system — suggests itself as a model for the organization of the cheap kindergarten. The kindergarten shall be a large one, located in a room of ample size to hold 5 to 10 tables, each table to have 15 children attending it, and presided over by a novitiate teacher; and the whole room shall be placed under the charge of a thoroughly competent teacher."[117]

chapter 6   **Kindergarten in the Case-Study Countries**

AT THE END OF the nineteenth century, when private and public kindergartens were instigated in Canada, Australia, and New Zealand, the three countries were self-governing nations within the British Commonwealth. In 1891, the population of Canada was 4.2 million, with the great majority, about 75 percent, living on farms and in villages.[1] The 1901 *Canada Year Book* compared the urbanization of Ontario with that of Utah and Quebec's with that of Wyoming and Montana.[2] In stark contrast, the states just south of these provinces — New York, Massachusetts, and Rhode Island — were highly urbanized, with city-based populations of 71.2 percent, 86.9 percent, and 91.6 percent respectively. Canada contributed labour to American industries throughout New England. Some mill towns, such as Fall River, Massachusetts, and Woonsocket, Rhode Island, were predominantly made up of French Canadians. Canada was not highly industrialized. The largest Canadian cities in 1891 were Montreal and Toronto, with populations of 216,650 and 181,000. Although both had undergone tremendous growth during the 1880s, they were home to just 10 percent of the nation's population. With the exception of Quebec City, no other Canadian city had a population exceeding 50,000. Cities in the eastern provinces grew slowly: the capital cities of Charlottetown (established 1768) and Fredericton (established 1785) remained small throughout the nineteenth century, reaching 11,400 and 6,500 respectively.

There were signs that, by the 1880s, industrialization was on the rise in Canada: during this decade, the numbers of persons employed in handwork such as blacksmithing declined, whereas those in industries such as ironworks and foundries increased. In 1871, 15,770 handwork labourers were employed in 8,438 separate workplaces. By 1881, this had increased to 18,551 in 10,563 workplaces. However, by 1891, the sector had decreased to 12,668 persons employed in 9,570 shops. In contrast, workers in foundries increased from 7,789 in 548 establishments (1881) to 13,374 in 648 businesses (1891).³

In the 1870s, Canada's rate of immigration fluctuated from 27,773 in 1871 to 50,050 in 1875, dropping to 27,082 in 1877. In 1882, it surged to 112,458 and remained high throughout the 1880s. However, by 1896, it had decreased to less than 17,000. Many immigrants used Canada as a staging point for a move to the United States. In the decade 1880 to 1890, 11.3 percent of the population of Canada migrated to the United States, a total of 450,000.⁴ From 1878, the Government of Canada encouraged immigration through commercial enterprises, such as the Canadian Pacific Railway (CPR). The CPR established colonization offices in Britain and Europe, and assisted immigrants through various sponsorship schemes. One result was the westward push of settlement into Manitoba and the North-West Territories (Saskatchewan and Alberta). However, migration to the United States meant that the population of Canada remained fairly stable, despite the need for new industrial workers and the government's desire to colonize the West. This changed dramatically in 1895 with the appointment of a new minister of the interior, Clifford Sifton, who encouraged immigration from Southern and Eastern Europe. In the ten-year period known as the "Sifton Years," immigration increased from 16,835 in 1896 to 141,464 in 1905.

One consequence of this was the greater visibility of non-British Canadians and the rise of a racist opposition and calls for Canada to close the gates on this "mass of human ignorance, filth and immorality."⁵ Moreover, despite the focus on agricultural immigration, as in Australia, towns and cities continued to grow. Although the balance of the population did not shift from rural to urban until 1921, the trend was clear from the beginning of the twentieth century. In 1891, 32 percent was urban, in 1901, 37 percent, and in 1911, as immigration reached its historic peak, 45 percent.⁶

The year 1888 marked the end of Australia's first century as a self-governing British colony. Its settler population was 3 million in 1888, from an initial settlement of about one thousand in a single colony in 1788.⁷ By the mid-1840s, the numbers of freeborn settlers had overtaken the convict population. In 1888, 60 percent of Australia's population had been born there, and almost all of these were of British descent. Of the remaining 40 percent, 34 percent had been born in the British Isles, and 6 percent were of European origin, mainly from Germany and Scandinavia.[8] The population had grown unevenly, with larger numbers of immigrants arriving at times of economic promise and smaller numbers during recessions.

Immigrants, who came mainly from industrial regions in Britain, stayed in the cities despite the government's desire for predominantly agricultural immigrants to settle on farms and colonize the land. In 1888, half the European population lived in cities or towns, with 30 percent in the capital cities of Melbourne, Sydney, Adelaide, Brisbane, Hobart, and Perth. The two southeastern cities of Melbourne and Sydney were home to almost one-third of Australia's population. At 470,000 and 400,000 respectively, Melbourne and Sydney were among the ten largest cities in the British Commonwealth. They were comparable in size to Boston, which in 1890 had a population of 448,000. Industry in Melbourne and Sydney was dominated by the trades and conducted in small workshops. Workers employed in the traditional handwork associated with horses — saddle makers, coachbuilders, wheelwrights — were more numerous than those in the new railway and tramway industries.[9]

In 1886, the European population of New Zealand was 576,524, almost all of whom had arrived during the previous thirty years. European settlement was minor until government and commercial immigration schemes got their start in 1840. In 1800, only 50 settlers of European origin lived in New Zealand. By 1841, there were 5,000. This number more than doubled to 12,000 in 1842. By 1850, there were 50,000, almost 100,000 by 1861, and 171,009 only three years later. However, by the mid-1880s and the onset of a trade recession, immigration again slowed, with a small loss of departures over arrivals of 132 between 1885 and 1889.[10] From 1878 to the 1920s, immigration was stable at about 20,000 per year. New Zealand's immigration pattern was thus marked by a surge in population from 1840 to 1880, followed by a long period of slow growth.

New towns and cities were created in association with immigration schemes: the New Zealand Company brought immigrants to New Plymouth; the Otago Association brought settlers from Scotland to Dunedin; the Canterbury Association brought immigrants from England to Christchurch. The population congregated in and around the new towns, supported economically by the surrounding farms. In 1854, the town of Auckland and its surrounding area had a population of eleven thousand.[11]

Other centres of European population were New Plymouth (two thousand), Nelson (six thousand), and Wellington (six thousand) on the North Island, and Canterbury (four thousand) and Dunedin (twenty-five hundred) on the South Island. The 1861 discovery of gold in the Tuapeka fields near Dunedin stimulated that city's growth, transforming the town from an "obscure Presbyterian outpost" to the "foremost commercial and industrial" centre in New Zealand.[12] Dunedin retained this distinction throughout the nineteenth century. By 1881, it was the largest city in New Zealand, with a population of forty thousand. However, by the mid-1880s and the beginning of a worldwide depression, Dunedin rapidly developed problems of poverty similar to those of its larger sister cities in Australia. Low wages and poor working conditions in industries, and the exploitation of women workers in sweat shops, re-created the poverty that had pushed some immigrants to leave the British Isles in the first place.

In the case-study countries, urban expansion was a common feature of immigration during the nineteenth and early twentieth centuries. In 1913, 400,870 immigrants entered Canada, a number never again reached in a single year.[13] The rapid increase in population over a short period of time placed a strain on the older cities, such as Montreal, to meet the needs of the newcomers for housing, employment, and education. It also led to the creation of new settlements and the quick growth of small frontier cities such as Dunedin, Perth, and Winnipeg. In Australia, the expansion of cities and their accompanying slums was phenomenally swift. Initially a small convict settlement, Sydney was transformed into a metropolis in the space of a hundred years. Melbourne grew from a tent city in the 1830s to almost half a million by the end of the century. The resulting problems were acute, stimulating attention from government and private charities. Overall, the mortality rate for infants (under one year of age) was high in the colonies but very high in cities. In rural Australia, for example, the death rate for infants of European origin was 100 per 1,000, whereas in Sydney and Melbourne, it was 166 and 171 respectively.

Free Kindergartens

Canada

The free-kindergarten movement in Canada was almost entirely averted by the establishment of kindergartens in urban public schools. Inspired by developments in the United States, James Laughlin Hughes began to open

Toronto kindergartens in 1883. They were established in all Protestant public schools in Montreal during the 1890s. The pattern followed trends in the United States, where free kindergartens were incorporated into public schools in New York, Philadelphia, Washington, and, in 1913, in San Francisco. In some cases, as in New York, a free-kindergarten association had been established only a short time before. The New York Association was formed in 1889, and public school kindergartens were opened in 1892.[14] In Canada, free kindergartens were taken up locally in only a few instances. Like their counterparts in Dunedin and Sydney, some turned for inspiration to San Francisco. Catherine Condon of Halifax corresponded with Elizabeth Peabody, who sent her a copy of a Golden Gate report. Condon went on to establish the Froebel Institute of Nova Scotia.[15] She described herself as an advocate of "Froebel's principles and praxis." In September 1887, she established a model kindergarten in the Truro Normal School. Her motto was to "make this a perfect kindergarten, one that the wisest American Kindergartener would gladly endorse." Her ultimate aim, as in New Zealand and Australia, was for kindergartens to be included in public schools. She asked Cooper for a letter to serve as moral support in anticipation of a large public meeting and a debate on kindergarten in the provincial legislature.[16] In 1888, due in part to her work, a kindergarten opened in a public school at Dartmouth, Nova Scotia.

The Winnipeg Free Kindergarten Association, which seems to have had no contact with the Golden Gate Association, opened a kindergarten in a storefront in 1892. From the beginning, it hired trained teachers, most of whom had graduated from schools in the United States. The association opened branch kindergartens, but they closed after a short time. It also operated two kindergarten programs in classrooms that it rented from the Winnipeg School Board. From the start, the association lobbied the school board to open kindergartens in public schools, but this did not occur for almost fifty years. Free kindergartens in Winnipeg were a welfare service, providing shelter, food, and clothing for children — and a means of assimilating the youngest immigrants into Anglo-Canadian society of the 1890s.

Australia

An Australian visited a Golden Gate kindergarten in 1884, her observations forming the basis of a Sydney newspaper report the next year.[17] Mary Walker notes that the San Francisco kindergartens were characterized as "missionary" and "reformatory," not educational, though this is unlikely to have been a discouraging factor.[18] There was little further interest in them until 1895, when Margaret Windeyer returned to Sydney from San Francisco with a copy of the Golden Gate Kindergarten Association annual report.[19] That same year, Windeyer and other middle- and upper-class women with an interest in helping poor women and children established the Kindergarten Union of New South Wales (KUNSW). It identified education goals alongside social-welfare objectives: its ambitious aim was to have kindergarten "principles introduced into every school in New South Wales."[20]

In January 1896, the KUNSW opened Australia's first free kindergarten, in a Sydney social service called the All Night Shelter. By February, it had moved to a residence in Woolloomooloo, Sydney. After ten years, the KUNSW was confident in its purpose and sufficiently established to construct its own building: the Newtown Free Kindergarten, which opened in 1905, was known as the first purpose-built free kindergarten in the southern hemisphere. The number of Sydney kindergartens grew to eight by 1907 and spread to other states due to KUNSW influence.

New Zealand

In New Zealand, the opening of free kindergartens during the late 1880s coincided with a slowdown in the movement in America as kindergartens were incorporated into public schools. However, community leaders in New Zealand, wanting the best for their children, sought to establish kindergarten programs, both as charities for poor children and within public schools. Free kindergartens were established in Auckland and Wellington, opening in 1887 and closing about 1891. A third, established in Dunedin in 1889, is generally accepted as New Zealand's first free kindergarten because it endured for a longer time. Andrew Burn Suter, bishop of Dunedin, had visited the Stanford Kindergarten during a visit to San Francisco about 1888. He had also met Cooper. The editor of the *Dunedin Evening Star,* Mark Cohen, was interested in the kindergarten as a means of social and educational reform. Thus, Suter, Cohen, and others corresponded with Cooper, seeking her guidance concerning their work in New Zealand.[21]

Cohen wrote to Cooper that he wished to see kindergartens as "stepping stones to primaries," pointing to the states of Tasmania and Victoria as examples. The Dunedin Free Kindergarten Association was formed, supported by leaders in the colony such as the former prime minister Sir Robert Stout, Anna Stout, Bishop Suter, and the Reverend Rutherford

Waddell of St. Andrew's Church. Dunedin resident Lavinia Kelsey had gained some direct knowledge of kindergarten work during a visit to England, and she used kindergarten activities at a school she operated in her home. She, Cohen, and Rachel Reynolds worked with Waddell to organize a free kindergarten.²² Reynolds, who had previously been involved in setting up a crèche in Dunedin, became the kindergarten association's first president. The kindergarten itself was housed in the Walker Street Mission Hall of St. Andrew's Church and was initially known as the Walker Street Kindergarten. The association wished to open additional kindergartens in Dunedin, but other church leaders were not enthusiastic, and none would offer a rent-free space.²³ Cohen noted that, despite the aid of high-profile citizens (Dr. Stuart, chancellor of the University of Otago, was later numbered among them), there was little support for the kindergarten.²⁴ Cohen resolved, "We should be content to jog along quietly till our foundations are firmly implanted; then we can spread our activities."²⁵

Kindergartens for First Nations Children

In the United States, kindergartens were briefly introduced into Indian schools during William Hailmann's four-year term as director of government schools for the Bureau of Indian Affairs, and a similar development occurred in Canada, where Indian education policy mirrored that of the US.²⁶ Hailmann, a Swiss immigrant, came to the US with his parents in 1852 at age sixteen. He was committed to kindergarten education, and as superintendent of public schools in LaPorte, Indiana, he reorganized schools in line with the principles of New Education emphasizing practical studies and a child centred approach in line with his Froebelian beliefs.²⁷ In 1894 he was appointed superintendent of Indian schools, and he implemented similar reforms in kindergartens for Indian children, including the employment of trained kindergarteners, a curriculum based partly on nature study, and the use of assistant teachers who spoke local Indian languages. His plans were thwarted by an insufficient budget and recalcitrant teachers who, because they subscribed to preset methods and ideas concerning Indian education, were reluctant to co-operate with his reforms. His ideas were clearly out of step with mainstream thinking regarding Indian education in the 1890s. The influential United States commissioner of education William Torrey Harris, a one-time champion of kindergarten, endorsed the more rigid pedagogical theory of George Herbart. Harris considered Indians a savage race that could be rehabilitated only through conversion and the adoption of Christian values.²⁸ The form this took was generally a military-like education with strict and even severe discipline, adherence to a rigid schedule, and a basic curriculum focusing on reading, writing, and the development of skills in trades or household management.

Prior to Hailmann's experiment, individual missionaries in Canada had shown an interest in applying kindergarten methods to Indian children. In 1889, Methodist missionary Charles Tate wrote to Sarah Cooper in San Francisco, soliciting advice on starting a kindergarten for First Nations' children near Chilliwack, British Columbia.²⁹ Tate and his wife, Caroline, had established a day school at Sardis in 1884 and began boarding children at their home in 1886. In 1894, this evolved into a residential school called the Coqualeetza Institute. Tate began to correspond with Cooper after he secured funding to establish a school with a trained teacher for the children whom he boarded at his home.³⁰ A kindergarten operated in the late 1890s, where children were taught weaving, sewing, and paper folding. Older students learned through vocational training "in the house and out in the fields, in the laundry and in the shoe-shop, in the dairy and at the carpenter's bench. Healthy, intelligent, useful, Christian citizenship is the aim of the earnest teachers in charge. Christianity and education are lifting them out of the old ways of indolence."³¹

While Hailmann was superintendent, a teacher at an American kindergarten for Indian children echoed the idea of redemption, remarking that industry and education could effect the children's "transition from their old, careless, free life into the world of knowledge."³² As she put it, "The old Indians cling to the customs and traditions of their tribe, and but a small per cent are influenced to any permanent change of life, but in the kindergarten we take these dark-skinned boys and girls while they are impressionable, and through its pleasant teaching form habits of observation and thought, preparing the way for the teachers who shall come after us."³³

The kindergarten system was in harmony with the mode of manual education popular in the 1880s. Manual education, which focused on vocational rather than intellectual training, was viewed by educationists and the business class as appropriate for immigrant and minority students. For First Nations children and youth, it developed from the manual labour schools of the 1840s, an early example of which was at Alderville, Ontario. These were later called industrial schools, and they proliferated in the North-West Territories as a cheap means of schooling Aboriginal children.

139

Kindergarten in the Case-Study Countries

A prospective student at St. Michael's residential school. The message written on the back of the image reads "The little Indian boy of this card shall be one of our pupils next year. Is he not nice?" Postcard sent from St. Michael's Indian School, Saskatchewan, May, 1909. Author's collection.

Most were organized according to a "half-time" system, in which students spent their mornings in the classroom learning basic academic skills and their afternoons undertaking chores. Indian industrial schools were not initially planned to accept preschool-aged children. However, in many instances, young children lived in the boarding schools along with older pupils and youth. One of these — the boy in the photograph above — was expected to attend St. Michael's residential school in 1909, an Oblate-run institution at Duck Lake, Saskatchewan.³⁴

Certainly, the Duck Lake school would not offer him kindergarten activities, but during the late 1880s, these began to be available in a very limited way at a few day and industrial schools, as described in annual reports to the superintendent general of Indian Affairs. The first were provided in day schools at Piapot's Reserve and on the reserves at Wabegon and Riding Mountain. At the Presbyterian mission at the Piapot's Reserve near Fort Qu'Appelle, the teacher, Miss Rose, used aspects of the kindergarten system.³⁵ An inspector described the situation at Riding Mountain. He observed that the teacher had considerable materials, though it would seem none of the building Gifts:

> The day school is taught by a most competent young lady and trained teacher, Miss Cameron, under the auspices of the Presbyterian Church; and has reached a very satisfactory stage of efficiency. When I visited the school eighteen children, from five to thirteen years old, were present; they were nearly all girls; they were all neatly and cleanly attired; and would favourably compare with white children in the same walk in life; their work in class was very satisfactory.
>
> Through the kindness of Eastern friends of the church, Miss Cameron has been enabled to introduce, in a measure, the kindergarten system. She has all sorts of appliances, both for amusement and instruction; plain sewing, carding and spinning wool and knitting form a regular part of the school work, which includes religious instruction and Bible history.³⁶

Principals at industrial schools seemed enthusiastic about the potential of the kindergarten system but generally vague regarding its specific impact or purpose. An exception was the principal of the Rupert's Land school, who asserted that it helped children to acquire English: "The difficulty of making the pupils speak English and speak out has been well overcome and we find the kindergarten classes a great help in this direction."³⁷ He had a particular interest in the work, expressing a desire to hire "some lady competent to teach the Kindergarten methods" in his 1890 report.³⁸

In 1892, the children's work at Rupert's Land was considered sufficiently advanced to be part of the school's display at the annual industrial exhibition, along with laundry work and homemade bread.[39] Developments quickened after 1896 — probably following Hailmann's lead in the United States — when the Department of Indian Affairs enlisted Elizabeth Bolton to demonstrate the system on a tour of the North-West Territories and Manitoba. Bolton, who directed the model kindergarten at the Ottawa Normal School, visited the Elkhorn, Rupert's Land, and Regina Industrial Schools, which were convenient to train lines. The following year, Indian Affairs ordered more than $200 worth of kindergarten supplies for boarding and industrial schools, and smaller amounts were spent over the next few years. This would have resulted in an overabundant supply of materials for the Manitoba and North-West Territories schools — Rupert's Land, Battleford, Crowstand, and Regina — that are known to have had kindergartens during the 1890s. The Milton Bradley Company sold Gift number three for twenty cents and sewing cards for a penny each.[40]

Although most of the schools waited for the materials to arrive before they started up their programs, the teacher at the Crowstand Boarding School organized six five-year-olds in a "kindergarten or infants' class," located in the unused "sick room" where they "were exercised in sounds, counting, etc., and in the evening they were amused and instructed in sewing figures upon cardboard."[41] However, the principal and the teacher were "very anxious to be furnished with a full kindergarten outfit." Older children were similarly involved in handwork, but with very rough materials: "After school hours, between four and five o'clock, under the direction of the seamstress, nine girls and eleven boys were engaged at straw plaiting, the straw used was the best obtainable, but it was discoloured and coarse."[42] The next year, some materials arrived, though they were insufficient even for the eleven children then at the kindergarten. Nevertheless, the principal called the experiment a success: "The kindergarten class has justified its existence by the results. Although our appliances were few and crude, they were sufficient to prove that many applications of kindergarten methods can be made, to a great advantage, in such a school as this. These kindergarten pupils have made remarkably good progress in speaking English and reading; and they grasp ideas expressed in English much more quickly than pupils who have not had some such training."[43] Indeed, the kindergarten was the largest class at Crowstand. There were a few students in each of standards one to three, the highest level in which students were enrolled. The teacher was Catherine Gillespie, who had earlier used kindergarten methods at the File Hills school with children aged three to seven.[44]

Public Kindergartens

Canada

A small number of kindergartens were formed in Canadian public schools during the early 1880s. Among the first were classes in Berlin (now Kitchener), Ontario, in 1882, Toronto in 1883, and Hamilton in 1885. In 1885, the Ontario Public School Act was amended to permit funding for any school boards wishing to establish kindergartens for children between the ages of three and five. The act also provided for teacher training. In the same year, a kindergarten department opened at the Toronto Normal School. Kindergartens had strong support from Minister of Education George W. Ross, later premier of Ontario, and James Hughes, chief inspector of schools for Toronto. By the end of the decade, additional kindergartens were established in schools in Hamilton, London, and Ottawa, the three largest cities in Ontario after Toronto. In 1892, there were sixty-six kindergartens in the province, each with an average enrolment of one hundred pupils. By 1900, kindergartens existed in many smaller communities as well, though none in rural schools.

In Montreal, the Protestant Board of School Commissioners discussed kindergartens as early as 1872, but none were opened until 1885. They took the form of a preparatory class called a "modified kindergarten."[45] The board sponsored an elementary school teacher to travel to St. Paul, Minnesota, to receive kindergarten training before operating its own training program from 1892 to 1897. A kindergarten diploma was included at the McGill Normal School in 1895. However, the teachers in the first kindergartens were trained elsewhere, since by 1890, all schools operated by the Protestant Board of School Commissioners had kindergartens. The program consisted of scripture reading and moral lessons, morning talks, songs and games, the weather record, and play with Froebel's Gifts and occupations.

In western Canada, 1892 legislation permitted kindergartens, but few were sustained for long. Regina had established public kindergartens the previous year, and by the early twentieth century, they were common in Manitoba, Saskatchewan, and Alberta. The Manitoba Public Schools Act (1890) allowed for kindergarten schools, "if deemed expedient, for children between three and six years of age in schools."[46] Kindergartens for three-year-olds were proposed as part of the North-West Territories School Bill (1892).[47] Debate centred on the age of admission. A journalist reported that one member of the legislature believed that "No doubt ... infants of three years of age could be taught to do and say some funny things and their mammas and papas would be very proud of them, but he did not believe in relieving mothers from the responsibility which properly belongs to them. He would have no serious objection, however, if the age of admission be raised to four or five."[48]

The issue was raised several more times for debate, although the clause had been passed, with the final result being an increase in the age from three to four.[49] For community boosters, the presence of a kindergarten signalled their town's modern thinking, and the local boards of trade used it as a promotional tool for attracting newcomers.[50] In 1900, the same year it was incorporated as a town, Yorkton boasted a kindergarten in its newly built Victoria School. A newspaper reporter thought it would be useful as a childcare service and for drawing younger children into the schools, though this was probably not the intent of the school board: "In the west nearly all the incoming settlers are young people with large families, and that the kindergarten system has resulted in the schoolhouses being filled with children of all sizes — with the exception of mere babes in arms. This is without doubt a great benefit to the mothers, who have so little chance of obtaining 'hired help' even if they can afford it."[51]

The Dawson City kindergarten opened in 1900, at the same time as the public school formed.[52] By 1907, fully equipped with kindergarten materials, it hired teacher Laura Thompson — mother of author Pierre Berton — from Toronto, where she had trained at the Normal School. Beset by falling attendance and an economic shortfall, it closed in 1919. Kindergarten was not resumed in the city until the 1960s. A similar situation occurred in Alberta, where kindergartens were established in Edmonton and a number of towns — Wetaskiwin, Drumheller, Medicine Hat, and Lethbridge — following the incorporation of the province in 1905. All closed by the mid-1920s.

Toronto and Winnipeg

The Toronto kindergartens involved two pioneers in the North American movement, James Hughes and Adaline Augusta Marean.[53] Hughes visited the 1876 Philadelphia Centennial Exhibition in his capacity of inspector of schools for Toronto. Among those demonstrating kindergarten work at the exhibition was Maria Kraus-Boelte. She had emigrated from London to New York, where she opened a private kindergarten-training college in 1873. The exhibition included photographs of kindergartens and displays

Demonstration kindergarten at the Philadelphia Centennial Exhibition, 1876, with Froebelian building Gifts on the table. Stereographic card, Centennial Photographic Company. Author's collection.

of materials. The main attraction, however, was a demonstration kindergarten that operated for eight months with children borrowed from a local orphanage.[54] Their teacher, who had been trained by Peabody, followed her interpretation of a Froebelian approach.

Although the impact of this experience on the children is unknown, certainly Hughes was deeply impressed by what he observed, and he used his influence as inspector of schools to promote the kindergarten in Toronto. As a first step, he asked Kraus-Boelte to recommend one of her graduates to come to Toronto to direct a private kindergarten. She chose American-born Adaline Augusta Marean, who opened the Toronto kindergarten in September 1877, directly across from the Normal School, though it moved the next year.[55] It offered two classes, with one described as "higher than the kindergarten proper, in which the pupils will not only have the advantage of a thorough course in English by an efficient teacher, but will also devote a portion of each day to the regular Kindergarten exercises." The kindergarten accepted boarders, and Hughes personally screened the applications. As an added draw, tuition was claimed to be lower "than in any genuine kindergarten in America."[56]

Over the next few years, Hughes gathered support for public kindergartens in Toronto. In this same period, public kindergartens were established in additional cities in the United States, and a kindergarten department had opened at the Oswego Normal School in New York State. In 1882, Hughes toured the kindergartens in St. Louis, along with a Toronto School Board trustee, recommending on their return that the board establish a trial kindergarten and teacher training.[57]

Winnipeg's Protestant Board of School Trustees watched the developments in Toronto closely. In the early 1870s, Winnipeg women's groups such as the Christian Woman's Union had undertaken "the Kindergarten agitation" for the adoption of kindergarten in public schools but with no effect.[58] However, interest intensified during 1883 following news that public school kindergartens had been established in Toronto in January of that year. Over the course of 1883, the Winnipeg Protestant School Management Committee prepared a report on kindergartens, which borrowed heavily from one written by Hughes in 1882 and was based on the committee's communication with school officials in Toronto, New York, St. Louis, Philadelphia, Baltimore, and Boston. The Winnipeg report, which was subsequently adopted by the Protestant Board of School Trustees, concluded that kindergartens should be introduced into two schools on an experimental basis and that "proper steps be taken to secure the services of at least one thoroughly trained Kindergartener, together with the necessary supply of materials."[59] However, the implementation of these recommendations was postponed for financial reasons. A satirical editorialist in the *Manitoba Daily Free Press* congratulated the board, agreeing that the cost of public kindergartens, with their small class sizes, was too great for "a city like this."[60]

Whereas Winnipeg lacked a leader to continue the effort, Hughes led developments in Toronto, selecting Marean as kindergartener and arranging for her to tour the St. Louis kindergartens and meet their director, Susan Blow. Another of Kraus-Boelte's students, Blow prepared the way for the Toronto kindergartens by lecturing at the Normal School in 1882, establishing a strong connection with both the St. Louis schools and Froebelian orthodoxy. From 1886 to 1892, the director of the kindergarten

Student teachers at the Toronto Normal School demonstration kindergarten, c. 1898. RG 2-257 Acc. 13522, Archives of Ontario, Toronto.

department at the Toronto Normal School was Blow's student Caroline Hart, who helped standardize training throughout Ontario.[61] The graduates of this period provided leadership in kindergarten work in Toronto and elsewhere in Canada for decades.

The St. Louis kindergartens were in decline even as Hughes toured them in 1882. In the early 1870s, William Torrey Harris, at that time superintendent of schools in St. Louis, had enlisted Susan Blow to direct the first kindergarten in a North American public school; this opened in 1873 at St. Louis' Des Peres School. When Harris resigned in 1880, the kindergarten was brought under the supervision of the elementary division, a move that threatened the administrative independence of the program. To protest this move, Blow resigned in 1884, as did many of the teachers she trained, Caroline Hart among them.[62]

In Toronto, eighty children enrolled in the Elizabeth Street School kindergarten in 1883, its first year. Marean worked with seven student teachers training under her. However, the initial interest waned, and enrolment dropped off. When Caroline Hart came to Toronto to take charge of kindergarten training in 1886, it was to rescue the "languishing playschool," as only six children attended a single kindergarten class. A report looking back on this time noted, "She brought with her a faith in Froebelism that was not daunted by the gloomy state in which she found the kindergarten."[63] By 1898, the situation had improved, and the Toronto Normal School demonstration kindergarten, established by Bessie Hailmann in 1885, was training teachers for increasing numbers of kindergartens.[64]

Marean's own teaching career in public kindergartens was brief. She directed the class at the Elizabeth Street School for two years before marrying Hughes and resigning in 1885. Adaline Hughes continued involvement in kindergarten work through various professional organizations, including the Ontario Educational Association (OEA) and the International Kindergarten Union (IKU).[65] She was OEA president in 1900. In 1905, the IKU held its annual meeting in Toronto, and at the next year's meeting in Milwaukee she was elected president. It seems likely that her association with James Hughes enhanced her standing in the kindergarten world.

She was also a member of the Committee of Nineteen, which was appointed by the International Kindergarten Union to study the philosophical differences that had developed between the Froebelians, who were led by Susan Blow, and the Reconstructionists, who advocated a progressive approach. It has been noted that Adaline Hughes sided with Blow, understandable in light of their similar training and Blow's contribution to the Toronto kindergartens.[66] The IKU's 1905 Toronto meeting occurred at the height of the union's debate over the future of Froebelism. The meeting ended with a series of speakers, each having three minutes to state his or her case. Susan Blow counselled the assembly to "depart not from Froebel and his genius."[67] In Toronto, the approach to kindergarten departed little from Froebel, at least as interpreted by US-based German teachers such as Kraus-Boelte and her students. Kindergarten pedagogy in Toronto public schools remained largely unchanged until the 1930s.[68]

James Hughes' reading of Froebel was literal, as detailed in his writings, such as *Froebel's Educational Laws for All Teachers*. He attributed this title to Bertha von Marenholtz-Bülow, to whom he credited the words, "By and by Froebel's educational law will be accepted as distinctly and independently as Newton's law of gravitation." He explained the process whereby kindergarten activities developed "self-activity within law," directing children's innate love of work toward good instead of evil. As he explained, "The same power that is intended to make the child constructive makes it destructive if wrongly used. The same tendency that undirected makes the anarchist will make a law-respecting citizen if guided wisely."[69] As historian W.E. Marsden suggests, "The innovative Froebelian pedagogy concealed a rigid moral code. Nature's first law was not autonomy but order."[70]

The drill and directed and imitative play that were common in the kindergartens of the period fit James Hughes' interest in citizenship education.[71] This involved patriotism and allegiance to Britain. Hughes was an active Orangeman, serving as a grand master, as was his brother Samuel, who led Canada's war effort in the First World War. In 1916, James Hughes gave a talk to the Clinton School kindergarten class: titled "Lessons from the Front," it was based on his recent trip to France.[72] The directed play in kindergarten was generally tied to moral training. Hughes had written a number of short texts for student teachers, among which was his *Manual of Drill and Calisthenics*, with an extended title listing its contents: *Squad Drill, Calisthenics, Free Gymnastics, Vocal Exercises, German Calisthenics, Movement Songs, the Pocket Gymnasium, and Kindergarten Songs and Games.*[73] Adolf Douai described kindergarten gymnastics as an essential part of the curriculum, with the aim to discipline minds and bodies: "Every exercise ought to have its particular name, so that the teacher's short word of command may set the entire little band at once into the desired motion or position." The routines "ought not to be converted into fun or farce."[74]

A belief in the inherent law of the system contributed to what Evelyn Weber calls a cult of Froebelism, in which Gift work was ritualized and Froebel himself revered.[75] As Susan Blow implored, "Depart not from Froebel." In 1910, at the height of the IKU's debate over the relative merits of Gift work versus free play, Lucy Wheelock organized a pilgrimage to "Froebel Land" for US kindergarteners. James Hughes met the tour group in London and, along with Kate Douglas Wiggin, gave lectures on Froebel's educational laws. The pilgrimage occurred as support for the conservative position was weakened by reform-minded kindergarteners such as Patty Smith Hill and Alice Temple.

Three years later, the Committee of Nineteen published its final findings, which consisted of separate liberal and conservative reports and a third that took a middle-of-the-road position. The majority of committee members signed the conservative report. In Wheelock's description, the supposed reconciliation of diverse views exemplified "the Froebelian law of mediation."[76] However, support for the conservative view quickly dissolved among those US kindergarten movement leaders who were not members of the Committee of Nineteen. Furthermore, Froebelian theorist Susan Blow, who authored the conservative report, died in 1916. Those outside the kindergarten world, unconcerned with matters of theory, focused mainly on the relation between kindergarten and first grade, and the IKU quickly moved to build relationships with schools, forming a subcommittee to study the kindergarten curriculum. One version of its report was published as a Bureau of Education bulletin in 1919 and was used as an unofficial curriculum guide by kindergarten teachers for many years.[77]

The subcommittee's chair was Alice Temple, director of the Kindergarten-Primary Department at the University of Chicago. Of the other members, only Elizabeth Harrison had sat on the Committee of Nineteen, serving as chair of the middle-ground "liberal-conservative" report. The curriculum described in the subcommittee's report was strongly influenced by Temple's understanding of unified kindergarten-primary work and experiments at the Laboratory School at the University of Chicago, which had been influenced by John Dewey. Formal Gift work was abandoned, but the blocks were retained: "Blocks may consist of Froebel's building blocks enlarged, large floor blocks in the form and relative proportion of the Froebelian building blocks but enlarged six times, and boards of different dimensions to be combined with these; or the Patty Hill floor blocks and boards can be made to order by a planing mill or the school manual training department."[78]

New kindergartens were opened in Toronto schools, even as criticism grew regarding their value. In 1895, there were forty kindergartens in schools. By 1914, there were seventy-eight. Kindergartens in the new schools were provided with double rooms containing specialized moveable tables and chairs. In 1913, the Board of Education began to install stained-glass panels in about half its kindergarten rooms, a move that beautified the classrooms and marked them as a unique and important part of the school.[79] It also drew attention to their cost, long a focus of concern for school trustees. A *Toronto Globe* editorial, written after the 1905 IKU meeting, cut through the finer points of the Froebelian-Reconstructionist debate, which seemed important only to members of the IKU. The writer admitted that "a good kindergarten is a better place for a child than a bad home" but added that other interventions such as supervised playgrounds could serve as well for less cost.[80] He also targeted the esoteric elements of the kindergarten system: "In [playgrounds] the children might be left, as free as possible from interference and discipline, to amuse and educate one another. 'Free play' was one of the things pleaded for at the convention, and free play is impossible in a kindergarten."[81]

For Hughes, the kindergarten was useful in directing children's play toward a more appropriate social purpose than could be achieved if they spent their time outside school and on the street. He also supported the playground movement and other initiatives associated with the child-saving movement. In her study of Toronto kindergartens, Julie Mathien notes that the rationale for kindergartens changed during the late nineteenth century: in the 1880s, kindergarten was presented as a useful intervention for poor children; in the 1890s, Hughes and others argued that it was an integral part of the school system, one appropriate for youngsters from all circumstances.[82] In fact, it was most popular among the middle classes, probably because they could afford the materials fee required by the school board. Kindergarten, with its focus on crafts and specialized materials, was an expensive program.

Hughes maintained his commitment to kindergartens over his lifetime, even celebrating his seventy-fifth birthday with the children at the Lansdowne Kindergarten.[83] However, his retirement in 1913, after thirty-nine years as inspector of schools, opened the way for a discussion of new ideas, one of which was unified kindergarten-primary work. This had a limited impact; the changes may have seemed too radical. One suggestion was that, as class progressed from kindergarten to grade three, its teacher would not change. Another was that kindergartens would be located "in small homes suitably equipped, rather than in large public schools whose accommodation is made for larger pupils," an idea that would also have solved the severe overcrowding at the time.[84] Some schools were wholly unable to accommodate children in kindergarten.

Evelyn Weber observes that, when kindergartens were introduced into public schools, they were exposed to "the currents of thought playing upon the schools at large."[85] This exerted pressure on kindergarteners to bring their program into line with that of the primary grades. For many years, with the support of Hughes and the conservative Normal School training, Toronto kindergarteners resisted this impetus. Nonetheless, a 1918 speech by F.E. Coombe, of the University of Toronto's Faculty of Education, heralded the changes to come. Addressing the kindergarten section of the Ontario Education Association, Coombe stated the obvious — that some of Froebel's writing was entirely incomprehensible — uttering a criticism that could not have been imagined a few years earlier. In its coverage of his speech, the *Toronto Globe* revealed that, "where understandable," Coombe "found [Froebel] singularly wise and sane." However,

> Some paragraphs he had pondered over for hours and had found absolutely void of meaning. Froebel and Froebel's kindergarten, he declared, must ever remain as a city set on a hill which cannot be moved. "Have no fear for the future status of the kindergarten," he said. "Transformations must come; transformations are coming; transformation should come in the kindergarten. Much in it that is dead and inane needs the pruning hook, but that condition is not peculiar to the kindergarten. Granted that it must shake off its own body of symbolism, of fixed gifts and prescribed program, that shaking off of the empty husk will but free the spirit. Froebel's kindergarten can never be lost; it is immortal."[86]

The transformation occurred over the next decade. In 1923, Chief Inspector of Schools R.H. Cowley announced plans to drastically modify kindergarten classes, including more "academic work of an abstract nature, such as the use of symbols in the form of letters and figures placed upon a blackboard."[87] For kindergarten teachers, these were fighting words, and they engaged the school board in vigorous and oftentimes acrimonious debate for more than a year.

Proposed changes included the loss of the position of kindergarten supervisor, whose work would be undertaken by the primary supervisor. Mary Adair, a graduate of the Toronto Normal School and then head of the kindergarten department at the Philadelphia Normal School, spoke out, stating, "There were inspectors of meat, of clothing, and of almost every commodity of life. How much more necessary, therefore, was the need for inspection of things that were so subtle as the child mentality?"[88]

Hughes, though long retired, joined in, calling the scheme "utterly and diabolically bad."[89] Elizabeth Harrison, president of the Toronto Kindergarten Association, declared that it would "set back infant education 100 years."[90] She mocked Cowley's suggestion that the kindergarten be renamed a "childerfold," a move she believed would make Toronto "the laughing-stock of the whole continent."[91] The term "fold" was occasionally used in nineteenth-century infant schools to refer to the structure containing the youngest children — William Wilson employed it in the 1820s — but was certainly unused in the 1920s.[92] The association explained the kindergarten's distinctive character, focusing on its links with the home and not the school, and referencing Froebel's philosophy of development with the term *unfolding:* "The pure kindergarten bridges the jump from home life to school life — sympathetically and understandingly — softening the terrors of leaving home and mother for the first time. Carefully, scientifically, day by day, the course proceeds. Every play, every song, everything, has a purpose in the unfolding of the young mind and the development of character, preparatory to the more serious primary academic work ahead, to which the pupil is passed just as soon as ready."[93]

Support for purity came primarily from the kindergarten association itself, which had an interest in continuing its professional isolation. The association also felt a new pressure and a new source of criticism. Nursery school experts from the University of Toronto supported the recommendation of the Board of Education to move children out of kindergarten on their sixth birthday. Helen Bott, who would later head parent education at St. George's Nursery School, declared, "A child who is not retarded should not be doing kindergarten work at the age of six."[94] On one level, the debate was between the value of traditional kindergarten work and that of formal instruction in reading and writing. Also at stake was the kindergarteners' independence, marked by their unique professional knowledge, and the primary school division's interest in retaining the status quo. Teaching reading was a key area of the division's expertise, best left to the formal instruction of first grade.

In a 1925 speech, the president of the Toronto Kindergarten Association observed that "throughout Canada the kindergarten is suffering something of an eclipse, and we need constantly to assure ourselves that an eclipse is only of short duration; the sun is shining as bright as ever." She continued with a new metaphor: "We must feed the kindergarten fire and fan it into a flame which all the world can see."[95] Although the eclipse was not total, the pressure to change was relentless. The Primary Teacher Association, which had earlier supported kindergarten teachers in their struggle for professional control, asserted that children should be tested for readiness prior to their promotion to grade one. Apparently, the association believed that some children were overripe for their move to grade one, whereas others were ill-prepared and needed to wait. The call for testing could also be seen as a challenge to the ability of kindergarteners to prepare students for the rigours of first grade.

In 1927, the new director of the kindergarten department at the Philadelphia Normal School spoke in Toronto of the reformed kindergarten as one in which the "idea was not to lose any of the beauty or the idealism of the kindergarten, but to emphasize habit formation in the young child." She believed the kindergarten must link to school, and she further stated that she would "like to live to see the day when the kindergarten was called the first grade."[96] Kindergarten teachers in Toronto were not so quick to shift from traditional kindergarten activities. At the teachers' convention earlier in the year, kindergartener Lillian Dent had titled her session "The Use of the Building Gifts."[97] Nevertheless, by the 1930s, teachers considered Gift work old-fashioned, the small blocks were collected into larger containers for free block play, and "teachers nailed down the lids of the large Gift boxes which they then painted to use as floor blocks."[98]

Australia

In Sydney, Australia, infants' departments and separate infants' schools were formed for children from the age of five to ease overcrowding in primary classrooms in public schools. These classes used formal instruction as preparation for later education and though they were tailored for infants, they were not patterned on the infant school invented by Owen. From the 1880s, kindergarten methods were adopted in some infants' classes, where some "babies" and "alphabet" classes were recast as kindergarten and transition classes. The Australian development resembled the British pattern of introducing modified kindergarten pedagogy in infants' classes. In the modified kindergarten, "gifts and occupations" were a subject in the timetable, along with reading, writing, and drills in number work. This mix of approaches sprang from a pragmatic decision, according to Kevin Brehony, who argues that, because the Froebelians in England "could not hope to supplant the infant schools and departments with the kindergarten, their only viable strategy was to try to reform or supplement them."[99]

This was certainly true in Australia and, as we shall see later, in New Zealand as well. Once infants' classes gained a foothold in public schools, they were remarkably resistant to change despite attempts to introduce new ideas. In the 1850s, William Wilkins trialed a pre-primary class based on the ideas of Froebel and Pestalozzi during his time as headmaster at Sydney's Fort Street Model School. Wilkins, who had recently arrived from England, set about introducing contemporary British and Continental ideas in New South Wales schools, an effort he continued upon becoming under secretary in the New South Wales Department of Public Instruction. Under his direction, the department developed systems for school inspection and for the classification of teachers according to their knowledge and skill; it also improved teacher training and, overall, put measures into place to raise the quality and efficiency of instruction.[100] In 1856, Wilkins established what he called a "nursery school" at the Fort Street Model School, which was described in the annual report of the commissioners of national education in New South Wales:

> In the lowest department, called the Nursery School, children are received whose ages range from two to five years, provided they are able to talk. Here their formal instruction may be said to commence, and the methods adopted are those which experience has proved to be best suited to develop and strengthen the dawning intellect. An attempt has been made to introduce, with the modifications necessary in the peculiar circumstances of the school, the system of F. Froebel, the originator of the "Kinder Gärten" (Children's Gardens). The spacious and airy school grounds at Fort-street permit the carrying out of this system with great facility, the only drawback being the want of some of the requisite appliances. It has not been deemed expedient to adopt Froebel's views in their entirety, many of his notions being impracticable with Australian children, although perhaps perfectly suitable to the temperament of natives of Germany. But his fundamental principle of mingling employment with instruction, and combining amusements with both, has been successfully observed. This department is very popular with the parents, chiefly, I believe, because their children are therein afforded opportunities of healthful exercise and recreation, while at the same time their safety is made a matter of paramount importance. They also receive that moral training and instruction which their tender years permit. The 120 children in his department are trained, cared for, and instructed by an assistant teacher, with the help of a pupil teacher.
>
> The separation of the very young children, by leaving the remainder more nearly equal in point of age and intellectual development, has considerably increased the efficiency of the Infant Department. The advantages of well-conducted Infant Schools in cities and large towns cannot be disputed; and keeping in view the probable increased demand for institutions of this kind, every exertion has been used to select good methods from the systems of Stow, Wilderspin, and others who have made Infant Education their special study. The modes of teaching employed in this department, though of a kind to

interest young children, partake of a more intellectual character than those before spoken of. The result is so far successful, that some of the most promising scholars in the senior department are those whose early training was received in the Infant School. On the removal of the boys and girls to the new schoolrooms, the infant children were transferred to the ground floor of the old building, having previously occupied one of the upper rooms. This circumstance greatly facilitated the introduction of a more suitable organization, and enables the teacher to carry out the principles of the Infant System more completely than under the former arrangements.[101]

The timing of the experiment followed the well-publicized kindergarten display at London's 1854 International Exhibition of Educational Materials, reported on by the American Henry Barnard. Barnard's brief review of the exhibit in the 1856 *American Journal of Education* inspired Elizabeth Peabody's interest in the kindergarten and may have stimulated Wilkins' interest as well.[102] However, a number of educational thinkers influenced Wilkins, and there is no evidence that the Fort Street class was based solely or strongly on Froebel or that it employed any kindergarten materials. Wilkins' own preparation at the Battersea Training School in England was under the direction of James Kay-Shuttleworth, who had conducted a study of educational systems. In Kay-Shuttleworth's view, Pestalozzi's "'synthetic method' held the key for children's learning."[103] This meant that new knowledge was built on old in a natural, even unconscious way. As headmaster at Fort Street, Wilkins considered the infants' department to be the weakest in the school and wished it "to be conducted upon enlightened principles and approved methods."[104]

One result was the creation of the nursery school. Students who attended the nursery class graduated to the infants' class, which had a more academic focus. Wilkins expected that nursery and infants' classes patterned after his system at the Fort Street Model School would spread to public schools. However, the Fort Street experiment of "combining amusements with instruction" was short-lived and appears not to have had any generalized influence on pedagogy in infants' schools. Wilkins continued as inspector and superintendent of schools in Sydney, finishing his career as under secretary in the Department of Public Instruction and retiring in 1884.

In the 1880s, kindergarten was no longer novel, yet the New South Wales minister for public instruction considered it untested and experimental. He reasoned that "the results of the method are not immediately apparent, and for that reason would not recommend themselves to the approval of the working classes and others who are anxious that their children should reach the standard of education prescribed by the [Education] Act as soon as possible."[105] Thus, the infants' class continued to focus on literacy, and pupils were retained in the class until they had learned to read, resulting in a wide range of ages.[106] For the youngest pupils, the infants' class provided care while their mothers were at work. At the Fort Street National School in 1859, the youngest pupil was two and a half years of age. When compulsory school laws came into effect in New South Wales in 1881, older girls were freed from childcare duties, and their younger siblings followed behind them to take their place in the babies class. At the end of the first school year following the compulsory school law, 20 percent of pupils in New South Wales primary schools were underage.

Infants' education in other states followed similar lines and was influenced by developments in New South Wales.[107] In Victoria, the first public school kindergarten opened in 1907 under the direction of Emmeline Pye, who had trained with the British kindergartener Eva Hooper at the Melbourne Teachers College. The principal of the teachers college, John Smith, hired Pye to lecture on kindergarten work and to demonstrate the system at the practice school. All urban schools in Victoria had infants' classes by the mid-1930s. At this time, kindergartens were rare despite the continued place of kindergarten work in teacher training. Although the teachers college had four practice kindergartens, there were only seven public school kindergartens in the entire state.

The South Australia Department of Education sent two teachers to the Melbourne Teachers College to study with Pye and Smith. On their return to Adelaide, one was appointed inspector of infants' schools and the other the lecturer on infants' school methods at the teachers college. In little more than a decade, there were infants' classes in larger schools and twenty-seven infants' departments in primary schools by the mid-1930s.

During an 1889 visit to schools in other states, the general inspector of education for Queensland became interested in kindergarten, but the economic downturn of the 1890s slowed its implementation. Initiatives included some experimentation with kindergarten work in infants' schools and the purchase of sets of Gifts and other materials. The number of infants' schools remained stable to the mid-1930s: eight existed in 1889 and nine in 1936. Kindergarten work was included as a subject in the Queensland Department of Education syllabus from 1908. The approach was termed a unified kindergarten-primary school.

Separate infants' departments were established in Western Australia primary schools to meet the needs of an increase in population after 1900. After the age of admission was changed in 1920 for economic reasons, the babies class that had enrolled four- and five-year-olds was eliminated. With older children in the infants' classes, the focus turned to primary class work.

In Tasmania, the attention to New Education in 1904, remembered as the year of reconstruction, prompted links with the teachers college in Sydney, to which Tasmanian students were sent. Teachers were also "loaned" to Tasmania to work in schools for a few years at a time. The first separate infants' department was formed in 1914, at the Elizabeth Street Training School. By the mid-1930s, all large primary schools had a kindergarten class.

Sydney

A teacher who came to Sydney via Christchurch, New Zealand, undertook an experiment with kindergarten work in an infants' school. In New Zealand, the Education Act of 1877 made free schooling available from age five and compulsory from seven. Therefore, what were optional pre-primary classes in Australia were a mandated part of the school system in New Zealand. The first non-compulsory pre-primary stage of education in New Zealand was the infants' class. Although this mostly followed the British infants' class model, experiments were made with the kindergarten approach, as in Australia, although at a later date. The first was in Christchurch in 1878, when the Normal School established a model kindergarten. The teacher was Amelia Quinney (later Crowley), hired from England and trained in kindergarten methods at the London School Board.[108]

When interest in the kindergarten work waned along with funding, she resigned and went to Sydney, where her husband had business prospects. In Sydney, she wrote to William Wilkins, seeking a teaching position "with the view to introduce the Kindergarten system of education in the colony."[109] Wilkins accepted her proposal, and, as a three-month experiment, she was offered a class at the Crown Street Public School. This was an interesting development, in which an experienced teacher undertook to initiate a public school kindergarten, apparently with little support or interest from the Department of Public Instruction. The kindergarten at the Crown Street school opened in October 1881, giving Crowley the distinction of directing the first public school kindergarten in both New Zealand and Australia.[110]

J.S. Jones, chief inspector of schools, was pessimistic from the start, believing that Crowley would face significant problems in implementing the full kindergarten system in Sydney's overcrowded infants' classes. He seemed aware of kindergarten methods, indicating that a kindergarten needed a "covered in playground, or juvenile laboratory, well stocked with well devised means of manual operations," amenities lacking in most Sydney schools.[111] The infants' classes were overcrowded, with children packed in galleries, whereas, according to Crowley, the system could not be implemented with more than twenty-five pupils. Crowley toured the infants' classes and agreed they were unsuitable for kindergarten work, but she nevertheless undertook the challenge. She produced a list of materials and furnishings for outfitting her classroom: "2 tables (with squares); 4 forms; 1 blackboard; 1 easel; 30 Gift I; 30 Gift III; paper of various colors; cardboard; wool of selected colors; 30 slates; 2 tables, 3 feet wide and 10 feet 6 inches long."[112]

The experiment was plagued with problems: sufficient numbers of "kindergarten appliances" were never ordered, and the twelve-foot by fifteen-foot room provided no freedom of movement. Nonetheless, plans were under way to erect a special room for the kindergarten, and the initial reports on Crowley's work were positive. Inspector Jones spoke approvingly of its two achievements: One was to "train them [pupils] to think and Obey in preparation for the school effort and discipline." The other was to place "them in the hands of a trained person ... instead of leaving them to the influence of the too frequent neglect of indifferent parents."[113] Given this view, he recommended that, since kindergartens were really only "play schools," they should be adopted on a wider scale but with larger class sizes. Although this would require a more structured program, he believed that it would not "sacrifice anything essential to the system."[114] In essence, he recommended a modified kindergarten within the existing infants' classes.

Other reports continued these themes: they perceived value in having young poor children attend school, but, applying a cost-benefit analysis, they feared that the expenditure was too high for too little instruction or learning. At the same time, the reports reveal a degree of sympathy for the system: "The disciplinary condition of the class is sound and healthy; the government is mild ... and intelligent, far less rigid and more natural than that of ordinary Infants Schools, but nevertheless effective and philosophical."[115] Jones was apparently familiar with free kindergartens. Though none was yet established in Sydney, he compared their work to that at the Crown

Street kindergarten. He also recommended that Crowley be provided with a proper room and equipment, and that students work under her as assistants. Further, he believed that student teachers should be aware of kindergarten methods and that Crowley should give lectures at the Normal School. Wilkins was unmoved. In his response to the inspector, he wrote,

> In old thickly peopled countries, where masses of mere infants have from one cause or another to be placed under the charge of strangers, Kindergarten teaching is one of a variety of methods devised to amuse children and to give them, at the same time, some mental training. Probably in most of these systems the claims made as to "mental training" are greatly exaggerated. It has been struggling in its natural home for nearly 50 years to make headway but with very little success. The objection urged against it is, that it teaches nothing, that parents as a rule value, and that for the healthy, artless play of children, it substitutes games regulated by the pedantry of school routine.[116]

Wilkins recommended that the class be maintained as it existed. Three months later, the inspector issued the notice that it "should be closed forthwith."[117] The aim of the experiment was to discover whether the approach could be generalized; due to the cost and Wilkins' lack of support, it was determined that it could not.

In a strange and unexplained turn of events, the next year Crowley was offered a position as teacher of a kindergarten at Castlereagh Public School in Sydney.[118] This time, the inspector's reports were immediately critical, though now he focused on the quality of instruction rather than cost. To evaluate the kindergarten, he employed an assessment devised for the infants' classes, believing that, if the kindergarten were to prove its worth, the performance of its pupils must equal or outstrip that of the students in an infants' class. Though some attention was paid to reading and writing in the kindergarten, its pupils were judged not properly prepared in these areas for primary school work.[119] Crowley reasoned that she needed more time: the inspector argued that efficiency was required.

The inspector prepared a report in which he compared the Castlereagh kindergarten to an infants' class. The former consisted of three divisions, in which children were placed according to their age: the average age of pupils in the first division was four and a half, that of the second was six, and that of the third was seven years and eight months. Crowley taught the oldest division. The kindergarten was compared with the first three divisions of infants' classes. The average age of the kindergarten children was higher than that of the infants' class in the second and third divisions. However, the latter outperformed the former in almost all categories. The inspection forms used to assess student capabilities had been devised for infants' classes, in which object lessons, reading, and writing were taught. The kindergarten children, who had not received much instruction in these areas, naturally proved deficient in them. The absence of a lesson plan or timetable, a contrast with infants' classes, also drew the inspector's attention. Following the gathering together of the kindergarten class, the day was spent in the typical rotation of activities — drill, hymns, meditation, reading, Gift three, recess, role games, writing, drawing, singing, discussion, weaving, folding, Gift one, and story.[120] It is interesting to see Gift one, devised for a mother's play with her baby, used with children who were nearly eight.

The kindergarten was a matter for public debate and was discussed in the Legislative Assembly of New South Wales in 1884. A brief prepared for the minister of public instruction, reflecting the view of Wilkins, stated that it was not desirable to continue "or enlarge its operation as a separate or independent system."[121] It added, "This system, which is spoken of as 'regulated play,' is not one that should form the first basis of the school life of our Public School children, that it is a system which would very probably act ... against children when they came to be moved into the higher classes, where this system of playing at learning would be impracticable."[122] The Castlereagh kindergarten closed in 1884, and there is no evidence that the full kindergarten system was subsequently used in Sydney infants' classes, though kindergarten principles were a required subject in the Normal School at this time, and a recommendation was made to engage Amelia Crowley as lecturer.[123]

The kindergarten approach to early education differed radically from any other that had been conducted in infants' schools for sixty years. The Department of Public Instruction exhibited some understanding of its philosophy and a recognition that, at least in its relatively gentle discipline of children, its practice was superior to that in current infants' schools. There was, however, no reason for the department to embrace kindergartens, given that schools already existed for young children, that classroom architecture did not facilitate kindergarten activities, that parents did not seem to support the approach, and that the cost was higher than existing provisions. What were called "modified kindergartens" were no more than a crude compromise. Several years after the original kindergarten experiment at Crown Street Public School, the architect for the Department of Public Instruction was called upon to design a new kindergarten classroom. A plan was approved to erect a gallery in the infants' department for the kindergarten. Specifications included that it should have four tiers, with backs to the seats and hinged flaps for the table.[124] Jane Read has shown that kindergarten work in low galleries was also common in Britain at the time, where it was accommodated within the existing pedagogy.[125]

Kindergarten work did not disappear in Sydney schools with the conclusion of the Crown Street experiment. However, where it was integrated into infants' schools, it lost its distinct character as Froebelian theory and Gifts were set aside. The contribution of Martha M. Simpson, in charge of the Blackfriars demonstration kindergarten from 1906, and later lecturer on methods, exemplified the way in which kindergarten work was undertaken in infants' schools.

Simpson's approach is evident in her detailed description of a 1908 curriculum unit on Aboriginal Australians, which was employed in several Sydney kindergartens. The general subject was "Primitive Man — his life and Customs with special reference to the Australian Black."[126] Simpson explained her reasons for selecting this topic: "The Herbartians hold that the child's mental development corresponds to that of the race; and this view is, I think, generally held by all thinkers on education at the present time. If this be so, and if the child's mental development be an epitome of the evolution of humanity, then the life of any primitive people should furnish material from which the skilled kindergartner may draw sufficient for her needs."[127] For reasons undisclosed, the curriculum unit was abandoned in the two kindergartens whose students were mostly four years of age, but it "was very successful indeed" in three classes of older pupils.[128] In all of this work, Simpson made little use of the standard materials, believing the kindergarten spirit was key: "It may be noticed in the plan that no mention is made of the Kindergarten Gifts. From this it must not be inferred that the gifts were not used, or that they are in any way undervalued. I might say, however, that I do not think the Kindergarten depends for its existence on the Gifts. The spirit and tone and atmosphere of the Kindergarten — these are the important things. The material, whatever it may be, is only secondary, and much good Kindergarten work can be done with very simple and inexpensive material."[129] In actuality, the Gifts may not have been available in the classes. Equipment and materials records dating from 1908 show that only blackboards, three tables, and thirty small chairs were ordered for a new kindergarten class at the demonstration school.[130]

Simpson was keen to try new ideas, experimenting with Montessori methods in an infants' school kindergarten in 1912. In her unique interpretation of Montessori's program, using materials made by the teachers themselves with some crafted by men in a prison workshop, she did not subscribe to Montessori's philosophy.[131] Speaking before the Sydney Kindergarten Club in 1912, Simpson emphasized the use of materials such as the sandpaper letters for teaching writing and asserted that kindergarten work and the Montessori method were compatible, each stressing "nature work, rhythm, musical training, freedom, and discipline."[132] Through use of the Montessori materials, children would individually "work out their own salvation."[133] Her experiment did not aim to replicate Montessori's method, but "cull" from it some useful ideas.[134] A.C. Carmichael, New South Wales minister for public instruction and a supporter of Simpson's experiments, desired to see "what branches of the Montessori scheme can be best grafted on to Froebelian studies, as practiced in our schools."[135] One commentator noted bluntly, "Her apparatus is not final, nor are some of the occupations necessary to Australian children. They find no difficulty in boot lacing."[136]

In 1913, Simpson travelled to Rome to partake in Montessori's first international offering of her course. Upon returning to Sydney, she stated, wrongly, that Montessori, no purist, encouraged teachers to experiment with her method, retaining only its spirit of liberty for children, as, for example, in allowing them to choose whether to attend story time. On this basis, a Montessori class operated as an experiment for four years. When the chief inspector reviewed it in 1916, he found the students to be good readers and advanced in English, with excellent study skills and "no wandering of attention and no unemployment."[137] However, the teachers were not trained in Montessori methods, and the class was isolated from practice in the rest of the school, "nearly a Montessori island in a Non-Montessori ocean."[138]

New Zealand

As in Australia, kindergartens in New Zealand were mainly philanthropic, and the system had little impact on the infants' school.[139] Kindergarten activities in infants' schools were made to fit the existing curriculum. A lesson in bead threading from 1894 was a simple counting exercise: "Children stand with arms folded in front round the table. At the word *one* boxes are opened; *two,* children take hold of the bead that is fastened and lift the string, when the beads slip into the box. Teacher tells a tale — 'I found a nest with two white eggs in it.' Children put two white beads on. Teacher — 'I bought three rosy apples.' Children string three red beads, and count 'Two and three are five.' Teacher — 'I eat one apple.' Children take one bead off. 'One from five leaves four,' etc."[140]

Of the two public school kindergartens founded in the nineteenth century — in Christchurch and Wellington — only the latter survived for an extended period. Under the direction of Catherine Augusta Francis, the Mount Cook Infants' School in Wellington was for many years the leader in kindergarten and infants' school practice in Wellington Province.

Wellington

Francis emigrated from England to Australia with her family as a young girl.[141] She trained as a pupil-teacher and taught in Adelaide infants' schools during the 1860s and '70s. In 1878, the same year Crowley (Quinney) went to Christchurch, Francis moved to Wellington on the invitation of Robert Lee, inspector of schools for the Wellington Education Board, where she became "Principal Teacher" at the Mount Cook Infants' School. The school had opened in 1875 as one of three divisions, the others being a boys' school and a girls' school for children over the age of seven. Initially, all three schools shared a building, but each had their own quarters by 1878.[142] The start-up of the school coincided with the appointment of Robert Lee as school inspector, an initiative intended to support the new centralized Wellington Education Board, which was formed to create a more standardized and high-quality system of education in the province.[143]

Francis had a great interest in kindergarten work, but her training is undetermined. The Adelaide Training College was established in 1876, and she may have gained some background in kindergarten methods there.[144] Lee nonetheless recruited her as a kindergarten expert, and she introduced kindergarten-like materials and activities in the first level of the infants' school for five-year-olds.[145] Initially, restrictions for the work were evident, few kindergarten materials were available, and several different classes shared the room. The galleries, constructed in 1878 on the infant school model, would have made kindergarten work highly challenging.[146] The kindergarten materials available to Francis consisted of a single incomplete set of Gifts.[147]

Regardless of its adherence to Froebelian principles, the Mount Cook class stood out from the older classes, according to a journalist in 1884. For the five-year-olds, "learning is moulded into a pastime to suit infantile understanding, and knowledge acquired without that forcing of the mind, which may result in pale faces, weak limbs, and fretful temperaments."[148] Francis' specialization in music and the quality of the children's singing were most often noted in inspectors' reports. Activities included object lessons carried out in a quite regimented manner, leading one commentator to conclude, "The Kinder-Garten system is somewhat different to the object lessons, but so far as we could see, it is similar in principle."[149] A member of the Mount Cook Infants' School Committee similarly struggled to describe the methods, determining them to be a combination of the infant system promoted by the Home and Colonial Training Schools in London with "Kinder-Garten lessons as an auxiliary."[150] Francis' demonstration of an object lesson in her kindergarten was similar to infants' school methods:

> [Francis] took for her subject a small card of carpenters' tools — of course on a diminutive scale — and by means of one after the other succeeded in eliciting, by more questions, a wonderful amount of information from the children before her, herself supplying it when it could not be given by the little scholars. The card contained a hammer, a saw, a chisel, a screwdriver, a brad awl, etc., and it is needless to say that the history of any one of these instruments, closely followed up, embraces a great variety of subjects. Take the hammer, for instance — What does it consist of? What is iron, a vegetable or a mineral? How is it obtained? How is it brought into its present condition? Its relative weight? How forged and smelt? And numerous other questions of a similar character.[151]

Lee praised the kindergarten work that did occur, noting that lessons in form and colour were included along with the object lessons.[152] Some additional materials were added in 1884, including two kindergarten tables, and during the next year, Francis experimented with the system with a small group of twenty students.[153] In 1889, Lee and Francis were sufficiently confident in the Mount Cook kindergarten work that Francis spent two months demonstrating lessons at the New Zealand and South Seas International Exhibition in Dunedin.[154] Thus, Francis had the opportunity to influence infants' schools elsewhere in New Zealand, as well as the development of private fee-paying kindergartens. Her two daughters, who trained with her at the Mount Cook Infants' School as pupil-teachers, opened a private kindergarten in St. Andrew's on the Terrace Church, Wellington, in 1884.[155] By the end of the century, the Mount Cook kindergarten offered an array of activities, with the notable exception of the building Gifts.[156] Francis retired in 1905 after twenty-eight years at the Mount Cook school.

Common Features

The kindergarten movement had its start in the private charity sector as upper-class women embraced Froebel's notion of maternalism and child education. In her study of developments in the United States, Catherine Cosgrove describes the push for kindergartens in public schools occurring as the largely middle-class women teachers sought greater recognition and status for their work in public school systems, an analysis that has little relevance for the three nations reviewed here.[157] School administrators also sought more appropriate teaching strategies for the youngest children in the infants' classes. Although the older generation of administrators such as William Wilkins doubted its value, the kindergarten was at least the subject of experiments.

Free-kindergarten associations in Australia and New Zealand served children who were below school-starting age and thus were not in direct competition with public school kindergartens for students. Their teacher training remained separate, and in the case of the Kindergarten Union of South Australia, it remained so as a result of a hard-fought battle. In Canada, James Hughes initiated public kindergartens in the absence of a local free-kindergarten union. In all three countries, government, school authorities, and teacher-training colleges eventually assumed control over curriculum and training.

Free kindergartens in all three countries reflected local concerns and the personalities and interests of the individuals involved, but they quite faithfully represented the American model. In New Zealand, the Dunedin kindergarten had ties with church work, although supporters represented several denominations. Its first teacher, who was apparently devout, included Christian education as an important part of her lessons. The first free kindergartens in Melbourne were branches of church work. In 1906, the Reverend T.S. Woodfull, who was in charge of a Methodist mission in the city, established a kindergarten and hired a teacher trained in the United States.[158]

The American free-kindergarten movement also had a religious, even evangelical, strain, with organizations such as the Woman's Christian Temperance Union adopting kindergartens as an important branch of their work.[159] At the same time, key figures in the movement, such as Felix Adler and Elizabeth Peabody, instilled it with a humanist philosophy. Adler, for example, was a liberal religious thinker and social reformer.[160] He was a founder of the Ethical Culture Society, a group that, later in his life, he described as a "religious society imbued with the spirit of religion without its dogmas."[161] In California, Sarah Brown Cooper was taken to court on a charge of heresy for refusing to teach about hell and salvation in her kindergarten Bible class.

Other colonial kindergartens were non-sectarian. The Unitarian Mary Richmond established the Wellington free kindergartens. Born in Wellington in 1852, Richmond was the daughter of a supreme court judge.[162] She was familiar with kindergarten ideas through her reading and her knowledge of local initiatives in Dunedin on the South Island. In 1896, at the age of forty-four, she travelled to London to undergo three months of training at the Froebel Institute College. Upon her return a year later, she opened a private school in Wellington and organized a Froebel Society. Almost a decade went by before she established the Wellington Free Kindergarten Association for poor children in 1905. Free kindergartens developed slowly in Wellington, despite the activity in Dunedin from 1889. In this early period, the kindergarten movement was a regional rather than a national phenomenon, with city-based associations starting in Auckland in 1909 and Christchurch in 1911.

A feature of the free-kindergarten associations was the early introduction of private teacher-training schemes. This resulted in the rapid creation of a group of teachers trained according to a single interpretation of kindergarten work. In Dunedin, the first head teacher began training other women in kindergarten methods almost from the start, and by 1891, she had six students working under her. This created a very favourable ratio of adults to children at her kindergarten, considering that the average number of pupils attending the program was forty-six.[163] The number of graduates from the new training programs meant that, initially, there were far more trained teachers than free kindergartens, and many went on to establish private schools, to work as governesses, or to teach in Australian and Canadian public schools.[164] In New Zealand, journalist Mark Cohen bemoaned the poor training standards and lack of progressive ideas in the Dunedin program as a blow to the kindergarten movement. In 1891, he wrote to Sarah Cooper that the director whom the organizing committee had hired in 1889 was "kind, patient, and very religious" but that "her methods are not those of what I have been led from my reading to believe should be those of a true kindergartener."[165] She apparently disliked music, and in his view, her teaching had no system. He continued:

> None of our people have any practical acquaintance with any real kindergartener. We are all well meaning enough, and each desires to do the right thing, but we are all quite helpless in this important matter ... I fear if we turn out a number of indifferently instructed young women, many of them, finding their occupation a profitable one, will establish kindergartens of their own with unsuitable result that our methods will fall into disrepute, and that the New Education will get a setback that may take years to recover ... I opine that if we got a bright loveable girl we should have little difficulty persuading her to cast in her lot with us.[166]

In Australia, the centre of training was the Sydney Kindergarten Teachers College (SKTC). Free-kindergarten associations based on the New South Wales model developed outward from Sydney to other states, as newly trained teachers took up positions of leadership, first in Adelaide, then in Perth and Melbourne. The early excitement over the free-kindergarten idea gave rise to remarkable careers, such as that of Australian kindergartener Lillian de Lissa. Like Mary Richmond of New Zealand, de Lissa was a child of the colony, born in Sydney in 1885. Captivated as a young woman by the kindergarten idea, she entered the SKTC training program at age seventeen.[167] Graduating at nineteen, she taught briefly in a Sydney kindergarten before adding duties as administrator and teacher educator. In 1907, she was director of the first free kindergarten in Adelaide and became the first principal of the Adelaide Kindergarten Training College during the same year. Her 1911 visit to Perth inspired the formation of the Kindergarten Union of Western Australia. In 1914, she travelled to Rome to study with Maria Montessori.[168] Her return to Adelaide left a strong Montessori influence on South Australia kindergartens. In 1917, de Lissa left Australia to take up the position as principal of the Gipsy Hill Training

College, a teacher-training institute in Surrey, England, where she lived until her death in 1967.[169] Her distinguished career, and in the end, her relatively brief tenure as an educationist in Australia, had a lasting effect on kindergarten in that country. An excellent public speaker with a commitment to early education, she was at least partly responsible for spreading kindergartens beyond Sydney and Melbourne.

Another feature of the kindergartens was a belief that they had a social value as a safeguard against crime. The 1891 report of the Dunedin Free Kindergarten Association reflected the influence of the Golden Gate Association: "The moral uplift that this work will give to our population may be gathered from the fact that not one name of the 7,000 children who have passed through the free kindergartens of San Francisco has been found upon the police records."[170] This statistic was held up as proof that kindergartens were worthwhile investments. Strangely, the colonial programs persisted in citing the San Francisco statistics even after their own programs had operated for several decades. According to the Kindergarten Union of New South Wales (KUNSW), even by 1922, only one child had gone astray: "Out of the eight thousand children arrested in San Francisco only one had been trained at a kindergarten, and the Chief of Police there said that he believed Kindergarten training to be a perfect protection against criminal tendencies."[171] The origin of this statistic is obscure, and remarkably, as the number of children served by the Golden Gate kindergartens grew year by year, there continued to be just the one wayward child.

A kindergarten education, it was argued, could deter delinquent behaviour. Like the Golden Gate Association, the KUNSW compared the small operating costs of kindergartens with the price of remedial treatments: "Every prisoner in [New South Wales] eleven years ago cost annually £52. The annual cost of a child in the Kindergarten was 45s; and let us bear in mind that every neglected child is a potential criminal, a waster or pauper."[172] The oft-repeated sentiment was that "formation is cheaper than reformation."[173] Similar arguments were made on behalf of infant schools and ragged schools.[174]

The rhetoric surrounding kindergartens revealed a fear of civil and political unrest led by poor working-class immigrants. This view of immigrants was held by Francis Wayland Parker (1837-1902), who looked to the kindergarten as a solution to the "terrible problems of anarchy, of socialism, of trade oppression, [and] of trade-unionism."[175] A fear of anarchy also occupied the Winnipeg Free Kindergarten Association, which claimed that "many of the criminal families and anarchists could be traced to some neglected children."[176] In the words of a Sydney newspaper report, kindergarten would "inoculate" poor children so that they would not become "centres of infection for the better brought up children" whom they would join in the melting pot of the public elementary school.[177] Similar ideas, expressed in somewhat softer terms, persisted for decades: without kindergartens, the Kindergarten Union of New South Wales claimed, young children "grow feeling they are a nuisance to everyone, and that tends to give them a natural hatred for authority, and this is a very bad beginning for our future citizens."[178] On the other hand, the normalizing role of kindergarten education was viewed positively as a solution to the problem of the growing gap between rich and poor. In Parker's view, anarchists and trade unionists were taking advantage of the uneducated masses: "Education, not collective bargaining [was] the means of integrating industrial wage slaves into the new industrial society."[179]

The social-welfare role of free kindergartens in the colonies was firmly established by 1910. The teacher-training branch of the Kindergarten Union of New South Wales was Froebel-based, but the fundraising material focused entirely on child saving, not child development. As described by Maybanke Anderson (Wolstenhome) in her history of the Australian movement, "In a scientific kindergarten, every occupation is a training in industry, every game is a lesson in citizenship ... Each kindergarten is a centre for social work in the home surrounding it."[180] In this volume, Froebel is never mentioned, nor is any educational benefit — the complexity of the kindergarten idea giving way to a singular social-welfare ideology.

Charity infant schools, free kindergartens, and later, free nursery schools shared similar goals of redemption and basic education for poor children. The academic infant school evolved into the public schools as the infants' class. Kindergarten work in the context of the infants' class supported academic goals as preparation for the next grade level. Teachers in infants' classes seemed to appreciate the work of the kindergartener. One of these, a Dunedin teacher, commented approvingly on pupils who had attended kindergarten: "In teaching them, I have scarcely any trouble; they are more tractable, their little faculties are more developed, and they settle to their work with more heartiness of purpose than other incoming pupils."[181] There appeared to be a transfer of learning from the kindergarten to the primary school. The secretary of the Dunedin Free Kindergarten Association pointed to the inroads that the free kindergarten had made in the United States, particularly to the integration of kindergartens into public schools. The association's annual report recorded her view: "Surely a progressive and astute nation like America would not be likely to make a mistake in this matter, and she believed this colony could not do better than copy her example."[182]

chapter 7   **Winnipeg Free Kindergarten Association**

THE WINNIPEG FREE KINDERGARTEN Association (Winnipeg FKA) opened its first kindergarten in November 1892, at about the same time as the Methodist All People's Mission (APM) was organized. Over the years, the two charities were closely tied in Winnipeg's small kindergarten network. A student in the Winnipeg FKA training school apprenticed at the APM, and for a time an APM kindergarten was in the charge of a former director of the Winnipeg FKA. However, though kindergarten work in both organizations included a religious dimension, the Winnipeg FKA was principally an educational and social-welfare service. Its statement of purpose affirmed its link to Froebel's ideals: "The work of this Association is based upon the principles laid down by the founder of the system, Fredrick Froebel. Wherever such free kindergartens exist, little children are kept off the streets, and in the pleasantest manner possible their faculties are bent in the right direction; the first principles of correct living, such as good manners, habits of cleanliness, and industry, are unconsciously learned."[1] The association was formed in 1892, spearheaded by Winnipeg resident Martha Colby. Trained as a teacher in Quebec, she came west during the 1880s and had travelled to Chicago to study at a kindergarten college. For a time, she operated a private kindergarten in Winnipeg's wealthy South End, bringing her pupils to the free kindergarten to demonstrate the program to the mothers.[2]

Although the association never developed a network of kindergartens — it operated for most of its history at a single site — it sought a permanent physical presence in the area it served.[3] Its territory was the working-class neighbourhood, home to many newcomers, adjacent to the Canadian Pacific Railway terminal and the immigration halls. Enrolment increased rapidly, from five on the first day to forty-seven after five months. The kindergarten initially operated out of rented quarters, moving five times in the first five years. The board's main consideration for location was that the kindergarten be near its targeted clientele. In 1896, the kindergarten relocated because the board "did not feel satisfied with the number or class of children we were then reaching."[4] In its new location, the administrators enthused, "We have nearly all our old pupils, with a great many new and more destitute children living in the north end."[5] This suggests that the pupils were being drawn south to the kindergarten from across the vast CPR yards. A move north of the railway tracks in 1898 into the Swedish Lutheran church at the corner of Ellen and Logan Streets marked the beginning of a long period of stability. This became the association's permanent address and site of a newly built kindergarten known as the Ellen Street Kindergarten. Construction began in 1903 and the Ellen Street Kindergarten opened in December 1904. The building included a gymnasium in the basement for club work with boys, a workroom on the ground floor, and the kindergarten on the upper floor.[6] It was also designed to accommodate meeting rooms for sewing classes and clubs. Although the development was a mark of progress for the association — in a period of twelve years, it had exchanged a shack for a structure of some importance — the move into a purpose-built school helped entrench kindergarten in Winnipeg as a social-welfare service. This was not the association's original intent: in 1890, the Manitoba Schools Act had made provision for the public school kindergarten, but the Winnipeg School Board decided not to open its own programs, so the Winnipeg FKA attempted to spur interest in their instigation.

Believing that the twentieth century demanded new ways of thinking, the Winnipeg FKA board initiated fundraising with great expectations. An address by the board president at the annual meeting in 1902 outlined an ambitious agenda for the association, in language mixing religious imagery with kindergarten philosophy:

> The new Free Kindergarten building we hope will be the Mother House of our work. Within another decade we hope to see other crowded districts, provided with Kindergartens where other little

folks will have the same lovely opportunity to unfold along right lines that those in this neighborhood enjoy ... In our new building each department will have space and equipment. Our aim is to make this new house a home of wholesome Christian influence, presided over by a kind and wise House-Mother, whose duties will be to keep in touch with the homes of the poorest and their needs, to encourage parents to send their little ones to the sunny, cheerful kindergarten, to welcome mothers at the mothers' meetings and give them wise counsel at all times, and, in the evenings, keep an attractive home for the boys or factory girls (who are obliged to board), where they may read, sew, or study.[7]

Initial attendance was disappointing: though eighty students were enrolled, the average daily attendance was forty. The president's review of the first year's work in the new building was guarded. Drawing on an agricultural image of rust fungus interfering with crop growth, she observed: "While the work has not grown as rapidly as we hoped it would, and we sometimes feared the 'rust' had attached [to] it, still there has been considerable progress."[8]

Entrenchment

The slow attendance growth at the new kindergarten did not halt the board's expansion plans. By 1906, the president announced "we now feel enabled to extend our work in a more thickly settled district" and added that a new school would be opened "when the weather is mild for the little ones to walk."[9] The next year, the board opened a branch school in the Sherman Street Presbyterian Church, just a few blocks west of the Ellen Street Kindergarten. The area proved fertile ground for kindergarten work, with high enrolment from the start, and the board undertook to raise funds to construct a second purpose-built kindergarten at this location. This branch, called the Froebel School, opened at 676 Alexander Avenue in 1909. The choice of name was significant, occurring in the heat of the debate in US kindergarten circles regarding the merits of Gift and handwork versus free play; it placed the Winnipeg association on the side of the conservatives.

The director at the Froebel School observed that homes in the neighbourhood were poor — "Just the sort we want to reach."[10] Other charities recognized the same need and concentrated their work in the area. Like the Froebel School, the Mother's Association Day Nursery opened in 1909, as did the Stella Avenue Mission, a Methodist settlement house that also had a kindergarten. At this time, attendance at both the Ellen Street Kindergarten and the Froebel School was high, and it seems that no child was ever turned away. On one day in 1909, 109 children attended the single session at the Froebel School, and it was not unusual for 75 to attend each of the two sessions at the Ellen Street branch.

The schools had obviously found acceptance among parents, though they would probably not have agreed with the association's assessment of their home life, as expressed by long-time Winnipeg FKA teacher Jeannie Lothrop: "Many of the homes our children come from are homes where the children grow up like weeds, with such environments as tend to develop only the lower nature of the child. The parents are in many cases unfit to train their children, or when the mother is a bread-winner, the children are left to themselves."[11] She believed in the malleability of the developing child and that changes in individuals could occur through instruction in social and moral codes, leading "a child to choose good in obedience to a command from within, rather than from without."[12] This benefit would ripple outward from individuals into the community, from children to their parents.

As it approached its ten-year anniversary, the president of the association remarked on the "steady movement upward amongst our Kindergarten families." She explained, "Many have moved into better homes with more comforts, and mothers have learnt to have a more thoughtful care for their little ones. The children themselves have become imbued with a love for school (an important item where there is no compulsory school law). Into the old shacks and dwellings come other families who are promptly visited and invited to send their children to the Kindergarten, and so the process of elevating goes on."[13]

This was a larger task than could be achieved via kindergarten activities alone. From the first year, the kindergarten provided for the children's physical needs by serving a "light lunch"; in the winter of 1897, when it was discovered that some children came to school without eating breakfast, hot soup was added to the menu. A sewing machine was donated so that mothers could make their children's clothing on-site, and the kindergarten teacher organized a sewing club. Individuals or groups outside the Winnipeg FKA offered services at the Ellen Street branch after hours. In the first few years of its operation, the Winnipeg FKA either sponsored or supported mothers' meetings, girls' and boys' clubs, and a Sunday school in addition to the kindergarten, the range of programs remaining unchanged over the next fifty years.

Even before building the Ellen Street Kindergarten, the Winnipeg FKA identified its approach as settlement work. In 1901, the president, who was inspired by kindergartens she had observed in settlements in New York City, believed the Winnipeg FKA should move more firmly in this direction. A 1915 name change to the Kindergarten Settlement Association of Winnipeg (KSAW) formalized this orientation. As the president explained, "It was pointed out that our work being both charitable and educational, in fact true settlement work, the proposed change would convey a more correct idea as to the scope of our activities."[14] These included direct services for adult family members and others in the community who may have had no connection to the kindergarten. The aim for adult clients was the same as for children: Anglo-conformity and citizenship education alongside philanthropic aims to support families by helping them meet basic needs. It was supposed that the "interesting lectures on Canada" held at the Winnipeg FKA "may develop loyalty to our King and Government in the hearts of those who have come from other lands to make their home amongst us."[15]

Settlement organizations in Winnipeg, including the secular kindergarten association and church-organized neighbourhood houses, shared a mission orientation toward their clients. In this way, they were more similar to the settlements described by Howard Jacob Karger in Minneapolis than to Hull House in Chicago or Toynbee Hall in London.[16] The Minneapolis settlement houses, including Wells Memorial House, where several Winnipeg FKA kindergarteners continued their training, were paternalistic in their approach, with programs that rarely followed through on settlement ideology's desire to empower clients.

A common concern in Winnipeg FKA reports was that the settlement was not reaching the neediest children or parents. The mothers' meetings organized by the kindergarten director in the early years were poorly attended. On occasion, the director was the only person present, a situation described as being "not quite satisfactory."[17] Not having a common language was a hindrance to greater attendance; although many mothers were German speaking, the meetings were run entirely in English. Leaders of other programs at the settlement also questioned their impact. The supervisor of the Boys' Brigade, a youth club, believed that, though attendance was satisfactory, he was not reaching the right boys: "Boys who had good homes should be at home in the evenings, and it was only the *homeless* ones *he* wanted."[18]

Searching out the neediest children was a role of the kindergarten director. Each school day, she went door to door, collecting children for school and spreading the word about kindergartens in the neighbourhood. Until 1899, her afternoons were filled with additional home visits; after this point, her work with teacher-training classes limited them to three days a week. As Jeannie Lothrop suggested, thus immersed in the community, the teacher could see firsthand "amid what poverty and degradation some human flowers are developing."[19]

Home visits became a specialized area of work in 1906, when a deaconess joined the staff. She was a graduate of a deaconess-training school in Toronto, which offered practical training for community work along with a theological education.[20] At least three deaconesses worked at the Winnipeg FKA from 1906 to 1913. The extent of their casework highlights the load previously carried by the kindergarten director. In 1907, the deaconess conducted eleven hundred visits. This was too much for one of them, who was reported to have had "a serious nervous breakdown ... due to overstrain."[21] In some instances, the deaconess offered help on the spot, seeking medical aid for the sick or providing warm clothing for families experiencing their first Winnipeg winter. At other times, she conducted home investigations in the manner of a social worker to determine appropriate aid, referring some cases to the Associated Charities.

The first Winnipeg FKA kindergarten director was Miss Fleming (first name unknown), for whom there is little record other than that she was a local resident who had trained in an unidentified Chicago school. She was replaced in 1894 by Jeannie King Barnett (who became Lothrop upon her 1901 marriage). With brief periods of absence, Lothrop continued as a director until 1910.[22] She directed the Maple Street Mission Kindergarten, opened in the former Congregational Church in 1902. From 1903 to 1904, Lothrop directed the Methodist All People's Mission Kindergarten. A need for assistants led the association to launch a formal pupil-teacher scheme under her direction, in which girls aged seventeen and over were offered a year's training through a combination of afternoon lectures and practical work with children in the morning.

From 1897, students were given the option of writing an examination, similar to the one set by the Toronto Normal School, which mainly tested their knowledge of Gifts and occupations. Starting about 1900 this examination was used by the Manitoba Department of Education for its

Methodist All People's Mission Kindergarten class, Winnipeg, 1904, with teacher Jeannie King Lothrop at the right. N13261, Archives of Manitoba, Winnipeg.

kindergarten teacher-training course, which was taught by Lothrop.[23] The Winnipeg FKA provided the only kindergarten training in Manitoba, and four of Lothrop's students passed the department's exam in the first year. This led her to remark, "We are getting the teachers ready for the schools we hope to have some day."[24] The day did not arrive for forty years, and most Winnipeg FKA trainees who pursued a teaching career found employment elsewhere. Those who stayed in Winnipeg had limited options. Two completed a second year of training at Wells Memorial House in Minneapolis and opened a private kindergarten upon their return to Winnipeg. The superintendent of Winnipeg schools told a teacher newly graduated from Oberlin Kindergarten Training School in Ohio that the only class available for her to teach would be "a backward grade 1."[25] She opted to open a private kindergarten in her family home for children from wealthy families. By the time the Winnipeg FKA training scheme ended in 1920, thirty students had graduated; those who were still teaching worked in schools throughout Canada and the United States. At least, if there were no public kindergartens in Winnipeg, graduates were working elsewhere, "helping prepare the way for a kindergarten for every child and every child in kindergarten."[26]

Some trainees were employed at the Winnipeg FKA or mission kindergartens as assistants. However, most worked as unpaid assistants in exchange for free tuition.[27] Most directors had credentials from two- or three-year training programs at educational institutions outside Winnipeg. Some were local women returning home after a time away, whereas others were new to the city.

Under Jeannie Lothrop's direction the Froebel kindergarten system was emphasized. She had trained in Ontario, most likely at the Hamilton or Toronto Normal School, where she would have learned a formal approach. Miss Copus (first name unknown), director in the new Ellen Street Kindergarten, is known to have trained at the Toronto Normal School. It was during her tenure that a deaconess was recruited to conduct community work, including collecting children from their homes in order to bring them to the kindergarten. This reassignment of roles may have been due to the opening of an afternoon session. Copus resigned in 1907 and was replaced by Alma Anthony (training unknown), who stayed for one year. Jeannie Lothrop returned in the same year to take charge of the branch school at the Sherman Street Presbyterian Church.

When the Froebel School opened in 1909, Lothrop was appointed its director. Her former student Isabel Coulter — the first Manitoban to graduate from the in-house training program in 1902 — directed the Ellen Street branch. After an initial period of varying attendance, there was an average of forty-five children in the morning-only program at the Froebel School. Lothrop resumed the practice of collecting the children and bringing them to school. Except for brief periods, neither branch had a paid assistant, and both operated with the help of student teachers. Lothrop was put in charge of training, operating what was called an assistants' training class. A total of six students trained in 1910, completing their apprenticeships at Ellen Street, the Froebel School, and a kindergarten at a branch of the All People's Mission. Classes were held on two afternoons each week, and students probably assisted in the kindergarten at other times.

In May 1893 Elise Payne Adams gave a lecture in Winnipeg on kindergartens, outlining the social and educational aims of the work. Her visit was timed to draw attention to the Winnipeg effort. Her credentials were excellent: principal of the kindergarten association in Minneapolis, she had trained with Alice Putnam at the Chicago Froebel Association Training

School and had graduated from the Cook County Normal School.[28] Her lecture stressed that, through their time in kindergarten, children could build their "character for good citizenship" and could get a head start on schooling, enabling them to "do two years' of work of the schools in one year with great ease and ability."[29] She added that kindergartens could ameliorate social problems. Citing Sarah Cooper's "statistics" from the Golden Gate kindergartens in San Francisco, she noted that only one of their nine thousand graduates had ever been arrested.

The discourse surrounding kindergartens in Winnipeg tended to feature moral purpose far more often than any academic benefit. If children were seen as "human flowers," they were also considered potential criminals. Years later, the San Francisco kindergartens were again the focus of a talk, this time given by Congregationalist minister J.B. Silcox at the Winnipeg FKA annual meeting. He appealed to the business community to understand the importance of kindergartens as a wise economic, social, and political investment. In San Francisco, he claimed, "Many of the criminal families and anarchists could be traced back to some neglected children. The making of good citizens of our boys and girls was the only safeguard for the future."[30] This repeated a theme of the secretary's report at the 1899 Winnipeg FKA annual meeting, in which it was claimed that, left unsupervised to play on the streets, "children are taught to be criminals before they know the awful meaning of the word; and to prevent this is the aim of the kindergarten."[31] Rhetoric on crime prevention was particularly strong during this time, when the association was seeking support for additional kindergartens. However, the Winnipeg FKA did not dwell so much on crime prevention, choosing to focus on adjustment education for the children of immigrants through English-language immersion and instruction in manners and social behaviour.[32] Easing children's transition to grade one was not a goal during the early years.

Children attending the kindergarten ranged in age from three to eight. They were ethnically diverse: in 1908, half were foreign-born, but the makeup changed over time, reflecting immigration and local mobility patterns. The national and ethnic origins of children were generally noted in annual reports. In 1893, children's families were Swedish, Scottish, English, and German; in 1896, they were German, Polish, Jewish, and English. Children from Britain were almost always in the majority, and by 1907, 80 percent were English speaking and 20 percent spoke German. The director noted, "What few real foreigners we have are very observing, picking up the language readily, showing a willingness and desire to do all the work. Many of them are very clever indeed."[33]

While the Winnipeg FKA sought to assimilate newcomer children, non-English-speaking immigrant communities such as the German Catholics and Lutherans strived to preserve their ethnic identity and religion by establishing parochial schools, often as part of a church and headed by trained teachers.[34] In the case of the German community, these proved difficult to sustain and were not supported by all parents, some of whom believed that students attending parochial schools were poorly prepared for a later transfer to public schools. However, parochial schools and secular organizations such as benevolent associations, clubs, and newspapers promoted bilingual education. Although the aims of the Winnipeg FKA concerning the rapid assimilation of foreigners matched the government position, they were at odds with the desire of some immigrant communities to pursue bilingual education and sustain their national identity.

In addition, newcomer families were mobile, and often the Winnipeg FKA's impact on children was only briefly felt. In 1904, the board characterized attendance as "floating," with an average of 40 from a total enrolment of 80 to 120.[35] Sixty-six children moved out of the neighbourhood during the year, and fifty-two left to attend public school.

Classes were initially offered in the morning only, with an afternoon kindergarten at the Ellen Street branch started for children who lived too far away to arrive on time for the morning session. Attendance increased on a periodic basis, notably at the start of the school year. In September 1906, seventy-five children attended, some of them underage siblings: "So many little girls brought the baby also, that the school sometimes looked like a nursery, for on hot days the little ones would get sleepy and need a nap. At such times the need of an extra department in our work is keenly felt. It would be a splendid idea to convert the downstairs room into a nursery, where mothers who have to go out working can leave the babies. At present the older children must either stay at home or else bring the baby to kindergarten."[36] An 1893 experiment with a crèche terminated when it was determined that the service was not needed, there being only one baby in attendance — though "not always the same one" — over the four months of its operation.[37]

The kindergarten combined group activities such as marching, singing, and storytelling with individual work using Gifts and occupations, during which children sat at long tables. Indicating that occupations and Gifts were used, a newspaper reporter noted the children's "careful interlacing of bright coloured bits of paper."[38] Moral training involved teaching Anglo-Canadian social manners and work habits, developing children's ability to "exercise their powers of choice wisely."[39] The prevalent idea was that foreign families in the frontier city were ill-equipped to rear their children in accordance with the standards for Canadian citizenship, as the Winnipeg FKA president made clear in her address at the tenth anniversary annual meeting: "Preventative work is always easier and cheaper than punitive or corrective work ... In this Western land of ours there is an absence of restraint on the part of parents and guardians that one regards with foreboding, there is therefore the highest wisdom in providing such helps as the Kindergarten in assisting parents in the noble work of training and restraining their children."[40] Kindergarten operated for eleven months of the year, closing for vacation in July. The Ellen Street branch held two sessions each day, starting at 10:00 a.m. and 2:00 p.m. Teacher Alma Anthony described the daily schedule and program philosophy in the 1907 annual report:

> Each session is opened with a child's prayer and songs of praise. The child is brought in contact with nature, and through his physical viewing of the life about him he is led gradually and unconsciously to feel that God is everywhere, and he loves every little animal, every flower, and that without God our world would not be so beautiful. Each week has its special thought, illustrated by stories, songs, pictures, talks, games, and in some of the handwork at the tables. In this way lessons of self-control, politeness, kindness, courage, bravery, patriotism, unselfishness, and neatness are brought to the children ... The table work comprises handwork, as sewing, weaving, cutting, pasting, freehand drawing, lessons with the blocks, sticks and rings, giving him his first ideas of form, measurement, building and designing. The kindergarten is a bridge between the home life and public school life. It is learning through play, the younger children having more play with their work than the older ones. Games have also an important place in the work, as play is an expression of what is within us and the true nature of the child is shown in his play.[41]

Having a first-hand look at the homes of children made some kindergarten directors more critical than sympathetic. Isabel Coulter offered, "In our work we find much poverty and sin; and the poverty is too often the result of shiftlessness or sinful indulgence."[42] To make up for impoverished home conditions, "we make our kindergarten as beautiful as we can, that he may see good things." She elaborated: "We teach songs and tell stories that have the right sentiments, that he may hear good things; and we train him to use his hands at work period, and play games that have right underlying principles, that he may do good things. Even such seeming trifles as building his blocks on the squares of the table, marching in good time, folding his hands in prayer, and so on, help in making him exact in his work, methodical in his ways, and reverent in his feelings."[43]

Other programs offered directly by the Winnipeg FKA targeted older children, but for similar reasons. In the Kitchen Garden, girls aged six to twelve were taught "housework with toys." Prior to initiating this class, the Winnipeg FKA secretary corresponded with the founder of the Kitchen Garden idea, Emily Huntington, matron at the Wilson Industrial School in New York City. The board then purchased the necessary material, called the "Kitchen-garden Outfit," which cost $100 for a class of twenty-four.[44]

The Kitchen Garden was planned as a means to train domestic servants.[45] Children used tools of regular and miniature size to learn household work via song and drill. A report in the *New York Times*, part of a series on the topic of domestic servants, described the situation at the Wilson Industrial School:

> One of the features of the mission work is the dinner which is given every day at noon to the children who attend school. Four little kitchen and two little parlor maids are selected from these children to assist in the work each week ... The little parlor maid dusts, sweeps the bare floor of the halls, and answers the bell, being excused from duty long enough to go to the school on an upper floor and recite her lessons. Just before dinner is served she dresses up neatly in a clean, white apron, to be ready to wait on the tables. In the meantime, the kitchenmaids have set the table for the children and for the teachers in their private dining room ... The afternoon kitchenmaids wash the dishes from the teachers' table and assist with those the children have used.[46]

Reconstruction

Economic difficulties brought on by wartime dealt a harsh blow to the Winnipeg FKA. With two kindergartens to staff and two buildings to maintain, the association struggled from year to year, dependent for funding on subscriptions and donations. A severe financial shortfall in 1914 caused it to consider closing the Froebel School temporarily. Though it remained open, costs were cut, with the greatest saving coming from the free labour provided as part of their training by larger numbers of student teachers. Despite the flourishing training school, the association was forced to close the Froebel School in 1917. Its German name may also have been a factor. Hostilities toward Winnipeg's German community during the First World War included destruction of property, physical attacks, and boycotts of businesses and products with German names.[47] The association retained the building until 1926, when it was sold and converted to a private residence.

The end of the Froebel School and the association's financial problems coincided with the input of a new group of teachers who infused the kindergarten program with progressive ideas. The directors following Jeannie Lothrop were Ella Aikman (McKellar) (1911-16) and Helen McLean (1917-19). Both had trained at US schools oriented toward kindergarten-primary work. For Lothrop, the purpose of the kindergarten was purely "character building," laying the stress on work habits.[48] At the same time, some evidence does indicate that she saw the purpose of kindergarten as developing the whole child. Coulter, the director for part of 1911, whom Lothrop had trained, was clearly influenced by psychology. In explaining the role of play, she observed, "The shy or self-conscious child gains confidence by losing himself in some simple play, in which he imitates something he has seen."[49] By this time, the idea that play involved social imitation was perceived as a Froebelian principle.[50]

Ella Aikman attended Manitoba College for one year, and at about age twenty, she trained informally under a Toronto Normal School graduate at the Robertson House Kindergarten in Winnipeg, a mission of Robertson Memorial Presbyterian Church.[51] In 1911, she completed formal training at Kalamazoo's Western State Normal School, which was headed by Lucy Gage, earning both a kindergarten and a life teaching certificate.[52] Gage had trained at the Chicago Free Kindergarten Institute with Anna Bryan and later at Teachers College, Columbia University with Patty Smith Hill. She developed the kindergarten-training curriculum at Western State Normal School as its first director in 1909 (see Table 1). Her program included texts by psychologists John Dewey, William Kilpatrick, and William James alongside Froebel and content from *Mother-Play*.[53]

Aikman's training incorporated recent thinking on kindergarten education, which was critical of literal interpretations of Froebel, and she carried

Table 1. Kindergarten courses at Western State Normal School, 1909

Name of course	Key author or theorist
An introductory course dealing with the child, his interests, his play	Amy Tanner, James Sully
Study of such phases of development as imagination and habit	William James
Techniques: Introduction to play materials; study of their values	—
A review of the process of interaction between the child and play materials with emphasis upon the teacher as mediator	Friedrich Froebel, William Kilpatrick
The application of principles as found in *Mother-Play*	Friedrich Froebel, John Dewey
Observation in city and Normal School Kindergartens	—
Study teaching: Each student teacher responsible for group 2 hours daily under supervision	—

Source: Agnes Snyder, *Dauntless Women in Childhood Education 1856-1931* (Washington: Association for Childhood Education International, 1972), 336–37.

these views back to Winnipeg. She began her first director's report in 1911 with a quotation from Teachers College philosophy professor John Mac-Vannel, not Froebel: "The kindergarten may be defined as a society of little children engaged in play and its various forms of self-expression, through which the child comes to learning something of the values and methods of social life without as yet, being burdened by its intellectual technique."[54] Aikman demonstrated her concern for the role of kindergarten in preparing children for grade one:

> We consider the whole child — his physical, mental and moral nature — and give each a chance for development. Physically — the child's body is the tool with which he must work through life. Children are exceedingly active and we give them fitting environment and right channels for the expression of the activity in hand work, games and rhythmic marching. Mentally — the Kindergarten furnishes a background for the formal study of reading, writing, arithmetic, geometry, music and geography. As regards reading, a child who has been in Kindergarten enters the public school with a stock of good stories and poems, and is at home with the subject matter of reading, and therefore soon masters its symbols. Writing — the processes involved in writing the child gets in Kindergarten from

holding and directing a pencil, crayon or brush, from observing models, reproducing copy, and connecting symbols and ideas. Arithmetic — number and form are characteristic of much handwork and many games so that the child obtains ideas of geometry and simple combinations of numbers. Geography — through the use of sand children delight in laying out riverbed and mountain, etc. Music — the children hear good, simple songs and music, and much attention is given to rhythm work. In short, the Kindergarten saves wasted time and power, and conserves the energy of the child, giving him increased power and control, through organized play. Morally — the child learns of God, of His beneficence to man in the changing seasons, and His loving care for His creatures. Thus the child is better fitted for school and for life for having had a Kindergarten training.[55]

Aikman's whole-child approach was distinct from Lothrop's stress on character building and industrial education, and at least on paper, it suggested a curriculum revolution at the Winnipeg FKA. Yet, changes were subtle. Although children used materials such as the Froebel blocks in less prescribed ways, the Gifts remained a mainstay of the program.

The association's perception of poor families as problem families also persisted. In 1912, prior to the economic downturn, a building boom and expansion of the business area encroached on the neighbourhood of the Winnipeg FKA, but there was "no dearth of children."[56] After twenty years, the association continued as a popular service with parents in the neighbourhood, but it remained unlikely that they understood the manner in which the Winnipeg FKA viewed them. In selling the program to donors, the association retained its earlier approach of instilling fear in the wealthy classes, stressing the low morals and criminal tendencies of the poor and immigrant families that were its clients. The problems listed in the 1914 annual report as besetting kindergarten families — drunkenness, idleness, and the absence of a compulsory schooling law — were similar to the "shiftlessness" and "sinful indulgence" cited in the 1910 report.[57] Reports from the organizing committee retained the flavour of the old, claiming, "There is work both of prevention and of up-building which may be done before the school age and the omission of which at that time can never be made up. Is it not unwise to overlook the earliest seed time?"[58]

The training program, now formally called the Winnipeg FKA Training School, grew under Aikman's direction to a record high of twelve students in 1915, the most it would ever enrol. Training consisted of lectures on the theory and practice of kindergarten Gifts and handwork, child study, and kindergarten principles with practical work involving songs, games, music, and stories. The three new students who joined the training school in 1917 were judged "rich in qualities and womanly traits which will tend to make them successful teachers of little children."[59] Most graduates from the one-year course successfully sat for the departmental examination, but not all went on to teach in a kindergarten. Nonetheless, it was considered an "ideal profession for a young woman, for the one reason that it carries over into the home better than most professions."[60] Whatever her ambitions, a graduate was enabled "to become an intelligent social server, a kindergartener, having a conscious insight into the principles and methods of elementary education, and an understanding and appreciation of the principles that govern the home and society with the power and ability of adjustment."[61]

Despite the larger numbers of students, Aikman believed there were too few to sustain the association's kindergartens, a state of affairs she attributed to a lack of public support and the limited teaching opportunities in Winnipeg.[62] At various periods, Aikman directed the Froebel School as the sole trained teacher, with students working at the Ellen Street Kindergarten under her supervision.

The association (called the Kindergarten Settlement Association of Winnipeg from 1915) commonly hired former students after they had completed their studies in the US. Two of these, Mabel Lindsay and Olive Smith, returned to become directors: Lindsay had studied at Miss Wheelock's Kindergarten Training School in Boston, and Smith at Oberlin Kindergarten Training School in Ohio.[63] Helen McLean, who was given the title of lecturer at the KSAW, also graduated from Oberlin after studying with Aikman.[64] The Oberlin connection to Winnipeg was strong: seven additional KSAW students went to Oberlin during McLean's time as director. Despite the interest in kindergarten work in Canada, there were no private schools offering two-year diplomas and no Normal School kindergarten training in western Canada during this period. This differed from the United States (in Chicago alone, there were five private training schools) and from Australia and New Zealand, where local kindergarten unions had established kindergarten colleges with two- or three-year programs. As one result of this, kindergarteners in western Canada had diverse training. The director of kindergartens at the Regina Public Schools, for example, received her initial training under Aikman at the Winnipeg FKA in 1913, continuing her studies at the Pestalozzi-Froebel Kindergarten Training School in Chicago.[65]

Aikman's vision for the curriculum stressed social aims: "Our chief aim in our Kindergarten this year is to make a little world of our own, which shall follow as closely as possible the main features of the great world in which the children will soon have to struggle."[66] This goal was accomplished through a mix of structured play and lessons. The class began with a "morning talk," with children seated in chairs in a circle. They shared their news of the day with the group and sang hymns and other songs.[67] In dramatization, they enacted the roles of workers — here called community helpers — such as a carpenter, blacksmith, baker, and street cleaner. In handwork, they used simple materials to construct representations of the weekly theme. Rhythm work, storytelling, and games rounded out the program.

Teachers continued to use kindergarten Gifts alongside sets of larger blocks for free play. In 1915, students in a high school manual training class donated twenty-five sets of small blocks, ensuring an abundant supply. Other materials included a sandbox and goldfish bowl, and the children tended a garden outdoors.[68] The aim, as in the earlier years, was character building, teaching children to acquire good work habits, to distinguish between right and wrong decisions, and to be self-reliant, creative, and able to make good choices. Although this was seen as citizenship training, the earlier overt references to acquiring Anglo-Canadian values had disappeared, a situation that may have been due to the reduced numbers of children from non-English-speaking families.

Ella Aikman made a fine distinction between the educational and vocational role of kindergarten: it was educational insofar as children's energies were directed into useful activity and vocational as they received training in doing useful things. For school-aged girls, this meant Kitchen Garden activities such as setting tables, dusting, and making beds, work led by Aikman as training for domestic service. For younger children, it meant training through their play. Though called "free play," it was structured by Aikman to fit vocational training objectives. Play in kindergarten was not the same as children's free-time activities on the street or at home, which Aikman did not perceive as purposeful play. Children were therefore taught to play in the kindergarten mode, where play was a teaching strategy.

Teachers based play activities on their interpretation of children's interests. This involved their observation of favourite play themes, such as the work of the milkman or postman, along with a theory of learning that held that children learned most effectively through their own exploration. In the words of Aikman, "The little child is interested in seeing things ... doing things ... talking about things ... playing with things."[69] The emphasis on learning to do useful things changed under Helen McLean, who highlighted child development rather than training, perhaps due to the influence of her training with Clara May at Oberlin. Again, this was a fine distinction, and what was determined development as opposed to training was not clearly evident. Clara May assumed her position as Oberlin director during 1915 in which McLean arrived there.[70] May was herself a graduate of the first class at Oberlin in 1894. In 1914, before becoming director, she attended Maria Montessori's training course in Rome, the same year as the Australian Lillian de Lissa, and she introduced Montessori materials to the kindergarten at Oberlin.[71]

McLean described six domains of child development: locomotion, communication, construction, exploration, invention, and social interest.[72] In her vision of the "new" kindergarten, emphasis was placed on skill training, using content with a high appeal to young children. As an example, McLean described her variation on Froebel's occupation in the 1916 annual report:

> There are certain steps to be followed when presenting materials to children. For example, it has been found that clipping and fringing paper is the simplest form of cutting, but how tiresome it would be unless there was some purpose in view. This has been one of our problems, to use the child's efforts and bring about a definite result. We have fringed paper and then made it into brooms, mats for doll houses and various other things. The other materials have been used with the same aim. Instead of cutting Teddy bears from brown paper as we sometimes have done in outline cuttings, we gave the children the parts and had them put the Teddy bear together with fasteners, so that the head, arms and legs would move easily.[73]

Although it seemed innocuous, this account of a craft activity well known to subsequent generations of kindergarten children was a strong statement that the formal sequence of occupations and Gifts needed to be abandoned. The elimination of occupations, McLean wrote, was a response to criticism from psychologists and physicians as well as educators. No such criticism had been voiced in Winnipeg, so the idea must have come from her training at Oberlin. She consciously conceived the changes as progress:

"Kindergartners now are striving to hold fast to that which is good, while pressing forward in the endless quest for the better — the best — the ideal."[74]

McLean continued to push for curriculum change: in the next year, she initiated what she termed the "experiment method," which was similar to William Kilpatrick's project work and John Dewey's theory of experience.[75] In fact, her description of the method was freely drawn from an article written by Meredith Smith regarding a lecture Dewey had given at Teachers College in 1913.[76] As McLean explained,

> Last year we were using the experiment method trying to lead the children to think to work out problems for themselves and develop reasoning powers. This power cannot be added to, we believe, but unless it is kept active it will decrease. This falling away may be caused by three things (1) frittering away of time by using materials with no definite end in view; (2) by too much dictated work; (3) by presenting ready made, finished toys which are complete in themselves, calling for no energy from the child and leaving no place for invention and experimentation. An effort was made last year to work out a programme based on purpose and freedom in use of materials leading to experimentation. These plays started with suggestions from the children such as making milk bottles of clay, during a free play lesson. We then needed the milkman's basket, wagon, horse, cows, farm, etc., and in this way the whole community was built up even to streetcars, car barns and subway. In such absorbing occupation the children were really living and if it is true that children become like what they imitate we must believe that character will be influenced and modified for the better in this reproduction of human life through play.[77]

Isolation

For their first twenty years of operation, the KSAW kindergartens were isolated from developments in primary schooling. Although the association directors desired to demonstrate the educational benefits of kindergarten, the belief that it was properly a charity service was part of their thinking in the early years. Marion Bryce, Winnipeg FKA president in 1899, believed that the association would still be needed even if public kindergartens came into existence, as it offered services "quite outside the duties of teachers in the public schools."⁷⁸ Superintendent of Winnipeg Schools Daniel McIntyre served on the Winnipeg FKA's board from 1900. A champion of New Education in Winnipeg, McIntyre was responsible for introducing manual training into public elementary schools, but he showed no interest in making kindergarten a part of the scheme.⁷⁹ His view was that, with an estimated fifteen hundred to two thousand children in the city who were aged four to seven, the cost of providing up to forty kindergartens was too high.⁸⁰ However, he did speak before the City of Winnipeg Financial Committee to ask for a grant for building the Ellen Street Kindergarten.⁸¹

In 1916, at the height of its financial emergency, the association considered requesting financial support from the public school board, as was done in settlement house kindergartens in New York City and elsewhere, but it took no action at that time. In 1920, the Winnipeg School District agreed to pay the association teachers, an arrangement that continued until 1923. At that point, the school board discontinued it for its own financial reasons, claiming as well that the number of trained teachers was insufficient and that the kindergarten had not yet proven itself, though the KSAW had operated more than thirty years.⁸² After this time, the newly created Winnipeg Federation for Community Services paid teachers' salaries.

This solidified the KSAW's role as a small-scale child-welfare service. It lacked a teacher-training program, and kindergartens were not expected to be included in schools. However, through the influence of directors trained at Normal Schools, and the brief involvement of the school board, the curriculum resembled that in public school kindergartens elsewhere, including academic readiness activities and project work. There was also some increased co-operation between the association and the neighbourhood school. In September 1926, eighteen six-year-olds remained at the kindergarten beyond compulsory school age because the local school was overcrowded, joining the grade one class at Christmas.

At this time, KSAW pupils came from diverse national origins reflecting the general immigration patterns in western Canada as well as the occasional influx of religious or ethnic groups. In 1926, there was a rise in the number of Mennonite children whose families had settled in the district. Once again, as in the early years of the kindergarten, it was noted that some students could not speak English.

Greater attention was paid to children's health than in previous years. During the period in which the school board paid the teachers' salaries, this had been monitored by a school nurse. In addition, a paid staff member replaced the deaconess in 1925. Though she was called a social worker, she was trained as a registered nurse. She established links with various agencies in Winnipeg, making 113 referrals in her first year to the Children's Aid Society, YMCA, Children's Bureau, Social Welfare Commission, Juvenile Court, Psychopathic Hospital, Day Nursery, and the City Health Office. Within a few years, her future was assured: her portion of the annual report became longer than that of the kindergarten director. Like the deaconess before her, she visited every home in the area having a child of kindergarten age. Families were not only encouraged to send their children — they were seen as suspect if they did not. The social worker discussed this situation in 1926, when she revealed that "there were several families in the district in which the parents presented a problem. They persisted in keeping their children (of kindergarten age) at home for no apparent reason."[83]

The KSAW ceased its training program in 1920, when the school board assumed responsibility for teachers' salaries, and assistant teachers were untrained and changed from year to year. Lacking any branch kindergartens, and with no plan for expansion, the KSAW no longer needed a training program. Some programs were given over to non-professionals to manage, including the Kitchen Garden, which had been the responsibility of the kindergarten teacher. In 1924, it was run by a group of board members who led the girls, aged six to ten, as they used "toy apparatus" to "learn to wash clothes, iron, sweep, dust, set tables, make beds, and also to sew."[84]

Helen McLean left the KSAW to join the teaching staff at the Oberlin Kindergarten Training School, where she directed a practice kindergarten, worked as a "critic teacher" with students, and taught handwork.[85] (For a list of Oberlin's kindergarten-training courses, see Table 2.) In 1928, she spent a semester at Teachers College, Columbia University.[86] *Childhood Education,* the International Kindergarten Union journal, noted that almost all critic teachers at Oberlin had degrees by this time. In 1932, McLean completed her master's degree at Teachers College, and in 1938, she left Oberlin to become director of kindergarten at the State Teachers College in Indiana, Pennsylvania.[87]

The influence of Ella Aikman and Helen McLean was long-lasting: after their departure, the KSAW undertook no new initiatives in pedagogy. From 1920 until 1932, all directors at the KSAW received their initial training with either Aikman or McLean: Phyllis Middleton in 1915, Gladys Best in 1917, and Edith Deacon in 1919. Best and Deacon went on to Ohio, where they graduated from Oberlin. Middleton completed her training at

Table 2. Kindergarten courses at Oberlin Kindergarten Training School, 1924-25

Name of course	Readings and course format
Art for kindergarten-primary teachers	Walter Sargent and Elizabeth Miller, *How Children Learn to Draw* (1916)
Blackboard drawing	—
History of art	Charles Caffin, *How to Study Pictures* (1910)
Bible	Gospel of Mark
Current events	—
Kindergarten introduction	—
Kindergarten methods	Naomi Norsworthy and Mary Whitley, *Psychology of Childhood* (1918)
Primary methods A and B	—
History of education	Ellwood P. Cubberley, *History of Education* (1920); Augustus Field Beard, *Story of Oberlin* (1909)
Principles of education	Friedrich Froebel, *Education of Man* (edition unknown); John Dewey, *School and Society* (1900); Grace Owen, *Nursery School Education* (1920). Suggestions are found for improvement and modification of original tendencies as demanded by experience and present circumstances.
English composition	—
Child literature	Porter MacClintock, *Literature in the Elementary School* (1904)
Games 1 and 2	Henry Curtis, *Education through Play* (1915); Charles Ward Crompton, *Folk Dance Book No. 1* (1916)
Physical exercise	—
Handwork (one semester, first year)	—
Hygiene	Lewis Terman, *The Hygiene of the School Child* (1914); May Ayers, Jesse F. Williams, and Thomas D. Woods, *Healthful Schools* (1918)
Music	—
Pianoforte	—
Nature	Study of birds and common trees
Elementary psychology	Walter Pillsbury, *Essentials of Psychology* (1911)
Child psychology	Study of Binet-Simon tests
School management	Ellwood P. Cubberley, *Public School Administration* (1916)
Sociology	Edward Ross, *Outlines of Sociology* (1923)
Teaching observation	2 hours weekly, second semester
Practice teaching	5 mornings for 24 weeks, second year

Source: *Oberlin Kindergarten Training School, 1924-1925* (Oberlin, OH: Oberlin Kindergarten Training School, 1925), 33-42.

Chicago's National Kindergarten and Elementary College in 1916 and returned to supervise the KSAW kindergarten from 1920 to 1922. Deacon held this post from 1922 to 1928, and Best from 1928 to 1932. Best continued her career with Winnipeg Public Schools: from 1944, she worked for eighteen years as a kindergarten and primary-class teacher.[88]

Professional development for KSAW teachers continued through study tours or brief courses at leading US programs. In 1926, Deacon took a one-month leave and toured kindergarten programs in New York City, including the Horace Mann Kindergarten at Columbia University. Prior to becoming supervisor, Best took a summer course at the National Kindergarten and Elementary College, which had moved to Evanston, Illinois. Ruth Holden was supervisor from 1932 to 1944. Her training is unknown, though she visited the National College of Education in Evanston, and later taught with the Winnipeg School Board.

The curriculum under directors Middleton and Deacon followed that of McLean, emphasizing individual growth and development as well as a balance between freedom and social responsibility. Play themes stressed cleanliness and thrift in the mode of the earlier era of charity kindergartens. "Training in health habits" and "banking as it is taught in schools in association with the Canadian Bank of Commerce" are examples of play themes.[89] The traditional kindergarten purpose of leading children to understand their relationship with God and the universe was reformulated as bringing a child to "a consciousness of his relationship to his environment and his kinship with all living things."[90] Deacon continued in this vein when she took over in 1922. In accordance with this aim, children's activities were planned to include social studies topics similar to those in a public school curriculum.

The program was organized around the calendar. The year began with a study of the child and his or her family, followed by harvest, Christmas, the New Year, and spring.[91] In 1925, the study of children elsewhere in Canada and around the world was added so that students could "see how other children lived." In the spring, the theme was local bird life.[92] These basic themes continued with a few changes from year to year. In 1926, the pupils studied Eskimos and the Dutch, and added Indians in Canada, health, and gardening. Canada's indigenous peoples were a popular topic of study, repeated for over a decade under the watch of three different teachers. In 1928, the children memorized "Indian Children," a poem by Annette Wynne, for their "Indian project."[93] They recited,

Where we walk to school each day,
Indian children used to play,
All about our native land,
Where the shops and houses stand:
And the trees were very tall
And there were no streets at all,
Not a church and not a steeple,
Only woods and Indian people.
Only wigwams on the ground,
And at night bears prowling 'round;
What a different place today,
Where we live and work and play.[94]

In 1932, after investigating home, family, and community helpers, the children studied "Life Amongst the Indian People," a project with roots in nineteenth-century Herbartian theory.[95]

Despite the kindergarten's isolation as a "one of its kind" in Winnipeg, the KSAW directors of the 1920s were aware of new ideas. In some cases, time might elapse between their initial appearance and their eventual discussion within the KSAW; in others, new approaches were rejected as unworkable. The first annual report to mention Montessori dated from 1925, when the president addressed the issue of the teacher's role in the kindergartens that appeared to give children more freedom. Her comments imply that pedagogy had changed between 1917 and 1925, presumably through the influence of Winnipeg's Oberlin-trained kindergarteners:

> Since the Montessori influence, to a casual observer the external means employed in the Kindergarten may seem to have changed. Truly less accentuated, less accurate, less convincing direction is given, but in the hands of a trained Kindergartener, one of high endeavor of culture, one who knows resources, and has complete control over herself and environment, the result is ever the same as the founder, Frederick Froebel had in mind, viz: to study the child as a child of nature in order that its unfolding might be gradual; and that the teacher may construct or combat whatever the tendency — good or evil.[96]

The president's address of the following year pursued a similar theme: "In the Kindergarten the child is fitted for the art of living by being allowed to make his own plans — to discover his own errors and to correct them — and in the supervised games as he becomes one of a group, he recognizes that every other child has the same rights as his own, and that liberty but not license is paramount. Knowledge gained in this way is the *result of development* rather than the *aim*."[97]

Director Edith Deacon understood that the trend in kindergarten education was to give more attention to children's independence, but she doubted that this was possible at the KSAW. She reached this conclusion after her month-long study tour of 1926, during which she visited New York City kindergartens both "well-to-do and poor." In her report on the Horace Mann Kindergarten at Teachers College, she noted that materials were larger than before. She was impressed by the potential of blocks to support group play, although two years passed before a set of Patty Smith Hill Blocks was ordered for the KSAW. Deacon had less enthusiasm for what she understood to be a greater focus on children's initiative: "The teachers are always ready to help the children if they ask, but feel that the children gain more by working out their own problems."[98] She added,

> Observing as I did in many different Kindergartens I felt that in the better districts where the children came from well-to-do homes rich in firsthand experiences this method worked out very well, and the children did express themselves through their play. In the poorer districts, one might say the Slums, I did not feel it was so successful. Some of the children were such poor drab little things they seemed devoid of ideas and couldn't enter into the spirit of the Kindergarten. One teacher told me frankly she didn't like this new method, and felt that the children got very little out of it as they had no background in the home. Other teachers had adopted the method to suit the district.
>
> While I can see a certain amount of value in allowing the child to experiment with different materials I do not feel that in a district such as we are working in it is an altogether wise plan. The children in this Kindergarten love the organized rhythms and singing games and I would feel to do away with them would be to deprive the children of something which gives them real pleasure as well as physical benefit. I do think that large materials are excellent and a certain amount of freedom in the work with them will cultivate initiative, the ability to work with others and originality in expressing their own ideas.

During our whole Kindergarten year we have tried to give the children health lessons, little lessons in politeness and through our stories and games develop a spirit of fair play, and consideration for others, in the hope that the foundation laid in the Kindergarten may help them to become healthy, happy and useful young Canadians.[99]

Deacon's New York experience reinforced her perception that the KSAW approach, which focused on training in light of the children's deficits, was the correct one. "Our children have limited experiences and therefore limited expressions," she wrote. "It is our work to supply the needed experiences or a substitute for them."[100]

Endings

Annual reports dating from the last decade of the KSAW give few details concerning the children, the teachers, or the program.[101] The year 1942 marked the fiftieth anniversary of the association, and the annual report of that year outlined its achievements. Most of its information seems to have been drawn from earlier reports, and its main focus is the opening, but not the closing, of the various branches. In 1942, there were still sufficient numbers of children to warrant morning and afternoon classes. Ruth Holden was supervisor and teacher, and a social worker remained on staff. The building was still shared with the same groups that had rented space at the Ellen Street Kindergarten for forty years, and a Kitchen Garden class still met, as did a Mother's Circle.

In 1943, the Winnipeg Public Schools start-up of kindergartens as childcare for mothers who were employed in war work signalled the end of the KSAW. Kindergartens had gained public and school board support by the war's end, expanding to thirty-seven schools in 1948. Spurring the change was a reform agenda pursued by Winnipeg Public Schools to infuse the latest ideas in its programs. Early childhood education had achieved a high profile during the war years.[102] Plans for change were further stimulated by the 1946 introduction of a new provincial curriculum and by a highly critical assessment of Winnipeg Public Schools in 1948 by a committee of experts from the University of Chicago.[103] After gathering information on the city's new kindergartens via questionnaires sent to teachers and principals, the committee published its findings in what became known as the Reavis Report, named after committee chair William C. Reavis. Although the report criticized Winnipeg's antiquated school buildings and pointed to the lack of materials and poor accommodation in its kindergartens, it also revealed that the kindergarten idea had finally taken hold in the public school system. Already, eighteen existed in twenty-five schools, with an additional four programs set to open the next year. Two sessions were offered in each one, with an average of twenty-two children in each half-day. All but one of the teachers had specialist training in kindergarten work, and overall the program was rated highly as preparation for grade one.

Once public support was realized, the KSAW kindergarten was no longer needed. In the end, the association played no role in stimulating public support. The association's leaders and kindergarten directors had no intellectual connections with child study, no political links that resulted in support. The eventual takeover of the KSAW by the Community Chest reinforced its isolation from the education field. Stronger voices came from elsewhere. One was Winnipeg lawyer Joe Zuken, a communist city councillor and school trustee. Zuken and other socialist school trustees called for increased numbers of kindergartens during wartime, beyond the small-scale "experiment" started in a few schools in 1942.[104]

While the KSAW board contemplated the future, it continued to offer a children's program. The Welfare Council of Winnipeg commissioned a survey of the KSAW, which resulted in a strongly critical report in 1951.[105] It found that, though attendance was small, the kindergarten continued to operate two sessions, each of which was staffed by a teacher and two assistants. The program was described as a "supervised play program" lacking any educational purpose. Pupils were as young as two years of age; the oldest were almost six. Neither the teacher, the social worker, nor any of the staff were trained, and the teacher spent a large part of her time "encouraging people to attend."[106] The building was outdated, retaining features from an earlier era such as a large bathtub in the children's washroom.

The report was blunt in its assessment of the association's six decades of charity work: "Throughout the years the Kindergarten Settlement Association operated along traditional lines varying its program only slightly in spite of considerable development of welfare services, both public and private, for people of this area ... The present program is somewhat of a hodge-podge and too much is being attempted by staff who are not qualified."[107]

The council's recommendation that the KSAW cease operation was not surprising. In 1952, the Winnipeg Neighbourhood House opened in the old Ellen Street Kindergarten building, with a nursery school as its main children's program.[108] A few years earlier, another committee had considered developing a community centre in the area, concluding that the Ellen Street Kindergarten was an ideal site. The community-centre idea stemmed from a report on juvenile delinquency in the area in 1949, and the "neighbourhood house" was conceived as a "preventative service," training youngsters in social responsibility and keeping them off the street. The nursery school was the keystone upon which all other services would depend:

> [Its aim is] not just to keep the children out of mischief, but is to help to strengthen family ties, and to teach each member of the family a better way of life ... When the tiny tots come to nursery school, the mothers become interested in a mothers' club, and perhaps later in a sewing class, or music group. The boys come to play games, and stay on for crafts, and perhaps eventually interest Dad in coming over to do some woodwork. Dad might stay on for a chat with other fathers, and never know he was learning citizenship. Girls come for fun, and learn to paint, or to cook. The old folks come because it's warm and friendly — and receive some educational companionship. Parent education, health — there is no end to what might be learned through a neighborhood house.[109]

From settlement house to neighbourhood house, the spirit of the KSAW as a mission to the poor continued.

chapter 8   **Kindergarten Union of New South Wales**

THE FIRST FREE KINDERGARTEN established by the Kindergarten Union of New South Wales (KUNSW), also the first in Australia, opened in January 1896 in a mission for the poor on Sussex Street, Sydney.[1] As it was poorly attended in this location, the next month it was moved to a residence in Woolloomooloo, Sydney, where enrolment grew to about twenty children. The organizers expressed the importance of kindergarten work as a preventative measure in the face of the social, moral, and economic poverty of its targeted clientele:

> The moral, physical, and intellectual benefit of true Kindergarten work was considered specially needful for the poor — those children of busy mothers, who have neither the necessary time nor training to look after their little ones, so that the children have often to spend the most valuable portion of their lives in the gutter or the streets. Here the innocent baby eyes and ears take in sights and sounds, the remembrance of which may never by wholly effaced, however happy the after circumstances of the children may be. To prevent the first germs of vice from taking root in the impressionable minds of these little ones, to inculcate good habits and desire for work, to awaken the first dim appreciation of the beautiful in nature and art, was the wish of the Kindergarten Union.[2]

The KUNSW administrators worked quickly, building a small network of kindergartens and a teacher-training school by the end of their first decade. The first teacher they hired adhered to a strict Froebelian approach, but the organizers had a different vision in mind, believing that, for poor children, the strength of kindergarten lay in its potential for skills training and moral education. When the teacher left to open a private school, they sought a replacement who could direct the kindergarten according to their understanding of the style of the Golden Gate Kindergarten Association. They hired the American Ridie Lee Buckey, who was teaching in a Honolulu kindergarten.

Americans

Buckey's training, however, bore no relation to the Golden Gate approach to kindergarten work. She graduated from Chicago's Cook County Normal School in 1895. In the 1890s, Cook County offered one of the few professional training programs for kindergarten teachers in the United States. The Cook County faculty included key figures in the US kindergarten movement.[3] Its director was Francis Wayland Parker, who was well known for his experimental approach to teacher education, which combined observation and practice with expertise in subject matter.[4] Parker's ideas were grounded in a Herbartian "theory of concentration," setting the child at the centre of the educational experience, with traditional subjects — geology, biology, history — considered pathways to understanding the natural law of the world.[5]

The Cook County approach to kindergarten work was more pragmatic than the esoteric theory of concentration would suggest. Alice Putnam, who had trained with Susan Blow, directed the demonstration kindergarten. Putnam abandoned the symbolism of Blow's approach, subscribing instead to the progressive view associated with John Dewey, G. Stanley Hall, and Patty Smith Hill, in which the ritualistic aspects of kindergarten work involving such activities as beadwork and paper folding were considered useless and even harmful to children's development. Buckey worked for a time at the demonstration kindergarten, and it is likely that she shared these ideas.

The Free Kindergarten and Children's Aid Association of the Hawaiian Islands (FKCAA) formed the year before the Sydney association. The

FKCAA was a union of five existing mission kindergartens, segregated by racial or the national origins of children — Chinese, Portuguese, Japanese, Hawaiian, and foreign (*haole,* or white). As revealed by photographs, signs above the doorways of the showplace kindergarten at Queen Emma Hall designated separate Japanese and Hawaiian entrances. The original five kindergartens were segregated until about 1900.

Buckey taught at a newly opened sixth kindergarten in a settlement house in the Palama district of Honolulu.[6] Although it was the only integrated FKCAA kindergarten, it served mainly Portuguese children.[7] Before she left for Honolulu, Buckey told a reporter that she intended to learn Portuguese, though she believed that the language of play was universal: "Kindergarten teaching ... is the same in all tongues. It is so much gesture that I am sure I will be able to make the little people understand me until I can understand them."[8] In preparation for her work at the charity kindergarten, she spent ten days visiting at the Golden Gate Kindergarten Association before leaving San Francisco en route to Honolulu.

The superintendent of the FKCAA was Buckey's friend Frances Lawrence, who had graduated from Cook County in 1893 and worked with Buckey as an assistant at the demonstration kindergarten.[9] Lawrence was hired to replace FKCAA superintendent Hannah Eastman. Eastman trained in the Golden Gate kindergartens and had ten years' experience before coming to Honolulu.[10] However, Lawrence was highly critical of Eastman's approach, which she believed to be outdated, and she claimed that the time had come to move beyond Froebel, for "other great thinkers to take up the work where he left off."[11] Soon after she arrived, Lawrence replaced the Gifts and occupations with "free play, rhythms, construction, and creative art."[12] Her approach, outlined in a newspaper report at the time of her takeover from Eastman, was based on "continual child study, an insistence on the play principle and disapproval of intellectual forcing, a minimum of required handiwork in training directors and the constant aim of character building that discountenances display and precocity."[13] She continued as head of the FKCAA for thirty-nine years until her death in 1935. Over time, she developed a progressive kindergarten program, in which "child education was connected to child life." For Lawrence, this meant translating the urban experience, including its commerce, transportation systems, and everyday chores, into play in the kindergarten. The focus was on building healthy habits — of work, of hygiene, and of nutrition. Describing a child's play, she wrote, "He served luncheon, he watered his garden, he swept the steps. Out of waste lumber and old spools he constructed a locomotive and cars following a visit to the Oahu Railway, or he built Aloha tower and a variety of ships on his return from the waterfront. After a visit to a neighborhood shop, he played store and learned incidentally about the best foods for health and toothbrushes for better teeth."[14]

Hygiene and health were an important part of the program at the Palama kindergarten: Buckey bathed the children on their arrival, and a nurse visited families in their homes. The educational aspects of Buckey's program were probably consistent with the ideas expressed by Lawrence. After just seven months in Honolulu, Buckey left for Australia to direct the KUNSW.[15] When she arrived in Sydney in August 1897, the Woolloomooloo kindergarten had been open for just over one year.

The KUNSW had high expectations for Buckey, and her role as director encompassed the threefold purpose of promoting the kindergarten ideal, training teachers, and establishing kindergartens in "poor neighbourhoods."[16] She taught in the Woolloomooloo kindergarten and directed teacher training, which was initially a two-year program leading to a certificate from the KUNSW. In 1899, the program was extended to three years, allowing students to earn a diploma. Buckey believed that a longer and more in-depth program was essential for the future of kindergartens in Australia and that all "thoughtful parents will decline to place their children in the hands of untrained teachers."[17] The three-year program, though not yet matching her ideal for four-year programs, such as existed at a few "lead training schools" in the United States, gave students a more mature understanding of kindergarten work. As Buckey described the process, "the three [years] embody a drama in which each experience is necessary to the whole" and where instinct gives way to purposeful and knowledgeable teaching. Whereas "the junior student finds the first year filled largely by confusion and toil, the senior gives far greater insight, while freedom and breadth of thought replace confusion of ideas. In the post-graduate year work becomes genuine pleasure, instinct becomes definite effort."[18]

Students were admitted into training at seventeen, though they were required at this age to take the full three-year diploma course to better ensure a "mature" graduate. Lyndsay Gardiner, commenting on the 1924 introduction of a third year of training at the Kindergarten Union of Victoria's Melbourne college, suggests that other motives were in play. The additional year meant an extra year of fees, with little more required from the college. It was a kind of "bonding scheme" in which students provided volunteer labour as teaching assistants in order to acquire the certificate.[19]

In Sydney, the first training scheme under director Mary Hooper was initiated to provide her with extra help when it was found that "she could not manage without assistance."[20] In the early years of the Sydney KUNSW, as at Melbourne, more students were taken on than could ever find positions in the few existing kindergartens. Options for graduates included opening private schools for children from wealthy families or, should they marry and have children of their own, applying their training to their offspring. The latter constituted the largest drain on the supply of kindergarten teachers. As the Australian Maybanke Anderson (Wolstenhome) explained of the situation at the Golden Gate Association, the San Francisco kindergartens "require constant additions, and replenishment, for kindergarten mistresses make remarkably useful wives, and their marriage is almost a matter of course."[21]

During their mornings, students undertook practical work with children in the kindergarten, attending lectures in the afternoons. Their work with children was essential, and in 1900, when the graduating class departed, Buckey noted a "very noticeable break in our teachers' ranks."[22] During that year, the first local teacher who had trained under Buckey took charge of the Woolloomooloo kindergarten, relieving Buckey of her teaching duties and allowing her to concentrate on training. Also in this year, the Kindergarten Training College moved into a former private residence in Elizabeth Bay, a fashionable suburb some distance from the Woolloomooloo kindergarten.

The promotion of the kindergarten ideal was partly achieved by setting high teacher-training standards and creating a uniform approach to practice. During Buckey's tenure, the KUNSW annual report also helped promote the work, expanding from three pages in 1897 to forty-one the next year, with articles, testimonials, dramatic before-and-after stories with photographs, and advertisements. In "A Plea for Free Kindergartens," her essay in the 1898 annual report, Buckey pointed to its power to change lives. However, she argued that this would require sustained community support similar to the philanthropic aid that gave rise to the Golden Gate Kindergarten Association. Buckey was a good writer, particularly in her sensitive observations of children. However, parts of her reports were derivative, drawing on the journalistic style used by Sarah Cooper in her Golden Gate reports.[23] The rhetoric of the kindergarten as a crime-prevention program, so effectively exploited by Cooper, was the Golden Gate's most significant influence on the KUNSW kindergartens.

Curriculum

Aiming to "inculcate good habits and desire for work" in children and to "awaken the first dim appreciation of the beautiful in nature and art," the KUNSW combined traditional child-welfare strategies with progressive kindergarten pedagogy.[24] These intentions were expressed more simply in a sign above the entranceway, which read, "As the twig is bent the tree inclined," leaving one to wonder how parents interpreted the message.[25] The teachers were meant to influence these human plants — individual children and their families — in the physical and the moral realms. Buckey's initial purchase for the Woolloomooloo kindergarten was a bathtub; sending children home freshly bathed was a message to mothers to attend to the hygiene of their offspring, according to a standard set by the KUNSW. The other furnishings included fifty small chairs, four tables, and two chairs for adults. Walls were decorated with inspirational images meant to engage and train children's aesthetic sense and connection with faith and the empire: pictures of Raphael's *Sistine Madonna* and Queen Victoria, and prints from Froebel's *Mother-Play*.[26] A canary and a goldfish were kept as class pets, living lessons in responsibility.

The curriculum was organized around a single theme or subject undertaken throughout an entire school year. The interests of individual children were not central here, as lesson plans were set long in advance of their implementation. The 1898 theme was the "trades"; that of 1899 was Froebel's *Mother-Play*. The latter, as Buckey noted, also stressed the trades.

The kindergarten's development as a branch of manual education was evident: it served as the first step on the ladder of a working-class education and the inculcation of knowledge, skills, and a work ethic. Poverty was believed to be associated with lax morals and poor motivation, making behaviour and cognitive change the aim. In her description of the full year devoted to the "trades," Buckey affirmed her belief that manual education was of value for the children of Woolloomooloo:

> Mechanical skill receives an impulse in the Kindergarten which, if continued in the schools, would cause a revolution in the manufacturies of the country, and the demand for skilled labour would be met satisfactorily. Our sand boxes were refilled by masons who were working on a terrace of new houses near us, and who were greatly interested in the Kindergarten. They kindly loaned us a number of

tools which the children modeled in clay. The trades of masons and carpenters were chosen for that time, so that the children could make their observations and illustrate those trades by drawing (blackboard), modeling, gifts and occupations.[27]

The KUNSW lessons on trades resembled what the Golden Gate kindergartens called "sociological work," an approach apparently rejected by Buckey in her attention to "modern" methods. In the Golden Gate curriculum, children were taught "social games and songs on trades and occupations, teaching a love and respect for all who labor honestly, and directed in building houses, constructing railroads, canals, bridges, tunnels, etc., on the sand table."[28]

Buckey emphasized the importance of the kindergarten experience for children with special needs, such as those who were "nervous and backward." She advocated a hands-off, non-interventionist teaching approach, believing that the answer to developmental problems could be found through patient observation. Here, she drew on the favoured kindergarten metaphor — children are like plants — but suggested that they should be watched instead of watered: "Froebel insisted that children are like plants, and need the same patient consideration that Mother Nature gives her offspring. Child development, like that of plants, should not be forced, but be gradual, all-sided and perfect. A little child may be developed *into* a dullard, as well as from a dullard into an intelligent child. Thousands of children would be blessed if they were allowed a more natural growth and a less forced development."[29]

She included an illustrative case of a girl who was so socially withdrawn that, as her parents reported, she did not talk until she was three. "Her shyness we can hardly describe," Buckey remarked, adding,

When spoken to she would look at you for minutes without change of expression — especially if addressed suddenly. She could concentrate on nothing, and was interested in nothing — spasmodically active at one time, and utterly impassive at others. I was frequently met with the question, "What shall I do with Ethel?" "We will study her and find out how to help her." This is my remedy for every case, and it never fails. As I knew she would, she gave us the key to her own nature through her unconscious expressions and attitudes, thus furnishing the best means of helping her.[30]

After nine months at the kindergarten, Ethel participated in activities and often led the other children in "marching and games."[31] Buckey's teaching strategy appears mainly to have involved encouraging and helping Ethel on the basis of careful and sustained observations. Buckey used the case to chide teachers in public schools, reminding them that "the children under their care are something more than phonographic instruments — they are living specimens of humanity, future citizens of a commonwealth."[32]

For Buckey, progressive kindergarten pedagogy featured a mix of old and new ideas. She combined her focus on overall child development with concern for moral uplift and the cost saving produced by "reclaiming" children from criminal life. Here, she advocated a more interventionist approach. Perhaps anticipating that the apparent contradiction between hands-off and hands-on teaching strategies might confuse her readers, she wrote, "But how about heredity? You will probably ask, and it is a most natural question, for it is a most potent force, but experience has proven that environment is a greater one. Let the impressions and habits in the human organism registered in childhood be wholesome ones, and he can afford to take other changes."[33]

Buckey left Sydney in 1901, at the end of her agreed-upon stay. She sailed from there to India and Europe, visiting kindergartens in Madras (Chennai), an *école maternelle* in Paris, the Pestalozzi-Froebel House in Berlin, kindergartens in Belgium, and the Froebel Institute College in London. In June 1902, she returned to the United States, "making the circle complete." Through her world tour and work in Honolulu and Sydney, Buckey concluded that kindergarten had achieved a global reach over a period of fifty years, yet she observed that practice often fell short of Froebel's ideal:

> Many times the words of the apostle of childhood have come to me — "If three hundred years after my death my method of education shall be completely established according to its idea, I shall rejoice in heaven." As to whether it is "established according to its idea" yet, I have grave doubts, but that it has reached the four corners of the earth I have tried to show you. Beside me, as I write, is an autograph portrait of my dear old teacher and friend, Col. Francis Parker, on which is also written in his hand: "A little child shall lead you." It still does.[34]

Buckey's replacement was another American-trained kindergartener, Frances Newton (1865-1938).[35] Newton arrived in Sydney in 1902 from

Chicago, where she had been a director of Gertrude House, noted by the KUNSW administrators to be "one of the principal training schools in America."[36] Like Buckey, she had trained at the Chicago Normal School (the Cook County Normal School was known as the Chicago Normal School after 1896). After her arrival, it was noted that "the standard of the work in connection with training of the students (the foundation of the whole system) has been immensely raised."[37] The annual report was silent on Buckey's earlier efforts in this regard. Newton's assistant was another American, Elizabeth Jenkins, recruited by her from the Chicago Kindergarten Training School.[38]

Gertrude House, established about 1895, was a branch of the Chicago Kindergarten Institute, which was closely involved with social settlements such as the Chicago University Settlement. The inspiration for its name was Pestalozzi's ideal woman, a mother who directed her child's moral growth toward love for God. Students boarded at Gertrude House as they trained in "homemaking ideals."[39] At the Gertrude House kindergarten, industrial and manual training dominated as the youngsters developed practical skills by working at household chores. A *Kindergarten Magazine* (US) report on Gertrude House praised its manual training while it parodied the ritual use of Froebel's Gifts and occupations: "[Were children] bending with flushed cheeks and trembling hands over a piece of pricking or fine sewing? Moving little one-inch cubes around, making imaginary wonders at the dictation of their teacher? No ... They were doing what is the heart's delight of all normal children, helping in the work of their elders."[40]

It could be supposed that the KUNSW administrators selected Newton due to her progressive approach. More generous toward Buckey than they were, Newton acknowledged that training had become well established under her direction but had now been made more rigorous. What this entailed for students was that some were required to repeat a year at the junior level or were demoted to the kindergarten nurses' class, a program begun by Buckey in 1897. Evidently, no interested applicants were turned away; students not meeting even minimum educational requirements were placed in a "preparatory class" prior to starting their training.[41] For Newton, these steps were necessary in order to raise kindergarten work to a professional standard.[42]

At the same time, students were given more responsibility for the children's program, ostensibly as part of their training. After the director of the flagship Woolloomooloo kindergarten resigned in 1902, it was staffed entirely by senior students for the remainder of the term. Despite the tightening of standards, few students left the program, and forty-six were enrolled across all training programs in 1905. Newton believed that kindergarten-teacher training was more popular with young women than it had been even a few years before: "It not only puts into their hands the power to win their bread in a womanly way, but at the same time provides the means for a broad and general personal culture."[43]

The quest for professional standards also included attention to minimum age requirements for children attending the program, reaffirming that the kindergarten was not a babysitting service. As an educational program, Newton argued, kindergarten should admit children only from age three. She proposed that a day nursery be attached to each kindergarten for children of working mothers, serving also as a training site for students in the kindergarten nurses' course, but this was never done.[44]

In 1904, whereas children under age three were excluded from the kindergarten, older children were added and enrolled in a "transition" class with a focus on school readiness. Newton explained that the expanding academic focus did not mean that the KUNSW had abandoned its concern for the physical well-being of its pupils. At least milk was available at the kindergarten for underfed children; a girl had fainted after arriving there "breakfastless and starving."[45] The staff no longer bathed children. After Newton made attendance dependent on the KUNSW standard of cleanliness, "their mothers learned that unduly soiled faces and hands kept them out of their heaven until they were clean."[46] Under Newton's direction, the kindergarten became more rule-bound overall; entrance doors were locked after starting time to encourage punctuality. This desire to teach children and their mothers good habits is reminiscent of Wilderspin, who also dismissed dirty children and shut them out when they were late.[47]

Enrolment increased in individual kindergartens, and the number of program sites expanded.[48] Occasionally, children were singled out in annual reports as worthy of special mention due to their race. At the Surry Hills kindergarten, four children were categorized as "half-castes" — presumably of mixed Aboriginal and European heritage — and a number were Chinese, the latter judged to be "wonderfully bright." Few were noted to have special needs, although a child who was blind attended a kindergarten in 1905.[49]

When the Day Nursery for Babies of Working Mothers opened in Woolloomooloo in 1906 under the administration of the newly formed Sydney Day Nursery Association, the KUNSW training college used it as a site in which students would benefit from a greater developmental perspective. The 1906 KUNSW annual report remarked that, though the nursery was "not officially connected with the KU [KUNSW], it has kindly given our students the opportunity to learn in a practical way something of the care of very young children. We feel it quite as necessary that a Kindergartener should know children before the kindergarten age, as that she should know them after that age. The Crèche gives the one experience; the primary class the other. Only so can the teacher know what to expect of the children in the Kindergarten, and appreciate the educational significance of Kindergarten training."[50]

Children's services in Sydney became more specialized, with separate private organizations targeting children from birth to age three (the Sydney Day Nursery Association) and from three to school-starting age (the KUNSW). Although both served children from poor families, nurseries offered custodial care along with social and moral training, and kindergartens sought to provide an educational program with some attention to physical development.

At this time, free kindergartens spread beyond New South Wales to South Australia, where Newton and her former student Lillian de Lissa gave lectures and demonstrations on kindergarten work in Adelaide in 1905. Later, de Lissa became director of the Kindergarten Union of South Australia's first kindergarten; her first annual report highlighted the manner in which kindergarten work developed both mind and body:

> While it is the high privilege of the Kindergartener to watch and control the development of the inner nature of the child, it is no less her duty to see that the activities of his body are allowed the full and proper play. To this end Froebel introduced the exercises connected with the gifts, occupations, and games. While these have a deep significance entirely apart from the effect on the body, they nevertheless are admirably adapted to give the growing limbs and muscles of the children just the work they most need. Care is taken, in preparing and using the material for the different occupations, that there shall be nothing to strain the eyes or other tender organs of the little ones.[51]

In 1906, Newton and two Sydney Kindergarten Teachers College (SKTC) students visited the United States. Connections with Chicago training schools were reinforced when the three travelled to Chicago; the two students remained there to study kindergarten work, and one returned to Sydney at the end of her program. During Newton's absence, Elizabeth Jenkins took over as principal. When Newton did not return, Jenkins was appointed to the position.[52]

Entrenchment

In 1911, Jenkins left on a tour of Europe, on the understanding that she would return to her position in Sydney. Australian-born Harriet Dumolo, who had her kindergarten certificate from the Teachers' Association (1897) and a diploma from the SKTC (1905), served as interim principal.[53] When Jenkins resigned without returning, Dumolo was appointed principal, with Sophia (Zoe) Benjamin, who graduated in 1905, as her assistant. Dumolo became the first locally trained principal of the training college. She would lead the college for the next twenty-two years. Benjamin remained on staff as assistant to the principal, lecturer, and, on occasion, acting principal until 1937. In 1910, Dumolo supplemented her training under Jenkins with studies at the Froebel Institute College in London, beginning the practice of sending Australian teachers overseas in anticipation of their assumption of leadership positions in the KUNSW.

Under Dumolo's direction, the KUNSW entered a long period of stability, with little change in the children's program or student training. Dumolo's contributions to annual reports were perfunctory. Hiring a locally trained principal seemed to slow the introduction of new educational ideas. Over the next twenty-five years, she made few changes to the interpretation of modern kindergarten pedagogy imported during the earlier period by the American-trained directors.

Visitors' accounts of the KUNSW noted the American-style program and the dominance of practical teacher training. A visitor from the United Kingdom described teacher training at the Sydney college in 1912:

> The students have about two years' training, most of it being practical, as they spend every morning in a free Kindergarten, in the same Kindergarten for six months at a stretch. There are about sixty children as a rule under the management of the Director, who is a

trained Kindergartener, and is paid. She is responsible also for the students, four to six at a time, who are under her control and criticism for six months. There are a few lectures and handwork classes held in the afternoons, but the academic and theoretical part of the course is not taken into so much account as over here, whereas the practical work is well provided for.[54]

When asked if her kindergarten was a copy of the US version, Dumolo responded defensively: "'No' the Principal said; 'our Kindergartens are Australian, not American.'"[55] In fact, the similarities to American kindergartens outnumbered the differences. Even the exception to the rule — instilling an allegiance to the Commonwealth — resembled citizenship training in the United States, focused as it was on the flag. The same visitor remarked, "It was quite thrilling to see the tinies saluting the flag and giving three cheers for King George, then with actions, saying, 'I give my head, my heart, and my hands to my country.'"[56] A visitor in 1909, given a tour by Elizabeth Jenkins, witnessed the same ceremony and reported on her experience in the UK-based kindergarten magazine *Child Life*:

> The organizers of the Sydney Free Kindergartens certainly inculcate reverence and patriotism for the mother country and the Empire in the children and their parents ... I think this feeling of unity, which the ceremony of saluting the flag seems to foster, is an excellent thing, especially as the present generation of colonial and English children will be the Empire's builders and supporters of the future. On one occasion the mothers' club of the Woolloomooloo and a neighboring Free Kindergarten held a crowded meeting of the Empire League, so that this spirit of Imperial loyalty is felt by the poor parents also.[57]

A source of new ideas in this period was the educational system promulgated by Maria Montessori. Martha Simpson and several SKTC graduates — Ruby Starling and sisters Norma and Rhoda Selfe — attended Montessori's training course in Rome in 1913. As well as providing training in Montessori's methods, the course enabled kindergarteners from around the world to meet and discuss their work.[58] The course consisted of three lectures each week, which were given by Montessori at her home, and one morning of observation in a school.[59] Upon their return, the Selfe sisters were hired to demonstrate the system at the teachers college at Blackfriars, and the KUNSW organized its own Montessori kindergarten in 1915 under the direction of Ruby Starling. The KUNSW noted that kindergarten pedagogy was in flux and, in light of Montessori's call that children be given greater freedom, regarded its own program as too formal. Yet, it was cautious and the Montessori kindergarten was devised as a testing ground through which "we shall then be able to judge fairly the advantage of the methods, and to introduce those we think well of into our Free Kindergartens."[60]

True to her training in Rome, Starling used "pure Montessori methods."[61] Because the kindergarten was experimental, it was not used as a training site, reducing its impact in the overall network of schools. To expand the experiment, a blend of Montessori and Froebel was initiated at a second kindergarten, "so that we shall soon be able to arrive at some conclusion as to the relative value of the two systems."[62] The experiment with "pure" methods was soon halted — judged by Dumolo and Starling to be "not sufficiently comprehensive" — and continued as a combined Montessori-Froebel program.[63] In 1920, Dumolo visited Montessori schools in Adelaide, where de Lissa had incorporated Montessori materials; in her report, she revealed her doubts regarding Montessori's relevance in the face of new ideas concerning children's freedom and self-expression in kindergarten.[64] The entire experiment was terminated in 1922. The KUNSW reasoned that the Montessori name did not reflect the nature of the actual program, which over time became similar to the other kindergartens, and the school was renamed in honour of Maybanke Anderson.[65]

The debate over KUNSW pedagogy that was stimulated by the Montessori experiments was rekindled by Dumolo herself after her 1925 study tour of schools in the United States, England, and Europe. Dumolo was particularly interested in the methods she observed at the Horace Mann Kindergarten, Teachers College, and in efforts to place kindergarten work on a scientific basis. She summarized what she learned:

1 That children must first of all be healthy
2 That children need the right social conditions to properly develop their social consciousness
3 That the work of the children avails nothing in the early stages if it is not based on actual experience
4 That materials through which the children express their ideas must be simple, large and easily obtainable.[66]

Children playing with Froebelian materials in a KUNSW kindergarten, Sydney, 1928. Kindergarten Union of New South Wales Collection Mitchell Library, Sydney.

Changes to kindergarten pedagogy, allowing children more choice and freedom, were slow to take hold. From the early 1920s, Margaret Ford, the Woolloomooloo kindergarten director, had achieved some success in independent experiments with freer approaches. She visited England and the United States in 1928, reporting to the local organizing committee on her return that the "finer materials were no longer used" and that "children need bigger things to handle."[67] By the late 1920s, Gift work and circle time, hallmarks since the opening of the first KUNSW kindergarten, were still employed. Contrary to Mary Walker's conclusion that the KUNSW programs "resembl[ed] in many respects the Laboratory School of John Dewey," the American-trained directors Buckey, Newton, and Jenkins retained Gift work along with progressive pedagogy.[68]

Dumolo suggested the introduction of materials to support self-expression and freedom through play, such as the enlarged Patty Smith Hill Blocks, but there is no record that any were purchased during her tenure. In 1930, the KUNSW added gymnastics to the program schedule; Dumolo and Margaret Ford had observed this in the United States, but in Australia, it was used for the student teachers, not the children.[69]

Reconstruction

During the 1930s, several events coincided to stimulate changes at the SKTC. The first was Dumolo's retirement in 1933, opening the way for Ella Slack's appointment as principal the next year. Slack immediately set about making changes in line with American-style nursery school education, opening a nursery school at the Golden Fleece Kindergarten with assistance from Mary Gutteridge, head of training at the Kindergarten Union of Victoria. Melbourne was at the centre of the nursery school movement in Australia. Gutteridge's initial training was at the Froebel Institute College, London. Her subsequent teaching experience was varied and included work in nursery schools in London and Paris. In 1922, she was appointed head of the Melbourne Kindergarten Training College. She completed her bachelor of science degree at Columbia University while on leave from the Kindergarten Union of Victoria in 1929.

Slack determined that kindergarten work had stalled at the KUNSW, writing in her first report as director, "Because people tend to cling so firmly to traditional methods, definitely progressive work for young children has in the past been confined to isolated centres."[70] To stimulate reforms, the KUNSW followed the initiative of the Victoria union by sending SKTC graduate Jean Wyndham to study at Teachers College in New York and to visit the Institute of Education in London. The intent of this was that she would return "with her mind enriched by her varied experiences, bringing back to us the latest methods that have been tested and accepted in the educational centres in England and America."[71] When Wyndham returned in 1937 with a bachelor of science degree from Columbia University, she initiated a demonstration nursery school for children aged eighteen to thirty months.

With Wyndham's appointment as principal in 1939, the reforms instigated under Slack continued. In describing the new principal, the KUNSW board highlighted her academic training in modern nursery school methods. As well, more staff had specific training in the methods. The teacher at the Golden Fleece Nursery School trained for two years in Melbourne after completing her kindergarten certificate at the SKTC. Under Wyndham's direction, the SKTC developed a nursery school option. After a common first year, students could continue training in kindergarten-nursery school or kindergarten-primary programs.

Wyndham was familiar with the current US trends in nursery school work. Her training at Teachers College included courses in child development, which involved structured observations at the City and Country School, Dalton School, and Walden School.[72] At the KUNSW, Wyndham included a child-development course for students at the college. In the 1940 annual report, which contained a lengthy explanation of her reasons for doing so, she took care to emphasize that the new approach placed child-development knowledge as core knowledge for nursery school, kindergarten, and primary teachers, with the three divisions considered "one complete unit — early childhood education."[73] She clarified: "Every teacher who teaches the child below ten should understand the child and his growth from infancy on, and whether she teaches the two-year-old or the eight-year-old, will depend on the few extra courses she has taken in method, and on her personality and the age group with which she identifies herself most naturally."[74]

In 1937, Wyndham described the nursery school as "the answer to many of the modern problems of early childhood."[75] During the Second World War, a sharper focus on mental health and parent-child relationships developed. Because social adjustment was believed to depend on emotional security gained through a strong parent-child relationship, parent education and home guidance were reaffirmed as essential to the KUNSW's work. According to Wyndham, a failed parent-child relationship was "the most potent factor in child delinquency."[76] Family life was itself potentially damaging to healthy child development. If their relationship with their parents was askew, children were at high risk, even if the situation presented an appearance of normalcy. The 1937 New Education Fellowship Conference held in Sydney concentrated additional attention on child development. Psychoanalyst Susan Isaacs was among the speakers, and one interpretation asserts that Australia's shift to child development as the core of the kindergarten curriculum occurred from this time.[77] However, Wyndham's experience in the United States and her training at Teachers College had already prepared the KUNSW for these ideas.

The increased need for childcare in wartime raised public awareness of kindergartens and changed the KUNSW's own image of its programs. At one time, it had three thousand children on its waiting list. In 1943, the twenty-two programs operated by the KUNSW were called "child centres," featuring twenty-one kindergartens and fifteen nursery schools along with seven supervised playgrounds. For the first time, the more generic term "preschool" appeared in the report for the year, indicating a further loosening of the kindergarten's grip on the early childhood field.

Following the Second World War, the KUNSW maintained its focus on its traditional target group, poor children, but also continued to develop programs for specialized groups. The Samuel Cohen Kindergarten for Deaf Children opened in 1946, and in 1949, the Chippendale Kindergarten developed a relationship with the Sydney Child Welfare Department to accept children "whose parents are threatened with charge of neglect; children from exceptionally poor homes; [and] children with special difficulties."[78] The Chippendale Kindergarten also aimed to include children from "better-class homes," the directors believing that "the group work with the mothers is enriched by a nucleus of women with higher standards and better education."[79]

In 1939, developments in nursery school work were given a significant boost countrywide, when, via the director general of health, the federal government funded preschool demonstration centres in each state capitol. Named the Lady Gowrie Child Centres after Lady Zara Gowrie, wife of the governor general of Australia and supporter of the project, they offered comprehensive children's services targeting all aspects of child development and using "the best nursery school and kindergarten procedure that could be attained with the finance available."[80]

The idea to establish the centres grew out of the Melbourne-based nursery school movement. In 1932, a Demonstration Nursery School Committee began to open several centres in Melbourne. The Kindergarten Union of Victoria had developed along unique lines from the start, with little influence from the KUNSW.[81] When director Mary Gutteridge left again for Teachers College in 1936, this time to start doctoral studies, Christine Heinig replaced her from 1937 to 1938. Heinig's initial teacher preparation was at the National College of Education in Chicago, which began as the Cook County Normal School. Heinig had been director of the laboratory nursery school of the Child Development Institute at Teachers College, brought to this position by the director of the Institute for Child Welfare Research, Helen Thompson Woolley.[82] In 1938, Heinig was appointed the first director of the Australian Association for Preschool Child Development.

Thus it was that a relatively small group of influential educators who had trained in England and the United States steered Australian preschools on a new course starting in the 1930s. Jean Wyndham directed the KUNSW teachers college until 1956, when she resigned due to illness. Mary Walker, who held a diploma in education (from Sydney Teachers College) rather than in kindergarten, replaced her.

IN 1917, LILLIAN DE LISSA left Australia for England to take charge of the Gipsy Hill Training College for Teachers of Young Children. She had trained at the KUNSW with American kindergartener Frances Newton, directed the Kindergarten Union of South Australia (KUSA), and had taken a part in the start-up of the Kindergarten Union of Western Australia (KUWA). In 1955, having returned to celebrate KUSA's fiftieth anniversary, she reflected that the ideas of the past — hers — still sounded fresh and forward-looking:

> I thought that these reports would read like a visit to a museum of ideas of long ago and I expected to be amused in comparing "then" and "now." Instead, I found these reports so modern in spirit and so sound in ideas and ideals, that could they be re-written and have some modern psychological phraseology substituted they could be presented as an address on education today ... In fact the ideas and ideals of nearly fifty years ago here in the kindergarten world are those that are being written and spoken of today as "progressive" and are being aimed for in the procedures now being adopted in most of the up-to-date schools of England for children of all ages.[83]

Her assessment was self-congratulatory, of course, but she was right: the ideas and ideals of 1905 and 1955 were similar in many respects.

chapter 9 **Wellington Free Kindergarten Association**

According to a story dating from the 1920s, a founding myth common in kindergarten history, the Wellington Free Kindergarten Association (Wellington FKA) was inspired by Mary Richmond's personal observations of poor children playing on the city streets: "Miss Richmond saw little ones, too small to go to school, sitting about in the dirt on the pavements, dusty and grubby, learning language which was certainly no good to them, and her tender mother-heart asked for these neglected babies. 'We must have kindergartens for these children,' she said and set to work to get them."[1] The account continued, relating that Rachel Reynolds, president and a founder of the Dunedin Free Kindergarten Association, spoke on kindergartens in Wellington at Richmond's invitation. Richmond then embarked on a personal campaign, speaking at a series of teas where she enlisted friends and other women in the community to join her cause.[2] Richmond, trained at the Froebel Institute College in London, had operated a Wellington kindergarten school for seven years and was thus knowledgeable about kindergartens. Historian Kerry Bethell notes that this school served older children and operated according to a general kindergarten philosophy rather than following the standard pedagogy.[3]

At a July 1905 organizational meeting, the kindergarten management was decided, with Richmond as president. The administrators included a secretary and treasurer, an executive council of twenty women who also managed financial matters, and a number of associates, subscribers, and friends, their designation determined by the amount of money they pledged. Finally, there was a male advisory board whose duties were to attend the annual meetings and "give advice when asked to do so."[4]

The association opened a kindergarten nine months later, just after the start of the new school term. On April 2, 1906, thirteen children gathered with their teacher in a church schoolroom for their first day of kindergarten. Numbers grew to thirty-eight in a few weeks, and the Wellington FKA moved to larger quarters: first to a church hall on Tory Street and once more before settling into rented rooms above a Chinese grocer on Taranaki Street in 1910.[5] In 1909, the New Zealand government introduced a subsidy scheme on a per-child basis to be matched by donations, which encouraged the association to open additional branches for a total of four. In 1910, Constance Freeman, holding a National Froebel Union certificate from England, was put in charge of staff and student training, as well as the children's programs. The student teachers worked with the children as part of their practice teaching, which enabled the Wellington FKA to staff the additional kindergartens.

Australians

In 1912, Nettie Birkenhead Riley was hired from Australia as the new headmistress, the first of two Australians to take this role. Riley had trained at the Sydney Kindergarten Teachers College and had been director of the KUNSW's Surry Hills kindergarten in Sydney from 1906 to 1912.[6] It is likely that she trained under the American, Frances Newton. For a period in 1911, she was interim director of the Kindergarten Training College in Brisbane.[7] Riley was headmistress, later designated principal, of the Wellington FKA until her retirement and return to Sydney in 1928.[8]

In 1918, a building campaign was undertaken, but it failed to raise sufficient funds to replace the inadequate rented quarters with a newly constructed kindergarten. Instead, the association purchased a factory on Taranaki Street and converted it, creating a kindergarten on the ground floor and classrooms for student training above. Riley compared the Wellington kindergartens to those in Sydney and Auckland, and found them lacking. Yet, she believed the new kindergarten college was vastly improved, remarking that it could no longer be called "an old maid's factory."[9] Nonetheless, the facility itself was cold, damp, and dark, flaws that prompted teachers' complaints for the next fifty years.[10] It contained the Wellington FKA's flagship program, housing a kindergarten and later a nursery school until 1965, and the training college until 1962.

Most student-teachers were from middle-class families in and around Wellington. Richmond believed that kindergarten training matched women's interests and reflected their natural inclination to be nurturing. Kindergarten work made demands of the heart, not the head, and Richmond especially encouraged those girls who were not academically gifted to consider teaching: "Women should be trained up primarily to deal with individuals; men to deal with society. Every ordinary girl from twelve years old to sixteen years old should be trained amongst baby children. Let the unusually intellectual girl go her own way, and let every facility be provided for her, but do not force the ordinary girl through an academic course which she detests."[11]

The inclination to expand without sufficient numbers of trained staff generated what became a frequent problem for director Riley and the association: reliance on the labour of student teachers meant that children's enrolment depended heavily on student-teacher recruitment. Riley estimated that each additional student teacher allowed the enrolment of ten to fifteen children.[12] When student numbers increased, additional children were taken in, creating a problem when students graduated or were in short supply. This was the situation in 1919 when Riley reported to the executive council that "we have six students to staff five Kindergartens — they are doing their best but it means a lower standard of work unless we reduce our numbers, which I am loath to do."[13] Riley believed that twenty "were too many children for anyone to look after." She "aimed at the student being a type of mother, to act the same to the children as they would have a mother do."[14] This implied a need for more individual attention.

The number of unpaid and untrained staff was a matter of real concern for the Wellington FKA. In 1920, three of the five kindergartens had one paid teacher and one paid assistant; the remaining two had one paid teacher and unpaid students.[15] The sole recorded payment to students occurred in 1916, when three students took charge of a kindergarten during a period of their supervising teacher's absence. They were awarded a small "bonus" to be shared among them.[16] Although no tuition fees were charged for training, it was understood that labour was compensation in kind.

Students were admitted to the training program at age seventeen, but when their numbers became critically low in 1913, Riley sought permission to accept them on probationary status at three months prior to their seventeenth birthday.[17] Some were recruited at schools where Riley gave talks and invited girls to visit the kindergarten. This was the case with sixteen-year-old Edna Scott.[18] She enrolled in the training and, after graduating in 1917, was hired as a teacher, a position she held for thirty-one years.

A shortage of staff in relation to the numbers of kindergartens — really a shortage of student teachers — meant long waiting lists and, in Riley's opinion, a damaged reputation with parents. At the start of the 1919 school year, she reported to the Wellington FKA council, "The lack of students necessitates the reduction of children and we have so many [illegible] in the Kindergarten that it becomes quite a serious matter. We lose the interest of the neighborhood when we have to refuse children when they have been waiting for a year to be admitted. At Wellington South we have fifty children waiting now."[19]

A factor influencing enrolment was the government subsidy, which was based on the number of children in a program. More children meant more money but also required greater numbers of staff and student teachers. Riley described the dilemma to the Wellington FKA executive council in 1921, judging that being assigned a class of fifteen children was "unfair for a beginner." She continued: "Even with these numbers in our five kindergartens and our Primary class we only total 200 children — and our expenditure would be practically the same for 300 and our subsidy a great deal more, and our students cost the same to train if there are 2 or 10."[20] In fact, as far as the records reveal, the training had no direct cost at all. A result was overcrowded and understaffed kindergartens, where additional children were admitted in order to obtain the government grant.[21] At the same time, large numbers of trained kindergarteners were produced.

Four days a week, students spent their mornings at work in the kindergarten, gaining practical experience under Riley's direction, and devoted their afternoons to study. Actual coursework occupied about half their afternoon time, as one group would be left to read while Riley worked with the other on specific lessons (see Table 3). In later years, lecturers were brought in, teaching the history of education, English, and blackboard drawing, among other subjects.

As Table 3 shows, their coursework covered practical and theoretical elements, with the emphasis on the former. Teaching practice was supported by methods courses. Theory included knowledge of child nature, nature study, and kindergarten principles. Coursework also focused on the physical care of children, where students gained "practical experience in bandaging little toes and knees properly ... [and] what to do in the cases of croup and other ailments."[22] Riley explained that studying children's na-

Table 3. Student schedule, Wellington Free Kindergarten Association, 1920

Day	Time	Student activities	
		Juniors	Seniors
Monday	2:00 to 3:00 3:15 to 4:15	Reading Program planning	Educational methods Reading
Tuesday	2:00 to 4:00	Games, singing, rhythm	
Wednesday	2:00 to 3:00 3:15 to 4:15	Reading Froebel's Gifts	Advanced Gifts Reading
Thursday	3:00 to 4:30	Handwork, including simple carpentry work with odd material	

Source: Wellington Free Kindergarten Association, "Council Reports" (Wellington, June 1920).

ture was really the "study of children and how to differentiate when imagination ends and lying begins; how to avoid punishment; how to administer it if unavoidable; and generally how to be judicious."[23] The training was planned as a well-rounded education, whereby students understood "the purpose and reason of existence, the development of personality, how to think, and the beginning of many arts and crafts."[24] The actual experience included a number of mundane tasks, and, as Table 4 reveals, students were responsible for housekeeping chores.

Entrenchment

From the mid-1910s and throughout the 1920s, the Wellington FKA served about forty children in each of its four or five kindergartens. Pupils were admitted between the ages of three and five, with a few starting at age two and a half, and for a time five- to seven-year-olds were enrolled in a separate primary class.[25] The youngest children may have accompanied older brothers or sisters to the kindergarten. The primary class was added in 1920, when parents lobbied the association to have their older children remain in the kindergarten until they reached the compulsory school-starting age of seven. The class operated throughout the decade.[26]

Why parents sent their children to kindergarten is mostly unknown, but their reasons probably varied depending on family circumstances. When space was unavailable in the state school, some sought to have their children remain in kindergarten.[27] Some of the association kindergartens,

Table 4. Student duties, Wellington Free Kindergarten Association, 1926

	Duties
All students	To bring flowers whenever possible. To keep clay in good order. Take home housekeeper's apron and wash. Keep own table scrubbed. Leave playhouse tidy. Monitor "B" and "C" to help with children's washing up on Fridays.
Monitor "A" only	
9:00 to 9:10 a.m.	Open all windows, attend to flowers, and dust circle room. Put out rusks and apples. Set morning tea tray. Outside in playground not later than 9:15.
10:40 a.m.	Put on kettle; see to housekeeper setting tables. Tidy circle room if necessary.
11:00 a.m.	Make tea and bring downstairs.
12:00 p.m.	See children over the road. Put away material, also rusk and apples, washbowl, board, and knife. Put out materials for next day. Set lunch table and buy necessary food.

Source: Scrapbook, 1908-30, Wellington Regional Free Kindergarten Association Inc. Records, MS-Group-0052, MSY 1921, Alexander Turnbull Library, National Library of New Zealand, Wellington.

located in suburbs, served middle-class parents who sought playmates for their preschool children. Taranaki Kindergarten served poor families, newcomers, and the nearby Chinese New Zealander community, in addition to middle-class families. Between 1916 and 1921, about equal numbers of the parents (fathers) of the children at this kindergarten were classified as professional or clerical workers, skilled labourers, or "unskilled."[28]

The argument was also made for kindergarten's social value in keeping vulnerable children out of the "playground of the public streets, with its contaminating influences."[29] The longer experience of the Dunedin kindergartens led the inspector of police in that city to conclude, in a now familiar use of "statistics," that "these schools had entirely checked the flow of children into the industrial schools."[30] By 1926, the Wellington FKA made its own claim: "The Free Kindergartens in Wellington have so far succeeded, that there are no known instances where children trained in them have come before the juvenile court."[31] The association suggested that this had been accomplished via a curriculum that "teaches the young child habits of punctuality, cleanliness and truthfulness. It teaches the dignity and value of necessary labour."[32] The children, however, did not always embrace this program. As Riley reported in 1921, "It has taken much longer this year than any other to get the children to respond, they seem so much duller." In the next month, she added, "It is quite time the children were showing some habits of order and method."[33]

These moral aims were embedded in children's activities emphasizing discipline and conformity. Handwork involved a variety of crafts and kindergarten occupations.[34] One Gift was used each morning but only the less complicated ones. Edna Scott recalled, "Some of the students [student teachers] would get out the more advanced Gifts which were collections of differently shaped and sized blocks and then spend all day trying to get them back into the box again."[35]

Children's activities were organized around weekly subjects or themes, such as "Mother's and Father's Work," which were elaborated in lesson plans governed by a "chief thought" (such as industry). The lessons started with a "talk," a discussion guided by teachers' questions (as, for example, Who works in the home? What can each one do to help?). They ended with "table work," in which the children sat in groups of about twelve and pretended to scrub, to chop and stack kindling, or to make bread.[36] Following their teacher's instructions and using small blocks, probably Gifts three and four, they "chopped" and "stacked" their "kindling" or made their "bread."

The curriculum was also organized via nature studies reflecting the seasons. A study of gardens, birds, and butterflies was undertaken in the spring.[37] Considerable time was devoted to holiday-themed work. Christmas crafts started in late October: older children made gifts for their parents, and the youngest children made paper chains for decorating the tree and the classroom. A 1918 newspaper report on kindergarten Christmas season activities described children making decorations, eating a snack, at circle time, and ending the morning by singing "God Save the King." The report concluded from this display, "Truly, the teaching of Froebel is being faithfully followed."[38]

Educational materials also included some Montessori apparatus.[39] In 1914, Mary Richmond had announced her intention to go to Rome and "see Dr. Montessori, to learn what she could of her methods, though the meeting never occurred."[40] Some Montessori materials were used in the kindergartens, though, in the experience of teacher Edna Scott, the children found some of these frustrating.[41] There is no record that the Wellington FKA teachers of this era had any Montessori training, and thus it is unlikely that the materials were used in accordance with the Montessori system.

Reconstruction

In 1928, Enid Thelma Wilson replaced Riley as principal. Like Riley, Wilson was from Australia. She trained at the Perth Kindergarten Training College, graduating in 1916 at twenty. Briefly director of a KUWA kindergarten, she resigned at the end of 1917 in protest at having been passed over for the position of training college principal. Her desire for a promotion with such little experience was typical of Australian kindergarteners during the period, who commonly experienced rapid career rises. She then took a position with the KUNSW. In 1919, she returned to Perth as director of a recently opened KUWA kindergarten and later in the same year was appointed principal, a post she held for seven years.

The KUWA was a younger organization than the Wellington FKA, having formed in 1912 after a visit from Lillian de Lissa in 1911, whose own career trajectory was remarkable. The first director, Ethel Donnel, a KUNSW graduate who was teaching in Adelaide, was appointed on de Lissa's recommendation. The association soon realized that training local teachers was necessary to sustain the nascent kindergarten movement in Perth, and Donnel organized a training college in a kindergarten in 1913. Additional kindergartens opened to provide students with opportunities for practice teaching. Wilson's own training was under Constance Finlayson, who also came to Perth from the Adelaide Kindergarten Teachers College, where she would have studied with de Lissa.[42]

Student training combined Froebelian kindergarten work with the new ideas of Montessori. The introduction of Montessori was stimulated by visits from Martha Simpson and de Lissa, who had stopped in Perth on their return from their international Montessori courses in Rome: Simpson in 1913 and de Lissa in 1915.[43] The KUWA course of study for 1915-16, when Wilson was undertaking her training, is given in Table 5. With the addition of Montessori work, it presents a contrast to Riley's program at the Wellington FKA (Table 3). The photograph below depicting children using Montessori materials in an infants' school in Perth, shows the strong influence of Montessori's ideas on education, presumably following visits by Simpson and de Lissa.[44]

Lillian de Lissa had been a major force for reform at the KUWA, pushing it to break with its very short history in a 1915 letter, three years after its founding: "The kindergarten today is very different from that of three years ago. Many customs and doings that we kindergartners had grown to love have had to go, as modern education science has thrown more light

Children using Montessori materials in a kindergarten in an infants' school in Perth, 1920. LC-USZ61-7008, LOT 5338, Library of Congress, Washington.

upon the path. It is often hard to part with old things and customs beloved — but progress demands it."[45]

Wilson had also been exposed to Montessori work at the experimental kindergartens operated by the KUNSW during her time in Sydney. She appeared to take de Lissa's challenge to heart. A 1919 newspaper article on

Table 5. Kindergarten Union of Western Australia Training College program of study, 1915–16

Student year	Student activity
Junior year	Froebel's Gifts, Montessori work, hygiene, physical culture and games, drawing, nature study, literature, singing, handwork (including basket work and modelling with clay)
Senior year	Child study, primary work, Montessori work, literature, history of education, Froebel's *Education of Man,* biology, drawing, handwork, physical culture and games

Source: Kindergarten Union of Western Australia, "Annual Report" (Perth, 1915–16), cited in Rosemary Kerr, *A History of the Kindergarten Union of Western Australia, 1911-1973* (Perth: Meerlinga Young Children's Foundation, 1994), 38.

the Perth kindergarten that she directed reported little trace of the standard Froebelian exercises. The class was made up of fifty children aged two to six, and the program was organized as a Montessori preschool, with practical life and sensorial curriculum areas predominant. The emphasis on sense training led the journalist to conclude, "The distinctive feature about the Montessori method is that in most of the problems put before the little students they have to rely solely on their sense of touch. Their eyes are blindfolded with special bandages, but even then after a little practice they are able to make the correct distinctions with ease."[46] After lunch, in the short time before they departed for home, the children participated in the more standard kindergarten group games, including marching and movement activities.

As principal of the Perth training college, Wilson developed the Montessori kindergarten further, promoting children's self-development through freely selected activities. Montessori materials were used every morning, and a plan was undertaken to establish a separate fee-charging demonstration Montessori school with a smaller enrolment of twenty. In 1919, student training began to include a psychology course.

In 1921, Wilson took leave to train in Montessori methods at Blackfriars demonstration school in Sydney. When she returned, she introduced the "Dalton Plan" into the new "sub-primary" class for children from age five to eight, and she purchased new Montessori materials for the kindergarten. In the Dalton Plan, students developed individual learning "contracts" in each subject. During her visit to Sydney, the KUNSW Montessori experiment terminated. Nevertheless, she returned convinced that Montessori was not only relevant, but that the KUWA methods were more advanced than those of its Sydney counterpart, an observation that the historical evidence seems to corroborate.

News regarding educational innovations such as the Dalton Plan moved quickly from the United States, where they often originated, to Sydney and Perth. In 1919, Helen Parkhurst, creator of the Dalton Plan, had introduced her reforms in a general way at the Children's University School, New York City.[47] In the upper-elementary and secondary school divisions, the focus was on freedom in terms of students' decisions regarding how best to learn and use their time, and process was emphasized over product. The plan was adapted for younger students aged seven to ten; called the "Sub-Dalton Plan," its main change was that students spent shorter periods on their learning contracts. Although the Dalton Plan was not designed for the kindergarten, similar principles were applied at this level; for example, large blocks of time were allotted for free play and individual enterprise. Parkhurst, who had studied under Montessori and had lived with her in Rome for several years, was influenced by her ideas.[48]

The Wellington FKA was in its twenty-second year when Wilson arrived in 1928 to assume her duties as principal. It had been under the direction of Riley for the last sixteen years. During her first few years in Wellington, Wilson continued to emphasize the social-welfare aspect of kindergartens, which was characteristic of the earlier period, including the idea that kindergartens were a sanctuary from city life. After touring Australian kindergartens in 1931, she reported to the Wellington FKA executive council, "Kindergarten aims to bring back to the city child that freedom, beauty and simplicity in life which is his right."[49] Her description of an Australian kindergarten detailed activities related to health routines in what appears to have been a full-day program: "I saw them all having a two-hour's rest. It really was a charming sight — tiny stretchers laid out in a cool, airy room, ready for weary little bodies. They all cleaned their teeth after the meal, removed their shoes, and quietly tip-toed into the sleeping room, with their dimpled fingers on rounded lips, to their own little bed for two hours of rest."[50]

In 1933, Wilson went on study leave to Teachers College, Columbia University. After returning to Wellington, she moved quickly to implement changes in the student training and the children's program that she believed would develop the work along more modern lines. Motivated by her new understanding of theory, she attempted to free teaching practice from its previous orientation, grounding it in a knowledge base that included scientific child study. Wilson undertook to make a break with past work and its welfare orientation. In some cases, this would be achieved through staffing — in 1934, she sought for a branch kindergarten director who could place it "on an educational basis rather than a charitable one."[51] However, she expended her greatest efforts on training a new cadre of teachers. For Wilson, teachers required a new reflective attitude toward child education, with the focus on individual children, and the training program was revised to meet this need. There is no evidence that Montessori methods were part of this change.

In the old program, though senior students assisted in the kindergarten during the mornings, they took charge of a classroom only at the end of their training, for a period of one week.[52] In the revised program, they took charge during one morning a week for ten weeks, suggesting a more developmental approach. Practical work was supported by knowledge gained about child development through observations, which were reported in a thesis. Students observed the mental, physical, and social development of two children, one younger and one older, including their home life. Staff from the Wellington FKA and Victoria University College supervised their observations.[53]

Wilson's report on the students' practice teaching reflected the new orientation:

> Each student was fully alive to the importance of a suitable environment. Cleanliness, order, beauty of colours and arrangement, light and fresh air and the provision of varied and suitable occupations and interest were features of each student's preparation for her morning's work. Their own personal appearance was as attractive as are the kindergartens for the forming of good habits for such socializing influence ... [The high standard of music selected] showed that they realized the importance of thought and practice in these things ... I was impressed with the very sympathetic and interested attitude of the students to the children and it is clear that the children feel that this interest and sympathy is genuine. The friendliness and absence of restraint shown by them to the students ... is remarkable.[54]

Another report described the teacher's role in the "new" kindergarten as one of a knowledgeable and detached observer, respectful of children's need to explore and learn on their own: "Several of the students have it seems to me developed in a marked degree the ability to keep themselves in the background, only directing and advising when necessary and so avoiding for the children over-stimulation, strain, and dependence on others."[55]

Wilson and her staff adopted a self-consciously modern approach, believing past practices inferior to the new. To emphasize this point, staff "dramatized an 'old time kindergarten' so as to give the students and some of the assistants an idea of the progress that has been made in our attitude towards child life and in our methods of handling children."[56] The new attitude "has to be realized by the teacher before she can hope to create an atmosphere worthy of the young children in her care. After it is realized, the teacher has to take stock of herself and as long as she is in a kindergarten or school atmosphere to be continually taking stock — everything comes back to *life* and real life situations."[57]

The children's program reflected the new thinking by introducing freely selected choices into the daily schedule.[58] The choices were termed "activities," and teachers and students were each responsible for one activity during free-choice period. In their role as observers, they recorded the children's behaviours, though the reasons for collecting the data are unspecified in the reports. The curriculum was still organized according to subject matter, but less emphasis was placed on learning facts and more on the process of the child's experience with the study subject. In the earlier period, the topic of gardens might have been explored via an initial discussion followed by table work, but in the new approach "various activities were grouped in a natural unforced way around such interesting things as hedgehogs, bees, and spiders, and one felt that at the end of the morning, what the children had seen and done had become part of themselves and had enlarged and enriched their appreciation of the world around them."[59]

IN 1931, THE NEW ZEALAND Department of Education ceased providing the subsidies and grants for kindergartens that it had initiated in 1909. The grants were terminated for economic reasons and due to a belief within the ministry that kindergarten had no educational value. In fact, some considered it to be harmful to child development. N.R. McKenzie, the former inspector of schools for Taranaki, waded into the controversy over the cutting of subsidies. He recalled that, while on leave in Toronto as part of an inspector exchange, he had learned of a longitudinal survey that had tracked Toronto students for fourteen years. This had revealed that, "on the average, children who entered school at the age of five completed the course only two months earlier than those who entered at six. In other words, teachers were paid twelve months' salary for the equivalent of two months' work."[60]

Kindergarten leaders and sympathetic community members spoke out on behalf of the program's educational benefits. In his address at the 1935 Wellington FKA annual meeting, Clarence Beeby, director of the newly formed New Zealand Council of Educational Research, highlighted the mental health benefits that would accrue from kindergarten experience: "The kindergarten really represented the psychological weaning of the child, the separation of the child mind from that of its parents."[61]

The removal of the subsidy, enacted in the midst of an economic depression, occurred at a time of increasing need for kindergarten services as mothers of preschool-aged children sought employment to support their families. The Wellington FKA pointed to the value of its service as an aid to child development rather than a support for mothers, collecting information on children's living conditions and concluding that those in poor circumstances "suffered retardation of some sort" and needed the advantages of a kindergarten program.[62] Funding for kindergartens was revived in 1936 under a new Labour government led by Prime Minister Michael Savage.

For part of this period, Wilson and Scott, who was then director of the Taranaki Kindergarten, were on a study leave at Teachers College, Columbia University. When she returned, Wilson spoke of introducing nursery schools as a modern step for New Zealand, noting their growth in the United States, England, and Melbourne. She challenged, "It now remains for New Zealand to awaken to this important aspect of education."[63] In explaining what nursery schools entailed, she included the principle that they were intended to supplement the home and stressed that they were not to replace a mother's care. She highlighted the four aims of nursery education: a psychological aim ("sense of security in an atmosphere of serenity"); a social aim ("the companionship of their [children's] contemporaries"); a curriculum and materials aim ("an environment equipped and planned from the point of view of the child's physical, mental and emotional needs"); and a teaching aim ("expert guidance by people enabled to understand the child's point of view and by their very impartiality to handle each child's idiosyncrasies successfully and well").[64]

Scott stayed two years in the United States, learning about American nursery school methods through coursework at Teachers College with leading scholars such as Patty Smith Hill.[65] That the dual emphasis of American nursery education — on self-expression and habit training — was incorporated into the Wellington program is evident in photographs contained in the 1935-36 annual report; these depict children involved in self-expression (painting at easels) and habit training (washing their hands).

In 1937, English psychoanalyst Susan Isaacs visited New Zealand under the auspices of the New Education Fellowship Conference. Partly as a result of hearing her speak, Wilson and Elizabeth Hamilton, director of the Wellington South Kindergarten, took leave to study with Isaacs at the Institute of Education at the University of London. Isaacs, a child psychologist, had been director of Cambridge's experimental Malting House School during the 1920s.[66] At Malting House, a small private school, Isaacs encouraged children's free exploration of intellect and emotion. Her observations over the three years during which the school operated formed the basis of a series of books, including *Intellectual Growth in Young Children* (1930) and *Social Development in Young Children* (1933).⁶⁷ During her lectures in New Zealand, she shared her ideas on children and education from her standpoint as a psychoanalyst and teacher, highlighting the importance of the early years for mental health and intellectual growth. She urged teachers to take active roles in provoking growth through questioning children and planning for real-world experiences. She privileged dramatic play as a multi-purpose teaching strategy for skill development, emotional release, and language and intellectual development. Isaacs had less to say about curriculum than she did about healthy child development.

Isaacs' approach to nursery education was very different from that at Teachers College, where Wilson and Scott had recently spent considerable time learning about the "conduct curriculum," with its focus on habit training and social adjustment. Nevertheless, despite the conflicting theoretical orientations of these various ideas, Wilson seemed able to accommodate them within her overall educational vision.

From 1940 to 1945, the Manpower Committee of the Organization for National Security controlled labour in New Zealand. The committee required that, subject to its discretion, single and married women with children over the age of sixteen were to be employed, a policy that raised the number of women in the paid workforce by thirty-six thousand in 1942.⁶⁸ Women with young children were employed in non-essential work. Kindergarten associations played a minor role in meeting the increased need for childcare. The common belief was that mothers of young children belonged in the home. In 1943, funded by the Government of New Zealand War Expenses Account, the Wellington FKA converted the Taranaki and Petone Kindergartens into nursery schools for children of mothers who were employed in essential war work.⁶⁹ The Taranaki Street Nursery School, led by Edna Scott, opened in 1943. Petone opened later the same year, continuing to offer a kindergarten program alongside the full-day nursery school.

Wilson retired in 1948, after twenty years as principal. Teacher Edna Scott left the same year, ending her long career at the association. Miriam Baucke served as acting principal for two years before being appointed to the position in 1950 as the Wellington FKA's first New Zealand-trained principal of teacher-training programs. Baucke immediately set to work to "free up" the approach of the Wellington kindergartens. In 1948, she and two branch kindergarteners went on a study visit to Australia, and she reported to the Wellington FKA on the "freer" methods in Melbourne:

"Taking into consideration the comparatively short period of each weekday spent by the children in our kindergarten — 15 hours out of approximately 84 waking hours — it was felt that some measure of direction each morning had advantages. 'Time to stand and stare,' however, should be considered as essential as sunshine and fresh air. It was regretted that the subsequent efforts of the Association to 'borrow' an experienced Director from the Victorian Free Kindergarten Union for one year in order to have these methods demonstrated was unsuccessful."[70]

The Wellington association remained oriented toward Australia and England after the Second World War. In 1951, Joyce Barns, the director of the Taranaki Street Nursery School, received a bursary from the British Council to study "the most up-to-date methods in work with young children" at London's Institute of Education. There, she would study under Dorothy Gardner, who had taken over from Susan Isaacs as head of the Department of Child Development in 1943.[71] Barns' reverence for Isaacs was evident in a news report of her experience: "'Miss Gardner told me that all the furniture in my room has an association with Susan Isaacs,' writes the New Zealander. 'Many times she ate from the table at which I work and sat in one of the easychairs. I cannot help feeling proud of the way we in New Zealand have tackled our problems and have kept up to date, as we have had to collect most of our ideas from books.'"[72]

chapter 10 Conclusion: Change and Continuity

THE INFANT SCHOOL SOCIETY described at the start of this book succumbed to ideological quarrels and dissolved after only a few years. Other, longer-lasting organizations such as the Home and Colonial Infant School Society and various missionary associations continued its work. In these efforts, the radical infant school pedagogy was modified as it was incorporated into state schooling for settler, and in some cases, indigenous children. A similar process occurred with the kindergarten, which lost its more esoteric elements when applied in free kindergartens for poor immigrant children.

According to the analysis of Dorothy Gardner and Joan Cass, this change was inevitable. Gardner was head of the Department of Child Development at the Institute of Education, University of London, for a quarter century. She and Cass observed pessimistically that, as was the case of the British nursery school, the generation that succeeded educational innovators tended to "follow a fashion ... having only a partial understanding of the purposes and principles behind the methods." Over time, "shorn of false and non-essential 'trappings,' the essence of each new influence inasmuch as it is based on the needs of children and on sound educational ideals, is assimilated into the educational ideas and practices of the school."[1] These practices developed within the constraints of what was possible, limited by the cultural, philosophical, and scientific beliefs concerning children, genetics, learning, poverty, and human rights.[2] The more radical approaches to early education sought to alter the social order by changing the trajectory of children's lives. The more conservative approaches aimed

Conclusion

to control aspects of children's lives as a means to maintaining the existing social order.

Few schools were grounded in Robert Owen's idealistic principles.[3] Teaching without corporal punishment and learning through amusements required a fundamental change from the dominant cultural belief regarding how education should occur. Just what was meant by amusements changed over time as various educationists sought to use children's inclination to play for a targeted purpose: learning letters or acquiring skills for group living.

In all settings, the enduring idea from the New Lanark experiment was that very young children were educable. This idea was not new, but there had previously been little interest in acting upon it by gathering toddlers into schools. Owen upheld a naive environmentalist view, believing that "the infants of any one class in the world may be readily formed into men of any other class." He added,

> It must be evident to those who have been in the practice of observing children with attention, that much of good or evil is taught to or acquired by a child at a very early period of its life; that much of temper or disposition is correctly or incorrectly formed before he attains his second year, and that many durable impressions are made at the termination of the first twelve or even six months of its existence. The children, therefore, of the uninstructed and ill-instructed, suffer material injury in the formation of their characters during these and the subsequent years of childhood and of youth.[4]

It was therefore important to bend the twig early and with a firm hand, training it to grow in a particular direction. In the infant school, this involved Bible study and rudimentary skills in the three R's. It was also a training of the will, aided by a child's love for and submission to his or her teacher. Accounts of infant schools in the colonies indicate that they were fairly effective in teaching basic literacy in local languages as well as English, through techniques that mixed monitorial methods with the New Lanark model.

From the outset, training at school was conceived as working in opposition to children's home and community upbringing in circumstances that, both "fascinated and repelled," Wilderspin recorded in his Spitalfields observations.[5] He described the children there as dirty, poorly clothed, and sexually precocious, as well as frequently cursing, begging, and thieving.[6] For teachers, their moral training presented a challenge equal to imparting basic literacy skills. London Missionary Society teacher Ebenezer Buchanan, in Tahiti in 1842, despaired over the local children's "obscene gestures" and "polluting conversations," and "the filthy habits of the children who may be seen sitting and standing about the beach quite naked, playing with their own and each others privates for want of other toys."[7]

Certainly, infant schools and kindergartens kept children's hands busy with other occupations. Aspects of infant school practices found their way into kindergarten classrooms. These included what Wilderspin identified as "babyisms" adopted in the infant school: the hand clapping, arm movements, and marching that kept children in motion for exercise and obedience. His ultimate punishment was "to insist on the child sitting still, without moving hand or foot for a given time, say half an hour at most."[8] Movement alternated with "seatwork," which, in the infant school, involved the entire class seated in a gallery. In kindergarten, though children worked individually with their Gifts, they performed their table work simultaneously in a large group. Few texts on kindergarten delineated punishment, though it doubtless occurred.[9] In kindergarten, as in infant school, quiet pursuits alternated with organized games, the large class sizes in public schools leading to highly regimented movement exercises. Teachers College (Columbia) professors Mary Runyan and Caroline O'Grady described a New York kindergarten of this type, where one hundred children were organized in "military discipline, even to the 'lock-step' in marching."[10] Marching was a teaching strategy carried over from infant school methods. As American author Mary Ware Howland explained in *The Infant School Manual,*

> When the leader gives a stamp with his foot, the children immediately begin clapping their hands and stamping the right foot in regular time. Lines chalked or painted upon the floor serve to direct their course. It is however found expedient to vary the course from time to time, that novelty may increase the interest. Perfect regularity is prerequisite in their marches, which, though difficult at first, may be acquired by the persevering effort of the teacher. This not only forms the chief beauty of the exercise, but, it is of very important use in furnishing the infant mind with a principle of order and regularity which will soon be found to affect their conduct in other things.[11]

Conclusion

Winnipeg kindergarten teacher Jeannie Lothrop, who included "marching in good time" as part of her program, recognized the importance of marching exercises for intellectual training. In Sydney, Ridie Lee Buckey judged her program a success when a withdrawn child developed enough confidence to lead the marching. In Wellington, children marched from their tables to sit on the floor for circle time.[12] In Winnipeg in 1924, older children led the drill, like infant school monitors from a century before, but with the piano used as a signal to reinforce verbal commands: "Light steps, high steps, kicking steps, all followed in quick succession. George was chosen captain and sustained the honor with dignity. No officer on the parade ground could do better. He watched the march past, shouted out the orders with precision and decision. George is almost six years old and will be going to primary school next term."[13]

The kindergarten circle was a gallery on a single plane, enabling the teacher to view each child as a means to maintain order. However, marching and circle games were interpreted as a playful teaching strategy involving children's minds and bodies. In infant schools, and earlier in monitorial schools, pupils were also arranged in a circle for their lessons. Joseph Lancaster detailed the use of this in a monitorial school: "Another method of teaching the alphabet is, by a large sheet of pasteboard suspended by a nail on the school wall; twelve boys, from the sand class, are formed into a circle round this alphabet, standing in their numbers, 1, 2, 3, etc., to 12. These numbers are pasteboard tickets, with number 1, etc. inscribed, suspended by a string from the button of the bearer's coat, or around his neck. The best boy stands in the first place; he is also decorated with a leather ticket, gilt, and lettered *merit,* as a badge of honor."[14] His description could apply equally well to an infant school, with the exception that its pupils were not ranked according to their academic performance.

In the infant school run by teacher James Buchanan, circles represented harmony.[15] In the kindergarten, they were a form of beauty explored through occupations such as the rings, the ninth Gift.[16] Kate Douglas Wiggin and Nora Archibald Smith described a circle as an "unending line traced from a given line back to itself," their language intentionally suggestive of transcendental meanings: the rings touch at one point, yet all are connected, making concentric circles show how one thing can enclose another.[17]

Circles also had high importance in kindergarten games, which Wiggin and Smith linked to Froebel and traditions of children's play:

Circle time in a KUNSW kindergarten, Sydney, 1928. Kindergarten Union of New South Wales Collection, Mitchell Library, Sydney.

The ring is formed with some appropriate song in the beginning, and thus the sense of connection is felt, while the shape of the circle at least, is kept to the end. The majority of children's games in all countries are played in this way, as Froebel, of course, had noted; and the form of the circle itself, the symbol of unity, he held to be essential, — the more so, as the principle of self-activity here comes into play, since the children make the ring themselves by their own efforts, and not one of them can be left out without breaking it.[18]

More prosaically, Elizabeth Harrison and Belle Woodson noted how circle games such as passing a ball (Gift one) taught skills of "cooperation and self control."[19] Arranging children in a circle was a means of organizing them for instruction as well as amusement. Harrison and Woodson's manual, as well as others, referred to being "on the play circle" and to a "play-circle period." A circle painted on the floor was a teaching aid, as were the lines in the infant school.

Conclusion

At Winnipeg's Ellen Street Kindergarten, teacher Edith Duncan led her class in a dance around a circle as part of the morning routine. According to reporter Ann King, who profiled the kindergarten, this had the larger intent of "teaching children of many nationalities to become useful Canadians" via group games and other co-operative activities:

> The little tots, 33 of them, were standing around on the big circle, singing lustily. Mabel was "it," and came to a stand in her gay dancing, before Pearl, the little Chinese girl. After performing certain merry turns, the two of them started off on a gay hippity-hop around the circle, the class singing. They divided and each chose another partner, and so on, until everybody had been chosen and the kindergarten room was one blur of bobbing heads, brown, black and yellow curls, straight bobs topped on big floppy bows, and smooth round clipped heads, all dancing around in a merry whirl.[20]

Whole-class action games alternated with table work, which made children's individual performance visible. It was obvious when children deviated from the required pattern, and the complexity of some kindergarten activities could make them dependent on their teacher's assistance. Harriette Melissa Mills, from the Speyer School Kindergarten at Teachers College, New York, explained that the principles of the Gifts were "known only to the teacher."[21] As the teacher chose the moment in which to divulge these principles, children were left with little that was under their control. This dependency carried over into the next grade, where primary teachers complained that kindergarten children were "always crying out for help, and seem incapable of taking a step alone."[22] The kindergartens in the three case-study countries showed no such evidence, though instances in which primary or infants' school teachers had anything to say about their kindergarten counterparts were rare.

However, children did have the opportunity to develop habits that prepared them for formal schooling, where punctuality, perseverance, concentration, and the ability to follow directions were highly valued, and self-initiative was less so. Its role as a readiness program assured kindergarten a level of acceptance in public schools. Patty Smith Hill described this as one of the two "survival" strategies adopted by kindergarteners as they sought a permanent place in public schools. Under constant pressure to prove their worth, kindergarteners adopted primary school methods, succumbing to what Hill called the "tyranny of the primary teacher."[23] She identified the second survival strategy as becoming stubbornly Froebelian and isolated from the primary grades. This was not the case with the free-kindergarten associations in Winnipeg, Sydney, and Wellington, which developed outside a public school system, but it was true of the situation in Toronto during the 1920s.

In the process of adapting to primary school expectations, the mystical or idealistic aspects of the kindergarten system, which were aimed at fundamentally altering child life through spiritual uplifting, were dampened. A hyper-religious kindergarten was an affront, even an embarrassment, to educators seeking to place early education on a scientific basis. As described by Froebel, manipulating blocks was more than a physical or cognitive exercise: "In the forms made with the fifth gift there rules a living spirit of unity. Even members and direction which are apparently isolated are discovered to be related by significant connecting members and links, and the whole shows itself in all its parts as one and living — therefore, also, as a life-rousing, life-nurturing, and life-developing totality."[24] This understanding was beyond the reach of young Daisy Cowper, a pupil at a Liverpool infants' school in 1895. Cowper's reminiscences provide us with a rare glimpse of a child's reaction to kindergarten work:

> Another daft-seeming lesson was up-turning a box of small bricks, cubes, triangles, etc., itself forming a cube, and withdrawing the lid of the inverted box, at the word of the command: "Now lift the box", and hi, presto, there was the cube (of bits). So far, so good: I could do that, but I hated the end proceedings. The cube was reformed, the box placed over it — all to the word of command — and now for the prestidigitation! The upturned box and contents had to be drawn off the desk, to rest exactly on its lid which the hapless child held jammed between chest and desk, and it was sure to collapse!
>
> But paper weaving was a pleasure indeed. You threaded strips of coloured, shiny paper held in a special clip-holder through a coloured paper frame of vertical strips, thus forming a pretty pattern.[25]

Wiggin and Smith may have asserted that, though she was a child, Cowper nonetheless failed to see the activities in "the child way, which is always the poetic way."[26] Evidently, she did not perceive the activity through what they called the "glasses of the imagination." Nor, it seems, did the many critics of the kindergarten philosophy and its attendant materials, who claimed not to see educational value in children's routinized and symbol-ridden play.

In the United States, criticism caused only a brief pause in the kindergarten movement, where aspects of the system were folded into existing and developing ideas and initiatives, particularly those targeting immigrant children in large cities. The home mission field drew on the vast experience of foreign missions, concentrating on English-language immersion and the inculcation of Anglo manners and morals. Historian William Marsden claims that, though it appeared to support freedom, Froebelism actually blocked progressive ideas because it was so controlling: "His [Froebel's] pedagogy's long-term bent was to deny key progressive principles held dear in a later period, namely, cherishing present experience for its own sake, and promoting autonomous thought. Froebel's underlying intention was to instill strict religious rules, serving to ensure a passive acceptance of the socioeconomic frameworks and moral codes to be met with in adult life."[27] However, progressive education through manual training and social adjustment had very conservative aims. Furthermore, the American kindergarten was imbued with religious ideas, though, unlike those of Froebel, they were evangelical in nature. In Canada, they were tied to the Social-Gospel movement, linking the work undertaken in free kindergartens with ideas of social justice and Christian doctrine. The repeated call to "free up practice" could not be realized, because the outcome was never actually desired in the face of other priorities.

Even secular kindergartens had a missionary outlook, starting with the first free kindergarten established by the Ethical Culture Society in New York.[28] Kindergartens in settlement houses offered an education in citizenship and basic life skills to hasten the assimilation of young immigrants and prepare them for public schooling. Kindergartens were often the nucleus for settlement work in communities. Parents sought them out, and settlement workers believed they would be a feeder for other services including adult education. When the kindergarten opened at the Chicago Commons in 1896, it was called the "starting point and basis of the educational effort and also of the social redemptive work."[29] Although other services were provided by the case-study kindergartens, even in Winnipeg, where the kindergarten was designed as a settlement, children's programs dominated.

In Australia and New Zealand, no formal connection existed between settlement houses and the Sydney and Wellington kindergartens. However, due to the input of American-trained kindergarteners, settlement-oriented ideas regarding manual education enjoyed a strong influence in all these kindergartens. In the case-study examples, children were taught to respect workers and to value manual labour. In many instances, their parents were labourers or were employed as domestic or factory workers.

Bertha Hofer Hegner, a graduate of the Pestalozzi-Froebel House in Berlin, directed the kindergarten at the Chicago Commons and devised its manual training curriculum, in which "industrial and domestic work has largely supplanted the more theoretical gifts and occupations."[30] Kindergarteners at Hofer Hegner's training school were instructed in sloyd work, an approach to manual education developed in Sweden, including basket weaving rather than paper weaving. Children at the Commons' kindergarten learned to "wash their own towels, napkins, and dust-cloths in their little washtubs, and iron them with real little irons."[31] Furthermore, "The industrial work is what the children love best, and some children who are helpless with blocks, or weaving or paper-folding will brighten up at the sight of the little washtubs."[32]

Poor children had always been set to work early in the home, and later, within industry. Child-labour laws regulated children's employment in workplaces, and schools were vocationalized as a means to become more relevant. This was an inconsistency of progressive education; work in schools was considered to be beneficial to children's development, but some forms of waged labour were abusive. It is doubtful whether four- and five-year-olds would have ironed clothes at home, and they certainly would not have done so in an industrial laundry. In England, laundry work had been part of the home economics curriculum from Standard IV since 1890, though, as Fanny Calder explained in her *Teachers' Manual of Elementary Laundry Work*, the aim was "not to prepare laundresses" but to enable girls to do laundry work at home "without the aid of machines."[33] In free kindergartens, via the Kitchen Garden program, the aim was precisely to prepare laundresses. In the Chicago Commons' kindergarten and other similar set-ups, children were not playing at work — they were working.

In 1917, Lewis Hine photographed children building dollhouses at the Horace Mann Kindergarten, in a series of "Work Portraits" created for the National Child Labor Committee. Twenty years later, work was interpreted as essential for children's social development and encouraged in the "Wendy corner," the activity area named in honour of the James Barrie character and designated for dramatic play on a household theme. In a photograph in the 1937 publication *The Horace Mann Kindergarten for Five-Year-Old Children*, two youngsters engage in co-operative housekeeping.

This was considered dramatic play, an element within the creative arts curriculum. Such play for the middle- and upper-class children at the Horace Mann Kindergarten was described as "stimulus to the imagination" and was perceived as important to social adjustment.[34]

Following the debacle of the Committee of Nineteen, which met for ten years before issuing three conflicting reports, the International Kindergarten Union (IKU) moved away from Gift work, incorporating the materials in re-creating "social situations" via "projects."[35] These achieved high realism, as can be seen in the two 1928 photographs below, of children at work in the Honolulu kindergarten. An IKU report classed such play under "manual activities":

> The grocery store may be an individual project, each child building with Froebelian blocks, counters and shelves, adding cans of fruit and vegetables and glasses of jelly represented by cylinders of the beads, large and small. Objects constructed of other materials may also be added to make the equipment complete. Later, the group may combine efforts to produce a store large enough for several children to enter at once, using the large floor blocks and boards for counters and shelves and the cylinders for cans of fruits and vegetables. Other material may be used with the blocks as the representation and play are carried forward and as the children discover a need for them. Real fruit, vegetables, and grains may be used, or clay fruit and vegetables may be made and painted, and boxes and baskets constructed to hold these. Money may be made, a pocketbook to carry it in, and a delivery wagon for the goods.[36]

The report was created by a subcommittee on kindergarten curriculum that included Elizabeth Harrison, then principal of the National Kindergarten and Elementary College in Chicago. A decade earlier, Harrison and Woodson had published *The Kindergarten Building Gifts with Hints on Program-Making,* in which teachers were also directed to use the Gifts in "role play." A child could pose as a fruit seller, going round the table or "play circle" with a basket containing the six coloured balls of the first Gift, selling her "cherries" and "oranges." Harrison and Woodson described how "the game can introduce the child to other activities of the trade-world, not only in the ideal play-form, but also in its financial form," using real fruit and real money. They ended their description with a nod to Froebel: "But deeper than this there lies in all such games of barter and trade the dim

Change and Continuity

Children at play, selling fruit at the Beretainia Kindergarten, Honolulu, 1928. SP 109669 – N 109669, Bishop Museum, Honolulu.

Children at play, doing laundry at the Beretainia Kindergarten, Honolulu, 1928. SP 109680 – N 109680, Bishop Museum, Honolulu.

perception of the interdependence of man and the Providence of God."[37] This sort of reference was entirely absent from the 1919 International Kindergarten Union report on the kindergarten curriculum.

Progressive kindergartens did not entirely abandon the Gifts, though when they were used, it was not always in relation to educational objectives. In the Horace Mann Kindergarten, where the "desired outcomes" of most activities were carefully listed, weaving was simply described "as a rather complicated process for children of this age," being "valuable chiefly because children enjoy the activity and the product is attractive."[38] Like young Daisy Cowper at the Liverpool infants' school, the upper-class children at the Horace Mann Kindergarten in New York City found weaving to be a pleasure. Weaving was an artifact from an earlier period in the development of the kindergarten, holding its place in the program because it was fun for children. However, it was a poor fit with what were understood to be the characteristics of child development: a short attention span, quickness to fatigue, and poor fine-motor coordination.

In Foreign Fields

Kindergarteners in Sydney, Wellington, and Winnipeg actively sustained links with American and British educators and colleges over several generations. Even from the early days of the infant school, this had ensured the transfer of educational ideas and practices, as graduates trained in England or the United States made their way to the colonies as missionaries or teachers. After a brief pioneering phase, the kindergarten associations entered periods of relative stability. Although economic concerns and recruitment of student teachers were ongoing and sometimes severe problems, there were few calls to change the orientation of the educational program itself. The rapid introduction of in-house training programs met the need for trained staff and extra hands, and set the stage for expansion. In Sydney, the early inauguration of a training school created a first generation of local graduates educated under a particular regime, who proceeded to spread the ideas they had absorbed from Chicago kindergarteners. A second phase occurred during the 1920s, somewhat earlier in Winnipeg, with directors urging that the children's program be freed up and brought into line with practice in the United States, and in the case of Wilson at the Wellington FKA, with kindergartens in Perth and Sydney. The Wellington directors looked to Australia for inspiration despite a perception within Australia that practice was outmoded. The Australian and New Zealand free kindergartens, as programs for younger children offered outside schools, eventually had more in common with nursery schools than with kindergartens, and after 1920, major reforms came from ideas in nursery education.

The case-study kindergarteners were keen to follow modern practices, though they sometimes seemed captive to the orientation of their college principal and further limited by their own success. In Winnipeg, Sydney, and Wellington in 1915, initial training for kindergarteners was offered by the respective associations, who were also the main employers. By contrast, Chicago was home to at least four training schools in 1915, all offering two-year diploma courses: the Chicago Kindergarten Institute, the Kindergarten Collegiate Institute, the National Kindergarten College, and the Pestalozzi-Froebel Kindergarten Training School. This did not mean that the case-study kindergartens were outmoded. However, experimentation was less likely in the absence of other models, and in the colonies, kindergarten depended largely on individuals to initiate significant shifts.

In all three settings, a reliance on the principal for leadership meant that calls for change often coincided with the appointment of new directors, a development that occurred only rarely. The New Zealand and Australian associations were notable for the length of their director's tenure: Australian-trained Nettie Riley headed the Wellington FKA for sixteen years; Harriet Dumolo directed Sydney's KUNSW for twenty-two. In Sydney, Ella Slack, the first director to hold a university degree, and Dumolo's successor, lost no time in separating herself from the old regime. She voiced her criticism in her first report: "Because people tend to cling so firmly to traditional methods, definitely progressive work for young children has in the past been confined to isolated centres."[39]

As in earlier years, study visits were planned as a means to change. The KUNSW sent Jean Wyndham to Teachers College, Columbia University, and to England in 1934 to 1936, the same tour Dumolo undertook ten years earlier. The association expected that she would return "with her mind enriched by her varied experiences, bringing back to us the latest methods that have been tested and accepted in the educational centres in England and America."[40] Other Australian and New Zealand staff spent time at Teachers College during the 1930s: Edna Scott (1932-34) and Enid Wilson from the Wellington FKA (1932-33); Mary Gutteridge from the Kindergarten Union of Victoria (1936-38); and Gladys Pendred from the Perth training college (1938). In the United States, the axis of influence in the kindergarten world, at least as it was played out in the academy, shifted

Conclusion

from Chicago and the Midwest to New York City early in the twentieth century.[41] Australian and New Zealand kindergarteners followed this path, whereas those in Winnipeg stayed closer to home.

A Winnipeg kindergartener who did visit the Horace Mann Kindergarten in 1926 found the program interesting but believed it to be irrelevant to conditions back home. Formal course work rather than brief visits or study tours made more lasting impressions, and some New Zealand and Australian kindergarteners completed course work and degrees during their time at Teachers College. Jean Wyndham from Sydney studied child development in a course offered by Child Development Institute staff, among whom were Christine Heinig.[42] Heinig, who subsequently travelled to Australia to take up a series of influential positions, was director of the laboratory nursery school at Teachers College. Canadian, Australian, and New Zealand kindergarten developments were influenced partly through the international movement of people and of ideas concerning education for young children. Evidence suggests, however, that new ideas did not bring about corresponding or immediate changes.

The teacher-training regime was based largely on learning via imitation, a Froebelian principle applied also to children. Grace Fulmer stressed the educational value in limiting children's choices, or, as she put it, "the value of starting out with a limited amount of material and a definite idea."[43] Kindergarteners in training programs in the three case studies were inducted into the kindergarten system via the same approach, through hands-on work with children. Novices did not have time to digest theoretical complexities — nor were they expected to — before leading lessons themselves. In this light, the notion that the principles underlying the Gifts were "known only to the teacher" is doubtful.[44] Perhaps neither children nor adults could articulate their arcane purpose.

Student teachers learned by using the materials, handling what were in some cases toys for babies — Gifts one and two — and making the crafts they would later teach the children. Exploring the materials in this way was a kind of initiation, fostering bonds among kindergarteners and commitment to the cause but not necessarily deep understanding. Kate Douglas Wiggin and her sister Nora Archibald Smith, who had been trainers at the Silver Street Kindergarten, described the effect of the Gifts on student teachers. Kindergarteners too needed to look at the materials through the glasses of imagination: "Those of us who have seen successive groups of young women in training-classes approach the first few gifts have noted that interest is commonly mingled at first with a slight surprise that the objects should be considered worthy of so much study, while underneath lies a half-concealed amusement at the simple forms produced. Yet this attitude of mind endures but for a season, for as soon as the gifts are studied and used practically, it is seen that they contain possibilities of indefinite expansion."[45]

Froebel's complex and puzzling educational philosophy was purposefully withheld from junior students. Mary Runyan cautioned, "The harm is not in the overdose, but in the disproportionate and premature administering of the dose."[46] Practice came before theory, if theory came at all. The materials revealed their meaning through manipulation, and student teachers were guided in play with the Gifts in the same way as were the children. Julia Abbott explained this process: "In using the same method with the students in the training class and with the children in the kindergarten, the student in her junior year is realizing the principles underlying the process through their constant application in response to the experimentation of the junior class. As the same principles emerge in the use of various materials, they begin to be defined as 'principles.'"[47]

In the case studies, the apprenticeship-type training combined with staff shortages to privilege practice over theory. In numerous instances, teachers worked with students to create a more favourable adult-child ratio, and it was not uncommon for trainees to work alone. Following an idea from training in the United States, students prepared "gift books," which were used for assessment and a source of ideas for their own teaching. Harriette Melissa Mills explained this aspect of training:

> Under the immediate supervision of an instructor, the [adult] students are led, through play, to find the meaning and use of the gifts. The results of this play are usually preserved in what is known as a Gift Book. The book contains descriptions of the gifts; lists of geometric forms illustrated in each; diagrams of the various classes building with the gifts; and numbers of sequences copied from manuals which contain designs in almost infinite variety. This Gift Book represents to many students the tangible result of one or two years' of work, by the aid of which the gifts may be administered in the kindergarten. At the conclusion of the study of each gift, the students are required to write an abstract on the gift in conformity to a more or less rigidly formulated scheme.[48]

Conclusion

Student teachers at the Wellington FKA, c. 1930. PAC011-0981-1-09-1, Wellington Free Kindergarten Association Collection, Alexander Turnbull Library, Wellington.

Gift books of this kind were a component of the provincial examination for Manitoba kindergarteners during the early 1900s and formed part of the training in Sydney (the Macquarie University archives houses a number of examples). In the 1920s, constructing wagons and dollhouses supplemented Gift work as part of teacher training. Helen McLean, the Winnipegger who became critic teacher at Oberlin Kindergarten Training School, taught a course in handwork for junior students. As described in the Oberlin school calendar, the "course includes the consideration of play materials as a means of understanding of how to direct the play activities of children in the kindergarten and first grade ... [and] and directed work with paper, cardboard, clay, raphia, textile materials, wood, paint, sand, blueprints, nature materials and miscellaneous materials."[49] In the photograph above, which dates from about 1930, student teachers at the Wellington FKA can be seen working with similar materials.

In the case-study countries as in United States, kindergartners could choose between the pedagogical progressives, on the one hand, and the Froebelians, on the other. The impression from standard and oft-cited histories is that, after Susan Blow and the debates by the Committee of Nineteen, progressive kindergarteners led the way. However, in most cases

Froebel's materials were not suddenly discarded on one day and replaced the next by Patty Smith Hill Blocks or Montessori's pink tower. School supply catalogues such as Milton Bradley's included Froebel's Gifts until the late 1930s, along with floor blocks. In her 1928 book on block building, Margaret Trace listed enlarged sixth Gifts as essential equipment for kindergarten and grade one.[50] These were to be used with a set of "double enlarged" Trace Building Blocks, available from the Milton Bradley Company, for both experimental and directed building. Trace was supervisor of kindergartens in Cleveland, Ohio. In her guide to block building, children used large numbers of blocks in experimental building, including the cubes from Gift three, to create patterns according to teachers' suggestions. This was followed by "imaginative play" with the construction. In directed construction, children practised creating elements of structures and were then guided to co-operate in creating large-scale models of familiar buildings or other items. The results, though on the floor and very much enlarged, were similar to the types of constructions made during an earlier era with the small-sized Gifts.

At the same time, traditional approaches continued full strength during a kind of Froebelian renaissance. Trace acknowledged the work of Grace Fulmer, who published *The Use of Kindergarten Gifts* in 1918.[51] Fulmer had been an assistant professor at Teachers College, Columbia. After Patty Smith Hill was appointed head of the Department of Kindergarten Education, she left Teachers College to take a post as assistant superintendent of schools in Los Angeles. In 1917, she established her own training school there, which she headed until her retirement in 1935. In *The Use of Kindergarten Gifts,* she acknowledged the contribution of the ideas of John MacVannel and John Dewey at Columbia University, but the spirit of Froebel dominated her thinking: "The materials peculiar to the kindergarten were selected because of their value in the organization and control of human experience — because of their universal significance — and not because they happened to be the few things in which the founder of the kindergarten had become interested, or because of their appeal to a few individuals."[52]

Notes

Chapter 1: Childhood and Education

1. "Infant School Society, Meeting," *Times* (London), June 6, 1825, 4.
2. "Infantile School Society Meeting," *Times* (London), June 8, 1824, 3.
3. "Infant School Society, Meeting," *Times* (London), June 6, 1825, 4.
4. "Infantile School Society Meeting," *Times* (London), June 8, 1824, 3. A report in the *Times* describing the work of the opposing church-based infant school society highlighted the intense need for such a service: "The City of London Infant School Society have opened their first school in Liverpool-street, Bishopsgate-street. The building consists of a large airy school-room, in a semi-circular form, a class-room, and a couple of rooms for the mistress and her assistant. A play-ground, with a shed for the use of the children in wet weather, is attached to the building. The school receives 200 children, who pay each a penny a week. It is conducted by a mistress and one female assistant. The applications for admission have been much more numerous than the means of accommodation. These schools only take charge of the children during those hours when by the necessary avocations of the parents their children are unavoidably separated from them. They are taught habits of obedience, order, and cleanliness." "Infant Schools," *Times* (London), May 13, 1826, 3.
5. Quoted in "Infant School Society, Meeting," *Times* (London), June 6, 1825, 4.
6. William Wilson, *A Manual of Instruction for Infants' Schools* (New York: G. and C. and H. Carvill, 1830), 25 (emphasis in original).
7. Phillip McCann and Francis A. Young, *Samuel Wilderspin and the Infant School Movement* (London: Croom Helm, 1982), 167.
8. United Nations Educational, Scientific and Cultural Organization (UNESCO), *Strong Foundations: Early Childhood Care and Education. EFA Global Monitoring Report 2007* (Paris: UNESCO, 2007).

9 Selected examples include Margaret Clark and Tim Waller, eds., *Early Childhood Education and Care: Policy and Practice* (London: Sage, 2007); Marcia K. Meyers and Janet C. Gornick, "Public or Private Responsibility? Early Childhood Education and Care, Inequality, and the Welfare State," *Journal of Comparative Family Studies* 34, 3 (2003): 379-411; Michelle J. Neuman, "Governance of Early Childhood Education and Care: Recent Developments in OECD Countries," *Early Years: An International Journal of Research and Development* 25, 2 (2005): 129-41; UNESCO, *Strong Foundations;* Emily Vargas-Barón and Sian Williams, eds., "Funding the Future: Strategies for Early Childhood Investment, Costing and Financing," *Coordinators' Notebook* 30 (2008): http://www.ecdgroup.com/pdfs/ECD-CoNo30.pdf; Jane Waldfogel, "Early Childhood Policy: A Comparative Perspective," in *Blackwell Handbook of Early Childhood Development,* ed. Kathleen McCartney and Deborah Phillips (Malden, MA: Blackwell, 2005), 576-94; and Linda A. White, "Trends in Child Care/Early Childhood Education/Early Childhood Development Policy in Canada and the United States," *American Review of Canadian Studies* 34, 4 (2004): 665-88.

10 Peter Moss, "Beyond Early Childhood Education and Care" (paper presented at the early childhood education and care conference organized by the OECD, and the Ministry of Education and Science, Sweden, and the Swedish National Agency for Education, Stockholm, June 13-15, 2001), 9-10 (emphasis in original).

11 Marc Depaepe, "Demythologizing the Educational Past: An Endless Task in History of Education," *Historical Studies in Education* 9, 2 (1997): 219.

12 Agnes Snyder, *Dauntless Women in Childhood Education 1856-1931* (Washington: Association for Childhood Education International, 1972), 48; V. Celia Lascarides and Blythe F. Hinitz, *History of Early Childhood Education* (New York: Falmer, 2000), 256. Lascarides and Hinitz include a genealogical chart of teacher education in the United States.

13 Nikolas Rose describes critical history as "a way of utilising investigations of the past to enable one to think differently about the present, to interrogate that in our contemporary experience which we take for granted, through an examination of the conditions under which our current forms of truth have been made possible." Rose, "Power and Subjectivity: Critical History and Psychology," in *Historical Dimensions of Psychological Discourse,* ed. C.F. Graumann and K.J. Gergen (New York: Cambridge University Press, 1996), 160.

14 Maurice Gontard, *Les Ecoles Primaires de la France Bourgeoise (1833-1875)* (Toulouse: Institut Pédagogique National, n.d.), 16. De Pastoret's own inspiration was reportedly Jean-Frédéric Oberlin's "knitting schools." Because one of the activities of the schools was knitting, a practical skill in a cold climate, Oberlin called his establishments knitting schools. The popular name for them, however, was *poêles à tricoter* or simply *poêles,* meaning rooms with a stove. John W. Kurtz, *John Frederic Oberlin* (Boulder: Westview Press, 1976).

15 James Pierrepont Greaves served as Millet's interpreter during her visit. McCann and Young, *Samuel Wilderspin and the Infant School Movement,* 139-40. As Buchanan is not known to have written about his methods, the book would have been one of the guides by Samuel Wilderspin, David Goyder, James Brown, or

William Wilson, published by about 1830. For information on Millet, see Linda Clark, *The Rise of Professional Women in France: Gender and Public Administration since 1830* (Cambridge, UK: Cambridge University Press, 2000), 14. In 1833, Jean Denys Cochin published his *Manuel des Fondateurs et des Directeurs des Premières écoles de l'enfance, connues sous le nom de Salles d'Asile* (Paris). Millet was married to painter Frederic Millet. She spent two months in London visiting infant schools. In 1827, these could have included Westminster, Spitalfields, Walthamstow, and numerous others. See E. Millet, *Observations sur le système des écoles d'Angleterre pour la première enfance établies en France sous le nom de salles d'asile* (Paris: Henri Servier, 1828).

16 Hugh Cunningham, *The Children of the Poor: Representations of Childhood Since the Seventeenth Century* (Oxford: Blackwell, 1991).

17 Perry Le Fevre, "Evolutionary Thought and American Religious Education," *Journal of Religion* 40, 4 (1960): 301.

18 Mary F. Ledyard and Bertha H. Breckenfeld, *Guide to Primary Manual Work: A Suggestive Outline for a Year's Course in First and Second Grades* (Springfield, MA: Milton Bradley, 1912), 8.

19 Grace Fulmer, *The Use of Kindergarten Gifts* (Boston: Houghton Mifflin, 1918), 196.

20 Notebook, c. 1909-10, Mrs. Florence Elder (née Thompson) Papers, MG30 D121, Library and Archives Canada, Ottawa.

21 Ibid.

22 Helmut Walser Smith, "The Talk of Genocide, the Rhetoric of Miscegenation: Notes on Debates in the German Reichstag concerning Southwest Africa, 1904-1914," in *The Imperialist Imagination: German Colonialism and Its Legacy,* ed. Sara Friedrichsmeyer, Sara Lennox, and Susanne Zantop (Ann Arbor: University of Michigan Press, 1998), 107-24.

23 Lora Wildenthal, *German Women for the Empire* (Durham, NC: Duke University Press, 2001), 162.

24 Depaepe, "Demythologizing the Educational Past," 217. Franz-Michael Konrad describes the kindergarten as a "counter-world for school," in Konrad, "Care — Not Education! The Beginnings of Early Childhood Education and Care in Germany (1800-1850)" (paper presented at the twenty-ninth session of the "International Standing Conference for the History of Education," Hamburg, July 25-28, 2007).

25 "Dr. Montessori's Aim," *New York Times,* December 9, 1913, 8.

26 Peter Pierce, *Country of Lost Children: An Australian Anxiety* (Oakleigh: Cambridge University Press, 1999).

27 Bill Ashcroft, "Primitive and Wingless: The Colonial Subject as Child," in *Dickens and the Children of Empire,* ed. Wendy F. Jacobson (New York: Palgrave, 2000), 184-202.

28 Amy Susan Green, "Savage Childhood: The Scientific Construction of Girlhood and Boyhood in the Progressive Era" (PhD diss., Yale University, 1995), 97.

29 Waldorf Schools are based on the ideas of the Austrian scientist and philosopher Rudolph Steiner. The first was established for the employees of the Waldorf-Astoria cigarette factory in Germany in 1919. The approach to teaching and

learning in Waldorf schools follows Steiner's philosophy of anthroposophy. A Waldorf kindergarten does not focus on academic instruction and does not include books. See Tom Stehlik, "Thinking, Feeling, and Willing: How Waldorf Schools Provide a Creative Pedagogy That Nurtures and Develops Imagination," in *Pedagogies of the Imagination: Mythopoetic Curriculum in Educational Practice*, ed. Timothy Leonard and Peter Willis (New York: Springer, 2008), 231-44.

30 Lucie Calista Maley, "Kindergarten Benefit to Indian Children," *Kindergarten Magazine* 10, 7 (1898): 440.
31 Jan Kociumbas, "Childhood History as Ideology," *Labour History* 47 (1984): 1-17.
32 Lillian Arundel, "Some Educational Work in Other Lands Part II," *Child Life* 11, 46 (1909): 53.
33 "Empire Day," *Australian Kindergarten Magazine* 2, 6 (1912): 12.
34 Ibid.
35 On the proverb applied to child development, see Jesús Palacios, "Proverbs as Images of Children and Childrearing," in *Images of Childhood,* ed. C. Philip Hwang, Michael E. Lamb, and Irving E. Sigel (Mahwah, NJ: Lawrence Erlbaum, 1986), 75-98. Although the proverb has long been a favoured metaphor in early childhood education, it gained new popularity in the 1970s with reference to compensatory programs and the US Head Start programs. See titles of such publications as the following: Consortium for Longitudinal Studies, *As the Twig Is Bent — Lasting Effects of Preschool Programs* (Hillsdale, NJ: L. Erlbaum, 1983); see also Robert H. Anderson and H.G. Shane, eds., *As the Twig Is Bent: Readings in Early Childhood Education* (New York: Houghton Mifflin, 1971); and Fernand Dutile, Cleon Foust, and Robert Webster, eds., *Early Childhood Intervention and Juvenile Delinquency: As the Twig Is Bent* (New York: Simon and Schuster, 1982). *As the Twig Is Bent* is the title of at least two films on early education. One, produced by the New South Wales Department of Education in 1954, focuses on school furniture fitted to children's bodies. The other, which concerns Maori children in New Zealand, was produced by the New Zealand National Film Unit in 1966.
36 Barbara Beatty, *Preschool Education in America: The Culture of Young Children from the Colonial Era to the Present* (New Haven: Yale University Press, 1995), 89.
37 Dorothy W. Hewes, "Fallacies, Phantasies, and Egregious Prevarications in ECE History" (paper presented at the annual conference of the National Association for the Education of Young Children, Anaheim, CA, November 14, 1997), 6, Eric Reproduction Document Number ED414058.
38 M.J. Lyschinska, "Henriette Schrader-Breymann: Life and Letters" (unpaginated translation in manuscript of M.J. Lyschinska, *Henriette Schrader-Breymann: Ihr Leben* [Berlin and Leipzig: Walter de Gruyter, 1922]), quoted in Jane Read, "Froebelian Women: Networking to Promote Professional Status and Educational Change in the Nineteenth Century," *History of Education* 32, 1 (2003): 21.
39 Kindergarten Union of New South Wales, *Annual Report* (Sydney, 1904), 10. Annual reports of the KUNSW are in the KUNSW Collection, ML MSS 5945, 51(52), Mitchell Library, State Library of New South Wales, Sydney.

40 John Joseph Kelso, *Early History of the Humane and Children's Aid Movement of Ontario, 1886-1893* (Toronto: L.K. Cameron, 1911), 47.
41 Thomas S. Popkewitz and Marianne N. Bloch, Administering Freedom: A History of the Present — Rescuing the Parent to Rescue the Child for Society, in *Governing the Child in the New Millennium,* ed. Kenneth Hultqvist and Gunilla Dahlberg (New York: Routledge, 2001), 85-119.
42 Martha Vicinus, *Independent Women: Work and Community for Single Women 1850-1920* (Chicago: University of Chicago Press, 1985), 219.
43 Quoted in Henry and Dorothy Castle Memorial Kindergarten, *The Story of the Henry and Dorothy Castle Memorial Kindergarten* (Honolulu: Paradise Engraving, n.d.), 23.
44 Allen F. Davis, *Spearheads for Reform: The Social Settlements and the Progressive Movement 1890-1914* (New York: Oxford University Press, 1967), 44.

Chapter 2: Infant Schools in Britain

1 Jean-Jacques Rousseau, *Jean-Jacques Rousseau: His Educational Theories Selected from "Émile," "Julie" and Other Writings,* ed. R.L. Archer (Woodbury, NY: Barron's Educational Series, 1964), 259.
2 James R. Brown, *The Infant School Echo; or, A Practical Compendium of the System of Infant Education,* 2nd ed. (London: Simpkin and Marshall, 1843), 1, 19 (emphasis in original).
3 Samuel Wilderspin, *On the Importance of Educating the Infant Poor from the Age of Eighteen Months to Seven Years. Containing an Account of the Spitalfields Infant School, and of the New System of Instruction There Adopted,* 2nd ed. (London: Hoyder, 1824), 1.
4 In their proposal for infant schools in Glasgow in 1827, the provisional committee highlighted the moral purpose of the schools. "In tracing the history of many of the inmates of our Bridewells and Jails, it is found that their habits of violence or dishonesty have had their commencement before the period of usual education begins. If we would apply an effectual remedy, therefore, we must go up to the very source of the evil; and the full effects of education cannot be experienced till it commences at the earliest period at which the mind is capable of being benefited by it." "Proposal for Establishing Infant Schools in Glasgow" (Glasgow: E. Khull, 1827), Printed Ephemera, J/6, Glasgow University Library, Glasgow.
5 Wilderspin, *On the Importance of Educating the Infant Poor,* 23.
6 Ibid., 19.
7 Robert Owen, *A New View of Society: Or, Essays on the Formation of the Human Character, Preparatory to the Development of a Plan for Gradually Ameliorating the Condition of Mankind* (Edinburgh: J. and J. Gray, 1826), 20; Robert Owen, *The Life of Robert Owen Written by Himself with Selections from His Writings and Correspondence,* vol. 1 (1857; repr., New York: Augustus M. Kelley, 1967), 83-84.
8 Samuel Wilderspin, *Infant Education; or, Remarks on the Importance of Educating the Infant Poor,* 3rd ed. (London: W. Simpkin and R. Marshall, 1825), 4 (emphasis in original).

9 Broad Street Infant School, *Annual Report* (Boston: J.H. Eastham, 1857), 4.
10 Robert Dale Owen, *An Outline of the System of Education at New Lanark* (Glasgow: Wardlaw and Cunninghame, 1824), 6-7.
11 James F. McMillan, *France and Women, 1789-1914: Gender, Society and Politics* (New York: Routledge, 2000), 56.
12 Robert Owen, *New Lanark* (London: n.p., 1849), 1.
13 Robert Owen, *A New View of Society; or, Essays on the Principle of the Formation of the Human Character, and the Application of the Principle to Practice* (London: Cadell and Davies, 1813), 12.
14 Robert Owen, *An Address Delivered to the Inhabitants of New Lanark, on the First of January, 1816, at the Opening of the Institution Established for the Formation of Character* (London: Richard and Arthur Taylor, 1816), 13.
15 Ibid., 14.
16 Robert Dale Owen described the infants' class as being for children from two to five years, in *An Outline of the System of Education*, 32.
17 It is not clear whether the classes were led by James Buchanan's successor (Buchanan left earlier in the year) or the headmaster of the school for older children.
18 Owen, *An Outline of the System of Education*, 34.
19 Henry Grey Macnab, *The New Views of Mr. Owen of Lanark Impartially Examined, as Rational Means of Ultimately Promoting the Productive Industry, Comfort, Moral Improvement, and Happiness of the Labouring Classes of Society, and of the Poor; and of Training Up Children in the Way in Which They Should Go: Also Observations on the New Lanark School, and on the Systems of Education of Mr. Owen, of the Rev. Dr. Bell, and That of the New British and Foreign System of Mutual Instruction* (London: J. Hatchard and Son, 1819), 221-22.
20 Margaret Nicolson and Ian Donnachie, "The New Lanark Highlanders: Migration, Community, and Language 1785-c. 1850," *Family and Community History* 6, 1 (2001): 19-32.
21 Michael Sanderson, "Education and the Factory in Industrial Lancashire, 1780-1840," *Economic History Review* 20, 2 (1967): 268.
22 Sidney Pollard, "The Factory Village in the Industrial Revolution," *English Historical Review* 79, 312 (1964): 519.
23 G.A. Fleming, *A Day at New Lanark: And a Sketch of Its Present Condition by the Editor of the "New Moral World"* (Edinburgh: F.B.S. Flindell, 1839), 9.
24 Ibid., 6-7.
25 Ian Donnachie, "Historic Tourism to New Lanark and the Falls of Clyde 1795-1830: The Evidence of Contemporary Visiting Books and Related Sources," *Journal of Tourism and Cultural Change* 2, 3 (2004): 145; Jonathan V. Farina, "Characterizing the Factory System: Factory Subjectivity in *Household Words*," *Victorian Literature and Culture* 35 (2007): 41-56.
26 Donnachie, "Historic Tourism."
27 Ibid., 147.
28 Many histories record her name as Molly Young. However, Mary Young is listed in the cash books from the institute and in the autobiography of Owen's son, Robert Dale Owen, *Threading My Way: Twenty-Seven Years of Autobiography* (New York: Trübner, 1874), 90.

29 Jeffrey G. Machin, "The Westminster Free Day Infant Asylum: The Origins of the First English Infant School," *Journal of Educational Administration and History* 20, 2 (1988): 49.
30 Barbara Buchanan, *Buchanan Family Records: James Buchanan and His Descendants* (Cape Town: Townshend, Taylor and Snashall, 1923), 2.
31 Owen himself later recalled the opening date for the New Lanark School — "the first infant school in the world" — to be January 1, 1816. Robert Owen to the Lord Chancellor, *Times* (London), November 10, 1834, 6.
32 Buchanan, *Buchanan Family Records*, 2.
33 Owen, *A New View of Society; or, Essays on the Principle;* Howard Silver, "Owen's Reputation as an Educationist," in *Robert Owen, Prophet of the Poor: Essays in Honour of the Two Hundredth Anniversary of His Birth,* ed. Sidney Pollard and John Salt (Lewisburg: Bucknell University Press, 1971), 65-83.
34 Owen, *The Life of Robert Owen,* 175.
35 William Chambers and Robert Chambers, eds., *Education from Two to Six Years of Age: Applicable to the Infant School and the Nursery,* 4th ed. (Edinburgh: William and Robert Chambers, 1837), 2.
36 Gordon S. Haight, ed., *The George Eliot Letters,* vol. 4, *1862-1868* (New Haven: Yale University Press, 1954), 141n.
37 Thomas Pole, *Observations Relative to Infant Schools: Designed to Point Out Their Usefulness to the Children of the Poor, to Their Parents, and to Society at Large* (London: S. Goyder, 1823), 8.
38 See Machin, "The Westminster Free Day Infant Asylum," for an account of the school. In his 1823 *Observations Relative to Infant Schools,* Thomas Pole referred to the institution as the Westminster Infant School.
39 Henry Brougham, "Mr. Brougham's Account of an Establishment in Switzerland," in appendix to *Mr. Brougham's Letter: Containing Minutes of Evidence Taken before the Education Committee* (London: Longman, Hurst, Rees, Orme, and Brown, 1818), 99.
40 Ibid., 100.
41 Ibid., 101.
42 Ibid.
43 Jeremy Bentham, *Panopticon; or, The Inspection-House* (Dublin: T. Payne, 1791), 137.
44 The Two Goliaths (pseudonym for Thomas Bilby and R.B. Ridgway), To the Editor of Educational Magazine, *Educational Magazine,* July 1835, 57.
45 Robert Owen to David Ricardo, Esq., M.P., in *Mr. Owen's Proposed Arrangements for the Distressed Working Classes, Shown to Be Consistent with Sound Principles of Political Economy: In Three Letters Addressed to David Ricardo, Esq. M.P.* (London: R. and A. Taylor for Longman, Hurst, Rees, Orme, and Brown, 1819), 90.
46 "Minutes of Evidence from the Select Committee on State of Police in the Metropolis," *British Parliamentary Papers* (hereafter, *Parliamentary Papers),* 1816, vol. 1, 30.
47 Machin, "The Westminster Free Day Infant Asylum."
48 Wilderspin, *On the Importance of Educating the Infant Poor,* 180.

49 Phillip McCann, "Samuel Wilderspin and the Early Infant Schools," *British Journal of Educational Studies* 14, 2 (1966): 193.
50 Phillip McCann, "Popular Education, Socialization and Social Control: Spitalfields 1812-1824," in *Popular Education and Socialization in the Nineteenth Century*, ed. Phillip McCann (London: Methuen, 1977), 8.
51 "Minutes of Evidence from the Select Committee on Cause of Increase in Number of Commitments and Convictions in London and Middlesex, and the State of Police of Metropolis," *Parliamentary Papers*, 1828, vol. 1, 96.
52 Quoted in McCann, "Popular Education," 27.
53 Mathew Carey, "Infant Schools," in *Miscellaneous Essays* (Philadelphia: Printed for Carey and Hart, 1830), 469.
54 "Report on the Select Committee on Education in England and Wales," *Parliamentary Papers*, 1835, vol. 7, 31.
55 Buchanan, *Buchanan Family Records*, 30.
56 Joseph Lancaster, *Improvements in Education*, 3rd ed. (London: printed and sold by Darton and Harvey, 1805).
57 Phillip McCann and Francis A. Young, *Samuel Wilderspin and the Infant School Movement* (London: Croom Helm, 1982), 79-81.
58 Quoted in ibid., 271.
59 Quoted in ibid., 272.
60 Buchanan, *Buchanan Family Records*, 7.
61 Samuel Wilderspin, *Infant Education; or, Practical Remarks on the Importance of Educating the Infant Poor, from the Age of Eighteen Months to Seven Years; Containing Hints for Developing the Moral and Intellectual Powers of Children of All Classes*, 4th ed. (London: W. Simpkin and R. Marshall, 1829).
62 David Goyder, *My Battle for Life: The Autobiography of a Phrenologist* (London: Simpkin, Marshall, 1857), 109.
63 Pestalozzi was a Swiss educator influenced by Rousseau's view of natural education. He formed a school for poor children and orphans based on his educational philosophy. His specialized method involved learning from nature using sensory information. Learning was structured according to object lessons, moving from concrete experience with objects to abstract concepts.
64 John Minter Morgan, *Hampden in the Nineteenth Century; or Colloquies on the Errors and Improvement of Society* (London: Edward Moxon, 1834), 23. On Greaves, see Jackie E.M. Latham, "Pestalozzi and James Pierrepont Greaves: A Shared Educational Philosophy," *History of Education* 31, 1 (2002): 59-70; J.E.M. Latham, *Search for a New Eden: James Pierrepont Greaves (1777-1842): The Sacred Socialist and His Followers* (Madison, NJ: Farleigh Dickinson University Press, 1999).
65 David George Goyder, *A Manual Detailing the System of Instruction Pursued at the Infant School, Bristol, etc.* (London: Thomas Goyder, 1824).
66 "Infant Schools," *Monthly Review* vol. 12 (London: G. Henderson, 1829): 83, 84.
67 Buchanan, *Buchanan Family Records*, 9; Josiah Miller, *Singers and Songs of the Church* (London: Longmans, Green, 1869), 413.
68 Richard Lines, "Education and the New Church," *New Church Lifeline* 348 (November 2006): 8.

69 Michael Stanley in Emanuel Swedenborg, *Emanuel Swedenborg: Essential Readings,* ed. Michael Stanley (Berkeley, CA: North Atlantic Books, 2003), 59.
70 McCann, "Samuel Wilderspin and the Early Infant Schools."
71 Quoted in Hester Burton, *Barbara Bodichon, 1827-1891* (London: John Murray, 1949), 6-7.
72 Edward Baines, *Leeds Mercury,* July 31, 1824, 3.
73 Ibid.
74 Wilderspin, *On the Importance of Educating the Infant Poor,* 39.
75 Appendix to the "Second Report of the Statistical Society of London on the State of Education in Westminster, Being a Detailed Account of Each Endowed or Charity School, and of Each Infant and Sunday School, in the Parishes of St. Margaret and St. John, Westminster," *Journal of the Statistical Society of London* 1, 5 (1838): 313.
76 Samuel Wilderspin, Letter to the Editor, *Educational Magazine,* July 1835, 149 (emphasis in original).
77 "Report on the Select Committee on Education in England and Wales," 13. Wilderspin elaborated that there were 200 infant schools in London with about 100 children in each. "Report on the Select Committee on Education in England and Wales," 26.
78 The figure of 270 is provided in "Infant Schools," *American Annals of Education and Instruction, and Journal of Literary Institutions,* vol. 7 (Boston: Otis, Broaders, 1837), 258; and McCann and Young, *Samuel Wilderspin and the Infant School Movement,* 167. Jewell Lochhead, providing no source, estimated that there were 150 infant schools in England in 1836. Lochead, *The Education of Young Children in England* (New York: Bureau of Publications, Teachers College, Columbia University, 1932), 22.
79 Samuel Taylor Coleridge, *Lay Sermons,* ed. Derwent Coleridge, 2nd ed. (London: Edward Moxon, 1852), 45.
80 Carl Kaestle, *Joseph Lancaster and the Monitorial School Movement* (New York: Teachers College Press, 1973), 15.
81 D.A. Turner, "1870: The State and the Infant School System," *British Journal of Educational Studies* 18, 2 (1970): 153.
82 Denison Deasey, *Education under Six* (London: Croom Helm, 1976), 130.
83 Turner, "1870," 153.
84 Thomas Bilby and R.B. Ridgway, *The Infant Teacher's Assistant,* 3rd ed., enlarged (London: Printed by Widow Tilling, 1834), 168.
85 British and Canadian Infant School Society, *Annual Report* (Montreal, 1834), 4.
86 Lawrence Cremin, *American Education: The National Experience* (New York: Harper and Row, 1980), 389.
87 "Minutes of Evidence before the Select Committee on Education of Poorer Classes in England and Wales," *Parliamentary Papers,* 1837-38, vol. 7, 138.
88 A.F.B. Roberts, "A New View of the Infant School Movement," *British Journal of Educational Studies* 20, 2 (1972): 157.
89 John Burnett, ed., *Destiny Obscure: Autobiographies of Childhood, Education, and Family from the 1820s to the 1920s* (Harmondsworth, UK: Penguin, 1984).

90 Wilderspin, who became too busy to write at least one of the books published in his name, utilized the service of a friend. Samuel Wilderspin, *Early Discipline Illustrated, or, the Infant System Progressing and Successful* (London: Westley and Davis, 1832), 3. The result was a lively book, recounting the spread of the system and his adventures on the road.

91 "Report on the Infant School Society (London)," in *Christian Observer* (August 1824), quoted in William Russell, "Infant Schools," *American Journal of Education* 1, 1 (1826): 14.

92 Samuel Wilderspin, *On the Importance of Educating the Infant Children of the Poor from the Age of Eighteen Months to Seven Years. Containing an Account of the Spitalfields Infant School, and of the New System of Instruction There Adopted* (London: Hoyder, 1823). Though the publication date was 1823, it was advertised as "just published" and available for sale in December 1822. *Times* (London) December 25, 1822, 4.

93 In 1823, Thomas Pole published *Observations Relative to Infant Schools*. He claimed to have completed his book without having read Wilderspin's. Pole, *Observations Relative to Infant Schools*, 48.

94 Russell, "Infant Schools," 14.

95 Samuel Wilderspin, Letter to the Editor, *Times* (London), August 8, 1846, 7.

96 David Salmon, "Grammatical Mnemonic Jingle," *Notes and Queries*, 12th ser., 4 (October 1918): 286.

97 A.E. Dyson and Julian Lovelock, eds., *Education and Democracy* (London: Routledge and Kegan Paul, 1975), 71.

98 Thomas Bilby and R.B. Ridgway, Letter to the Editor, *Educational Magazine*, July 1835, 57. Bilby and Ridgway were teachers at the Chelsea and Hart Street Infant School.

99 Bilby and Ridgway, Letter to the Editor, *Educational Magazine*, July 1835, 57.

100 Bilby and Ridgway, *The Infant Teacher's Assistant*, iii.

101 Owen, *An Outline of the System of Education*, 32.

102 Goyder, *My Battle for Life*, 188.

103 Dyson and Lovelock, *Education and Democracy*, 71.

104 *Christian Observer*, May 1823, quoted in Russell, "Infant Schools," 14.

105 Wilderspin, *Infant Education; or, Remarks*, 55.

106 "Report on the Select Committee on Education in England and Wales," 14-15.

107 Wilderspin, *Infant Education; or, Remarks*, 73.

108 Ibid., 251.

109 McCann, "Samuel Wilderspin and the Early Infant Schools," 200.

110 Wilderspin, *Infant Education; or, Remarks*, 102.

111 Years later, this was named a gonigraph (also spelled gonograph) and sold as a kindergarten material called the sixteenth Gift.

112 Thomas Pole, *A History of the Origin and Progress of Adult Schools, with an Account of Some of the Beneficial Effects Already Produced on the Character of the Labouring Poor* (Bristol: Printed and sold by Samuel Wood, 1815), 118.

113 Wilderspin, *Infant Education; or, Remarks*, 208.

114 *The Reports of the Society for Bettering the Condition and Increasing the Comforts of the Poor, London* (London: Society for Bettering the Condition and Increasing the Comforts of the Poor, 1814), 175-76 (emphasis in original).
115 William Wilson, *A Manual of Instruction for Infants' Schools* (New York: G. and C. and H. Carvill, 1830), 27.
116 Pole, *Observations Relative to Infant Schools*, 53.
117 "Report on the Select Committee on Education in England and Wales," 20.
118 Wilderspin, *Infant Education; or, Remarks*, 71.
119 "Report on the Select Committee on Education in England and Wales," 16.
120 Ibid., 22.
121 Wilderspin, *Infant Education; or, Remarks*, 112.
122 Wilderspin, *On the Importance of Educating the Infant Poor*, 2nd ed. (1824), 54.
123 Wilderspin, *Infant Education; or, Practical Remarks*, 245.
124 Pole, *Observations Relative to Infant Schools*, 57.
125 Ibid., 61.
126 Wilderspin, *On the Importance of Educating the Infant Poor*, 212.
127 "Report on the Select Committee on Education in England and Wales," 17.
128 Wilson, *A Manual of Instruction*, 21.
129 Francis Bond Head, *A Faggot of French Sticks* (London: John Murray, 1852), 121.
130 "Report on the Select Committee on Education in England and Wales," 28.
131 William Wilson, *The System of Infants' Schools*, 3rd ed. (London: G. Wilson, 1826), 91.
132 Ibid., 92.
133 Ibid., 28.
134 Ibid., 121.
135 McCann and Young, *Samuel Wilderspin*, 75.
136 Thomas Bilby, *A Course of Lessons, Together with the Tunes, to Which They Are Usually Sung in Infant Schools, and Also a Copious Collection of Hymns and Moral Songs, Suitable for Infant Instruction, Either in Schools, or in Private Families*, 3rd ed. (London: J.G. and F. Rivington, 1836), ix.
137 Ibid., 34.
138 Wilson, *A Manual of Instruction*, 19.
139 Ibid., 20.
140 Avril Wilson, "Ferrante Aporti — Apostle of Infancy," *British Journal of Educational Studies* 27, 3 (1979): 221-31.
141 "First Report of the Commissioners on Education in Ireland," *Parliamentary Papers*, 1825, vol. 12, 804. This school is recorded by Wilderspin, in *Early Discipline Illustrated*, 63. He makes no mention of training the teacher but writes that the sponsor (Lady Powerscourt) had visited a school in London.
142 McCann, "Samuel Wilderspin and the Early Infant Schools," 194.
143 Wilderspin, *Early Discipline Illustrated*, 139.
144 Glasgow Infant School Society, *First Annual Report* (Glasgow: William Collins, 1829), 19.
145 Wilderspin, *Early Discipline Illustrated*, 29.
146 McCann, "Samuel Wilderspin and the Early Infant Schools," 195.
147 Wilderspin, *Early Discipline Illustrated*, 163-64.

148 Ibid., 164.
149 Glasgow Infant School Society, *First Annual Report*.
150 Ibid., 20.
151 Alexander Dallas Bache, *Report on Education in Europe to the Trustees of the Girard College for Orphans* (Philadelphia: Lydia R. Bailey, 1839), 161, 164.
152 Henry Barnard, *School Architecture,* ed., with an introduction and notes, by Jean McClintock and Robert McClintock (1848; repr., New York: Teachers College Press, 1970), 230, 231.
153 John George Hodgins, *The School House, Its Architecture, External and Internal Arrangements: With Additional Papers on Gymnastics, the Use of Apparatus, School Discipline, Methods of Teaching, etc., etc., Together with Selections for Public Recitations in Schools* (Toronto: Department of Public Instruction for Upper Canada, Lovell and Gibson, Printers, 1857), 88.
154 Samuel Wilderspin, *The Infant System for Developing the Intellectual and Moral Powers of All Children, From One to Seven Years of Age,* 8th ed. (London: J.S. Hodson, 1852), 181.
155 Caroline Winterer, "Avoiding a 'Hothouse System of Education': Nineteenth-Century Early Childhood Education from the Infant Schools to the Kindergartens," *History of Education Quarterly* 32, 3 (1992): 294.
156 T.S. Ashton, "The Records of a Pin Manufactory, 1814-21," *Economica* 15 (1925): 288.
157 Sanderson, "Education and the Factory in Industrial Lancashire," 256.
158 "Royal Commission on Employment of Children in Factories Second Report, Minutes of Evidence; Reports of Medical Commissioners," *Parliamentary Papers,* 1833, vol. 12, 200.
159 "Royal Commission on Employment of Children in Factories. First Report, Minutes of Evidence; Reports of District Commissioners," *Parliamentary Papers,* 1833, vol. 12, 35. This may have been the owner of a factory in Staffordshire described by Wilderspin in *Early Discipline Illustrated,* 27. Wilderspin noted that there was considerable "prejudice" against the school at the start.
160 Rhodes Botson, *The Ashworth Cotton Enterprise: The Rise and Fall of a Family Firm, 1818-1880* (Oxford: Clarendon Press, 1970), 127.
161 Ibid., 129.
162 Olwyn M. Blouet, "Earning and Learning in the British West Indies: An Image of Freedom in the Pre-emancipation Decade, 1823-1833," *Historical Journal* 34, 2 (1991): 396.
163 "Select Committee on Extinction of Slavery in British Dominions, Report, Minutes of Evidence, appendix, Index," *Parliamentary Papers,* 1831-32, vol. 20, 533.

Chapter 3: Infant Schools in the Case-Study Countries

1 School starting ages are found in United Nations Educational Scientific and Cultural Organization, Institute for Statistics, *Global Education Digest 2008: Comparing Education Statistics Across the World* (Paris: UNESCO, 2008).
2 In Australia, the Public Instruction Act (1880) made education compulsory from age six to fourteen. In a 1916 amendment to the act, the age was raised to

seven. The age of the onset of compulsory schooling was again set at six by the Child Welfare Act (1939).
3 Charles Phillips, *The Development of Education in Canada* (Toronto: W.J. Gage, 1957). Some provision for compulsory schooling was made in Ontario in 1871, British Columbia in 1873, Manitoba in 1876, Prince Edward Island in 1877, Nova Scotia in 1883, the North-West Territories in 1888, New Brunswick in 1905, and Newfoundland and Quebec in 1942.
4 E.A. Roberts, *A Short History of Infants Education in New South Wales* (Sydney: New South Wales Federation of School Community Organisations, 1983), 9; Sue Middleton and Helen May, *Teachers Talk Teaching 1915-1995: Early Childhood Schools and Teachers' Colleges* (Palmerston North, NZ: Dunmore, 1997).
5 Deborah E.B. Weiner, *Architecture and Social Reform in Late-Victorian London* (Manchester: Manchester University Press, 1994).
6 Ibid., 104.
7 Ibid., 105.
8 John George Hodgins, *The School House, Its Architecture, External and Internal Arrangements: With Additional Papers on Gymnastics, the Use of Apparatus, School Discipline, Methods of Teaching, etc., etc., Together with Selections for Public Recitations in Schools* (Toronto: Department of Public Instruction for Upper Canada, Lovell and Gibson, Printers, 1857), 211-12.
9 Ibid., 211.
10 Royal Commission on Aboriginal Peoples, "Including First Nations and Inuit Peoples," *Report of the Royal Commission on Aboriginal Peoples*, vol. 1, *Looking Forward, Looking Back* (Ottawa: Ministry of Supply and Services, Canada, 1996).
11 Richard Broome, *Aboriginal Australians: Black Responses to White Dominance, 1788-2001* (Sydney: Allen and Unwin, 2001), 15. Broome estimates that, at the point of contact with Europeans in 1788, there were 300,000 Aborigines living in five hundred separate tribes.
12 Helen May, *School Beginnings: A 19th Century Colonial Story* (Wellington: NZCER Press, 2005).
13 "Examination of York Infant School," *York Courier of Upper Canada*, May 9, 1832, quoted in *The Town of York, 1815-1834: A Further Collection of Documents of Early Toronto*, ed. Edith G. Firth (Toronto: Champlain Society, 1966), 1.
14 Infant School Society, *Annual Report* (Halifax, 1834), 4-5.
15 Ibid., 4.
16 *Continuation of the Appendix to the Forty-Second Volume of the Journals of the House of Assembly of the Province of Lower Canada, Session 1832-1833* (Quebec City: King's Printer, 1833), Appendix I.1, February 2, 1833, II-26.
17 Percy Pope, "The Church of England in Prince Edward Island," in *Past and Present of Prince Edward Island Embracing a Concise Review of Its Early Settlement, Development and Present Conditions, Written by the Most Gifted Authors of the Province*, ed. D.A. MacKinnon (Charlottetown: B.F. Bowen, 1906), 278.
18 *Appendix to the Third Volume of the Journals of the Legislative Assembly of the Province of Canada, 1843* (Kingston: E.J. Barker, 1844), Appendix P.P., December 9, 1844.
19 Ibid.

20 Toronto Public School Board, *First Annual Report of the Local Superintendent of the Public Schools of the City of Toronto for the Year Ending 1859* (Toronto: Printed at the Wesleyan Methodist Book and Job Establishment, 1860).

21 "Report on Instruction in Lower Canada for the Year 1857," *Appendix to the Sixteenth Volume of the Journals of the Legislative Assembly of the Province of Canada, 1858* (Toronto: John Lovell, 1858), Appendix 43.

22 "Report of the Superintendent of Education for Lower Canada for the year 1859," *Sessional Papers*, vol. 4, *Third Session of the Sixth Parliament of the Province of Canada* (Quebec City: Thompson, 1860), no. 50, 50–57.

23 In 1834, this was the annual salary paid by the Infant School Society in Halifax. *Annual Report* (Halifax, 1834).

24 "Committee on Education Report," *Journal and Proceedings of the House of Assembly for the Province of Nova Scotia* (Halifax: R. Nugent, 1843), Appendix 50, 179.

25 "Infant School Pictou," *Halifax British Colonist*, April 10, 1851, 2.

26 "Committee on Education Report," *Journal and Proceedings of the House of Assembly for the Province of Nova Scotia* (Halifax: Richard Nugent, 1851), Appendix 53, 189–90.

27 Montreal Infant School Association, General Minute Book, February 15, 1868, John Dougall and family fonds, MG29 C34, vol. 2, Library and Archives Canada (hereafter, LAC), Ottawa.

28 Ibid.

29 Ibid.

30 William McDougall to the Montreal Protestant School Commissioners, Montreal, 10 April 1869, Correspondence, MG29 C34, vol. 1, file 3, LAC.

31 Montreal Infant School Association, General Minute Book, February 1, 1870, MF28 I405, vol. 2, LAC.

32 The boys' home was the start of Batshaw Youth and Family Centres, which continue as a social service provider for troubled youth in Montreal.

33 Most accounts credit Hill with establishing the first infant school in Australia. However, it is likely that private infant schools already operated for children from wealthy families. A much earlier infant school, which served as a Sunday school, is recorded by Stephen Henry Smith and George Thomas Spaull, in *History of Education in New South Wales (1788-1925)* (Sydney: George B. Philip, 1925), 18. However, founded as it was in 1797, it predates the infant school system. Hill was assisted in the organization of the infant school at St. James' by the attorney general of New South Wales, Saxe Bannister. See James Macarthur, *New South Wales, Its Present State and Future Prospects, Being a Statement, with Documentary Evidence, Submitted in Support of Petitions to His Majesty and Parliament* (London: D. Walther, 1837), 216.

34 Kenneth Cable and Rosemary Annable, *St. James, 1824-1999* (Sydney: St. James' Church, 1999); the Reverend Richard Hill, Letter to the Editor, *Sydney Gazette*, December 16, 1824.

35 Samuel J. Rogal, *The Children's Jubilee: A Bibliographical Survey of Hymnals for Infants, Youth, and Sunday Schools Published in Britain and America, 1655-1900* (Westport, CT: Greenwood Press, 1983), 72.

36 Hill, Letter to the Editor, *Sydney Gazette,* December 16, 1824.
37 Ibid. Other versions of this metaphor surface in infant school literature in addition to the one used by Hill, which was borrowed from Samuel Wilderspin's *Infant Education; or Remarks on the Importance of Educating the Infant Poor,* 3rd ed. (London: W. Simpkin and R. Marshall, 1852), 14. In the report of the Glasgow Infant School Society, the focus was on the activity of the teacher, "the soil being constantly stirred, the weeds are prevented from springing up." Glasgow Infant School Society, *First Annual Report* (Glasgow: William Collins, 1829), 14.
38 Hill, Letter to the Editor, *Sydney Gazette,* December 16, 1824.
39 Smith and Spaull, *History of Education in New South Wales,* 32-33.
40 New South Wales, *Governor's Despatches to the Secretary of State for the Colonies,* vol. 16 (June-December 1829), ML A1205, ML, State Library of New South Wales, Sydney.
41 Ibid.
42 Alan Barcan, *A History of Australian Education* (Melbourne: Oxford University Press, 1980).
43 Roberts, *A Short History of Infants Education,* 4.
44 Ibid.
45 William Westbrooke Burton, *The State of Religion and Education in New South Wales* (London: J. Cross, 1840), 148.
46 Ibid., 149. The St. James' teacher was James Roberts.
47 Ibid., 152.
48 The private infant school in Sydney is described in the *Sydney Gazette,* August 25, 1828.
49 Ibid.
50 Ibid.
51 Ibid.
52 Ibid.
53 Ibid.
54 Stanley James Curtis, *History of Education in Great Britain* (London: University Tutorial Press, 1948), 211; John L. Ewing, *Origins of the New Zealand Primary School Curriculum* (London: Oxford University Press, 1961).
55 May, *School Beginnings: A 19th Century Colonial Story.*
56 Phillip McCann, "Samuel Wilderspin and the Early Infant Schools," *British Journal of Educational Studies* 14, 2 (1966): 202.
57 William Buchanan to the Hon. J. Montagu, Cape Town, February 4, 1847, in *The Westminster and Foreign Quarterly Review* 47 (1847): 485.
58 Emigration Register, *Adelaide,* Alexander Turnbull Library (hereafter, ATL), Wellington. His assistant, Wilmott Huxtable Tilke, travelled under the name of Ann. She was born on January 22, 1809, to John Tilke and Wilmott Huxtable.
59 Janice Burns Woods, "Evans, George Samuel (1802-1868)," *Australian Dictionary of Biography,* vol. 4 (Melbourne: Melbourne University Press, 1972), 142-43. For Tilke's genealogical record, see "Joseph LAWRANCE / Wilmott (Wilmett) Huxtable TILKE," http://www.telusplanet.net/public/juz/pages/geneal/family/F12.html#I38.

60 Helen May, *School Beginnings: Case Study Two: Dreams and Realities for the Youngest Colonial Settlers, 1840s-50s,* Research and Policy Series No. 3 (Wellington: Institute for Early Childhood Studies, Victoria University of Wellington, 2004).
61 John Ward, *Information Relative to New-Zealand Compiled for the Use of Colonists,* 2nd ed. (London: John W. Parker, 1839), 137.
62 Ibid.
63 Gilbert Herbert, *Pioneers of Prefabrication: The British Contribution in the Nineteenth Century* (Baltimore: Johns Hopkins Press, 1978), 22.
64 Philip Temple, *A Sort of Conscience: The Wakefields* (Auckland: Auckland University Press, 2002), 260-61; Patricia Burns, *Fatal Success: A History of the New Zealand Company* (Auckland: Heinmann Reed, 1989), 163.
65 For more on the Buchanan family in Africa, see Barbara I. Buchanan, *Pioneer Days in Natal* (Pietermaritzburg: Shuter and Shooter, 1936), and *Natal Memories* (Pietermaritzburg: Shuter and Shooter, 1941).
66 Helen May, *School Beginnings: A 19th Century Colonial Story* (Wellington: NZCER Press, 2005).
67 Louise E. Ward, *Early Wellington* (Auckland: Whitcome and Tombs, 1928).
68 May, *School Beginnings.*
69 2 Corinthians 10:16.
70 Olive P. Dickason, *Canada's First Nations: A History of Founding Peoples from Earliest Times* (Don Mills, ON: Oxford University Press, 2002).
71 Ibid.
72 Helen May, *The Discovery of Early Childhood: The Development of Services for the Care and Education of Very Young Children, Mid Eighteenth Century Europe to Mid Twentieth Century New Zealand* (Auckland: Auckland University Press, 1997).
73 "Report from the Select Committee on Aborigines (British Settlements)," *Parliamentary Papers,* 1836, vol. 3, 200. For an analysis of the report with a focus on Australia, see Elizabeth Elbourne, "The Sin of the Settler: The 1835-36 Select Committee on Aborigines and Debates over Virtue and Conquest in the Early Nineteenth Century British White Settler Empire," *Journal of Colonialism and Colonial History* 3, 3 (2003). http://muse.jhu.edu/journals/journal_of_colonialism_and_colonial_history/v004/4.3elbourne.html.
74 "Report from the Select Committee on Aborigines (British Settlements)," *Parliamentary Papers,* 1836, vol. 3, 538.
75 James Axtell, *After Columbus: Essays in the Ethnohistory of Colonial North America* (New York: Oxford University Press, 1988), 53.
76 "Report from the Select Committee on Aborigines (British Settlements)," *Parliamentary Papers,* 1836, vol. 3, 531.
77 Cornelius J. Jaenen, "Education for Francization: The Case of New France in the Seventeenth Century," in *Indian Education in Canada,* vol. 1, *The Legacy,* ed. Jean Barman, Yvonne Hébert, and Don McCaskill (Vancouver: UBC Press, 1986), 45-63.
78 "The Canadian Chiefs," *Times* (London), April 12 1825, 2; "Infant Schools," *Times* (London), June 6, 1825, 4; "Visit of the Wyandot Indian Chiefs to the Lord Mayor," *Times* (London), April 22, 1825, 4; "A Few Days Ago," *Times* (London), July 5, 1825, 3.

79 Evan Haefeli and Kevin Sweeney, *Captors and Captives: The 1704 French and Indian Raid on Deerfield* (Cambridge, MA: University of Massachusetts Press, 2003), 61.
80 *Jesuit Relations and Allied Documents,* vol. 57, Relation of 1672-73, ed. Reuben Gold Thwaites (Cleveland, OH: Burrows Bros., 1899), 11.
81 Dominion of Canada, *Annual Report of the Department of Indian Affairs for the Year Ended 31st December, 1890* (Ottawa: Brown Chamberlin, 1891), xxiii.
82 Ibid., 26.
83 Ibid.
84 Ruth Clarke, *Before the Silence: Fifty Years in the History of Alderville First Nation, 1825-1875* (Alderville, ON: Alderville First Nation, 1999).
85 "Travels in Upper Canada," *Kingston Chronicle and Gazette,* September 6, 1834, 1.
86 Michael Ripmeester, "'It Is Scarcely to Be Believed ...': The Mississauga Indians and the Grape Island Mission, 1826-1836," *Canadian Geographer* 39, 2 (1995): 157-68. See also Peter S. Schmalz, *The Ojibwa of Southern Ontario* (Toronto: University of Toronto Press, 1991).
87 Alan Taylor, *The Divided Ground: Indians, Settlers, and the Northern Borderland of the American Revolution* (New York: Knopf, 2006), 350.
88 Ibid., 407.
89 Ibid., 131.
90 Clarke, *Before the Silence.*
91 Frank Eames, "Pioneer Schools of Upper Canada," *Papers and Records* 18 (1919): 101. In *Before the Silence,* Clarke reports the indenture date as October 16. Two versions of the Mississauga name for the island have been recorded — Zhoomin Mniss and Shaweemin shang. The former comes from Clarke, *Before the Silence,* the latter from "Travels in Upper Canada," *Kingston Chronicle and Gazette,* September 6, 1834.
92 Clarke, *Before the Silence.*
93 George Copway, *The Life, History and Travels of Kah-ge-ga-gah-bowh (George Copway)* (Philadelphia: J. Harmstead, 1847).
94 Peter Jones, *Life and Journals of KAH-KE-WA-QUO-NO-BY: (Rev. Peter Jones)* (Toronto: Anson Green, 1860), 284-85.
95 "Letter of William Case," *Toronto Christian Guardian,* October 2, 1833, 186. Britannia ware, a "cheap alternative to silver," was popular in America in the first half of the nineteenth century. See Nancy A. Goyne, "Britannia in America: The Introduction of a New Alloy and a New Industry," *Winterthur Portfolio* 2 (1965): 195.
96 Jones, *Life and Journals,* 279.
97 J.B. Benham, "Grape Island Mission," *Toronto Christian Guardian,* February 13, 1830, 98.
98 Quoted in "Credit River Mission," *Toronto Christian Guardian,* January 29, 1831, 46.
99 J.B. Benham, "Grape Island Mission," *Toronto Christian Guardian,* February 13, 1830, 98.
100 "Letter to the Editors of the Christian Guardian," *Toronto Christian Guardian,* January 30, 1830, 83.

101 Quoted in William Case, Letter to the Editor, "Credit School," *Toronto Christian Guardian,* March 13, 1830, 131.
102 William Lyon Mackenzie, *Sketches of Canada and the United States* (London: E. Wilson, 1833), 131-32.
103 *Second Annual Report of the Central Auxiliary Society for Promoting Education and Industry among the Indians and Destitute Settlers of Canada: Submitted to the Public Meeting Held in the Masonic Hall Hotel, Montreal, April 8, 1829* (Montreal: Printed at the Montreal Herald and the New Montreal Gazette Office, 1829), 27-28.
104 J.B. Benham, "Grape Island Mission," *Toronto Christian Guardian,* February 13, 1830, 98 (emphasis in original).
105 Quoted in, "Rice Lake Mission," *Toronto Christian Guardian,* January 30, 1830, 83.
106 John Carroll, *Case and His Contemporaries,* vol. 3 (Toronto: Wesleyan Conference Office, 1871), 281.
107 James Rodger Miller, *Shingwauk's Vision: A History of Residential Schools* (Toronto: University of Toronto Press, 1996).
108 Quoted in *Toronto Christian Guardian,* May 12, 1858, 127.
109 Wesleyan Methodist Church, Missionary Society Reports, quoted in Neil Semple, *The Lord's Dominion: The History of Canadian Methodism* (Montreal and Kingston: McGill-Queen's University Press, 1996), 172.
110 Miller, *Shingwauk's Vision,* 76. Teacher John B. Benham is noted in *Dictionary of Canadian Biography,* vol. 6, ed. Francess Halpenny (Toronto: University of Toronto Press, 1987), 335. Teacher William Smith, who came to Grape Island in 1827, is recorded in Eames, "Pioneer Schools of Upper Canada."
111 Joseph Edward Sanderson, *The First Century of Methodism in Canada* (Toronto: W. Briggs, 1908), 210.
112 Sources on the Grape Island Mission contain no record of Stockton's residency there. However, Stockton's mission experience in Hawaii is well documented. See Gerald H. Anderson, ed., *Biographical Dictionary of Christian Missions* (New York: Macmillan Reference, 1998), 643; A. Scott Moreau, ed., *Evangelical Dictionary of World Missions* (Grand Rapids, MI: Baker Books, 2000), 909; Constance K. Escher, "She Calls Herself Betsey Stockton," *Princeton History* 10 (1991): 87; Eileen F. Moffett, "Betsey Stockton: Pioneer American Missionary," *International Bulletin of Missionary Research* 19 (1995): 71-76; and John A. Andrew, "Betsey Stockton: Stranger in a Strange Land," *Journal of Presbyterian History* 52 (1974): 157-66. Stockton's involvement at Grape Island is alluded to but not sourced in John Webster Grant, "Two-Thirds of the Revenue: Presbyterian Women and the Native Indian Missions," in *Changing Roles of Women within the Christian Church in Canada,* ed. Elizabeth Gillan Muir and Marilyn Färdig Whiteley (Toronto: University of Toronto Press, 1995), 103.
113 Charles Samuel Stewart, *A Visit to the South Seas in the U.S. Ship Vincennes during the Years 1829 and 1830* (New York: John P. Haven, 1831), 159. A general contemporary description of the mission is recorded in "Mission to the Sandwich Islands," *The American Baptist Magazine and Missionary Intelligencer* 4, 1 (1823): 23-26.
114 James Waddel Alexander to John Hall, February 14, 1840, in James Waddel Alexander, *Forty Years' Familiar Letters of James W. Alexander, D.D., Constituting,*

with the Notes, a Memoir of His Life. Edited by the Surviving Correspondent, John Hall (New York: C. Scribner, 1860), 294.
115 Carl Kalani Beyer, "Manual and Industrial Education for Hawaiians during the 19th Century," *Hawaiian Journal of History* 38 (2004): 8.
116 Carroll, *Case and His Contemporaries*, 225. Case and the boys arrived in early April 1829. Jones joined them a few weeks later. The visit to Philadelphia coincided with the annual meeting of the Philadelphia Conference Missionary Society.
117 Schmalz, *The Ojibwa of Southern Ontario*, 153.
118 James Rodger Miller, *Skyscrapers Hide the Heavens: A History of Indian-White Relations in Canada*, 3rd ed. (Toronto: University of Toronto Press, 2000), 134.
119 Brian E. Titley, "Indian Industrial Schools in Western Canada," in *Schools in the West: Essays in Canadian Education History*, ed. Nancy M. Sheehan, J. Donald Wilson, and David C. Jones (Calgary: Detselig, 1986), 133-53.
120 Quoted in G.S. French, "Rev. William Case," *Dictionary of Canadian Biography*, vol. 8, ed. Francess Halpenny (Toronto: University of Toronto Press, 1985), 134.
121 Moses Henry Perley, *Reports on Indian Settlements, etc.* (Fredericton: J. Simpson, 1842), 18.
122 Ibid.
123 Ibid. Some fifty years later (1901), the US superintendent of Indian schools Estelle Reel expressed a similar idea, but in a more explicitly racist manner: "Association with good white people is the best civilizing agency that can be devised." Quoted in Margaret L. Archuleta, Brenda J. Child, and K. Tsianina Lomawaima, eds., *Away from Home: American Indian Boarding School Experiences* (Phoenix: Heard Museum, 2000), 36.
124 Perley, *Reports on Indian Settlements*, 7.
125 Dickason, *Canada's First Nations*.
126 Miller, *Shingwauk's Vision*; John S. Milloy, *A National Crime: The Canadian Government and the Residential School System, 1879-1986* (Winnipeg: University of Manitoba Press, 1999).
127 Miller, *Shingwauk's Vision*.
128 William Hailmann, "Education of the Indian," in *Education in the United States*, ed. Nicholas Murray Butler (New York: American Book Company, 1910), 5.
129 Ibid., 10.
130 Ibid.
131 Bernard Schissel and Terry Wotherspoon, *The Legacy of School for Aboriginal People* (Don Mills, ON: Oxford University Press, 2003), 51.
132 Jack Brook and J.L. Kohen, *The Parramatta Native Institute and the Black Town: A History* (Sydney: New South Wales University Press, 1991), 16.
133 Quoted in ibid., 22.
134 Ibid., 30-31.
135 Quoted in ibid., 62.
136 Niel Gunson, "Shelley, William (1774-1815)," *Australian Dictionary of Biography*, vol. 2 (Melbourne: Melbourne University Press, 1967), 438-39.

137 T.H. Scott to William Hall, 6 February 1827, "Thomas H. Scott Letter Book, 1825-29," no. 1, 357-58, in *Documents in the History of Aboriginal Education in New South Wales,* ed. J.J. Fletcher (Sydney: Southwood Press, 1989), 34.
138 Brook and Kohen, *The Parramatta Native Institute,* 205.
139 Ibid., 223.
140 Quoted in *Church Missionary Record* 5, 2 (1834): 30.
141 Hilary M. Carey and David Roberts, "Smallpox and the Baiame Waganna of Wellington Valley, New South Wales, 1829-1840: The Earliest Nativist Movement in Aboriginal Australia," *Ethnohistory* 49, 4 (2002): 821-69.
142 William Watson, December 4, 1832, Papers of William Watson, Journal 2, Class Mark: C N/O 92/13, MS page no: 2-090, Church Missionary Society Archives, Birmingham University Library, Birmingham, UK. Watson's journals are reproduced in Hilary M. Carey and David Andrew Roberts, eds., *The Wellington Valley Project: Papers Relating to the Church Missionary Society Mission to Wellington Valley, New South Wales 1830-42. A Critical Electronic Edition,* 2002, http://www.newcastle.edu.au/centre/wvp/group/amrhd/wvp/vol2/188.html.
143 Jan Kociumbas, *Australian Childhood: A History* (St. Leonard, NSW: Allen and Unwin, 1997), 16.
144 Watson, Journal 7, March 1, 1834, CMS Archives.
145 Ibid.
146 Watson, Journal 9, July 11, 1834, CMS Archives.
147 Keith R. McConnochie and A. Russell, *Early Childhood Services for Aboriginal Children* (Canberra: Australian Government Publishing Service, 1982).
148 Suzanne Parry and Julie Wells, "Schooling for Assimilation: Aboriginal Children in the Northern Territory, 1939-1955," *History of Education Review* 26, 2 (1997): 49-62.
149 Roweena MacDonald, *Between Two Worlds: The Commonwealth Government and the Removal of Aboriginal Children of Part-Descent in the Northern Territory* (Alice Springs: IAD Press, 1995).
150 Helen May, *School Beginnings: A History of Early Years Schooling, Case Study One: Missionary Infant Schools for Maori Children, 1830s-40s,* Research and Policy Series No. 1 (Wellington: Institute for Early Childhood Studies, Victoria University of Wellington, 2003); May, *School Beginnings: A 19th Century Colonial Story.*
151 Tanya Fitzgerald, "Missionary Women as Educators: The Church Missionary Schools in New Zealand," *Historical Studies in Education* (Canada) 6, 3 (1994): 139-49.
152 *Missionary Register,* December 1826, 612. Mitchell Library, State Library of New South Wales, Sydney.
153 Quoted in *Missionary Register,* December 1827, 625.
154 Angela Middleton, "Silent Voices, Hidden Lives: Archaeology, Class and Gender in the CMS Missions, Bay of Plenty, New Zealand, 1814-1845," *International Journal of Historical Archaeology* 11, 1 (2007): 1-31.
155 Quoted in *Missionary Register,* February 1834, 119.
156 *Missionary Register,* October 1835, 471.
157 Ibid.

158 Quoted in *Missionary Register,* June 1848, 285.
159 *Missionary Register,* July 1836, 341.
160 Ibid., 341.
161 Quoted in *Missionary Register,* February 1844, 110.
162 William Yate, *An Account of New Zealand and of the Formation and Progress of the Church Missionary Society's Mission in the Northern Island,* 2nd ed. (London: R.B. Seeley and W. Burnside, 1835), 183.
163 Ibid., 195-96.
164 William Bambridge, Diary, November 16, 1843, Willaim Bambridge Diaries, MS-0129-0132, ATL.
165 Bambridge, Diary, November 13, 1843.
166 Bambridge, Diary, September 18, 1843.
167 Native School Attendance Books, 1844-1845, qMS-1408-1413a, ATL. This attendance figure is similar to that at the Paihia Infant School, where twenty-six Maori and European children were enrolled. *Missionary Papers* 73 (1834).
168 Shef Rogers, "Crusoe among the Maori: Translation and Colonial Acculturation in Victorian New Zealand," *Book History* 1, 1 (1998): 182-95.
169 Judith Simon and Linda Tuhiwai Smith, eds., *A Civilising Mission? Perceptions and Representations of the New Zealand Native School System* (Auckland: Auckland University Press, 2001), 159.
170 New Zealand General Assembly, *Education: Native Schools* (Wellington: Government Printers, 1880), cited in Simon and Smith, *A Civilising Mission?* 327.
171 Simon and Smith, *A Civilising Mission?* 162.
172 Barbara Buchanan, *Buchanan Family Records: James Buchanan and His Descendants* (Cape Town: Townshend, Taylor and Snashall, 1923); John Philip to Samuel Wilderspin, July 29, 1831, cited in Samuel Wilderspin, *Early Discipline Illustrated, or, the Infant System Progressing and Successful* (London: Westley and Davis, 1832), 14-18.
173 Helen Ludlow, "'Working at the Heart': The London Missionary Society in Cape Town, 1842-3," in *The London Missionary Society in Southern Africa, 1799-1999,* ed. John de Gruchy (Athens, OH: Ohio University Press, 2000), 109. John Philip indicates that the Buchanan brothers arrived in February 1830. John Philip to Samuel Wilderspin, cited in Wilderspin, *Early Discipline Illustrated,* 15. The more likely date of their arrival is December 1829, provided by Barbara Buchanan. Buchanan, *Pioneer Days in Natal,* 128.
174 Robert Ross, *Status and Respectability in the Cape Colony, 1750-1870: A Tragedy of Manners* (Cambridge: Cambridge University Press, 1999), 71, 89.
175 John Philip, *The Importance of Early Instruction: A Sermon, Preached for the Benefit of the South African Infant School Society* (Cape Town: P.A. Brand at "De Zuid Afrikaan" Office, 1831). In *Early Discipline Illustrated,* Wilderspin recorded a private infant school for European children that opened earlier in the same year under the direction of Elizabeth Lyndall.
176 "Obituary of Elizabeth Rolland," in *The Recollections of Elizabeth Rolland (1803-1901) with Various Documents on the Rolland Family and the Free State Mission of Beersheba,* ed. Karel Schoeman (Cape Town: Human and Rousseau, 1987), 117. Lyndall (later, Rolland) taught at the Cape Town Upper School until 1833.

177 Ludlow, "'Working at the Heart,'" 109.
178 Ross, *Status and Respectability*, 89.
179 According to Spencer, the Lower School "was mainly for children of slaves, but after Ebenezer's arrival a new department for white boys was opened under his charge." Shelagh O'Byrne Spencer, *British Settlers in Natal 1824-1857: A Biographical Register*, vol. 3 (Pietermaritzburg: University of Natal Press, 1985), 81. Lyndall trained teachers for the district schools established by William Buchanan. "Letter from Rev. William Anderson, January 14, 1833," *Christian Advocate*, vol. 11 (Philadelphia: A. Finley, 1833): 514-15.
180 Buchanan, *Pioneer Days in Natal*, 52. Alan F. Hattersley, *The British Settlement of Natal: A Study in Imperial Migration* (Cambridge: Cambridge University Press, 1950), 91.
181 Ludlow, "'Working at the Heart,'" 109.
182 Philip to Wilderspin, in Wilderspin, *Early Discipline Illustrated*.
183 Quoted in James Backhouse and Charles Tylor, *The Life and Labours of George Washington Walker of Hobart Town, Australia* (London: A.W. Bennett, 1862), 25.
184 George Champion, *The Journal of an American Missionary in the Cape Colony* (1835; repr., Cape Town: South African Library, 1968), 4.
185 William Watson, February 28, 1832, Papers of William Watson, Reverend Watson's Letters, Class Mark: C N/O 92/1, MS page no: 2-001, Church Missionary Society Archives, Birmingham University Library, Birmingham, UK. Watson's letters are reproduced in Hilary M. Carey and David Andrew Roberts, eds., *The Wellington Valley Project: Papers Relating to the Church Missionary Society Mission to Wellington Valley, New South Wales 1830-42. A Critical Electronic Edition*, 2002, http://www.newcastle.edu.au/centre/wvp/papersofwilliamwatson/letter211.html.
186 Josiah Bateman, *The Life of Daniel Wilson, DD, Bishop of Calcutta and Metropolitan of India* (Boston: Gould and Lincoln, 1860), 235.
187 Larry Prochner, Helen May, and Baljit Kaur, "'The Blessings of Civilisation': Nineteenth Century Missionary Infant Schools for Young Native Children in Three Colonial Settings — India, Canada and New Zealand, 1820s-1840s," *Paedagogica Historica* 45, 1-2 (2009): 191-210.
188 Edward H. Berman, "Christian Missions in Africa," in *African Reactions to Missionary Education*, ed. E.H. Berman (New York: Teachers College Press, 1975), 1-53.
189 Champion, *The Journal of an American Missionary*.
190 John Philip to Samuel Wilderspin, July 29, 1831, quoted in Wilderspin, *Early Discipline Illustrated*, 16-17.
191 Charles S. Horne, *The Story of the LMS, 1795-1895* (London: London Missionary Society, 1895), 41-42.
192 "Report from the Select Committee on Aborigines," *Parliamentary Papers*, 1836, vol. 1, 672.
193 John Williams to LMS Governors, Simons Bay, Cape of Good Hope, July 18, 1838, CWM/LMS, Incoming Letters, South Seas, Box 11, Folder 5, Jacket D, Council for World Mission Archive (hereafter, CWM Archive), School of Oriental and African Studies Library (hereafter, SOAS), University of London, London.

194 Ebenezer Buchanan to LMS Governors, Falealili, Upolu, May 14, 1839, CWM/LMS, Incoming Letters, South Seas, Box 12, Folder 6, CWM Archive, SOAS. My account of Ebenezer Buchanan's time in the South Seas is based mainly on his correspondence with the LMS governors. Some details given here differ from those presented by Ebenezer's daughter Barbara, in Buchanan, *Buchanan Family Records,* held at the British Library. The largest discrepancy concerns the reasons for Buchanan's departure from the mission field. For an analysis of Buchanan's work in the Pacific, see Sujit Sivasundaram, *Nature and the Godly Empire: Science and Evangelical Mission in the Pacific, 1795-1850* (Cambridge: Cambridge University Press, 2005).

195 Ebenezer Buchanan to Annie Buchanan, May 6, 1838, Cape Town. Cited in Buchanan, *Buchanan Family Records.*

196 John Williams to LMS Governors, Simons Bay, Cape of Good Hope, July 18, 1838, CWM/LMS, Incoming Letters, South Seas, Box 11, Folder 5, Jacket D, CWM Archive, SOAS.

197 This chronology of events is supported by Backhouse and Tylor, *The Life and Labours of George Washington Walker,* 304.

198 John Williams, *Missionary Magazine, a Periodical Monthly Publication, Intended as a Repository of Discussion, and Intelligence Respecting the Progress of the Gospel throughout the World,* January 1840, 40.

199 Mission work was abandoned in the New Hebrides until 1848, when a Canadian Presbyterian mission from Pictou, Nova Scotia, established a settlement on the island of Aneityum (Aneiteum). Barbara Lawson, "Collecting Cultures: Canadian Missionaries, Pacific Islanders, and Museums," in *Canadian Missionaries, Indigenous People: Representing Religion at Home and Abroad,* ed. Alvyn Austin and Jamie S. Scott (Toronto: University of Toronto Press, 2005), 237.

200 *Missionary Magazine,* December 1840, 178.

201 For clothing as a conversion strategy, see Barbara Lawson, "'Clothed and in Their Right Mind': Women's Dress on Erromanga, Vanuatu,'" *Pacific Arts* 23-24 (2001): 69-86; Lawson, "Collecting Cultures," 240; and Sivasundaram, *Nature and the Godly Empire,* 192-95. Clothing was also sought out and valued by Aboriginal people in some instances. See Peggy Brock, "Nakedness and Clothing in Early Encounters between Aboriginal People of Central Australia, Missionaries and Anthropologists," *Journal of Colonialism and Colonial History* 8, 1 (2007): http://muse.jhu.edu/journals/journal_of_colonialism_and_colonial_history/toc/cch8.1.html.

202 Lawson, "Collecting Cultures," 249.

203 George Pritchard, quoted in *Missionary Magazine,* December 1840, 178.

204 Ebenezer Buchanan to LMS Governors, Falealili, Upolu, May 14, 1839, CWM/LMS, Incoming Letters, South Seas, Box 12, Folder 6, CWM Archive, SOAS.

205 Ebenezer Buchanan to LMS Governors, On Camden at Tahiti, October 25, 1841, CWM/LMS, Incoming Letters, South Seas, Box 14, Folder 6, Jacket B, CWM Archive, SOAS; Ebenezer Buchanan to LMS Governors, Falealili, Upolu, October 26, 1839, CWM/LMS, Incoming Letters, South Seas, Box 12, Folder 6, CWM Archive, SOAS.

206 Ebenezer Buchanan to LMS Governors, Upolu, November 20, 1846, CWM/LMS, Incoming Letters, South Seas, Box 21, Folder 4, Jacket C, CWM Archive, SOAS.
207 Ebenezer Buchanan to LMS Governors, Upolu, May 27, 1848, CWM/LMS, Incoming Letters, South Seas, Box 21, Folder 4, Jacket C, CWM Archive, SOAS.
208 Ebenezer Buchanan to LMS Governors, On Camden at Tahiti, October 25, 1841, CWM/LMS, Incoming Letters, South Seas, Box 14, Folder 6, Jacket B, CWM Archive, SOAS.
209 Ebenezer Buchanan to LMS Governors, Upolu, February 28, 1848, CWM/LMS, Incoming Letters, South Seas, Box 21, Folder 4, Jacket C, CWM Archive, SOAS.
210 Ebenezer Buchanan to LMS Governors, Tahiti, August 29, 1842, CWM/LMS, Incoming Letters, South Seas, Box 15, Folder 2, Jacket C, CWM Archive, SOAS.
211 Ibid.
212 Ebenezer Buchanan to LMS Governors, Upolu, August 15, 1844, CWM/LMS, Incoming Letters, South Seas, Box 17, Folder 7, Jacket B, CWM Archive, SOAS.
213 Ebenezer Buchanan to LMS Governors, Upolu, June 1, 1849, CWM/LMS, Incoming Letters, South Seas, Box 21, Folder 4, Jacket C, CWM Archive, SOAS.
214 Ibid.
215 George Stallworthy to LMS Governors, Upolu, June 20, 1849, CWM/LMS, Incoming Letters, South Seas, Box 22, Folder 3, Jacket B, CWM Archive, SOAS.
216 George Stallworthy, Secretary, Samoan Mission, to LMS Governors, June 20, 1849, CWM/LMS, Incoming Letters, South Seas, Box 22, Folder 3, Jacket B, CWM Archives, SOAS.
217 *Missionary Register,* August 1850, 368; Buchanan, *Buchanan Family Records.* Ebenezer Buchanan was the Pietermaritzburg town clerk from 1860 to 1875. Hattersley, *The British Settlement of Natal,* 91. Also see Spencer, *British Settlers,* 81.
218 R. Murray Thomas, "American Samoa and Western Samoa," in *Schooling in the Pacific Islands: Colonies in Transition,* ed. R. Murray Thomas and T. Neville Postlethwaite (Oxford: Pergamon, 1984), 206-7. From 1918 to Samoan independence in 1962, the New Zealand government, which administered Western Samoa as a trusteeship, was responsible for public education there. In the scheme that was developed, the churches continued to direct the lower levels of education, whereas the upper levels became public schools. Over time, the public system became identical to that of New Zealand, including the use of New Zealand curricula and staff. Ibid., 220-21.
219 William Case, Letter to the Editor, "Credit School," *Toronto Christian Guardian,* March 13, 1830, 131.
220 Ibid.
221 Quoted in H.A. Robertson, *Erromanga; the Martyr Isle* (London: Hodder and Stoughton, 1903), 138.
222 "Report from the Select Committee on Aborigines," *Parliamentary Papers,* 1837, vol. 3, 2.
223 R. Cartwright to Governor Macquarie, December 6, 1818, "Instructions for Promoting Moral and Religious Instruction of Aboriginal Inhabitants of New Holland and Van Diemen's Land," *Parliamentary Papers,* 1831, vol. 19, 4.

224 Earl of Gosford to Lord Glenelg, July 13, 1837, "Correspondence since 1835, between Secretary of State for Colonies and Governors of British North American Provinces, Respecting Indians," *Parliamentary Papers,* 1839, vol. 34, 29.
225 Human Rights and Equal Opportunity Commission, *Bringing Them Home: Report of the National Inquiry into the Separation of Aboriginal and Torres Strait Islander Children from Their Families* (Sydney: Human Rights and Equal Opportunity Commission, 1997).
226 Axtell, *After Columbus,* 51.
227 David W. Adams, *Education for Extinction: American Indians and the Boarding School Experience, 1875-1928* (Lawrence: University Press of Kansas, 1995), 336.
228 A.F.B. Roberts, "A New View of the Infant School Movement," *British Journal of Educational Studies* 20, 2 (1972): 154-64.
229 Human Rights and Equal Opportunity Commission, *Bringing them Home,* 24.
230 Judith A. Simon, "State Schooling for Maori: The Control of Access to Knowledge" (paper presented at the annual meeting of the Australian Association for Research in Education, in *Creating Space in Institutional Settings for Maori,* ed. G. Smith and M. Hhepa. RUME Monograph no. 15 (Auckland: University of Auckland, 1993).
231 Barbara Beatty, *Preschool Education in America: The Culture of Young Children from the Colonial Era to the Present* (New Haven: Yale University Press, 1995); Carl Kaestle and Maris Vinovskis, *Education and Social Change in Nineteenth-Century Massachusetts* (Cambridge: Cambridge University Press, 1980); Caroline Winterer, "Avoiding a 'Hothouse System of Education': Nineteenth-Century Early Childhood Education from the Infant Schools to the Kindergartens," *History of Education Quarterly* 32, 3 (1992): 289-314.
232 Henry P. Chavasse, *Advice to a Mother on the Management of Her Children and on the Treatment on the Moment of Some of Their More Pressing Illnesses and Accidents* (Toronto: Willing and William, 1880), 140.
233 Weiner, *Architecture and Social Reform,* 111.
234 Quoted in Alan Barcan, *Two Centuries of Education in New South Wales* (Kensington: New South Wales University Press, 1988), 145.

Chapter 4: Childcare and Daycare

1 "Select Committee on Education of People of England and Wales, and Grants in Aid: Report, Minutes of Evidence, Appendix," *Parliamentary Papers,* 1835, vol. 7, 13.
2 Eneas Mackenzie, "Institutions for Education: Infant Schools," *Historical Account of Newcastle-upon-Tyne: Including the Borough of Gateshead* (Newcastle-upon-Tyne: n.p., 1827), 456, http://www.british-history.ac.uk/source.aspx?pubid=307.
3 Ruth K. McClure, *Coram's Children: The London Foundling Hospital in the Eighteenth Century* (New Haven: Yale University Press, 1981).
4 Wet nurses were lactating women who were employed to breastfeed other women's children. Dry nurses provided general childcare including feeding prepared foods to infants.

5 Reginald H. Nichols and Francis A. Wray, *The History of the Foundling Hospital* (London: Oxford University Press, 1935).
6 McClure, *Coram's Children*, 225.
7 Andrew Bell, *An Analysis of the Experiment in Education Made at Egmore, near Madras*, 3rd ed. (London: Printed by T. Bensley, for Cadell and Davies, 1807), v.
8 London Foundling Hospital, *An Account of the Hospital for the Maintenance and Education of Exposed and Deserted Children* (London: n.p., 1749), iv.
9 Ibid., 82.
10 A number of church-run foundling institutions, primarily Catholic, existed in the colonies.
11 London Foundling Hospital, *An Account of the Hospital*.
12 "Royal Commission to Inquire into State of Popular Education in England: Appendix to Minutes of Evidence," *Parliamentary Papers*, 1861, vol. 21, pt. 6, 402.
13 "Parish of St. Marylebone. Death from Culpable Neglect in Marylebone Workhouse," *Times* (London), November 28, 1840; "Report of Special Assistant Poor Law Commissioners on Treatment of Infant Pauper Children in Marylebone Workhouse," *Parliamentary Papers*, 1843, vol. 45.
14 "Report of Special Assistant," 37.
15 Ibid., 19.
16 Ibid., 25.
17 Ibid., 18.
18 "Proceedings of Directors and Guardians of the Poor of St. Marylebone, Relative to Infant Pauper Children in the Workhouse," *Parliamentary Papers*, 1843, vol. 45, 4.
19 Larry Prochner, "Quality-of-Care in Historical Perspective," *Early Childhood Research Quarterly* 11, 1 (1996): 5-18; Larry Prochner, "The American Crèche: 'Let's Do What the French Do, but Do It Our Way,'" *Contemporary Issues in Early Childhood* 4, 3 (2003): 267-85.
20 John Hollingshead, *Ragged London in 1861* (London: Smith, Elder, 1861).
21 Jack Tizard, Peter Moss, and Jane Perry, *All Our Children: Preschool Services in a Changing Society* (London: Temple Smith for New Society, 1976).
22 "Public Nurseries in England," *Living Age* 28, 351 (1851): 284-85.
23 A report in 1853 again recommended that a nursery be started in Manchester. "The Cotton Metropolis," *Living Age* 36, 455 (1853): 241-54.
24 Ibid., 248.
25 "Poor People's Children," *Living Age* 46, 580 (July 7, 1855): 187; "Paris — The Crèche," *Leisure Hour: A Family Journal of Instruction and Recreation* 187 (1855): 484-86.
26 Alfred Richard Sennett, *Garden Cities in Theory and Practice* (London: Bemrose, 1905), 518. There were approximately 55 crèches in London in 1904. "Mrs. Townshend, The Case for School Nurseries," in *Women's Fabian Tracts*, ed. Sally Alexander (London: Routledge, 1988), 93.
27 Sennett did not list crèches that had closed prior to the year of his survey. The founding dates of the thirteen that were surveyed were 1871, 1876, 1878 (three), 1884, 1887, 1888 (two), 1889, 1890, 1891, and 1903.

28 "Correspondence between Secretary of State and Governor of Van Diemen's Land on Convict Discipline," *Parliamentary Papers,* 1843, vol. 42, 7.
29 Halifax Infant School Society, Petition (Halifax: Halifax Infant School Society, 1856).
30 Suzanne Morton, "From Infants Homes to Day Care," in *Mothers of the Municipality: Women, Work, and Social Policy in Post-1945 Halifax,* ed. Janet Guildford and Judith Fingard (Toronto: University of Toronto Press, 2005), 116.
31 Bronwyn Dalley, *Family Matters: Child Welfare in Twentieth-Century New Zealand* (Auckland: Auckland University Press, 1998), 58.
32 Susan Lorne-Johnson, *Betrayed and Forsaken: The Official History of the Infants' Home, Ashfield, Founded in 1874 as the Sydney Foundling Hospital* (Sydney: Infants' Home, 2001). The name was changed from the Sydney Foundling Institution to the Sydney Foundling Hospital shortly after its opening in 1874.
33 Ibid., 37.
34 Ibid., 21.
35 Ibid.
36 "History of the Infants' Home," Infants' Homes of Toronto Fonds, SC1B, Box 6, file 6, City of Toronto Archives, Toronto, 1.
37 Ibid., 11.
38 "Infants' Home and Infirmary," *Toronto Globe and Mail,* November 18, 1881, 6.
39 Ibid.
40 John McCullagh, Gail Aitken, and Donald Bellamy, *A Legacy of Caring: The Children's Aid Society of Toronto* (Toronto: Dundurn Press, 2002).
41 Patricia T. Rooke and R.L. Schnell, "The Rise and Decline of British North American Protestant Orphans' Homes as Woman's Domain, 1850-1930," *Atlantis* 7, 2 (1982): 21-35.
42 Ibid., 27.
43 D. Suzanne Cross, "The Neglected Majority: The Changing Role of Women in Nineteenth Century Montreal," in *Canadian Cities: Essays in Urban History,* ed. Gilbert Stelter (Ottawa: Carlton University Press, 1984), 66-86; Micheline Dumont, "Julie Gaudry," *Dictionary of Canadian Biography,* vol. 13, ed. Ramsay Cook (Toronto: University of Toronto Press, 1994), 371-72.
44 Prochner, "Quality-of-Care."
45 The employment bureau could also be seen as part of the purely benevolent mission of the nurseries, as suggested by Rooke and Schnell in the case of orphans' homes. Rooke and Schnell, "The Rise and Decline," 24.
46 For accounts of the history of wet-nursing, see Linda Campbell, "Wetnurses in Early Modern England: Some Evidence from the Townshend Archive," *Medical History* 33, 3 (1989): 360-70; Valerie Fildes, *Wet Nursing: A History from Antiquity to the Present* (London: Basil Blackwell, 1988); Valerie Fildes, "The English Wetnurse and Her Role in Infant Care, 1538-1800," *Medical History* 32, 2 (1988): 142-73; Janet Golden, "From Wetnurse Directory to Milk Bank: The Delivery of Human Milk in Boston, 1909-1927," *Bulletin of the History of Medicine* 62, 4 (1988): 589-605; Gerry Hill, Grace Johnston, Sharon Campbell, and Judy Birdsell, "The Medical and Demographic Importance of Wetnursing," *Canadian Bulletin of Medical History* 4 (1987): 183-92; Mary Lineman, "Love for

Hire: The Regulation of the Wetnursing Business in Eighteenth-Century Hamburg," *Journal of Family History* 6, 4 (1981): 379-95; Nancy Senior, "The Nourrice in Paris, Past and Present," *Atlantis* 7, 1 (1981): 104-12; George Sussman, *Selling Mothers' Milk: The Wetnursing Business in France, 1715-1914* (Chicago: University of Illinois Press, 1982); Michael J. Thearle, "Infant Feeding in Colonial Australia, 1788-1900," *Journal of Paediatrics and Child Health* 21 (1985): 75-79; Jacqueline Wolf, "'Mercenary Hirelings' or 'A Great Blessing?' Doctors' and Mothers' Conflicted Perceptions of Wet Nurses and the Ramifications for Infant Feeding in Chicago, 1871-1961," *Journal of Social History* 33, 1 (1999): 97-120.

47   Golden, "From Wetnurse Directory to Milk Bank."
48   *Report of the Toronto Lying-In Hospital for the Year 1857* (Toronto: n.p., 1857), 1.
49   Charles E. Rosenberg, *The Care of Strangers: The Rise of America's Hospital System* (New York: Basic, 1987), 304.
50   C.H.F. Routh, "On the Selection of Wet Nurses from Among Fallen Women," *Lancet* 73, 1867 (1859): 580-82; Letter to the Editor, "Wetnurses from the Fallen," *Lancet* 74, 1851 (1859): 200-1.
51   Routh, "On the Selection," 581.
52   Hill. Johnston, Campbell, and Birdsell, "The Medical and Demographic Importance," 187.
53   Jan Kociumbas, *Australian Childhood: A History* (St. Leonard, NSW: Allen and Unwin, 1997), 84.
54   "Memorandum of Children Sent Out to Wet Nurses," 1862, Toronto House of Industry Papers, SC35D, Box 2, File 4, City of Toronto Archives, Toronto.
55   Georgina O'Hara, *The World of the Baby: A Celebration of Infancy through the Ages* (New York: Doubleday, 1989), 40.
56   Ivy Pinchbeck and Margaret Hewitt, *Children in English Society* (London: Routledge and Kegan Paul, 1969), 218.
57   *The Oxford Universal Dictionary on Historical Principles,* 3rd ed. (1933; repr., Oxford: Oxford University Press, 1955), 133. The date of the term is corroborated in J.B. Curgenven's 1869 "On Baby Farming and the Registration of Nurses," cited in Lionel Rose, *The Massacre of the Innocents: Infanticide in Britain 1800-1939* (London: Routledge and Kegan Paul, 1986), 191n24. However, Rose indicates that the term was first used as early as 1848. Baby farmer Margaret Waters was found guilty of murder and executed in London in 1870. Pinchbeck and Hewitt, *Children in English Society,* 613. Baby farmer Catherine D. Putnam was tried two years earlier in New York City. R. Meckel, *Save the Babies: American Public Health Reform and the Prevention of Infant Mortality 1850-1929* (Baltimore: Johns Hopkins University Press, 1990), 30.
58   Linda Gordon points out that, in North America, baby farms were also used by married women. Gordon, *Heroes of Their Own Lives: The Politics and History of Family Violence: Boston, 1880-1960* (New York: Viking, 1988), 45.
59   Pinchbeck and Hewitt, *Children in English Society,* 587.
60   G.K. Behlmer, "Deadly Motherhood: Infanticide and Medical Opinion in Mid-Victorian England," *Journal of the History of Medicine and Allied Sciences* 34, 4 (1979): 403-27.

61 Sherri Broder, "Child Care or Child Neglect? Baby Farming in Late-Nineteenth-Century Philadelphia," *Gender and Society* 2, 2 (1988): 128-48; Gordon, *Heroes of Their Own Lives,* 43.
62 Benjamin Waugh, *Baby-Farming* (London: Kegan Paul, Trench, Trubner, 1890), 1. Gordon provides an alternative explanation for the growth of the baby farm as a form of infanticide: "It may be that baby farming was replacing infanticide and abandonment done by the mother herself ... If so, the spread of baby farming might reflect, in a grotesque way, a greater tenderness toward infancy." Gordon, *Heroes of Their Own Lives,* 322.
63 David Stannard, "Recounting the Fables of Savagery: Native Infanticide and the Functions of Political Myth," *Journal of American Studies* (UK) 25, 3 (1991): 381-417.
64 For attitudes in England, see A.R. Higgenbotham, "'Sin of the Age': Infanticide and Illegitimacy in Victorian London," *Victorian Studies* 32, 3 (1989): 319-37; C.L. Krueger, "Literary Defenses and Medical Prosecutions: Representing Infanticide in Nineteenth-Century Britain," *Victorian Studies* 40, 2 (1997): 271-94; and D.A. Symonds, "Reconstructing Rural Infanticide in Eighteenth-Century Scotland," *Journal of Women's History* 10, 2 (1998): 63-84. For Canada, see Marie-Aimée Cliché, "L'infanticide dans la région de Québec," *Revue d'Histoire de l'Amérique Française* (Canada) 44, 1 (1990): 31-59. For the United States, see D.V. Shaw, "Infanticide in New Jersey: A Nineteenth-Century Case Study," *New Jersey History* 115, 1-2 (1997): 3-31; and K.H. Wheeler, "Infanticide in Nineteenth-Century Ohio," *Journal of Social History* 31, 2 (1997): 407-18. For Australia, see S. Swain, "The Concealment of Birth in Nineteenth-Century Victoria," *Lilith* (Australia) 5 (1988): 139-47.
65 Pinchbeck and Hewitt, *Children in English Society,* 613.
66 D. Owen Carrigan, *Crime and Punishment in Canada: A History* (Toronto: McClelland and Stewart, 1991), 241.
67 Ibid., 256.
68 Pinchbeck and Hewitt, *Children in English Society,* 612-13.
69 Ibid., 620.
70 Helen May, *The Discovery of Early Childhood: The Development of Services for the Care and Education of Very Young Children, Mid Eighteenth Century Europe to Mid Twentieth Century New Zealand* (Auckland: Auckland University Press, 1997).
71 Kathy Laster, "Frances Knorr: 'She Killed Babies, Didn't She?'" in *Double Time: Women in Victoria, 150 Years,* ed. Marilyn Lake and Farley Kelly (Ringwood, Victoria: Penguin, 1985), 148-55; Kerry Greenwood, ed., *The Things She Loves: Why Women Kill* (Sydney: George Allen and Unwin, 1996).
72 Laster, "Frances Knorr," 149.
73 Judith Allen, "Octavious Beal Re-considered. Infanticide, Babyfarming and Abortion in NSW 1880-1939," in *What Rough Beast? The State and Social Order in Australian Society,* ed. Sydney Labour History Group (Sydney: George Allen and Unwin, 1982), 111-29.
74 Larry Prochner, "'Share Their Care Mrs. Warworker': Wartime Day Nurseries in Ontario and Quebec, 1942-1945," *Canadian Journal of Research in Early Childhood Education* 5, 1 (1996): 115-26.

75 Broder, "Child Care or Child Neglect?"
76 Ibid., 130.
77 "Public Nurseries or Homes for Infant Children," *Toronto Globe and Mail*, March 30, 1857, 2.
78 Prochner, "Quality-of-Care"; Margaret O'Brien Steinfels, *Who's Minding the Children? The History and Politics of Day Care in America* (New York: Simon and Schuster, 1973).
79 May, *The Discovery of Early Childhood*, 99.
80 Carolyn Ann Christenson Saba, "Early Progressive Educational Reform: The Kindergarten and Industrial Education Movements in the United States from 1875 to 1890" (PhD diss., University of Maryland, College Park, 2000).
81 Beatty, *Preschool Education in America*, 101.

Chapter 5: Kindergarten from Germany to England and America

1 "Royal Commission on Employment of Children in Factories, Second Report, Minutes of Evidence; Reports of Medical Commissioners," *Parliamentary Papers*, 1833, vol. 21, 43. The pin-making process is wonderfully described in T.S. Ashton, "The Records of a Pin Manufactory, 1814-21," *Economica* 15 (1925): 281-92.
2 Marguerite Van Die, *An Evangelical Mind: Nathanael Burwash and the Methodist Tradition in Canada, 1839-1918* (Montreal and Kingston: McGill-Queen's University Press, 1989), 28.
3 Ibid., 21.
4 The institute was renamed "Kindergarten" in 1840.
5 Friedrich Froebel, *Mother-Play and Nursery Songs*, ed. Elizabeth Peabody, trans. Fannie E. Dwight and Josephine Jarvis (Boston: Lothrop, Lee, and Shepard, 1878).
6 Manfred Berger, "Von der Kleinkinder-Bewahranstalt zum Kindergarten als Bildungsinstitution," *Unsere Kinder* (Fall 2004): 2.
7 Edward Wiebé, *Golden Jubilee Edition of the Paradise of Childhood. A Practical Guide to Kindergartners* (Springfield, MA: Milton Bradley, 1917), 53.
8 Friedrich Froebel, *Friedrich Froebel's Education by Development: The Second Part of Pedagogics of the Kindergarten*, trans. Josephine Jarvis (London: Edward Arnold, 1899), 141-42.
9 Quoted in Josiah Wilkinson, "System of the Humanistic Schools," St. Pancras, 1861, in "Royal Commission to Inquire into the State of Popular Education in England: Reports of Assistant Commissioners," *Parliamentary Papers*, 1861, vol. 21, part 3, 464. For an extended discussion of punishment using solitary confinement, see Larry Prochner and Yeonwook Hwang, "'Cry and You Cry Alone': Time Out in Early Childhood Settings," *Childhood* 15, 4 (2008): 517-34.
10 Mary Hilton, "Revisioning Romanticism: Towards a Women's History of Progressive Thought, 1780-1850," *History of Education* 30, 5 (2001): 476.
11 Ann Taylor Allen, "Let Us Live with Our Children: Kindergarten Movements in Germany and the United States, 1840-1914," *History of Education Quarterly* 28, 1 (1988): 23-48; Meike Sophia Baader, "Froebel and the Rise of Educational

Theory in the United States," *Studies in Philosophy and Education* 23 (2004): 427-44.

12 Baader, "Froebel and the Rise of Educational Theory." The first of Froebel's works to be translated into English was *Mutter- und Kose-Lieder,* in 1885. Kristen D. Nawrotzki, "'Like Sending Coals to Newcastle': Impressions from and of the Anglo-American Kindergarten Movement," *Paedagogica Historica* 43, 2 (2007): 229.

13 Hermann Poesche, "Froebel's Propaganda on His Kindergarten," in *Froebel's Letters on the Kindergarten,* ed. Emilie Michaelis and H. Keatley Moore (London: Swan Sonnenschein, 1891), 176.

14 Ibid., 175.

15 W.E. Marsden, "'Mrs. Walker's Merry Games for Little People': Locating Froebel in an Alien Environment," *British Journal of Educational Studies* 38, 1 (1990): 18.

16 The first seven gifts were numbered by Froebel. He suggested a sequence for the remaining activities, but did not number them. For examples of popular numbering systems see Johannes and Bertha Ronge, *A Practical Guide to the English Kindergarten* (London: J.S. Hodgson, 1855); Maria Kraus-Boelte and John Kraus, *The Kindergarten Guide* (New York: E. Steiger, 1892). Edward Wiebé, *The Paradise of Childhood: A Manual for Self-Instruction in Friedrich Froebel's Educational Principles, and a Practical Guide for Kindergartners* (Springfield, MA: Milton Bradley Co., 1869); and Kate Douglas Wiggin and Nora Archibald Smith, *Froebel's Gifts* (Boston: Houghton Mifflin, 1895), and *Froebel's Occupations* (Boston: Houghton Mifflin, 1896).

17 The numbering described here is drawn from Wiebé, *The Paradise of Childhood.*

18 Friedrich Froebel, *Friedrich Froebel's Pedagogics of the Kindergarten or, His Ideas concerning the Play and Playthings of the Child,* trans. Josephine Jarvis (London: Edward Arnold, 1897), 123.

19 Wiggin and Smith, *Froebel's Occupations,* 6.

20 Froebel, *Friedrich Froebel's Pedagogics,* 204.

21 Ibid., 72-73.

22 Ibid., 220.

23 Wiggin and Smith, *Froebel's Occupations,* 23.

24 Froebel to the Wives and Mothers of Blankenburg, December 25, 1839, in Michaelis and Moore, *Froebel's Letters,* 218.

25 Kevin J. Brehony, "The Froebel Movement in England 1850-1911: Texts, Readings and Readers" (paper presented at the "Fifth International Froebel Symposium," Berlin, April 30-May 1, 2005).

26 Michaelis and Moore, *Froebel's Letters,* viii.

27 Evelyn Weber, *The Kindergarten: Its Encounter with Educational Thought in America* (New York: Teachers College Press, 1969), 56.

28 Ann Taylor Allen, "Children between Public and Private Worlds: The Kindergarten and Public Policy in Germany," in *Kindergartens and Cultures: The Global Diffusion of an Idea,* ed. Roberta Wollons (New Haven: Yale University Press, 2000), 24.

29 Bertha von Marenholtz-Bülow, *Handwork and Headwork: Their Relation to One Another, and the Reform in Education, According to Froebel,* trans. Alice M. Christie (London: Swan Sonnenschein, 1883).
30 Barbara Beatty, *Preschool Education in America: The Culture of Young Children from the Colonial Era to the Present* (New Haven: Yale University Press, 1995), 50.
31 Allen, "Children between Public and Private Worlds," 25.
32 Ann Taylor Allen, "Gardens of Children, Gardens of God: Kindergartens and Day-Care Centres in Nineteenth-Century Germany," *Journal of Social History* 19, 3 (1986): 433-50.
33 Maria Kraus-Boelte, "Reminiscences of Kindergarten Work," in Henry Barnard, *Kindergarten and Child Culture Papers,* rev. ed. (Hartford, CT: Office of Barnard's American Journal of Education, 1884), 545.
34 Nawrotzki, "'Like Sending Coals to Newcastle.'"
35 Francis W. Parker, "The Kindergarten of Boston," *Kindergarten Magazine* 1 (March 1889): 334-35, quoted in Beatty, *Preschool Education,* 74.
36 John Ramsland, "The Sydney Ragged Schools: A Nineteenth-Century Voluntary Approach to Child Welfare and Education," *Journal of the Royal Australian Historical Society* 68, 3 (1982): 222-37; John Ramsland, "The Development of the Ragged School Movement in Nineteenth-Century Hobart," *Journal of the Royal Australian Historical Society* 73, 2 (1987): 146-57; John Ramsland, "The Ragged School Systems in the Australian Colonies," *Victorian Historical Journal* 60, 2-4 (1989): 47-56.
37 Mary Lucy Walker, "The Development of Kindergartens in Australia" (master's thesis, University of Sydney, 1964), 96.
38 C.J. Montague, *Sixty Years in Waifdom; or, The Ragged School Movement in English History* (Montclair, NJ: Patterson Smith, 1970).
39 Charles Dickens, "Ragged Schools," cited in Philip Collins, *Dickens and Education* (London: Macmillan, 1963), 90.
40 Henry Morley, "Child-Gardens," *Household Words* 11 (July 21, 1855): 577-82. The authorship of "Child-Gardens" was established by John Manning in *Dickens on Education* (Toronto: University of Toronto Press, 1959).
41 Jane Read, "Bertha Ronge," *Oxford Dictionary of National Biography* (Oxford: Oxford University Press, 2004), http://www.oxforddnb.com/. Read indicates that the Ronges invented the material, a claim Johannes Ronge made in Wilkinson's report on the school. Quoted in Wilkinson, "System of the Humanistic Schools," 464.
42 Charles Dickens to Mrs. Gaskell, February 3, 1855, in *The Letters of Charles Dickens,* vol. 7, *1853-1855,* ed. Madeline House, Graham Storey, Kathleen Tillotson, and Angus Easson (Oxford: Clarendon Press, 1965), 520.
43 C. Seymour, *Ragged Schools, Ragged Children* (London: Ragged Schools Museum Trust, 1995).
44 Ibid., 34.
45 Quoted in Seymour, *Ragged Schools,* 30.
46 One was in Liverpool where children were provided with a hot meal at noon and religious instruction. "Thomas-Street Infant Ragged School, Third Annual Report," *Liverpool Mercury* (Liverpool), February 20, 1856, 3.

47 John Garwood, *The Million-Peopled City; or, One-Half of the People of London Made Known to the Other Half* (London: Wertheim and Macintosh, 1853), 5 (emphasis in original).
48 Joy Parr, *Labouring Children: British Immigrant Apprentices to Canada, 1869-1924* (Montreal: McGill-Queen's University Press, 1980).
49 Quoted in Zine Magubane, *Bringing the Empire Home: Race, Class, and Gender in Britain and Colonial South Africa* (Chicago: University of Chicago Press, 2004), 84.
50 Committee of the Halifax Ragged and Industrial Schools, *Annual Report of the Committee of the Halifax Ragged and Industrial Schools* (Halifax: Industrial School Printing Office, 1865).
51 A speech by the Earl of Shaftesbury, quoted in Joseph Kingsmill, *On the Present Aspect of Serious Crime in England: And the Means of Punishment and Repression by Government: With Remarks on the Reformatory School Movement* (London: Longmans, Brown, Green, Longmans and Roberts, 1856), 19.
52 Joseph Kingsmill, *Ojibwa Indians: A Letter to the Rev. Mesac Thomas ... Respecting the Indians of British America* (n.p., 1855), 4.
53 Ramsland, "The Ragged School Systems," 54.
54 Margaret Clyde, "The Development of Kindergartens in Australia at the Turn of the Twentieth Century: A Response to Social and Educational Influences," in *Kindergartens and Cultures: The Global Diffusion of an Idea,* ed. Roberta L. Wollons (New Haven: Yale University Press, 2000), 87-112.
55 Lyndsay Gardiner, *The Free Kindergarten Union of Victoria* (Hawthorn, Victoria: Australian Council for Educational Research, 1982), 11.
56 Philippians 2:4.
57 Jacob A. Riis, *How the Other Half Lives: Studies among the Tenements of New York* (1890; repr., New York: Hill and Wang, 1957), 138.
58 Friedrich Engels, Preface, *The Condition of the Working-Class in England in 1844,* trans. Florence Kelley Wischnewetsky (London: Allen and Unwin, 1892); Henry Mayhew, *London Labour and the London Poor; a Cyclopedia of the Condition and Earnings of Those That Work, Those That Cannot Work, and Those That Will Not Work* (London: Griffin, Bhon, 1861-62); John Thomson, *Street Life in London* (1877; repr., New York: B. Blom, 1969). For a discussion of social surveys, see Martin Bulmer, Kevin Bales, and Kathryn Kish Sklar, *The Social Survey in Historical Perspective, 1880-1940* (Cambridge: Cambridge University Press, 1991).
59 Riis, *How the Other Half Lives,* 59.
60 Charles Brace, *The Dangerous Classes of New York, and Twenty Year's Work among Them* (New York: Wynkoop, 1872), ii.
61 Children's Aid Society, *Annual Report* (New York: Children's Aid Society, 1910), 16.
62 Heather Wilson, "British Stock for a British Dominion: The New Zealand Government's Child Migration Scheme" (master's thesis, University of Auckland, 1996).
63 Charles Loring Brace, *The Stages of Human Evolution: Human and Cultural Origins,* 3rd ed. (Englewood Cliffs, NJ: Prentice-Hall, 1988).
64 F. Pensrose Philp, *The Emigration to Canada of Poor Law Children* (London: P.S. King and Son, 1903), 14.

65 Marvin Lazerson, *Origins of the Urban School: Public Education in Massachusetts, 1870-1915* (Cambridge: Harvard University Press, 1971).
66 Donald N. Bigelow, introduction to *How the Other Half Lives,* by Riis, xiii.
67 Riis, *How the Other Half Lives,* 140.
68 Shurlee Swain, "Derivative and Indigenous in the History and Historiography of Child Welfare in Australia" (paper presented at the "History of Childhood Conference," Washington, DC, August 5-6, 2000).
69 National Kindergarten Association, *Documentary for Kindergarten Association of America* (New York: Edison, 1911). The copy I viewed was located at the National Film and Sound Archive, Canberra. It matches Beatty's description of *At the Threshold of Life.* Beatty, *Preschool Education,* 106.
70 Quoted in Allen, "Let Us Live with Our Children," 29.
71 Merle Curti, *The Social Ideas of American Educators* (New York: Charles Scribner's Sons, 1935), 323-24.
72 William T. Harris, "The Kindergarten in a Nutshell," *Century Magazine* 45, 3 (1893): 475.
73 Felix Adler, "The Democratic Ideal in Education," *Century Magazine* 38, 6 (1889): 928.
74 Ibid.
75 Talcott Williams, "The Kindergarten Movement," *Century Magazine* 45, 3 (1893): 370-71. An intellectual, journalist, and educator, Williams was a friend of Walt Whitman and a member of the American Philosophical Society. Later, he would become the first principal of the School of Journalism at Columbia University.
76 Helen May, *The Discovery of Early Childhood: The Development of Services for the Care and Education of Very Young Children, Mid Eighteenth Century Europe to Mid Twentieth Century New Zealand* (Auckland: Auckland University Press, 1997), xvi.
77 Maria Montessori, *The Montessori Method,* trans. Anne Everett George (New York: Frederick A. Stokes, 1912), 53.
78 Ibid., 62.
79 Ibid.
80 Neil Postman, *Building a Bridge to the 18th Century: How the Past Can Improve Our Future* (New York: Vintage, 1999), 121.
81 Henry Y. Hind, *Explorations in the Interior of the Labrador Peninsula: The Country of the Montagnais and Nasquapee Indians, 1823-1908* (London: Longman, Green, Longman, Roberts and Green, 1863), 322.
82 Henry W. Elliott, "Wild Babies," *Harper's New Monthly Magazine* 57, 342 (November 1878): 829-30.
83 George S. Wilson, "How Shall the American Savage be Civilised?" *Atlantic Monthly* 50, 301 (November 1882): 604. For a discussion of the idea of "military colonization," see Thomas W. Dunlay, *Wolves for the Blue Soldiers: Indian Scouts and Auxiliaries with the United States Army, 1860-1890* (Lincoln: University of Nebraska Press, 1982).
84 David W. Adams, *Education for Extinction: American Indians and the Boarding School Experience, 1875-1928* (Lawrence: University Press of Kansas, 1995), 19.

85 In some instances, individual Indian missionaries and teachers established successful community-based schools. A famous example was the Elizabeth Peabody Indian School (1855-88) founded by Sarah Winnemucca for Paiute children in Nevada. The school included a kindergarten that was based on Peabody's ideas. V. Celia Lascarides, "Sarah Winnemucca and Her School" (paper presented at the annual meeting of the National Association of Educators of Young Children, Atlanta, November 10, 2000).

86 Adams, *Education for Extinction*.

87 Jon Reyhner, "American Indian Language Policy and School Success," *Journal of Educational Issues of Language Minority Students* 12, 3 (1993): 35-59.

88 J.H. Oberly, *Annual Report of the Commissioner of Indian Affairs to the Secretary of the Interior for the Year 1885* (Washington: Government Printing Office, 1885), cxiii.

89 Michael S. Shapiro, *Child's Garden: The Kindergarten Movement from Froebel to Dewey* (University Park: Pennsylvania State University Press, 1983), 96.

90 Elizabeth Peabody, *Record of Mr. Alcott's School Exemplifying the Principles and Methods of Moral Culture* (Boston: Roberts Brothers, 1874).

91 In 1859, the German-born journalist and educator Adolf Douai opened a bilingual German-English kindergarten in his Boston home.

92 Elizabeth Peabody, "Kindergarten: What Is It?" *Atlantic Monthly* 10, 61 (November 1862): 586.

93 Ibid., 589 (emphasis in original).

94 F.E. Fryatt, "A Free Kindergarten," *Harpers New Monthly Magazine* 57, 342 (November 1878): 801-7.

95 Ibid., 801.

96 Ibid., 803.

97 "Poppenhusen's Institute at College Point," *New York Times,* May 9, 1870, 2.

98 Campbell J. Gibson and Emily Lennon, *Historical Census Statistics on the Foreign-Born Population of the United States: 1850-1990,* Population Division Working Paper No. 29 (Washington: Population Division, US Census Bureau, 1999), Table 22: Nativity of the Population for Urban Places Ever among the 50 Largest Urban Places since 1870: 1850 to 1990, http://www.census.gov/population/www/documentation/twps0029/twps0029.html.

99 Williams, "The Kindergarten Movement," 372.

100 Beatty, *Preschool Education,* 92.

101 Golden Gate Kindergarten Association (GGKA), *Annual Report* (San Francisco: George Spaulding, 1887), 82. Sarah Brown Ingersoll Cooper Papers, #6543 (hereafter, CP), Series 3: Box 8, Folder 8, Kroch Library (hereafter, KL), Division of Rare and Manuscripts Collections, Cornell University Library, Ithaca, New York.

102 C.H. McGrew, *Symmetrical Outlines of Development and Training for the Golden Gate Kindergartens, Prepared for Sarah B. Cooper* (San Francisco: George Spaulding, 1893), 19.

103 Ibid., 20.

104 Carol M. Roland, "The California Kindergarten Movement: A Study in Class and Social Feminism" (PhD diss., University of California, Riverside, 1980).

105 GGKA, *Annual Report* (San Francisco: George Spaulding and Co., 1888), 13. CP, Series 3: Box 8, Folder 9, KL.
106 Kathryn P. Hearst, "Phoebe Apperson Hearst: The Making of an Upper-Class Woman, 1842-1919" (PhD diss., Columbia University, 2005), 237. See also Alexandra M. Nickliss, "Phoebe Apperson Hearst's 'Gospel of Wealth,'" *Pacific Historical Review* 71, 4 (2002): 575-605.
107 Jackson Street Free Kindergarten Association (JSFKA), *Annual Report* (San Francisco: George Spaulding, 1881), 19. CP, Series 3: Box 8, Folder 2, KL.
108 GGKA, *Annual Report* (San Francisco: George Spaulding, 1890), 78. CP, Series 3: Box 8, Folder 11, KL.
109 JSFKA, *Annual Report* (San Francisco: George Spaulding, 1882), 12. CP, Series 3: Box 8, Folder 3, KL.
110 JSFKA, *Annual Report* (San Francisco: George Spaulding, 1883), 24. CP, Series 3: Box 8, Folder 4, KL.
111 Ibid.
112 JSFKA, *Annual Report* (San Francisco: George Spaulding, 1880), 14. CP, Series 3: Box 8, Folder 1, KL.
113 JSFKA, *Annual Report* (San Francisco: George Spaulding, 1882), 12.
114 The incident inspired a novel by Frank Norris, which was adapted by Erich von Stroheim in his 1925 film *Greed*. Norris, *McTeague: A Story of San Francisco*, ed. Donald Pizer (1899; repr., New York: Norton, 1977).
115 "Twenty-Nine Fatal Wounds," *San Francisco Examiner*, October 10, 1893, 12.
116 Roland, "The California Kindergarten Movement."
117 William Torrey Harris, "Kindergarten in the Public School System," in Barnard, *Kindergarten and Child Culture Papers*, 640.

Chapter 6: Kindergarten in the Case-Study Countries

1 The precise figure is 73.88 percent. Department of Agriculture, *Canada Year Book for 1902* (Ottawa: Government Printers, 1903).
2 Department of Agriculture, *Canada Year Book for 1901* (Ottawa: Government Printers, 1902).
3 Department of Agriculture, *Canada Year Book for 1908* (Ottawa: Government Printers, 1909), 132.
4 Yolande Lavoie, *L'émigration des Québécois aux États-Unis de 1840 à 1930* (Quebec City: Conseil de la langue française, 1981), 53, 68.
5 *Calgary Herald*, 1899, quoted in *Immigration and the Rise of Multiculturalism*, ed. Howard Palmer (Vancouver: Copp Clark, 1975), 45.
6 *Historical Statistics of Canada* (Ottawa: Statistics Canada, 1983).
7 Graeme Davidson, J.W. McCarty, and Ailsa McLeary, *The Australians 1888* (Broadway, NSW: Fairfax, Syme and Weldon, 1987).
8 Ibid., 30.
9 Ibid., 217.
10 A.H. McLintock, *An Encyclopaedia of New Zealand* (Wellington: Government Printers, 1966), 132.
11 W.H. Oliver, *The Story of New Zealand* (London: Faber and Faber, 1960).

12 Ibid., 103.
13 "Immigrant Arrivals," *Historical Statistics of Canada.*
14 Barbara Beatty, *Preschool Education in America: The Culture of Young Children from the Colonial Era to the Present* (New Haven: Yale University Press, 1995), 104.
15 Catherine M. Condon, "Alba Casa," Lower Sackville, Halifax, Nova Scotia, to Sarah Cooper, February 2, 1888, Sarah Brown Ingersoll Cooper Papers, #6543 (hereafter, CP), Series 1: Box 4, Folder 9, Kroch Library (hereafter, KL), Division of Rare and Manuscripts Collections, Cornell University Library, Ithaca, New York.
16 Ibid.
17 GGKA, *Annual Report* (George Spauling, San Francisco, 1885). CP, Series 3: Box 8, Folder 6, KL.
18 *Sydney Morning Herald,* January 21, 1885, 9, quoted in Mary Lucy Walker, "The Development of Kindergartens in Australia" (master's thesis, University of Sydney, 1964), 188.
19 Walker, "The Development of Kindergartens," 186.
20 Ruth Harrison, *Sydney Kindergarten Teachers College, 1897-1981: A Pioneer in Early Childhood Education and Care in Australia* (Sydney: Sydney Kindergarten Teachers College Graduates Association, 1985), 18.
21 Kerry Bethell, "'Not for a Name That We Plead': Fashioning the Ideological Origins of Early Kindergarten in Dunedin and Wellington, New Zealand, 1870-1913" (PhD diss., Victoria University of Wellington, 2008).
22 Karen Duder, "Lavinia Kelsey," in *The Book of New Zealand Women: Ko Kui Ma Te Kaupapa,* ed. Charlotte Macdonald, Merimeri Penfold, and Bridget Williams (Wellington: Bridget Williams Books, 1991), 344. Also see Bethell, "'Not for a Name That We Plead,'" and Dorothy Dempster, "From Patronage to Parent Participation — The Development of the Dunedin Free Kindergarten Association, 1889-1939" (Diploma in education thesis, University of Otago, 1986).
23 Mark Cohen to Sarah Cooper, June 10, 1891, CP, Series 1: Box 4, Folder 34, KL.
24 Mark Cohen to Sarah Cooper, June 19, 1891, CP, Series 1: Box 4, Folder 34, KL.
25 Ibid.
26 Dorothy W. Hewes, "Those First Good Years of Indian Education," *American Indian Culture and Research Journal* 4, 3 (1981): 63-82.
27 Dorothy W. Hewes, "Organic Education in Public Schools in Late Nineteenth Century America" (paper presented at the International Standing Conference for the History of Education, Joensuu, Finland, July 27, 1988), Eric Reproduction Document Number ED299048.
28 David W. Adams, *Education for Extinction: American Indians and the Boarding School Experience, 1875-1928* (Lawrence: University Press of Kansas, 1995), 19.
29 Charles Montgomery Tate, Methodist Missionary, Chilliwack, British Columbia, to Sarah Cooper, February 15, 1889, CP, Series 1: Box 4, Folder 16, KL.
30 Harriet Louise Platt, *The Story of the Years: A History of the Woman's Missionary Society of the Methodist Church, Canada, from 1881 to 1906,* vol. 1 (Toronto: Women's Missionary Society, Methodist Church, 1908).
31 Ibid., 60-61.

32 Lucie Calista Maley, "Kindergarten Benefit to Indian Children," *Kindergarten Magazine* 10, 7 (1898): 439.
33 Ibid., 441.
34 The Duck Lake school officially admitted students from age seven. For a description of the school, see Arlene Roberta Greyeyes, "St. Michael's Indian Residential School 1884-1926: A Study within a Broader Historical and Ideological Framework" (master's thesis, Carleton University, Ottawa, 1995).
35 Dominion of Canada, *Annual Report of the Department of Indian Affairs for the Year Ended 31st December, 1886* (Ottawa: MacLean, Roger, 1887), 153.
36 Dominion of Canada, *Annual Report of the Department of Indian Affairs for the Year Ended 31th December, 1892* (Ottawa: S.E. Dawson, 1893), 63.
37 Dominion of Canada, *Annual Report of the Department of Indian Affairs for the Year Ended 30th June, 1896* (Ottawa: S.E. Dawson, 1897), 321.
38 Dominion of Canada, *Annual Report of the Department of Indian Affairs for the Year Ended 31st December, 1890* (Ottawa: Brown Chamberlin, 1891), 74.
39 "The Fair Opened," *Manitoba Daily Free Press* (Winnipeg), July 28, 1892.
40 *Milton Bradley Company's Catalogue* (Springfield, MA: Milton Bradley, 1894).
41 Dominion of Canada, *Annual Report of the Department of Indian Affairs for the Year Ended 30th June, 1895* (Ottawa: S.E. Dawson, 1896), 121.
42 Ibid.
43 Dominion of Canada, *Annual Report of the Department of Indian Affairs for the Year Ended 30th June, 1896* (Ottawa: S.E. Dawson, 1897), 329.
44 James Rodger Miller, *Shingwauk's Vision: A History of Residential Schools* (Toronto: University of Toronto Press, 1996). Gillespie was born in Ontario in 1866 and completed teacher training at an unknown Normal School. Moving with her family to the Qu'Appelle Valley in 1889, she taught at several Indian schools including the Crowstand Boarding School, before becoming principal at the File Hills school. John Webster Grant, "Two-Thirds of the Revenue: Presbyterian Women and Native Indian Missions," in *Changing Roles of Women within the Christian Church in Canada,* ed. Elizabeth Gillan Muir and Marilyn Färdig Whiteley (Toronto: University of Toronto Press, 1995), 99-116. See also L.L. Dobbin, "Mrs. Catherine Gillespie Motherwell, Pioneer Teacher and Missionary," *Saskatchewan History* 14, 1 (1961): 17-26.
45 Protestant Board of School Commissioners for the City of Montreal, *Annual Report* (Montreal: n.p., 1886), 10. English Montreal School Board Archives, Montreal.
46 "An Act Respcting the Department of Education," *Sessional Papers of the Dominion of Canada:* Vol. 17, *First Session of the Seventh Parliament, Session 1891,* Appendix A (Ottawa: B. Chamberlin, 1891), 63-32.
47 "Second Reading of the School Bill," *The Globe* (Toronto), August 17, 1892.
48 "North West School Act," *Manitoba Daily Free Press* (Winnipeg), August 20, 1892, 2.
49 "North West Assembly," *Manitoba Daily Free Press* (Winnipeg), August 23, 1892, 4.
50 "Kindergarten Class in Regina," *Regina Standard,* January 15, 1892; *Alexandra High School Souvenir* (Wetaskiwin: n.p., 1909); W.J. Roche, *The Yukon Territory: Its History and Resources* (Ottawa: Department of Interior, Government of

Canada, 1916), 214; Marjorie Almstrom, *A Century of Schooling: Education in the Yukon 1861-1981* (Whitehorse: n.p., 1991).
51 "Progress of Doukhobors," *The Globe* (Toronto), November 24, 1900, 5.
52 Almstrom, *A Century of Schooling*, 82.
53 Born in New York State in 1848, Marean attended the Albany Normal School. Both "Mareau" and "Marean" were contemporary spellings of her name. The former appeared in an advertisement for her kindergarten and in her byline in a newspaper article. In *Froebel's Educational Laws,* Hughes used "Marean," which is probably the correct version. James L. Hughes, *Froebel's Educational Laws for All Teachers* (New York: D. Appleton, 1899). Her *The Globe* (Toronto) obituary (December 26, 1929) gave a third variant, Morean.
54 The eighteen children came from the Northern Home for Friendless Children in Philadelphia. Francis Walker, ed., *International Exhibition 1876, Reports and Awards,* vol. 8 (Washington, DC: Government Printing Office, 1880), 328.
55 "Kindergarten School," *The Globe* (Toronto), September 8, 1877, 7. The school moved to 19 Homewood Avenue in 1878. Barbara E. Corbett established the opening date of Marean's private kindergarten to be January 1878. Corbett, *A Century of Kindergarten Education in Ontario, 1887 to 1987* (Dundas, ON: Froebel Foundation, 1989). If this were the case, applications were taken in the fall for the winter opening.
56 "Miss Ada Mareau's Kindergarten," *The Globe* (Toronto), August 31, 1878, 02.
57 Corbett, *A Century of Kindergarten Education*.
58 "The Kindergarten System," *Winnipeg Daily Times,* December 5, 1883, 8.
59 Ibid., 10.
60 "Kindergartens," *Manitoba Daily Free Press* (Winnipeg), December 20, 1883, 2.
61 "Prominent Kindergarten Worker Passes Away," *The Globe* (Toronto), May 23, 1919. Hart left to direct kindergartens at the Normal School in Milwaukee, Wisconsin, where she spent one year; she was director of training at the Baltimore Kindergarten Association in 1897. She led the Philadelphia Training School for Kindergarten Teachers from 1904 until her death in 1918.
62 On the post-1884 influence of the St. Louis kindergarteners, see Henry Morgan, *The Imagination of Early Childhood Education* (New York: Greenwood Press, 1999), 218.
63 "The Kindergarten System," *The Globe* (Toronto), November 15, 1890. The article filled the front page of the Saturday edition of *The Globe,* and included several illustrations of kindergarten activities.
64 The opening of the demonstration kindergarten is noted in "Educational Notes and News," *The Canada School Journal* 11, 2 (1886), 23. Bessie Hailmann was the daughter of William and Eudora Hailmann. She was director of the kindergarten at the Toronto Normal School from 1895 to 1896.
65 From 1885 to 1900 Adaline Hughes lectured to kindergartners training to teach in Toronto public schools. Corbett, *A Century of Kindergarten Education,* 43.
66 Corbett, *A Century of Kindergarten Education*.
67 Quoted in "Must Adhere to Froebel," *The Globe* (Toronto), April 22, 1905, 9.
68 Corbett, *A Century of Kindergarten Education*.

69 Hughes, *Froebel's Educational Laws,* 168.
70 W.E. Marsden, "'Mrs. Walker's Merry Games for Little People': Locating Froebel in an Alien Environment," *British Journal of Educational Studies* 38, 1 (1990): 17.
71 Mark Moss, *Manliness and Militarism: Educating Young Boys in Ontario for War* (Toronto: Oxford University Press, 2001).
72 "Pennies for Teachers, Dollars for Movies," *The Globe* (Toronto), November 17, 1916, 6.
73 James L. Hughes, *Manual of Drill and Calisthenics* (Toronto: W.J. Gage, 1879).
74 Adolf Douai, *The Kindergarten: A Manual for the Introduction of Froebel's System of Primary Education into Public Schools; and for the Use of Mothers and Private Teachers,* 4th ed. (New York: E. Steiger, 1872), 17.
75 Evelyn Weber, *The Kindergarten: Its Encounter with Educational Thought in America* (New York: Teachers College Press, 1969), viii.
76 Lucy Wheelock, "Report for the Committee of Nineteen of the International Kindergarten Union," *Elementary School Teacher* 8, 2 (1907): 79.
77 Subcommittee on Curriculum of the Bureau of Education Committee of the International Kindergarten Union, *The Kindergarten Curriculum,* Department of Interior, Bureau of Education Bulletin No. 16 (Washington: Government Printing Office, 1919).
78 Ibid., 23.
79 Marylin J. McKay, *A National Soul: Canadian Mural Painting 1860s-1930s* (Montreal and Kingston: McGill-Queen's University Press, 2002).
80 "The Kindergarten," *The Globe* (Toronto), April 21, 1905, 6.
81 Ibid.
82 Julie Mathien, "Children, Families, and Institutions in Late 19th and Early 20th Century Ontario" (master's thesis, University of Toronto, 2001).
83 "Toronto Kindergartners Honor Dr. J.L. Hughes," *The Globe* (Toronto), February 19, 1921.
84 "School Inspectors Suggest Innovations," *The Globe* (Toronto), November 26, 1915, 8; "Kindergartens and Playgrounds," *The Globe* (Toronto), July 15, 1916, 6.
85 Weber, *The Kindergarten,* 27.
86 "Froebel Model for Childhood," *The Globe* (Toronto), April 5, 1918, 8.
87 "Nothing Radical to Cowley's Plan," *The Globe* (Toronto), April 5, 1923, 12.
88 "Miss Adair to the Board," *The Globe* (Toronto), April 16, 1925, 11.
89 Quoted in "Say Cowley's Plan Retrogressive Step," *The Globe* (Toronto), March 28, 1923, 14.
90 Quoted in ibid.
91 "Board to Consider Inspector's Report," *The Globe* (Toronto), March 29, 1923, 14. Other proposed names were play school and nursery school.
92 William Wilson, *A Manual of Instruction for Infants' Schools* (New York: G. and C. and H. Carvill, 1830).
93 "Cowley's Report Draws Criticism," *The Globe* (Toronto), April 17, 1923, 14.
94 "Champions of Kindergarten Resentful of Interference," *The Globe* (Toronto), November 18, 1925, 11.

95 Quoted in "Kindergarten Lives, Criticism is Contrary," *The Globe* (Toronto), April 15, 1925, 12.
96 Quoted in "Forming of Habits Kindergarten Task," *The Globe* (Toronto), November 3, 1927, 14.
97 "New Topics Broached at Busy O.E.A. Session," *The Globe* (Toronto), April 20, 1927, 14.
98 Corbett, *A Century of Kindergarten Education*, 81.
99 Kevin J. Brehony, "The Kindergarten in England, 1851-1918," in *Kindergartens and Cultures: The Global Diffusion of an Idea*, ed. Roberta Wollons (New Haven: Yale University Press, 2000), 60.
100 C. Turney, "William Wilkins — Australia's Kay-Shuttleworth," in *Pioneers of Australian Education: A Study of the Development of Education in New South Wales in the Nineteenth Century*, ed. C. Turney (Sydney: Sydney University Press, 1969), 193-245.
101 *Board of National Education of New South Wales, Report for the Year 1856*, Votes and Proceedings of the Legislative Assembly of New South Wales (Sydney: n.p., 1856), 6-7.
102 Henry Barnard, "Froebel's System of Infant-Gardens," *American Journal of Education* 2 (1856): 449-51.
103 C. Turney, *William Wilkins: His Life and Work: A Saga of Nineteenth-Century Education* (Sydney: Hale and Iremonger, 1992), 23.
104 Ibid., 70.
105 Quoted in Alan Barcan, *Two Centuries of Education in New South Wales* (Kensington: New South Wales University Press, 1988), 145.
106 Ibid., 71.
107 The review of state initiatives is drawn mainly from P.R. Cole, *Education in Australia: A Comparative Study of the Educational Systems of the Six Australian States*, ed. G.S. Browne (London: Macmillan, 1927).
108 Helen May, *The Discovery of Early Childhood: The Development of Services for the Care and Education of Very Young Children, Mid Eighteenth Century Europe to Mid Twentieth Century New Zealand* (Auckland: Auckland University Press, 1997), 62; Walker, "The Development of Kindergartens," 131.
109 A.C. Crowley to W. Wilkins, Secretary of Public Instruction, May 16, 1881, Department of Education Subject Files: Kindergarten Files, 1881-1885 (hereafter, KF), 20/13376 A, State Archives New South Wales (hereafter, SANSW), Western Sydney Records Centre, Kingswood. Unless otherwise indicated, all material from the Kindergarten Files shares this call number.
110 Alison S. Elliott, "Mrs. Crowley: The First Kindergartner," *Unicorn* 16, 2 (1990): 129-32.
111 J.S. Jones, Local Inspector, to District Inspector McCredie, May 20, 1881, KF, SANSW.
112 Crowley to Jones, Inspector, October 8, 1881, KF, SANSW.
113 Memorandum to District Inspector McCredie, "Kindergarten Experiment Report," March 28, 1882, KF, SANSW.
114 Ibid.

115 Chief Inspector Jones, Memorandum, to District Inspector McCredie, April 18, 1882, KF, SANSW.
116 Under Secretary, "Kindergarten," May 3, 1882, KF, SANSW.
117 Inspector, July 31, 1882, KF, SANSW.
118 Under Secretary to Crowley, May 25, 1883, KF, SANSW.
119 Inspector's comparative report upon the Stanmore Infants' School and the Kindergarten in Castlereagh Street, "Programmes of Lessons," August 16, 1884, KF, SANSW.
120 Inspection Report, Castlereagh Public Kindergarten School, March 28, 1884, KF, SANSW.
121 Minute by the Minister of Public Instruction: Subject Kindergarten School, Castlereagh Street, September 6, 1884, KF, SANSW.
122 Ibid.
123 Inspector to the Minister of Public Instruction, February 25, 1885, KF, SANSW.
124 Memorandum to the Architect: Kindergarten System (Crown Street) as to the Provision of a Gallery, October 27, 1884, KF, SANSW.
125 Jane Read, "Free Play with Froebel: Use and Abuse of Progressive Pedagogy in London's Infant Schools, 1870-c. 1904," *Paedagogica Historica* 42, 3 (2006): 299-323.
126 Martha M. Simpson, "Work in the Kindergarten. An Australian Programme, Based on the Life and Customs of the Australian Black," *Records of the Education Society* 2 (1909): i.
127 Ibid.
128 Ibid.
129 Ibid., 10.
130 Government Architect, Department of Public Works, New South Wales, Blackfriars Practice School Repairs and Improvements, August 6, 1908, Blackfriars School Files, KF, 5/14945 A/B SANSW, SANSW.
131 R.C. Peterson, "The Montessorians — M.M. Simpson and L. de Lissa," in *The Development of Education in Australia, 1900-1950,* vol. 3, *Pioneers of Australian Education,* ed. C. Turney (Sydney: University of Sydney Press, 1983), 232-71. In 1912, Rachel Reynolds wrote on behalf of the Dunedin Free Kindergarten Association to the Victoria minister of education, requesting a set of Montessori materials. The letter found its way to the New South Wales Department of Public Instruction. Inscribed on the back was the note that "the materials at Blackfriars were made by the teachers there, a lady specially employed for two or three months, and the men at Cockatoo Island." Mrs. Reynolds to Minister of Education, State of Victoria, December 8, 1912, KF, 20/13376 A, SANSW. A set was sent to Reynolds in 1913. Undersecretary to the Minister of Public Instruction, New South Wales, to Reynolds, July 9, 1913, KF, 20/13376 A, SANSW.
132 *Australian Kindergarten Magazine* 3, 2 (1912): 12. Sandpaper letters were cutouts of letters of the alphabet from sandpaper mounted on cards. Pupils traced the letters with their finger.
133 Ibid.

134 B.M. Tavish, "The Montessori System: Remarks by a Sydney Teacher," September 1912, KF, 20/13376 A, SANSW.
135 Carmichael, Minister of Public Instruction, Sydney, September 2, 1913, KF, 20/13376 A, SANSW.
136 Cole, *Education in Australia*, 33.
137 Special Inspection, by Chief Inspector, July 4, 1916, KF, 5/14948, SANSW.
138 Ibid.
139 May, *The Discovery of Early Childhood*, 63.
140 Quoted in John L. Ewing, *Development of the New Zealand Primary School Curriculum, 1877-1970* (Wellington: New Zealand Council for Educational Research, 1970), 80.
141 Rolo Arnold, "Catherine Augusta Francis, 1836-1916," *Dictionary of New Zealand Biography*, http://www.dnzb.govt.nz/dnzb/.
142 Don Brown, *Mount Cook School* (Wellington: Mount Cook School, 1975).
143 Beatrice Bade, "The Foundation of School Inspection in the Wellington Province: A Study of the Work of Robert Lee" (master's thesis, University of New Zealand, 1943). Lee trained at St. Mark's College, England, in the pupil-teacher system devised by Kay-Shuttleworth. He left his position as headmaster at a school in Nelson to become school inspector.
144 Helen May, *School Beginnings: A 19th Century Colonial Story* (Wellington: NZCER Press, 2005), 209. Francis may also have acquired some familiarity with kindergarten ideas from John Anderson Hartley, who immigrated to Adelaide in 1871, working for four years as headmaster at Prince Alfred College. In 1875, he became president of the newly created Council of Education in Adelaide. One of his aims was to standardize training, and in relation to the curriculum, he was interested in the ideas of both Froebel and Pestalozzi. See Cole, *Education in Australia*.
145 Ibid., 207.
146 Read, "Free Play with Froebel."
147 1878 Inventory of Materials, Inspector's Report, Mount Cook Infants' School Logbook, Beaglehole Room (hereafter, BR), Victoria University, Wellington.
148 "Chit Chat," *New Zealand Mail*, October 10, 1884, 3.
149 "The Mount Cook Kindergarten School," *New Zealand Mail* (Wellington), September 13, 1879, 11. See also the report in "The Kindergarten System of Teaching," *Evening Post* (Wellington), September 16, 1878, 2, and the description of the system in Annie R. Butler, *Glimpses of Maori Land* (London: The Religious Tract Society, 1886), 59-60.
150 Quoted in ibid., 12.
151 Ibid., 11.
152 Robert Lee, Inspector's Report, October 1, 1880, Mount Cook Infants' School Logbook 1878-1927, BR.
153 1884 Inventory of Materials, Mount Cook Infants' School Logbook 1878-1927, BR; Robert Lee, Inspector's Report, July 3, 1885, Mount Cook Infants' School Logbook 1878-1927, BR.
154 Bade, "The Foundation of School Inspection."
155 "Chit Chat," *New Zealand Mail*, October 10, 1884, 3.

156 These included activities with clay, coloured letter sticks, counters, stick laying, bead laying, bead threading, pattern making, ring laying, word building, perforated bead cards, paper plaiting, paper folding, lath plaiting, cane for basket work, cork and wire work, sticks and brass joints, parquetry, paper cutting, scissors, ball work, stencilling, Japanese bamboo work, coloured chalks, rope, string and straw work, card pricking, card sewing, coloured shapes, and form and colour. Listed in the 1899 Inventory of Materials, Mount Cook Infants' School Logbook 1878-1927, BR.

157 Catherine Cosgrove, "A History of the American Kindergarten Movement from 1860 to 1916" (PhD diss., Northern Illinois University, 1989).

158 Ada M. a'Beckett, *The Growth and Development of the Free Kindergarten Movement in Victoria* (Melbourne: Hart Printing, 1939).

159 Nina C. Vandewalker, *The Kindergarten in American Education* (New York: Macmillan, 1908). The Woman's Christian Temperance Union in Canada, Australia, and New Zealand was also active in kindergarten work. See Sharon A. Cook, *"Through the Sunshine and Shadow": The Woman's Christian Temperance Union, Evangelicalism, and Reform in Canada, 1874-1930* (Montreal and Kingston: McGill-Queen's University Press, 1995); May, *The Discovery of Early Childhood*. Women who played central roles in supporting Australian kindergartens, such as Margaret Windeyer, were also involved in the Woman's Christian Temperance Union.

160 Howard Radest, *Felix Adler: An Ethical Culture* (New York: Peter Lang, 1998).

161 Felix Adler, "Some Characteristics of the American Ethical Movement" (address delivered in South Place Chapel, London, June 7, 1925), http://aeu.org/library/display_article.php?article_id=12.

162 Kerry Bethell, "In Search of Mary Richmond: A Journey of Discovery of Subject and Self" (paper presented at the "Tenth European Early Childhood Education Research Association Conference," London, August 29-September 1, 2000); Kerry Bethell, "To Bring into Play: Miss Mary Richmond's Utilization of Kindred Networks in the Diffusion of Kindergarten Ideals into Practice," *History of Education* 35, 2 (2006): 225-44.

163 Dunedin Free Kindergarten Association, *Annual Report* (Dunedin: n.p., 1891). Dunedin Free Kindergarten Association Papers, AG-287/001, Hocken Library (herafter HL), University of Otago, Dunedin.

164 Harrison, Sydney Kindergarten, 52.

165 Mark Cohen to Sarah Cooper, June 10, 1891, CP, Series 1: Box 4, Folder 33, KL.

166 Ibid.

167 Helen Jones, "de Lissa, Lillian Daphne (1885-1967)," *Australian Dictionary of Biography Online,* 2008, http://www.adb.online.anu.edu.au/biogs/A080294b.htm?hilite=de%3Blissa.

168 de Lissa left Australia for Rome in December, 1913.

169 The college was made part of Kingston University in 1970.

170 Dunedin Free Kindergarten Association, *Annual Report* (Dunedin: Dunedin Free Kindergarten Association, 1891), 7. HL.

171 Cuthbert Fetherstonhaugh, cited KUNSW, *The Kindergarten Union of New South Wales* (Sydney: Frederick White, 1922), 5-6.

172 Fetherstonhaugh, "Kindergarten," 6.
173 Maybanke Anderson, *The Story of the Free Kindergartens* (Sydney: KUNSW, 1912), 3.
174 They persist in the form of the cost-benefit analyses of investment in preschool education. Lawrence P. Schweinhart, H.V. Barnes, and David P. Wiekart, *Significant Benefits: The High/Scope Perry Preschool Study through Age 27* (Ypsilanti, MI: High/Scope, 1993).
175 Francis W. Parker, "The Kindergarten of Boston," *Kindergarten Magazine* 1 (March 1889): 334-35, quoted in Beatty, *Preschool Education,* 75.
176 Winnipeg FKA, Annual Report (Winnipeg: Winnipeg FKA, 1901), 6. Winnipeg Free Kindergarten Association Records, Social Planning Council Fond, Box P663, File 8, Archives of Manitoba, Winnipeg.
177 *Sydney Morning Herald,* June 1, 1896, 6, quoted in Walker, "The Development of Kindergartens," 6.
178 *The Work of Free Kindergartens* (Sydney: KUNSW, [1931?]), 5.
179 Jack K. Campbell, *Colonel Francis W. Parker: The Children's Crusader* (New York: Teachers College Press, 1967), 169.
180 Anderson, *The Story of the Free Kindergartens,* 3.
181 Dunedin Free Kindergarten Association, *Annual Report* (Dunedin, 1892), 7. HL.
182 Dunedin Free Kindergarten Association, *Annual Report* (Dunedin: Dunedin Free Kindergarten Association, 1893), 4. HL.

Chapter 7: Winnipeg Free Kindergarten Association

1 Winnipeg FKA, Annual Report (Winnipeg: Winnipeg FKA, 1897), 3. Winnipeg FKA and Kindergarten Settlement Association of Winnipeg (KSAW) annual reports are in Winnipeg FKA Records, Social Planning Council Fond, Box P663, File 8, Archives of Manitoba (hereafter, AM), Winnipeg.
2 "Free Kindergarten," *Manitoba Daily Free Press* (Winnipeg), November 25, 1892. The history was also related in Ann King, "Developing the Young Idea by the Play Route: Free Kindergarten Teaching Children of Many Nationalities to Become Useful Canadians," *Winnipeg Evening Tribune,* April 12, 1924, 3. In 1894, Colby married the Methodist preacher Walter A. Cooke. Her sister Mary French Colby, also a Quebec-trained teacher, married Winnipeg lawyer James Aikins, who was also Methodist.
3 In his official history of Winnipeg School Division No. 1, J.W. Chafe wrote that "as early as 1890 a Free Kindergarten Association began operating kindergartens in classrooms, rented from the Board for one dollar a month, in the Dufferin and Mulvey Schools." Chafe, *An Apple for the Teacher* (Winnipeg: Winnipeg School Division No. 1, 1967), 99. This does not appear to have been the Winnipeg FKA, according to more detailed evidence presented by Alice E. Paterson, "The Development of Kindergartens in Manitoba" (master's thesis, University of Manitoba, 1966), 130.
4 Winnipeg FKA, *Annual Report* (Winnipeg: Winnipeg FKA, 1897), 6.
5 Ibid. For a brief time in the 1890s, the association operated a private fee-charging kindergarten in the wealthy South End of Winnipeg. The school was

attended by the young Ella Aikman, who later became director of the Winnipeg FKA teacher-training program. An earlier private kindergarten operated in 1884. In March of that year, it advertised openings "for children between two and ten years of age. Instruction will be according to Froebel's system, improved and adopted by more recent Kindergartens." *Winnipeg Daily Times,* March 14, 1884, 8. The children who attended this school were aged two to six, their teacher was Miss Yeomans, and the school operated in the home of her father, Dr. Yeomans. "The Kindergarten: A Visit to the School in this City," *Winnipeg Daily Times,* June 7, 1884, 8.
6 "Kindergarten Building," *Manitoba Morning Free Press* (Manitoba), March 19, 1903.
7 Winnipeg FKA, *Annual Report* (Winnipeg: Winnipeg FKA, 1902), 7.
8 Winnipeg FKA, *Annual Report* (Winnipeg: Winnipeg FKA, 1904), 7.
9 Winnipeg FKA, *Annual Report* (Winnipeg: Winnipeg FKA, 1906), 8.
10 Winnipeg FKA, *Annual Report* (Winnipeg: Winnipeg FKA, 1908), 9.
11 Ibid. Lothrop's first name is sometimes written as Jennie.
12 Winnipeg FKA, *Annual Report* (Winnipeg: Winnipeg FKA, 1897), 10.
13 Winnipeg FKA, *Annual Report* (Winnipeg: Winnipeg FKA, 1901), 8.
14 Kindergarten Settlement Association of Winnipeg (KSAW), *Annual Report* (Winnipeg: KSAW, 1915), 10.
15 Winnipeg FKA, *Annual Report* (Winnipeg: Winnipeg FKA, 1902), 7.
16 Howard Jacob Karger, *The Sentinels of Order: A Study of Social Control and the Minneapolis Settlement House Movement, 1915-1950* (Lanham, MD: University Press of America, 1987).
17 Winnipeg FKA, *Annual Report* (Winnipeg: Winnipeg FKA, 1901), 16.
18 Ibid., 6 (emphasis in original).
19 Winnipeg FKA, *Annual Report* (Winnipeg: Winnipeg FKA, 1904), 14.
20 Sherri McConnell, "Canadian Deaconess and Missionary Education for Women — Training to Live the Social Gospel: The Methodist National Training School and the Presbyterian Deaconess and Missionary Training Home, 1893-1926" (master's thesis, University of Winnipeg, 2003).
21 Winnipeg FKA, *Annual Report* (Winnipeg: Winnipeg FKA, 1912), 9.
22 "Kindergarten Opens," *Manitoba Morning Free Press* (Winnipeg), September 3, 1904; "Delighted 60 Children," *Manitoba Morning Free Press* (Winnipeg), July 16, 1904.
23 Paterson, "The Development of Kindergartens in Manitoba," 56.
24 Winnipeg FKA, *Annual Report* (Winnipeg: Winnipeg FKA, 1901), 10.
25 Paterson, "The Development of Kindergartens in Manitoba," 91.
26 KSAW, *Annual Report* (Winnipeg: KSAW, 1918), 13.
27 "The Free Kindergarten," *Manitoba Morning Free Press* (Winnipeg), August 29, 1901.
28 "The Free Kindergarten," *Manitoba Daily Free Press* (Winnipeg), April 28, 1893.
29 "Kindergarten Work," *Manitoba Daily Free Press* (Winnipeg), May 15, 1893, 5.
30 Winnipeg FKA, *Annual Report* (Winnipeg: Winnipeg FKA, 1901), 6.
31 "The Free School," *Manitoba Morning Free Press* (Winnipeg), February 1, 1899, 2.
32 Winnipeg FKA, *Annual Report* (Winnipeg: Winnipeg FKA, 1902) 7.

33 Winnipeg FKA, *Annual Report* (Winnipeg: Winnipeg FKA, 1907), 9.
34 Arthur Grenke, *The German Community in Winnipeg 1872 to 1919* (New York: AMS Press, 1991), 58.
35 Winnipeg FKA, *Annual Report* (Winnipeg: Winnipeg FKA, 1904), 13.
36 Winnipeg FKA, *Annual Report* (Winnipeg: Winnipeg FKA, 1906), 11.
37 "Free Kindergarten," *Manitoba Daily Free Press* (Winnipeg), May 16, 1894, 5. The nursery was planned from 1893. "The Free Kindergarten," *Manitoba Daily Free Press* (Winnipeg), May 10, 1893.
38 "The Free Kindergarten," *Winnipeg Free Press,* n.d., Winnipeg FKA Records, Box P663, File 13, AM.
39 Winnipeg FKA, *Annual Report* (Winnipeg: Winnipeg FKA, 1902), 7.
40 Ibid., 6-7.
41 Winnipeg FKA, *Annual Report* (Winnipeg: Winnipeg FKA, 1907), 11.
42 Winnipeg FKA, *Annual Report* (Winnipeg: Winnipeg FKA, 1910), 8.
43 Ibid., 7.
44 Winnipeg FKA, *Annual Report* (Winnipeg: Winnipeg FKA, 1904), 7.
45 "The Kitchen Garden; What Is Being Done throughout the United States to Increase the Supply of Well-Taught House Servants," *New York Times,* November 25, 1880.
46 "Training for the Smallest: Kitchen Garden in the Wilson Industrial School for Girls," *New York Times,* February 24, 1895, 25.
47 Grenke, *The German Community.*
48 Winnipeg FKA, *Annual Report* (Winnipeg: Winnipeg FKA, 1908), 10.
49 Winnipeg FKA, *Annual Report* (Winnipeg: Winnipeg FKA, 1911), 11.
50 Samuel Chester Parker and Alice Temple, *Unified Kindergarten and First-Grade Teaching* (Boston: Ginn, 1925), 9.
51 In a letter to Alice Paterson, Aikman wrote that she had trained at the Alfred Mission. Paterson, "The Development of Kindergartens in Manitoba."
52 According to a profile of Aikman by Woods, she completed a kindergarten certificate in June, 1911 and a life teaching certificate in 1912. The latter date conflicts with information in Winnipeg FKA annual reports that she was in charge of the association kindergartens from September, 1911. W. Wilson Woods, "Ella F. Aikman, a Pioneer Student at Western Michigan University," Diether H. Haenicke Institute for Global Education, Western Michigan University, http://international.wmich.edu/content/view/294/99/.
53 Friedrich Froebel, *Mother-Play and Nursery Songs,* ed. Elizabeth Peabody, trans. Fannie E. Dwight and Josephine Jarvis (Boston: Lothrop, Lee, and Shepard, 1878).
54 Winnipeg FKA, *Annual Report* (Winnipeg: Winnipeg FKA, 1911), 14. Gage studied with MacVannel at Teachers College. He was author of *The Educational Theories of Herbart and Froebel* (New York: Teachers College, 1905).
55 Winnipeg FKA, *Annual Report* (Winnipeg: Winnipeg FKA, 1911), 15.
56 Winnipeg FKA, *Annual Report* (Winnipeg: Winnipeg FKA, 1912), 10.
57 Winnipeg FKA, *Annual Report* (Winnipeg: Winnipeg FKA, 1910), 8.
58 Winnipeg FKA, *Annual Report* (Winnipeg: Winnipeg FKA, 1914), 15.

59 KSAW, *Annual Report* (Winnipeg: KSAW, 1916), 17.
60 KSAW, *Annual Report* (Winnipeg: KSAW, 1915), 18.
61 Ibid.
62 Ibid., 11.
63 Other graduates continued training at social settlements in Minneapolis and the Pestalozzi-Froebel Kindergarten Training School in Chicago.
64 "Kindergarten Lecturer Appointed," *Manitoba Free Press* (Winnipeg), June 13, 1917.
65 Winnipeg FKA, *Annual Report* (Winnipeg: Winnipeg FKA, 1914), 16. Her name was Vera Musgrove.
66 Winnipeg FKA, *Annual Report* (Winnipeg: Winnipeg FKA, 1912), 14.
67 Ibid., 15.
68 School gardens were a popular aspect of Manitoba elementary schools at this time, figuring prominently in the Department of Education annual reports.
69 KSAW, *Annual Report* (Winnipeg: KSAW, 1916), 19.
70 May was a member of the first class at Oberlin (1894), under principal Belle Goodman. Goodman taught kindergarten methods and chalkboard drawing at Oberlin for decades.
71 No evidence indicates that Montessori materials were in use at the KSAW kindergartens at this time.
72 KSAW, *Annual Report* (Winnipeg: KSAW, 1916), 14.
73 Ibid., 15.
74 Ibid.
75 William Heard Kilpatrick, "The Project Method," *Teachers College Record* 19, 4 (1918): 319-35; John Dewey, *Experience and Education* (New York: Macmillan, 1938).
76 Meredith Smith, "Experimental Studies in Kindergarten Theory and Practice: The Development of Reasoning in Young Children," *Teachers College Record* 14, 1 (1914): 16-25.
77 KSAW, *Annual Report* (Winnipeg: KSAW, 1918), 12.
78 Mrs. George (Marion) Bryce, *Historical Sketch of the Charitable Institutions of Winnipeg* (Winnipeg: Manitoba Free Press, 1899), 25.
79 See William Wilson, "The School as an Instrument of Urban Reform Education in Winnipeg: 1890-1920" (PhD diss., University of Alberta, 1985).
80 "The Free Kindergarten," *Manitoba Morning Free Press* (Winnipeg), January 30, 1901.
81 "City Debentures Placed on the Market," *Manitoba Morning Free Press* (Winnipeg), April 20, 1901.
82 Chafe, *An Apple for the Teacher*, 99.
83 KSAW, *Annual Report* (Winnipeg: KSAW, 1926), 15.
84 King, "Developing the Young," 3.
85 *Oberlin Kindergarten Training School 1924-1925* (Oberlin, OH: Oberlin Kindergarten Training School, 1925).
86 "The New and Notable: Personal-Professional," *Childhood Education* 4, 5 (1928): 257.

87 Rollo G. Reynolds, "Some Larger Tasks for Elementary School," *Teachers College Record* 39, 5 (1938): 363-74.
88 Gladys Muriel Best graduated from Oberlin in 1918. In 1925 she taught first grade at St. James School (Winnipeg). *Oberlin Kindergarten Training School 1924-1925* (Oberlin, OH: Oberlin Kindergarten Training School), 45.
89 KSAW, *Annual Report* (Winnipeg: KSAW, 1925), 11.
90 KSAW, *Annual Report* (Winnipeg: KSAW, 1921), 12.
91 Ibid., 11.
92 KSAW, *Annual Report* (Winnipeg: KSAW, 1925), 10.
93 KSAW, *Annual Report* (Winnipeg: KSAW, 1928), 9.
94 Ibid.
95 KSAW, *Annual Report* (Winnipeg: KSAW, 1932), 3.
96 KSAW, *Annual Report* (Winnipeg: KSAW, 1925), 8.
97 KSAW, *Annual Report* (Winnipeg: KSAW, 1926), 9 (emphasis in original).
98 Ibid., 12.
99 Ibid.
100 KSAW, *Annual Report* (Winnipeg: KSAW, 1932), 3.
101 The collection at the Archives of Manitoba does not include the KSAW annual reports for the years 1943 to 1954.
102 Nelson B. Henry and N. Searle Light, eds., *National Society for the Study of Education Yearbook,* vol. 46, 2 (Chicago: National Society for the Study of Education, 1947).
103 Committee on Field Services, Department of Education, University of Chicago, *Report of the Directed Self Survey, Winnipeg Public Schools* (Chicago: Department of Education, University of Chicago, 1948).
104 Doug Smith, *Joe Zuken: Citizen and Socialist* (Toronto: James Lorimer, 1990).
105 The survey was undertaken by the Canadian Welfare Council Canadian Welfare Council, "A Study of the Kindergarten Settlement Association of Winnipeg," 1951, Winnipeg FKA Records, Box P663, File 14, AM.
106 Ibid., 18.
107 Ibid., 23.
108 "Logan Neighbourhood House," *Winnipeg Free Press,* May 28, 1955. The Winnipeg Neighbourhood House was later called the Logan Neighbourhood House.
109 Mrs. A.K. Stephens, Neighborhood House, May 8, 1952, History of Neighborhood House addressed to the Central Volunteer Bureau, Winnipeg FKA Records, Box P663, File 15, AM.

Chapter 8: Kindergarten Union of New South Wales

1 Mary Lucy Walker, "The Development of Kindergartens in Australia" (master's thesis, University of Sydney, 1964); Sandie Wong, "Early Childhood Education and Care in New South Wales: Historicising the Present" (PhD diss., Macquarie University, 2006).

2 KUNSW, *Annual Report* (Sydney: KUNSW, 1896), 5, Annual reports of the KUNSW are in the KUNSW Collection, ML MSS 5945, 51(52), Mitchell Library (hereafter, ML), State Library of New South Wales, Sydney.
3 Barbara Beatty, *Preschool Education in America: The Culture of Young Children from the Colonial Era to the Present* (New Haven: Yale University Press, 1995).
4 Jack K. Campbell, *Colonel Francis W. Parker: The Children's Crusader* (New York: Teachers College Press, 1967).
5 Francis W. Parker, *Talks on Pedagogics: An Outline of the Theory of Concentration* (New York: Kellog, 1894).
6 R.L. Buckey, "A Kindergartner's Tour around the World," *Australian Kindergarten Magazine* 15, 3 (1902): 162-71.
7 "Mixed Children," *Hawaiian Gazette* (Honolulu), March 29, 1898. In time, the children attending the Palama kindergarten were mainly Hawaiian and Japanese.
8 "To Teach Kanakas," *Daily News* (Frederick, MD), December 3, 1896, 3.
9 According to ibid., which was based on an interview with Buckey, Lawrence attended the Cook County Normal School. Her graduation from the Cook County Normal School is also reported in Mabel Wing Castle, "One Year's Work with Children," *Hawaiian Gazette* (Honolulu), October 20, 1896, 6.
10 GGKA, *Annual Report* (San Francisco: GGKA, 1886), 69. Sarah Brown Ingersoll Cooper Papers, #6543 (hereafter, CP), Series 3: Box 8, Folder 7, Kroch Library (hereafter, KL), Division of Rare and Manuscripts Collections, Cornell University Library, Ithaca, New York.
11 Frances Lawrence, "Child Study Talk," *Hawaiian Gazette* (Honolulu), October 8, 1897, 5.
12 Charlotte Peabody Dodge, *A History of the Free Kindergarten and Children's Aid Association of the Hawaiian Islands, 1895-1945* (Honolulu: Mercantile Printers, 1945), 5.
13 Castle, "One Year's Work with Children," *Hawaiian Gazette* (Honolulu), October 20, 1896, 6.
14 Quoted in Dodge, *A History of the Free Kindergarten*, 28.
15 Buckey, "A Kindergartner's Tour," 165. A newspaper report indicated she spent nine months in Honolulu. "Miss Buckey's Success," *Daily News* (Frederick, MD), October 6, 1897, 3.
16 KUNSW, *Annual Report* (Sydney: KUNSW, 1899), 6.
17 Ibid., 8.
18 Ibid., 17.
19 Lyndsay Gardiner, *The Free Kindergarten Union of Victoria* (Hawthorn, Victoria: Australian Council for Educational Research, 1982), 66.
20 Maybanke Anderson, "The Story of the Kindergarten Union of New South Wales," in *Maybanke: A Woman's Voice, the Collected Work of Maybanke Selfe-Wolstenhome-Anderson 1845-1927*, compiled by Jan Roberts and Beverley Kingston (Avalon Beach, AU: Ruskin Rowe, 2001), 215.
21 Maybanke Anderson, "Free Kindergartens," *Women's Voice*, November 23, 1895, 396, in Roberts and Kingston, *Maybanke*, 168.

22 KUNSW, *Annual Report* (Sydney: KUNSW, 1900), 12.
23 See Sandie Wong, "Looking Back and Looking Forward: Historicising the Social Construction of Early Childhood Education and Care as National Work, "*Contemporary Issues in Early Childhood* 8, 2 (2007): 152.
24 KUNSW, *Annual Report* (Sydney: KUNSW, 1896), 5.
25 KUNSW, *Annual Report* (Sydney: KUNSW, 1898).
26 Friedrich Froebel, *Mother-Play and Nursery Songs,* ed. Elizabeth Peabody, trans. Fannie E. Dwight and Josephine Jarvis (Boston: Lothrop, Lee, and Shepard, 1878).
27 KUNSW, *Annual Report* (Sydney: KUNSW, 1899), 15.
28 C.H. McGrew, *Symmetrical Outlines of Development and Training for the Golden Gate Kindergartens* (San Francisco: George Spaulding, 1893), 19.
29 KUNSW, *Annual Report* (Sydney: KUNSW, 1898), 16 (emphasis in original).
30 Ibid., 18, 17 (emphasis in original).
31 Ibid.
32 Ibid., 19.
33 Ibid., 22.
34 Buckey, "A Kindergartner's Tour," 171.
35 Jeannie Graham Dane filled in as principal of the training program until Newton arrived.
36 KUNSW, *Annual Report* (Sydney: KUNSW, 1902), 9.
37 Ibid.
38 This was formerly Miss Harrison's Training School and is now the National-Louis University.
39 Ruth Grey, "The Keilhau of America: An Experiment in Educational Home Training," *Kindergarten Magazine* 10, 10 (1898): 620.
40 Ibid., 621.
41 KUNSW, *Annual Report* (Sydney: KUNSW, 1905).
42 KUNSW, *Annual Report* (Sydney: KUNSW, 1902), 12.
43 KUNSW, *Annual Report* (Sydney: KUNSW, 1905), 6.
44 KUNSW, *Annual Report* (Sydney: KUNSW, 1902), 15. A related course for nursery governesses began in 1906.
45 KUNSW, *Annual Report* (Sydney: KUNSW, 1904), 10.
46 Ibid., 8.
47 Samuel Wilderspin, *Infant Education; or, Practical Remarks on the Importance of Educating the Infant Poor, from the Age of Eighteen Months to Seven Years; Containing Hints for Developing the Moral and Intellectual Powers of Children of All Classes,* 4th ed. (London: W. Simpkin and R. Marshall, 1829).
48 Woolloomooloo opened in 1896, Newtown in 1897, Commonwealth in 1901, North Sydney in 1902, and Surry Hills in 1904.
49 KUNSW, *Annual Report* (Sydney: KUNSW, 1902, 1904, 1905).
50 KUNSW, *Annual Report* (Sydney: KUNSW, 1906), 6.
51 Kindergarten Union of South Australia (KUSA), *Annual Report* (Adelaide: KUSA, 1905), quoted in KUSA, *KUSA through Seventy-Five Years* (Adelaide: KUSA, 1980), 3.

52 In 1912, the *Australian Kindergarten Magazine* reported that Newton was principal of a kindergarten-training school in Elmira, New York.
53 Walker, "The Development of Kindergartens."
54 "Miss G. Williams on Her Travels," *Link* 3 (1912): 19.
55 Ibid.
56 Ibid.
57 Lillian Arundel, "Some Educational Work in Other Lands Part II," *Child Life* 11, 46 (1909): 53.
58 "Mme. Montessori Plans 'Laboratory,'" *New York Times*, December 4, 1913, 9; Maria Montessori, "Montessori Schools," *New York Times*, August 19, 1913, 10.
59 "Study Montessori System," *New York Times*, November 12, 1912, C4.
60 KUNSW, *Annual Report* (Sydney: KUNSW, 1914), 13.
61 KUNSW, *Annual Report* (Sydney: KUNSW, 1915), 11, 23.
62 Ibid., 11.
63 KUNSW, *Annual Report* (Sydney: KUNSW, 1918), 21.
64 KUNSW, *Annual Report* (Sydney: KUNSW, 1920), 10.
65 KUNSW, *Annual Report* (Sydney: KUNSW, 1922), 6.
66 KUNSW, *Annual Report* (Sydney: KUNSW, 1927), 18.
67 Margaret Ford, "Report of the Woolloomooloo Kindergarten," February 1928, KUNSW Collection, ML MSS 5945, Box 35 (52), ML.
68 Walker, "The Development of Kindergartens," 279.
69 KUNSW, *Annual Report* (Sydney: KUNSW, 1930).
70 KUNSW, *Annual Report* (Sydney: KUNSW, 1934), 11.
71 Ibid.
72 "Syllabus in Child Development," Staff of the Child Development Institute, Teachers College, Columbia University, 1935 (Revision), Sydney Kindergarten Training College Records, 89/166, Box 40, Macquarie University, Sydney.
73 KUNSW, *Annual Report* (Sydney: KUNSW, 1940), 10.
74 Ibid.
75 KUNSW, *Annual Report* (Sydney: KUNSW, 1937), 14.
76 KUNSW, *Annual Report* (Sydney: KUNSW, 1942), 8.
77 S.V. McLean, B. Piscitelli, G. Halliwell, and G. Ashby, "Australian Early Childhood Education," in *International Handbook of Early Childhood Education*, ed. Gary Woodill, Judith Bernhard, and Larry Prochner (New York: Garland, 1992), 49-73.
78 KUNSW, *Annual Report* (Sydney: KUNSW, 1949), 13.
79 Ibid.
80 Edna Hill, *The Lady Gowrie Centres: A First Analysis of Case History Records of Children Attending the Lady Gowrie Child Centres (1939-1940)* (Canberra: Department of Health, 1949), 1.
81 Deborah Brennan, *The Politics of Australian Child Care: From Philanthropy to Feminism* (New York: Cambridge University Press, 1994).
82 Jane Fowler Morse, "Ignored but Not Forgotten: The Work of Helen Bradford Thompson Woolley," *National Women's Studies Association Journal* 14, 2 (2002): 121-47.

Notes to pages 218-20

83 "Lyceum Club Members Welcome Miss de Lissa," September 13, 1955 (talks given by Lillian de Lissa at the Golden Jubilee of the KUSA 1955), Gipsy Hill College of Education Archive, Lillian Daphne de Lissa Papers (records are uncatalogued), Archive and Special Collections, Kingston University, Kingston Hill Campus, Kingston upon Thames.

Chapter 9: Wellington Free Kindergarten Association

1 "Account of the Beginnings of the Wellington FKA," June 17, 1922, Scrapbook, 1908-30, Wellington Regional Free Kindergarten Association Inc: Records (hereafter, WRFKA Records), MS-Group-0052, MSY 1921, Alexander Turnbull Library (hereafter, ATL), National Library of New Zealand, Wellington. The name of the association changed over time from the Free Kindergarten Union to the Richmond Free Kindergarten Union in 1910; in 1918, it became the Wellington Free Kindergarten Association.
2 On Richmond's own kindergarten training, see Kerry Bethell, "To Bring into Play: Miss Mary Richmond's Utilization of Kindred Networks in the Diffusion of Kindergarten Ideals into Practice," *History of Education* 35, 2 (2006): 225-44.
3 Kerry Bethell, "Not for a Name That We Plead: Fashioning the Ideological Origins of Early Kindergarten in Dunedin and Wellington, New Zealand, 1870-1913" (PhD diss., Victoria University of Wellington, 2008).
4 Formative Meeting of the Richmond Free Kindergarten, July 29, 1905, "Minute Book of Richmond Free Kindergarten Union," WRFKA Records, MSX-2516, ATL.
5 The first teacher at the Tory Street School was Ida Banks. "Young Empire Builders," unsourced newspaper clipping, August 19, 1918. Articles cited as unsourced newspaper clippings, many of which have no precise date, come from unidentified newspapers and are found in the scrapbooks of the Wellington Free Kindergarten Association, WRFKA Records, MSY 1921 (1908-30), 1922 (1931-48), 1923 (1948-68), ATL.
6 The KUNSW report for the year 1912 noted that the Surry Hills Kindergarten "has had a year of some anxiety, for its esteemed Director felt constrained to leave it. After six and a half years of excellent work, Miss Nettie Riley has gone to do important organising and training work in New Zealand. Surry Hills and the KU generally, sorry as they are to lose her for New South Wales, can but rejoice at her promotion, and wish her all success in her new and important sphere." KUNSW, *Annual Report* (Sydney: KUNSW, 1912), 4.
7 *Australian Kindergarten Magazine* 2, 2 (1911): 12.
8 Riley died in 1934.
9 "Kindergarten Work," unsourced newspaper clipping, c. 1918.
10 Complaints surfaced in the 1922 Wellington FKA annual report and recurred periodically thereafter. Wellington FKA annual reports are held by the National Library of New Zealand, Wellington.

11 Quoted in "Women's Sphere, Some Candid Admissions," unsourced newspaper clipping, May 15, 1913.
12 Richmond Free Kindergarten, "Minute Book," April 12, 1915, WRFKA Records, MSX-2517, ATL; "Kindergarten Work," unsourced newspaper clipping, c. 1918; Wellington FKA, *Annual Report* (Wellington: Wellington FKA, 1920); "Free Kindergartens, Annual Meeting of the Association," unsourced newspaper clipping, January 17, 1922.
13 Wellington FKA, "Council Reports," May 1919, WRFKA Records, MSX-2517, ATL. "Council Reports" are unpaginated.
14 Quoted in "Kindergarten Work," unsourced newspaper clipping, c. 1918.
15 Wellington FKA, "Minute Book," December 6, 1920, WRFKA, MSX-2518, ATL.
16 Richmond Free Kindergarten, "Minute Book," February 7, 1916, WRFKA Records, MSX-2517, ATL.
17 Richmond Free Kindergarten, "Minute Book," March 3, 1913, WRFKA Records, MSX-2517, ATL.
18 Edna Scott, *An Early Wellington Kindergarten as Described by Ted Scott, compiled by Geraldine McDonald* (Wellington: New Zealand Council for Educational Research, 1975).
19 Wellington FKA, "Council Report," March 1919, WRFKA Records, MSX-2524, ATL.
20 Wellington FKA, "Council Report," February 1921, WRFKA Records, MSX-2524, ATL.
21 Wellington FKA, "Council Report," February 1934, WRFKA Records, MSX-2526, ATL.
22 "Free Kindergartens, Annual Meeting," unsourced newspaper clipping, c. 1917.
23 Ibid.
24 Ibid.
25 "The Work of the Free Kindergartens," unsourced newspaper clipping, June 9, 1908. In 1918, the Department of Education introduced a new admittance regulation for infants' schools: children were admitted on either January 1 or July 1, whichever most closely followed the date of their fifth birthday.
26 Richmond Free Kindergarten, "Minute Book," July 7, 1913, WRFKA Records, MSX-2517, ATL; Wellington FKA, "Council Report" December 1920, WRFKA Records, MSX-2524, ATL.
27 Wellington FKA, "Council Report," July 1934, WRFKA Records, MSX-2526, ATL.
28 Scott, *An Early Wellington Kindergarten.*
29 "Free Kindergartens, Are They to Continue?" *New Zealand Times,* April 10, 1915.
30 Quoted in "The Work of the Free Kindergartens," unsourced newspaper clipping, June 9, 1908.
31 Wellington FKA, *Annual Report* (Wellington: Wellington FKA, 1926), 1.
32 Ibid.

33 Wellington FKA, "Council Report," March 1921, WRFKA Records, MSX-2524, ATL; Wellington FKA, "Council Report," April 1921, WRFKA Records, MSX-2524, ATL.
34 Scott, *An Early Wellington Kindergarten*.
35 Ibid., 5.
36 "Wellington Free Kindergarten at Work, Masonic Hall, August 20-23," 1918, Scrapbook, 1908-30, WRFKA Records, MSY 1921, ATL.
37 Wellington FKA, "Council Report," October 1925, WRFKA Records, MSX-2525, ATL.
38 "Morning at a Kindergarten," unsourced newspaper clipping, c. 1918.
39 Wellington FKA, "Minutes of the Executive Council," Wellington, June, 1920, WRFKA Records, MSX-2518, ATL. A set of Montessori materials was sent to the Wellington FKA from Sydney in 1913. See chapter 6, note 131.
40 "Richmond Kindergarten: The Work of the Free Kindergartens," unsourced newspaper clipping, c. 1914.
41 Scott, *An Early Wellington Kindergarten*.
42 For information on Wilson's years with the KUWA, see Rosemary Kerr, *A History of the Kindergarten Union of Western Australia, 1911-1973* (Perth: Meerlinga Young Children's Foundation, 1994); and J.G. Miles, *Kindergarten Teacher Education in Western Australia* (Perth: Western Australian Institute of Technology, Faculty of Education, 1982).
43 Kerr writes that Simpson and Rachel Stevens "worked in Perth during the period 1914 to 1916." Kerr, *A History of the Kindergarten Union*, 13.
44 The kindergarten in the photograph was most likely the one at Beaconsfield Infants' School. See Register of Heritage Places – Assessment Documentation, Beaconsfield Primary School (Perth: Heritage Council of Western Australia, 2008), http://register.heritage.wa.gov.au/PDF_Files/B%20-%20A-D/Beaconsfield%20Primary%20School%20(I-AD).pdf.
45 Lillian de Lissa to KUWA, September 1, 1915, quoted in Kerr, *A History of the Kindergarten Union*, 39.
46 "Toddlers at Play," *Daily News* (Perth), October 31, 1919, quoted in Kerr, *A History of the Kindergarten Union*, 43.
47 Susan F. Semel, "Helen Parkhurst and the Dalton School," in *Founding Mothers and Others: Women Educational Leaders during the Progressive Era*, ed. Alan R. Sadovnik and Susan F. Semel (New York: Palgrave, 2002), 77-92. Note that Belle Rennie and Edmond Holmes were influential in promoting progressive educational ideas in England; interested in both the Dalton Plan and Montessori, they were instrumental in recruiting Lillian de Lissa for the Gipsy Hill Training College.
48 June Edwards, *Women in American Education, 1920-1955: The Female Force and Educational Reform* (Westport, CT: Greenwood Press, 2001).
49 Quoted in "The Young Mind," *Evening Post* (Wellington), undated, c. 1931.
50 "Free Kindergarten Work in Australia," unsourced newspaper clipping, c. 1931.

51 Wellington FKA, "Council Report," March 1934, WRFKA Records, MSX-2526, ATL.
52 Wellington FKA, "Council Report," October 1922, WRFKA Records, MSX-2524, ATL.
53 Wellington FKA, "Council Report," June 1931, WRFKA Records, MSX-2526, ATL.
54 Wellington FKA, "Council Report," October 1931, WRFKA Records, MSX-2526, ATL.
55 Wellington FKA, "Council Report," December 1932, WRFKA Records, MSX-2526, ATL.
56 Wellington FKA, "Council Report," May 1934, WRFKA Records, MSX-2526, ATL.
57 Ibid. (emphasis in original).
58 Wellington FKA, "Council Report," April 1931, WRFKA Records, MSX-2526, ATL.
59 Wellington FKA, "Council Report," December 1932, WRFKA Records, MSX-2526, ATL.
60 Quoted in "Babes at School," unsourced newspaper clipping, c. 1933. McKenzie's criticism of kindergartens was surprising. He had studied with Dewey in the United States and was remembered by school inspector Douglas Ball as a strong supporter of progressive education. John Barrington, "D.G. Ball," *Dictionary of New Zealand Biography,* http://www.dnzb.govt.nz/dnzb/.
61 "Address at Annual Meeting of the Wellington Free Kindergarten Association, 1935," quoted in "Child Difficulties," unsourced newspaper clipping.
62 "Hope in Government," unsourced newspaper clipping, c. 1937.
63 Wellington FKA, *Annual Report* (Wellington: Wellington FKA, 1933-34), 3.
64 Ibid.
65 "Student in America, Study of Kindergarten Methods," unsourced newspaper clipping, c. 1933.
66 Dorothy Gardner, *Susan Isaacs* (London: Methuen, 1969); Lydia A.H. Smith, *To Understand and to Help: The Life and Work of Susan Isaacs (1885-1948)* (Cranberry, NJ: Associated University Presses, 1985).
67 Susan Isaacs, *Intellectual Growth in Young Children* (London: G. Routledge and Sons, 1930); Susan Isaacs, *Social Development in Young Children: A Study of Beginnings* (London: G. Routledge and Sons, 1933).
68 Eve Ebbett, *When the Boys Were Away: New Zealand Women in World War II* (Auckland: Reed, 1984).
69 Wellington FKA, "Principal's Annual Report," 1943-44, WRFKA Records, MSX-2527, ATL.
70 Wellington FKA, "Principal's Annual Report," 1948, WRFKA Records, MSY-1916, ATL, 8.
71 "Nursery Schools in London Visited," *New Zealand Free Lance,* April 23, 1952, 8; Richard Aldrich, *The Institute of Education, 1902-2002: A Centenary History* (London: Institute of Education Publications, 2002), 121.

72 Quoted in "Nursery Schools in London Visited," *New Zealand Free Lance,* April 23, 1952, 8.

Chapter 10: Conclusion

1. Dorothy E.M. Gardner and Joan E. Cass, *The Role of the Teacher in the Infant and Nursery School* (Oxford: Pergamon, 1965), 3.
2. Larry Cuban, *How Teachers Taught: Constancy and Change in American Classrooms, 1880-1990,* 2nd ed. (New York: Teachers College Press, 1993).
3. An exception is the school at New Harmony in the United States.
4. Robert Owen, *A New View of Society; or, Essays on the Principle of the Formation of the Human Character, and the Application of the Principle to Practice* (London: Cadell and Davies, 1813), 4.
5. Phillip McCann and Francis A. Young, *Samuel Wilderspin and the Infant School Movement* (London: Croom Helm, 1982), 25.
6. For a description of the city child, see Kevin J. Brehony, "A 'Socially Civilising Influence'? Play and the Urban 'Degenerate,'" *Paedagogica Historica* 39, 1-2 (2003): 87-106.
7. Ebenezer Buchanan to LMS Governors, Tahiti, August 29, 1842, CWM/LMS, Incoming Letters, South Seas, Box 15, Folder 2, Jacket C, CWM Archive, SOAS.
8. Samuel Wilderspin, *The Infant System for Developing the Intellectual and Moral Powers of All Children from One to Seven Years of Age,* 8th ed. (London: J.S. Hobson, 1852), 213.
9. See Larry Prochner and Yeonwook Hwang, "'Cry and You Cry Alone': Time Out in Early Childhood Settings," *Childhood* 15, 4 (2008): 517-34. In matters of discipline, infant school manuals were far more detailed in their prescriptions, generally favouring the punishment of shaming children in the manner of Wilderspin.
10. Mary D. Runyan and Caroline G. O'Grady, "Kindergarten Education: Kindergarten Supervision and Critic Teaching," *Teachers College Record* 5, 5 (1904): 65.
11. Mary Ware Howland, *The Infant School Manual,* 4th ed. (Boston: n.p., 1831), 23.
12. "Morning at a Kindergarten," unsourced newspaper clipping, c. 1918, Scrapbook, 1906-30, WRFKA Records, MSY 1921, Alexander Turnbull Library.
13. Ann King, "Developing the Young by the Play Route: Free Kindergarten Teaching Children of Many Nationalities to Become Useful Canadians," *Winnipeg Evening Tribune,* April 12, 1924, 3.
14. Joseph Lancaster, *Improvements in Education,* 45 (emphasis in original).
15. Hester Burton, *Barbara Bodichon, 1827-1891* (London: John Murray, 1949), 6-7.
16. Maria Kraus-Boelte and John Kraus, *The Kindergarten Guide* (New York: E. Steiger, 1892). Rings were the eleventh Gift in Kraus-Boelte and Kraus' sequence.
17. Kate Douglas Wiggin and Nora Archibald Smith, *Froebel's Gifts* (Boston: Houghton Mifflin, 1895), 161, 164.
18. Kate Douglas Wiggin and Nora Archibald Smith, *Kindergarten Principles and Practice* (Boston: Houghton Mifflin, 1896), 152.
19. Elizabeth Harrison and Belle Woodson, *The Kindergarten Building Gifts with Hints on Program-Making,* 3rd ed. (Chicago: Central Publishing, 1908), 22.

20 King, "Developing the Young," 3.
21 Hariette Melissa Mills, "Kindergarten Education: The Kindergarten Gifts," *Teachers College Record* 5, 5 (1904): 80.
22 Wiggin and Smith, *Froebel's Gifts*, 196-97.
23 Patty Smith Hill, "Kindergarten Problems: The Future of the Kindergarten in the Light of Its Origin and Influence upon Modern Philanthropy and Education," *Teachers College Record* 10, 5 (1909): 48.
24 Friedrich Froebel, *Friedrich Froebel's Pedagogics of the Kindergarten, or, His Ideas concerning the Play and Playthings of the Child,* trans. Josephine Jarvis (London: Edward Arnold, 1897), 235-36.
25 Quoted in John Burnett, ed., *Destiny Obscure: Autobiographies of Childhood, Education, and Family from the 1820s to the 1920s* (Harmondsworth, UK: Penguin, 1984), 198-99.
26 Wiggin and Smith, *Froebel's Gifts*, 200, 201. For a review of kindergarten as a subject in English infant schools in this period, see Jane Read, "Free Play with Froebel: Use and Abuse of Progressive Pedagogy in London's Infant Schools, 1870-c. 1904," *Paedagogica Historica* 42, 3 (2006): 299-323.
27 W.E. Marsden, "Contradictions in Progressive Primary School Ideologies and Curricula in England: Some Historical Perspectives," *Historical Studies in Education/Revue d'histoire de l'éducation* 9, 2 (1997): 225.
28 Ellen Salzman-Fiske, "Secular Religion and Social Reform: Felix Adler's Educational Ideas and Programs, 1876-1933" (PhD diss., Columbia University, 1999), 108.
29 "The Kindergarten," *Chicago Commons* 1, 1 (1896): 2.
30 "The Kindergarten," *The Commons* 5, 53 (1900): 9.
31 Ibid., 10.
32 Ibid.
33 Fanny L. Calder, *A Teachers' Manual of Elementary Laundry Work* (London: Longmans, Green, 1901), 3.
34 Charlotte Gano Garrison, Emma Dickson Sheehy, and Alice Dalgliesh, *The Horace Mann Kindergarten for Five-Year-Old Children* (New York: Teachers College, 1937), 91. The children at the Horance Mann Kindergarten were described as coming "from families living in comfortable circumstances ... The fathers of the children are for the most part professional men: teachers, lawyers, doctors." Agnes Burke, Edna V. Hughes, Edith U. Conrad, Mary E. Rankin, Alice Dalgliesh, Alice G. Thorn, and Charlotte G. Garrison, *A Conduct Curriculum for the Kindergarten and First Grade* (New York: Charles Scribner's Sons, 1928), 1.
35 *The Kindergarten. Reports of the Committee of Nineteen on the Theory and Practice of the Kindergarten* (Boston: Houghton Mifflin, 1913).
36 Subcommittee on Curriculum of the Bureau of Education Committee of the International Kindergarten Union, *The Kindergarten Curriculum,* Department of Interior, Bureau of Education Bulletin No. 16 (Washington: Government Printing Office, 1919), 24.
37 Harrison and Woodson, *The Kindergarten Building Gifts with Hints on Program-Making,* 28.

38 Garrison, Dickson Sheehy, and Dalgliesh, *The Horace Mann Kindergarten*, 114.
39 KUNSW, *Annual Report* (Sydney, 1934), 11. KUNSW Collection, ML MSS 5945, 51(52), Mitchell Library, State Library of New South Wales, Sydney.
40 Ibid.
41 Barbara Beatty points out the shift from Chicago to New York that began to occur in the early twentieth century. Beatty, *Preschool Education in America: The Culture of Young Children from the Colonial Era to the Present* (New Haven: Yale University Press, 1995).For the connection between Australia and New Zealand and Teachers College, Columbia, see Charles Franklin Thwing, *Higher Education in Australia and New Zealand,* Department of Interior, Bureau of Education Bulletin No. 25 (Washington: Government Printing Office, 1922); and Lawrence A. Cremin, David A. Shannon, and Mary Evelyn Townsend, *A History of Teachers College, Columbia University* (New York: Columbia University Press, 1954).
42 "Syllabus in Child Development," Staff of the Child Development Institute, Teachers College, Columbia University, 1935 (Revision), Sydney Kindergarten Training College Records, 89/166, Box 40, Macquarie University, Sydney.
43 Grace Fulmer, *The Use of Kindergarten Gifts* (Boston: Houghton Mifflin, 1918), 126.
44 Mills, "Kindergarten Education: The Kindergarten Gifts," 80.
45 Wiggin and Smith, *Froebel's Gifts,* 200.
46 Mary Runyan, "Kindergarten Education: The Training of Kindergartners," *Teachers College Record* 5, 5 (1904): 8.
47 Julia W. Abbott, "Experimental Studies in Kindergarten Theory and Practice: The Use of Materials in the Kindergarten," *Teachers College Record* 15, 1 (1914): 42
48 Mills, "Kindergarten Education: The Kindergarten Gifts" 78.
49 *Oberlin Kindergarten Training School 1924-1925* (Oberlin, OH: Oberlin Kindergarten Training School, 1925), 40.
50 Margaret A. Trace, *Block Building: A Practical Guide for Mothers and Teachers* (Springfield, MA: Milton Bradley, 1928).
51 Fulmer, *The Use of Kindergarten Gifts.*
52 Ibid., 7.

Selected Bibliography

Adams, David W. *Education for Extinction: American Indians and the Boarding School Experience, 1875-1928.* Lawrence: University Press of Kansas, 1995.
Allen, Ann Taylor. "Children between Public and Private Worlds: The Kindergarten and Public Policy in Germany." In *Kindergartens and Cultures: The Global Diffusion of an Idea,* edited by Roberta Wollons, 16-41. New Haven: Yale University Press, 2000.
———. "Let Us Live with Our Children: Kindergarten Movements in Germany and the United States, 1840-1914." *History of Education Quarterly* 28, 1 (1988): 23-48.
Anderson, Gerald H. *Biographical Dictionary of Christian Missions.* New York: Macmillan Reference, 1998.
Ashcroft, Bill. "Primitive and Wingless: The Colonial Subject as Child." In *Dickens and the Children of Empire,* edited by Wendy F. Jacobson, 184-202. New York: Palgrave, 2000.
Axtell, James. *After Columbus: Essays in the Ethnohistory of Colonial North America.* New York: Oxford University Press, 1988.
Baader, Meike Sophia. "Froebel and the Rise of Educational Theory in the United States." *Studies in Philosophy and Education* 23 (2004): 427-44.
Barcan, Alan. *A History of Australian Education.* Melbourne: Oxford University Press, 1980.
———. *Two Centuries of Education in New South Wales.* Kensington: New South Wales University Press, 1988.
Beatty, Barbara. *Preschool Education in America: The Culture of Young Children from the Colonial Era to the Present.* New Haven, CT: Yale University Press, 1995.
Bethell, Kerry. "In Search of Mary Richmond: A Journey of Discovery of Subject and Self." Paper presented at the Tenth European Early Childhood Education Research Association Conference, London, August 29-September 1, 2000.

—. "'Not for a Name That We Plead': Fashioning the Ideological Origins of Early Kindergarten in Dunedin and Wellington, New Zealand, 1870-1913." PhD diss., Victoria University of Wellington, 2007.

—. "To Bring into Play: Miss Mary Richmond's Utilization of Kindred Networks in the Diffusion of Kindergarten Ideals into Practice." *History of Education* 35, 2 (2006): 225-44.

Blouet, Olwyn M. "Earning and Learning in the British West Indies: An Image of Freedom in the Pre-emancipation Decade, 1823-1833." *Historical Journal* 34, 2 (1991): 391-409.

Brehony, Kevin J. "The Froebel Movement in England 1850-1911: Texts, Readings and Readers." Paper presented at the Fifth International Froebel Symposium, Berlin, April 30-May 1, 2005.

—. "The Kindergarten in England, 1851-1918." In *Kindergartens and Cultures: The Global Diffusion of an Idea,* edited by Roberta Wollons, 59-86. New Haven: Yale University Press, 2000.

—. "A 'Socially Civilising Influence'? Play and the Urban 'Degenerate.'" *Paedagogica Historica* 39, 1-2 (2003): 87-106.

Brennan, Deborah. *The Politics of Australian Child Care: From Philanthropy to Feminism.* New York: Cambridge University Press, 1994.

Broome, Richard. *Aboriginal Australians: Black Responses to White Dominance, 1788-2001.* Sydney: Allen and Unwin, 2001.

Buchanan, Barbara. *Buchanan Family Records: James Buchanan and His Descendants.* Cape Town: Townshend, Taylor and Snashall, 1923.

Burnett, John, ed. *Destiny Obscure: Autobiographies of Childhood, Education, and Family from the 1820s to the 1920s.* Harmondsworth, UK: Penguin, 1984.

Campbell, Jack K. *Colonel Francis W. Parker: The Children's Crusader.* New York: Teachers College Press, 1967.

Cook, Sharon A. *"Through the Sunshine and Shadow": The Woman's Christian Temperance Union, Evangelicalism, and Reform in Canada, 1874-1930.* Montreal and Kingston: McGill-Queen's University Press, 1995.

Corbett, Barbara E. *A Century of Kindergarten Education in Ontario, 1887 to 1987.* Dundas, ON: Froebel Foundation, 1989.

Depaepe, Marc. "Demythologizing the Educational Past: An Endless Task in History of Education." *Historical Studies in Education* 9, 2 (1997): 208-23.

Dickason, Olive P. *Canada's First Nations: A History of Founding Peoples from Earliest Times.* Don Mills, ON: Oxford University Press, 2002.

Edwards, June. *Women in American Education, 1920-1955: The Female Force and Educational Reform.* Westport, CT: Greenwood Press, 2001.

Ewing, John L. *Development of the New Zealand Primary School Curriculum, 1877-1970.* Wellington: New Zealand Council for Educational Research, 1970.

—. *Origins of the New Zealand Primary School Curriculum.* London: Oxford University Press, 1961.

Fitzgerald, Tanya. "Missionary Women as Educators: The Church Missionary Schools in New Zealand." *Historical Studies in Education* (Canada) 6, 3 (1994): 139-49.

Gardiner, Lyndsay. *The Free Kindergarten Union of Victoria*. Hawthorn, Victoria: Australian Council for Educational Research, 1982.

Gardner, Dorothy E.M. *Susan Isaacs*. London: Methuen, 1969.

Gardner, Dorothy E.M., and Joan E. Cass. *The Role of the Teacher in the Infant and Nursery School*. Oxford: Pergamon, 1965.

Grant, John Webster. "Two-Thirds of the Revenue: Presbyterian Women and Native Indian Missions." In *Changing Roles of Women within the Christian Church in Canada*, edited by Elizabeth Gillan Muir and Marilyn Färdig Whiteley, 99-116. Toronto: University of Toronto Press, 1995.

Green, Amy Susan. "Savage Childhood: The Scientific Construction of Girlhood and Boyhood in the Progressive Era." PhD diss., Yale University, 1995.

Hamlin, David D. *Work and Play: The Production and Consumption of Toys in Germany, 1870-1914*. Ann Arbor: University of Michigan Press, 2007.

Harrison, Ruth. *Sydney Kindergarten Teachers College, 1897-1981. A Pioneer in Early Childhood Education and Care in Australia*. Sydney: Sydney Kindergarten Teachers College Graduates Association, 1985.

Hearst, Kathryn P. "Phoebe Apperson Hearst: The Making of an Upper-Class Woman, 1842-1919." PhD diss., Columbia University, 2005.

Hewes, Dorothy W. "Fallacies, Phantasies, and Egregious Prevarications in ECE History." Paper presented at the Annual Conference of the National Association for the Education of Young Children, Anaheim, CA, November 14, 1997 (Eric Reproduction Document Number ED414058).

—. "Those First Good Years of Indian Education." *American Indian Culture and Research Journal* 4, 3 (1981): 63-82.

Kaestle, Carl. *Joseph Lancaster and the Monitorial School Movement*. New York: Teachers College Press, 1973.

Kaestle, Carl, and Maris Vinovskis. *Education and Social Change in Nineteenth-Century Massachusetts*. Cambridge: Cambridge University Press, 1980.

Kerr, Rosemary. *A History of the Kindergarten Union of Western Australia, 1911-1973*. Perth: Meerlinga Young Children's Foundation, 1994.

Kociumbas, Jan. *Australian Childhood: A History*. St. Leonard, NSW: Allen and Unwin, 1997.

—. "Childhood History as Ideology." *Labour History* 47 (1984): 1-17.

Lascarides, V. Celia, and Blythe F. Hinitz. *History of Early Childhood Education*. New York: Falmer, 2000.

Ludlow, Helen. "'Working at the Heart': The London Missionary Society in Cape Town, 1842-3." In *The London Missionary Society in Southern Africa, 1799-1999*, edited by John de Gruchy, 99-119. Athens, OH: Ohio University Press, 2000.

Mabindisa, Isaac. "The Praying Man: The Life and Times of Henry Bird Steinhauer." PhD diss., University of Alberta, 1984.

Machin, Jeffrey G. "The Westminster Free Day Infant Asylum: The Origins of the First English Infant School." *Journal of Educational Administration and History* 20, 2 (1988): 43-56.

Magubane, Zine. *Bringing the Empire Home: Race, Class, and Gender in Britain and Colonial South Africa*. Chicago: University of Chicago Press, 2004.

Markus, Thomas. *Buildings and Power: Freedom and Control in the Origin of Modern Building Types*. London: Routledge, 1993.
Marsden, W.E. "Contradictions in Progressive Primary School Ideologies and Curricula in England: Some Historical Perspectives." *Historical Studies in Education/ Revue d'histoire de l'éducation* 9, 2 (1997): 224-36.
—. "'Mrs. Walker's Merry Games for Little People': Locating Froebel in an Alien Environment." *British Journal of Educational Studies,* 38, 1 (1990): 15-32.
May, Helen. *The Discovery of Early Childhood: The Development of Services for the Care and Education of Very Young Children, Mid Eighteenth Century Europe to Mid Twentieth Century New Zealand*. Auckland: Auckland University Press, 1997.
—. *School Beginnings: Case Study Two: Dreams and Realities for the Youngest Colonial Settlers, 1840s-50s*. Wellington: Institute for Early Childhood Studies, Victoria University of Wellington, 2004.
—. *School Beginnings: A History of Early Years Schooling, Case Study One: Missionary Infant Schools for Maori Children, 1830s-40s*. Wellington: Institute for Early Childhood Studies, Victoria University of Wellington, 2003.
—. *School Beginnings: A 19th Century Colonial Story*. Wellington: NZCER Press, 2005.
McCann, Phillip. "Popular Education, Socialization and Social Control: Spitalfields 1812-1824." In *Popular Education and Socialization in the Nineteenth Century*, edited by Phillip McCann, 1-40. London: Methuen, 1977.
—. "Samuel Wilderspin and the Early Infant Schools." *British Journal of Educational Studies* 14, 2 (1966): 188-204.
Miller, James Rodger. *Shingwauk's Vision: A History of Residential Schools*. Toronto: University of Toronto Press, 1996.
—. *Skyscrapers Hide the Heavens: A History of Indian-White Relations in Canada*. 3rd ed. Toronto: University of Toronto Press, 2000.
Nawrotzki, Kristen D. "'Like Sending Coals to Newcastle': Impressions from and of the Anglo-American Kindergarten Movement." *Paedagogica Historica* 43, 2 (2007): 223-33.
Nickliss, Alexandra M. "Phoebe Apperson Hearst's 'Gospel of Wealth.'" *Pacific Historical Review* 71, 4 (2002): 575-605.
Paterson, Alice E. "The Development of Kindergartens in Manitoba." Master's thesis, University of Manitoba, 1966.
Peterson, R.C. "The Montessorians — M.M. Simpson and L. de Lissa." In *The Development of Education in Australia, 1900-1950*. Vol. 3, *Pioneers of Australian Education*, edited by C. Turney, 231-71. Sydney: University of Sydney Press, 1983.
Phillips, Charles. *The Development of Education in Canada*. Toronto: W.J. Gage, 1957.
Pierce, Peter. *Country of Lost Children: An Australian Anxiety*. Oakleigh: Cambridge University Press, 1999.
Pinchbeck, Ivy, and Margaret Hewitt. *Children in English Society*. London: Routledge and Kegan Paul, 1969.
Prochner, Larry. "The American Crèche: 'Let's Do What the French Do, but Do It Our Way.'" *Contemporary Issues in Early Childhood* 4, 3 (2003): 267-85.
—. "Early Childhood Education Programs for Indigenous Children in Canada, Australia, and New Zealand: An Historical Review." *Australian Journal of Early Childhood* 29, 4 (2004): 7-16.

—."Quality-of-Care in Historical Perspective." *Early Childhood Research Quarterly* 11, 1 (1996): 5-18.
Prochner, Larry, Helen May, and Baljit Kaur. "'The Blessings of Civilisation': Nineteenth Century Missionary Infant Schools for Young Native Children in Three Colonial Settings — India, Canada and New Zealand, 1820s-1840s." *Paedagogica Historica* 45, 1-2 (2009): 83-102.
Ramsland, John. "The Ragged School Systems in the Australian Colonies." *Victorian Historical Journal* 60, 2-4 (1989): 47-56.
Read, Jane. "Free Play with Froebel: Use and Abuse of Progressive Pedagogy in London's Infant Schools, 1870-c.1904." *Paedagogica Historica* 42, 3 (2006): 299-323.
—. "Froebelian Women: Networking to Promote Professional Status and Educational Change in the Nineteenth Century." *History of Education* 32, 1 (2003): 17-33.
Ripmeester, Michael. "'It Is Scarcely to Be Believed ...': The Mississauga Indians and the Grape Island Mission, 1826-1836." *Canadian Geographer* 39, 2 (1995): 157-68.
Roberts, A.F.B. "A New View of the Infant School Movement." *British Journal of Educational Studies* 20, 2 (1972): 154-64.
Roland, Carol M. "The California Kindergarten Movement: A Study in Class and Social Feminism." PhD diss., University of California, Riverside, 1980.
Rose, Nikolas. "Power and Subjectivity: Critical History and Psychology." In *Historical Dimensions of Psychological Discourse,* edited by C.F. Graumann and K.J. Gergen, 103-24. New York: Cambridge University Press, 1996.
Saba, Carolyn Ann Christenson. "Early Progressive Educational Reform: The Kindergarten and Industrial Education Movements in the United States from 1875 to 1890." PhD diss., University of Maryland, College Park, 2000.
Semel, Susan F. "Helen Parkhurst and the Dalton School." In *Founding Mothers and Others: Women Educational Leaders during the Progressive Era,* edited by Alan R. Sadovnik and Susan F. Semel, 77-92. New York: Palgrave, 2002.
Semple, Neil. *The Lord's Dominion: The History of Canadian Methodism.* Montreal and Kingston: McGill-Queen's University Press, 1996.
Shapiro, Michael S. *Child's Garden: The Kindergarten Movement from Froebel to Dewey.* University Park: Pennsylvania State University Press, 1983.
Silver, Howard. "Owen's Reputation as an Educationist." In *Robert Owen, Prophet of the Poor: Essays in Honour of the Two Hundredth Anniversary of His Birth,* edited by Sidney Pollard and John Salt, 65-83. Lewisburg: Bucknell University Press, 1971.
Simon, Judith, and Linda Tuhiwai Smith, eds. *A Civilising Mission? Perceptions and Representations of the New Zealand Native School System.* Auckland: Auckland University Press, 2001.
Sivasundaram, Sujit. *Nature and the Godly Empire: Science and Evangelical Mission in the Pacific, 1795-1850.* Cambridge: Cambridge University Press, 2005.
Slack, Paul. *From Reformation to Improvement: Social Welfare in Early Modern England.* Oxford: Oxford University Press, 1999.
Smith, Lydia A.H. *To Understand and to Help: The Life and Work of Susan Isaacs (1885-1948).* Cranberry, NJ: Associated University Presses, 1985.

Snyder, Agnes. *Dauntless Women in Childhood Education 1856-1931*. Washington: Association for Childhood Education International, 1972.
Titley, Brian E. "Indian Industrial Schools in Western Canada." In *Schools in the West: Essays in Canadian Education History,* edited by Nancy M. Sheehan, J. Donald Wilson, and David C. Jones, 133-53. Calgary: Detselig, 1986.
Turner, D.A. "1870: The State and the Infant School System." *British Journal of Educational Studies* 18, 2 (1970): 151-65.
Walker, Mary Lucy. "The Development of Kindergartens in Australia." Master's thesis, University of Sydney, 1964.
Weber, Evelyn. *The Kindergarten: Its Encounter with Educational Thought in America*. New York: Teachers College Press, 1969.
Weiner, Deborah E.B. *Architecture and Social Reform in Late-Victorian London*. Manchester: Manchester University Press, 1994.
Winterer, Caroline. "Avoiding a 'Hothouse System of Education': Nineteenth-Century Early Childhood Education from the Infant Schools to the Kindergartens." *History of Education Quarterly* 32, 3 (1992): 289-314.
Wong, Sandie. "Early Childhood Education and Care in New South Wales: Historicising the Present." PhD diss., Macquarie University, 2006.

Index

Note: KSAW stands for Kindergarten Settlement Association of Winnipeg; KUNSW, for Kindergarten Union of New South Wales; KUWA, for Kindergarten Union of Western Australia; Wellington FKA, for Wellington Free Kindergarten Association; Winnipeg FKA, for Winnipeg Free Kindergarten Association; "(i)" after a page reference denotes an illustration; "(t)," a table

Abbott, Julia, 249
Adair, Mary, 152
Adams, David, 84, 124
Adams, Elise Payne, 179-80
Adelaide (ship), 51, 52
Adelaide Kindergarten Teachers College, 226
Adelaide Training College, 164
Adler, Felix, 121, 128, 167
Aikman, Ella: director of Winnipeg FKA Training School, 186-88; influence on KSAW, 192, 194; on play as a teaching strategy, 188-89; social aims of kindergarten curriculum, 188; whole-child approach to kindergarten education, 184-86
Alberta, 144
Alcott, Bronson, 40, 125
amusements, for instruction: in infant schools, 2, 12, 39, 81, 236; in nursery schools in Australia, 155; in ragged schools, 113
Anderson, Maybanke, 170, 204, 213
Anglican Church. *See* Church Missionary Society (CMS)
Anglo-American Kindergarten Movement, 111
Anthony, Alma, 179, 182
Aporti, Ferrante, 37
arithmeticon, 30
Ashworth, Henry, 40-41
At the Threshold of Life (film), 119-20
Aubert, Marie, 92-93, 101
Australia: Aboriginal rejection of residential schools, 84; age of compulsory schooling, 42; assimilation policies for "half-caste" children, 68; child migration schemes, 117; day nursery development, 100; Female Factories with nurseries, 92; impact of European settlement on

317

Index

Aborigines, 65; indigenous infant schools, 54, 65-68; legislation to regulate fostering or boarding of infants, 99; long- and short-term childcare, 92; population, European and Aboriginal (1825), 43-44; population and urban expansion in late 1800s, 133-34, 135; protection acts for Aboriginals after 1830s, 68, 82; Queensland, 157; ragged schools, 111, 114; Victoria, 99, 157, 215; Western Australia, 158. *See also* free kindergartens in Australia; infant schools in New South Wales, Australia; New South Wales, Australia; public kindergartens in New South Wales, Australia
Australian Association for Preschool Child Development, 217
Axtell, James, 55, 84

baby farms, 97-101
Bache, Alexander Dallas, 39
Baines, Edward, 24-25
Bambridge, William, 70-71, 72(i)
Barnard, Henry, 39, 156
Barnardo, Thomas John, 117
Barnardo's Homes, 117
Barnes, Eliza, 62
Barnett, Jeannie King, 177. *See also* Lothrop, Jeannie (née Barnett)
Barns, Joyce, 234
Barrett, Richard, 52
Barrett's Hotel (Wellington, New Zealand), 52
Baucke, Miriam, 233-34
Beatty, Barbara, 9
Beeby, Clarence, 231
Beecham, John, 54
Bell, Andrew, 26, 49, 88
Benham, John B., 59-60, 61
Benjamin, Sophia (Zoe), 211
Bentham, Jeremy, 19-20
Beretainia Kindergarten, 244, 245(i)
Best, Gladys, 192, 194

Bethell, Kerry, 219
Bilby, Thomas, 23, 27, 28, 36
Blacktown Native Institution (Australia), 66
Bliss, Sarah, 45
Bloch, Marianne, 10
Blow, Susan: advocate of Froebelism, 148, 149; death, 150; influence on Toronto kindergartens, 146; at St. Louis, Missouri, kindergartens, 121, 146, 147; on susceptibility of poor children to bad influences, 120
Bolton, Elizabeth, 142
Bott, Helen, 153
Brace, Charles Loring, 117
Breckenfeld, Bertha, 5
Brehony, Kevin, 109, 154
Brewer's Green school, 18, 20, 25-26
Bristol Infant School, 22-23, 34
Britain: compulsory schooling at age five (1870), 39; free kindergartens, 111; ragged schools, 111-14. *See also* infant schools in Britain; *and entries beginning with* Select Committee
British Education Act of 1870, 39
Broder, Sherri, 99-100
Brougham, Henry, 2, 18-19, 86
Brown, James, 13
Bryce, Marion, 190-91
Buchanan, Ann, 52
Buchanan, Barbara, 17, 21-22
Buchanan, David Dale, 18, 21-22, 51, 73
Buchanan, Ebenezer: on compulsory schooling and its effects, 78-79; death, 76; organization of infant schools in Cape Town, 74; organization of infant schools in South Seas, 51, 76-79, 80, 274n194; resignation as LMS teacher, 79-80; on Samoan approach to child rearing, 79, 237; work in Cape Town, 51
Buchanan, Isabella, 17, 18, 23, 25, 52
Buchanan, James: admiration for Pestalozzi, 23; approach to pedagogy,

318

22-25; circle time in infant school, 238; criticism by Wilderspin, 25, 28; death, 52; emigration to Cape Town, 51-52; involvement with Bristol Infant School, 22-23; involvement with Spitalfields school, 20, 21; organization of infant school pupils, 24-25, 37; religious beliefs and influence of Swedenborg, 23-24; teaching at New Lanark Infant School, 17-18; teaching at Westminster Infant Schools, 18, 22, 73
Buchanan, Jane, 77, 79
Buchanan, William, 51, 73
Buckey, Ridie Lee: on child development, 206; curriculum and pedagogical approach of New South Wales kindergarten, 205-7; emphasis on hygiene and health in kindergarten, 203; on global expansion of kindergarten, 207; on importance of marching exercises, 238; kindergarten work in Honolulu, 201-3; teacher-training in New South Wales, 203-4; training in Chicago, 201; on value of manual education in kindergarten, 205-6
Burton, William, 50
Buxton, Mary Ann, 52

Calder, Fanny, 243
Campe, J.H., 105
Canada: age of compulsory schooling, 42; Alderville Manual Labour School, 62; assimilationist policies toward indigenous peoples, 53-54, 64, 82; child migration schemes, 117; childcare in crèches in Quebec, 95-96; childcare in foundling homes/daycares in Toronto, 93-95; combination of infant schools and childcare, 92; Crown Lands Protection Act of 1839, 53; day nursery development, 100; Indian lands declared to be Crown lands, 53; legislation to regulate fostering or boarding of infants, 99; mortality rates in childcare centres, 94; population, immigration, industrialization, and urbanization in late 1800s, 132-33, 135; population in mid-1800s, 43; ragged schools, 111, 114; Royal Proclamation of 1763, 53; school architecture, 43. *See also* free kindergartens in Canada; indigenous infant schools in Canada; infant schools in Canada; public kindergartens in Canada; public kindergartens in Toronto, Ontario
"cannibal mothers," 98
Canterbury Association, 134
Cape Town infant schools (South Africa), 73-74
Carey, Mathew, 21
Carmichael, A.C., 163
Carroll, John, 60, 61
Cartwright, Robert, 82
Case, William, 58, 59, 62
Cass, Joan, 235
Champion, George, 74, 75
Charlottetown Infant School (Prince Edward Island), 46, 47
Chicago: centre of free-kindergarten movement, 127, 247-48; kindergarten part of settlement work, 128, 176; number of kindergarten training schools, 187, 247; training of Canadian teachers, 172, 177, 179-80, 184; training of New South Wales teachers, 201, 208, 211, 217, 246
Chicago Commons kindergarten, 242-43
Chicago Free Kindergarten Institute, 184
Chicago Kindergarten Institute, 208, 247
Chicago Kindergarten Training School, 111
Chicago Normal School, 208

child development: belief in malleability of young children, 9; Buckey on child development, 206; child socialization through early education, 7-9; Herbartian theories, 5, 138, 162, 201; importance of environment, 130, 236; mothers as central figures (Froebel's belief), 103; 19th-century view of children as savage by nature, 4-6; racial recapitulation theories, 4, 121, 124; six domains of, 189

Child Life, 212

Child Rescue Movement, 98

childcare for poor: in Australia, 92; baby farms, 97-101; in Canada, 92, 93-96; contention that Buchanan's school really a childcare centre, 86; foundling hospitals/homes, 87-89, 93, 94, 98; infant schools in institutions, 88, 89-90; mortality rates in foundling hospitals, 88, 93, 94; mortality rates in workhouses, 89-90; in New Zealand, 92-93; options for poor single mothers in early 1800s, 87; orphanages (children aged 2 and older), 95; wet nurses, 96-97; workhouses, 89-90, 97

Childhood Education, 192

Children of the Tenements (Riis), 116

Children's Aid Society of Toronto, 95

Children's Protection Act (Quebec, 1944), 99

Chippendale Kindergarten, 217

Christian Observer, 29

Christian Woman's Union of Winnipeg, 146

Church Missionary Record, 67

Church Missionary Society (CMS): education as evangelizing strategy, 53; indigenous infant schools in Australia, 66-67; indigenous infant schools in New Zealand, 68-70; missionary activity among indigenous peoples, 53, 68-69

Clarke, Ruth, 58
Cochin, Jean Denys, 4
Cohen, Mark, 116, 137, 138, 168
Colby, Martha, 172
Colenso, William, 69
Coleridge, Samuel Taylor, 26
colonial schooling: on British pattern for European children, 80; development of free kindergartens, 111-12; mixed population of children, 3; re-creation of civilization, 6; socialization, assimilation, and patriotism, 7-9; variations of the short-time system, 41. *See also* kindergartens; *and entries beginning with* free kindergartens; indigenous infant schools; infant schools; public kindergartens

Committee of Nineteen (International Kindergarten Union), 148, 149-50

Condon, Catherine, 136

conversion, religious, 10, 54-55, 56, 60

Cook County Normal School (Chicago): graduates, 180, 202, 208, 217; pragmatic approach to kindergarten work, 201; training of New South Wales kindergarten teachers, 201, 208. *See also* Chicago Normal School

Coombe, F.E., 151-52

Cooper, Sarah Brown: approach to kindergarten work, 129, 130; founder of free kindergartens in San Francisco, 128; founder of International Kindergarten Union, 129; kindergartens promoted through annual reports, 129-30; letter of support for Nova Scotia free kindergarten, 136; murder, 131; on religious teaching in kindergarten, 167

Coqualeetza Institute (British Columbia), 139

Cosgrove, Catherine, 166

Coulter, Isabel, 179, 182-83

Course of Lessons (Bilby), 36

Cowan, Jane. *See* Buchanan, Jane
Cowley, R.H., 152
Cowper, Daisy, 241
Crèche d'Youville (Montreal), 95
crèches, 90-92
Cremin, Lawrence, 27
Crowley, Amelia (née Quinney), 158-61
Crowstand Boarding School (Canada), 142

Dale, Ann Caroline, 16
Dale, David, 16, 89
Dalton Plan, 228-29
dame schools, 27-28, 52
Dame's School (Webster), 27-28
Dawson City kindergarten (Yukon), 144
day nurseries: associated with kindergartens, 209-10; charitable causes into 20th century, 101; development in Australia, 100; development in Canada, 95-96, 100; development in New Zealand, 100
Day Nursery for Babies of Working Mothers (Woolloomooloo, NSW), 210
daycare: "babies classes," 39; crèches or charity-sponsored public nurseries, 90-92; day nurseries, 95-96, 100-1; twinned with complementary services, 100-1; wet nurses, 96-97. *See also* childcare for poor
de Fellenberg, Phillip Emanuel, 18-19
de Lissa, Lillian: ideas and ideals of kindergarten, 1905 vs 1955, 218; inspiration for KUWA, 168, 226; kindergarten work in South Australia, 210; reform at KUWA, 226-27
Deacon, Edith, 192, 194, 196-97
Dean, Minnie, 99
Deasey, Denison, 26-27
denominational schools, 48-50, 53. *See also* missionary schools; *entries beginning with* indigenous infant schools; indigenous kindergartens
Dent, Lillian, 154
Depaepe, Marc, 3, 7
Dequire, Jeanne, 99
Dewdney, Edgar, 56-57
Dewey, John, 150, 184, 190, 201, 251
Dickens, Charles, 112-13
Divine and Moral Songs for Children (Watts), 48
Donnachie, Ian, 16-17
Donnel, Ethel, 226
Douai, Adolf, 149
Dugdale, Richard, 130
Dumolo, Harriet: education, 211; interest in Horace Mann Kindergarten methods, 213, 247; pedagogy at KUNSW under her direction, 211-12, 214-15, 247; teacher training with emphasis on practical, 211-12
Duncan, Edith, 240
Dunedin (New Zealand), 135, 165, 167
Dunedin Free Kindergarten Association, 137-38, 169, 171
d'Youville, Marguerite, 95

early childhood education (ECE): "babies classes," 39; child socialization through early education, 7-9; compulsory schooling at age five in Britain (1870), 39; current importance, 2-3; differences between monitorial and infant systems, 27-28; Herbartian theory, 5, 138, 162, 201; preventing later lives of crime, 9-10, 13-14, 21, 130, 169-71, 180, 200, 204, 207, 224-25; purpose of playgrounds, 32-33; social reform agenda, 12-14; as solution to poverty, 117-19. *See also* kindergartens; *entries beginning with* free kindergartens; indigenous infant schools; infant schools; public kindergartens

321

Early Discipline Illustrated (Wilderspin), 37-38
Eastman, Hannah, 202
ECE. *See* early childhood education (ECE)
Edgeworth, Mary, 4
Edgeworth, Richard, 4
Edinburgh Ragged School, 113-14
Education Act (New Zealand, 1877), 158
Education of Man (Froebel), 103, 104, 106
Education Ordinance (New Zealand, 1847), 72
Educational Magazine, 25
Elkhorn Industrial School (Canada), 142
Ellen Street Kindergarten (Winnipeg), 173, 175, 182, 240
Elliott, Henry W., 123-24
Engels, Friedrich, 116
Ethical Culture Society, 167, 242
Europe, 13, 14. *See also* German kindergartens
Evans, George Samuel, 51
Evans, Harriet, 52
Evans, James, 55

Federation of Day Nurseries, 101
Finlayson, Constance, 226
"folds" for young children, 35, 37
Ford, Margaret, 214, 215
Fort Street Model School, 154-57
Fort Street National School, 157
Francis, Catherine Augusta, 164
Fredericton Infant School (New Brunswick), 46
Fredericton Infant School Society (New Brunswick), 46
Free Kindergarten and Children's Aid Association of the Hawaiian Islands (FKCAA), 201-3
free kindergartens: benefits for poor children and parents, 119-21; in Britain, 111, 113; for childcare, instruction, and evangelism, 121; civilizing value of, 121-23, 130; compared with infant schools, 111; in Germany, 103-6, 110-11; for indigenous children, 138-42; missionary tradition and, 10; moral and social education, 120, 129, 130, 175, 180, 182; preventing later lives of crime, 130, 169-71, 180; private teacher-training schemes, 167-69; skill-based training and childcare for the poor, 110-11; social reform movements in the New World and, 115-16, 128; social-welfare role, 170-71; uptake in the colonies and United States, 111-12, 120-21, 126-28. *See also other entries beginning with* free kindergartens
free kindergartens in Australia: development of, 111, 112, 127, 136-37, 158, 166; influence of American model, 166-67; teacher training, 168-69; teaching of patriotism in kindergarten, 8. *See also* Kindergarten Union of New South Wales (KUNSW)
free kindergartens in Britain, 111, 113
free kindergartens in Canada: arrival of movement, 127, 135; development forestalled by public school kindergartens, 135-36; influence of American model, 166-67. *See also* Winnipeg Free Kindergarten Association (Winnipeg FKA)
free kindergartens in New Zealand: arrival of and support for movement, 127, 137-38, 163; civilizing value of kindergartens, 122; Dunedin free kindergarten, 137-38, 169, 171; influence of American model, 166-67; influences on development of, 111; private teacher-training schemes, 167-68; ties with church work, 137-38, 166-67; Walker Street Kindergarten, 138. *See also*

Wellington Free Kindergarten Association (Wellington FKA)
free kindergartens in United States: American model of free kindergartens, 166-67; growth of, 101, 111-12, 125, 128-30, 146; incorporation into public schools, 136; missionary and religious ideas, 242; in San Francisco, 125, 127, 128-31, 169, 204; in settlement houses, 242. *See also* Golden Gate Kindergarten Association
Freeman, Constance, 220
Froebel, Friedrich: children considered savage by nature, 4, 122; father of the kindergarten, 4; kindergartens for all children without consideration of class, 120; obtuse writing style, 105, 151-52, 249; philosophy of education, 103-4, 109-10, 249; racial recapitulation theory, 4; religious beliefs, 103-4. *See also* Froebelism; Gifts (Froebelian)
Froebel Association Training School (Chicago), 179-80
Froebel Educational Institute (Britain), 111
Froebel Institute of Nova Scotia, 136
Froebel School (kindergarten in Winnipeg), 174-75, 184, 187
Froebelism: attack by Reconstructionists, 148-50; child-centred approach, 121; children considered savage by nature, 4, 122; circle use, 239; criticized as controlling, 242; emphasis on hand (arts and crafts), rather than mind (intellectual), culture, 112; kindergarten as a structured, non-academic approach to early education, 102-3; kindergartens for all children without consideration of class, 120; learning through play and activities ("occupations"), 104, 105, 184, 189-90, 210; moral code in kindergarten pedagogy, 149, 242; mothers as central figures in child development, 103; move away from, 110, 111, 185, 202, 208, 250-51; obtuse writing and puzzling philosophy, 105, 151-52, 249; pedagogy in Toronto public school kindergartens until 1930s, 148-50; racial recapitulation theory, 4. *See also* Froebel, Friedrich; Gifts (Froebelian)
Froebel's Educational Laws for All Teachers (Hughes), 148-49
Fryatt, F.E., 126
Fulmer, Grace, 5, 248, 251

Gage, Lucy, 184, 185(t)
gallery instruction: in infant schools, 20, 27, 30(i), 31-32, 35-36, 39, 42-43, 237; in monitorial schools, 31-32; school architecture, 42-43. *See also* Lancasterian system
Gardiner, Lyndsay, 203
Gardner, Dorothy, 234, 235
Garwood, John, 114
German kindergartens: educational experiment, 103-6; in Namibia pre-WWI, 6; number (1840-51), 110; spread of kindergarten idea to England and US, 111-12, 128. *See also* Froebel, Friedrich; Froebelism; Gifts (Froebelian)
Gertrude House (Chicago), 208
Gifts (Froebelian): confusion regarding principles, 240, 248; creation of dependency, 240, 248; description, 104, 106-7, 108(i), 109; "gift books," 249-50; move away from, 111, 150, 185, 202, 208, 244-46, 250-51; student-teachers' reaction to, 248-50; use at KUNSW, 170, 201, 202, 214; use at Wellington FKA, 223(t), 225, 226; use at Winnipeg FKA, 181-82, 186, 188; use in teacher training, 143, 248-50;

323

value beyond physical or cognitive exercise, 241. *See also* Froebel, Friedrich; Froebelism
Gillespie, Catherine, 142
Gipsy Hill Training College, 168-69
Girls' Home (Toronto), 94, 96
Glasgow Infant School Society, 38
Golden Fleece Nursery School, 215
Golden Gate Kindergarten Association: considered missionary, not educational, 136-37; kindergarten as crime-prevention, 169, 180; founded through philanthropy, 128-31, 169, 204; influence on KUNSW kindergartens, 204; influence on visiting kindergarten teachers, 202; loss of teachers through marriage, 204; "sociological work," 206
Golden Gate Kindergarten Free Normal Training School, 128-29
gonigraph (jointed slats), 39, 104
Gordon, James, 81
Gowrie, Lady Zara, 217
Goyder, David, 22-23, 28, 34, 37
Gradual Assimilation Act (Canada, 1857), 54
Grape Island Mission in Upper Canada, 57, 58-62
Greaves, James Pierrepont, 23
Guide to Primary Manual Work (Ledyard and Breckenfeld), 5
Guthrie, Thomas, 114
Gutteridge, Mary, 215, 217, 247

Hailmann, Bessie, 148
Hailmann, William, 64, 138
Halifax Infant School, 44, 45-47, 92
Halifax Ragged School, 114
Hall, G. Stanley, 5, 121, 201
Hall, William, 66
Hamilton, Elizabeth, 232
Harper's New Monthly Magazine, 126
Harris, William Torrey: attitude toward Indians, 138-39; on cost-effectiveness of public kindergartens, 131; founding of public school kindergarten, 147; on need for kindergarten supervisor, 152; on "weaklings" in city kindergartens, 120-21
Harrison, Elizabeth, 150, 239, 244, 246
Hart, Caroline, 147, 148
Head, Francis Bond, 35
Hearst, Phoebe Apperson, 128, 131
Hegner, Bertha Hofer, 243
Heinig, Christine, 217, 248
Herbart, George, 138
Herbartian theory of child development, 5, 138, 162, 201
Herbert, Gilbert, 52
Hewes, Dorothy, 9
Hewitt, Margaret, 99
Hill, Patty Smith: Blocks, 196, 214, 251; on kindergarten as preparation for formal schooling, 240-41; progressive view of kindergarten education, 201; supporter of progressive approach to kindergarten, 149
Hill, Richard, 48-49, 265n33
Hilton, Mary, 105
Hine, Lewis, 243
Hobart Ragged School, 115
Hodgins, John George, 39, 43
Holden, Ruth, 194, 197
Home and Colonial Infant School Society, 42, 235
Home and Colonial Training Schools (London), 165
Hooper, Mary, 204
Horace Mann Kindergarten, 196-97, 213, 243-44, 246, 248
Horace Mann Kindergarten for Five-Year-Old Children (Garrison et al.), 243-44
House of Industry (ON), 97
Household Words, 113
How the Other Half Lives (Riis), 116
Howland, Mary Ware, 237

Hubbard, Hester (Hetty) Ann, 62
Hughes, Adaline Augusta (née Marean), 145, 148
Hughes, James Laughlin: establishment of public school kindergartens, 135-36, 143, 144-46, 166; patriotism and allegiance to Britain, 149; response to criticism of kindergarten's value, 151; supporter of Froebelism, 148-49
Hughes, Samuel, 149
Hull House (Chicago), 128
Huntington, Emily, 183

immigration: to Australia in late 1800s, 134; to Canada in 1800s, 132-33, 135; to New Zealand in late 1800s, 134-35
Indian Act (Canada, 1876), 64
indigenous infant schools: aims of, 80-82; in Cape Town, South Africa, 73-74; effectiveness of infant system for both indigenous and European students, 75; European attitude to indigenous parents, 82-83; gateway program to larger target community (parents), 11; indigenous vs European approach to child rearing, 79, 81; industrial schools, 19; political and economic interests of colonial governments and, 82; "remaking" indigenous children into Europeans, 82; in South Seas, 76-79. *See also* residential schools in Canada; *other entries beginning with* indigenous infant schools
indigenous infant schools in Australia, 54, 65-68
indigenous infant schools in Canada: Ancienne Lorette Jesuit mission, 56; assimilation and conversion the priorities, 53-54, 56, 60; Credit River school, 60, 81; English immersion replacing bilingual instruction, 60-61; few after 1830s, 62; first established in 1820s, 44-45, 55; Grape Island Mission in Upper Canada, 57, 58-62; Huron-Wendat, 56-57; in New France era, 55-56; Rice Lake Mission, 60-61
indigenous infant schools in New Zealand: abandonment during Land Wars (1860-67), 71-72; Anglican Church Mission Society infant schools, 68-70-1, 72(i); popularity and efficiency, 69, 71, 84; use of Maori language, 71, 72
indigenous kindergartens in Canada: "civilizing" value of, 123-24, 139; emphasis on manual education, 139; incorporation into residential schools, 139-42; Rupert's Land industrial school, 141-42; St. Michael's at Duck Lake, 140(i), 141. *See also* residential schools in Canada
indigenous kindergartens in United States, 124, 138-39
indigenous peoples: Canada's assimilation policies, 53-54, 64, 82; European attitude to indigenous parents, 62-64, 82-84, 124; indigenous vs European approach to child rearing, 79, 81
industrial schools. *See* residential schools in Canada
Infant Education (Wilderspin), 28, 29-30, 33(i)
Infant School Depot, 38
infant school guide books, 26-27, 34, 36-38
Infant School Manual (Howland), 237
Infant School Society (London), 1-2, 35-36, 37-38, 235, 252n4
infant schools: architecture, 42-43; basic format, 14; belief in malleability of young children, 9; child socialization one of the aims, 7-9; differences/similarities with

kindergartens, 125, 126; established by charities, 9-10, 43, 47; growth from 1825 to 1835, 2; marching as teaching strategy, 22, 34, 67, 104-5, 237-38; missionary tradition of civilization and conversion, 10; moral agenda of, 1-2, 13-14, 237; "objects" of schools, 2; pedagogical change when incorporated into state schooling, 235; as preventing later lives of crime, 9-10, 13-14, 21; religion and, 23, 26, 36; similarity across countries, 3; social reform agenda, 12; standardization of methods and materials, 38-39; training and discipline valuable for future work, 19, 40-41; vs kindergartens, 105; vs monitorial schools, 27-28. *See also* missionary schools; *entries beginning with* indigenous infant schools; *other entries beginning with* infant schools

infant schools in Australia, 54, 65-68. *See also* infant schools in New South Wales, Australia

infant schools in Britain: architecture, 42-43; Bristol Infant School, 22-23, 34; compulsory schooling at age five (1870), 39; expansion inside Britain and abroad, 26-28, 37-38; focus on early reading in, 15, 27; infant instruction by amusements, 2, 12, 39, 81, 236; in London, 18, 20-22, 24-26, 34; moral agenda, 13-14, 19, 33, 36; New Lanark school, 4, 12, 14-18, 29; play and playgrounds, 32-33; religious character, 23; social reform agenda, 12; St. Mary's Infant School, 34; standardization of methods and materials, 38-39; training and discipline valuable for future work, 19, 40-41; Wilderspin's "Infant System," 25, 26, 28, 29-32, 37-39; Wilson's system, 34-36, 37

infant schools in Canada: charity schools prior to 1860, 47; fees and funding, 47; Halifax Infant School, 44, 45-47, 92; management and organization, 44-46; material and staffing problems, 46; moral education, 45, 60; number, 43, 44; popularity, 85; York Infant School, 44-45. *See also* indigenous infant schools in Canada

infant schools in Cape Town, South Africa, 73-74

infant schools in New South Wales, Australia: Aboriginal children's schooling, 54; age of compulsory schooling, 42; expansion of denominational schools, 48, 49-50; Male Orphan School in Sydney, 49; moral instruction, 48; Pestalozzi system, 50-51; popularity, 85; schools with monitorial system, 49; St. James' Infant School in Sydney, 48-49, 50; St. Phillip's Infant School in Sydney, 50. *See also* public kindergartens in New South Wales, Australia

infant schools in New Zealand: first non-compulsory pre-primary class, 158; for European and Maori children (1825-40), 44; Lyttelton Infant School, 53; mission schools, 54; New Zealand Company school, 51-52

infant systems. *See* systems for infant schools

Infants' Home (Sydney), 93

Infants' Home (Toronto) (*later* Infants' Home and Infirmary, 1877), 93-95

Institute for the Formation of Character (New Lanark, Britain), 14, 19

Institute of Education (London), 215, 232, 234, 235

Institute of Education (Switzerland), 103

Intellectual Growth in Young Children (Isaacs), 233

International Exhibition of Educational Materials (London, 1854), 156
International Kindergarten Union (IKU): address by Montessori on children as savage by nature, 4-5; founding, 129; Froebelian vs Reconstructionist kindergarten pedagogy, 148, 149-50; Hughes as president, 148; move away from Gift work, 150, 244-46; study of kindergarten curriculum, 150; support for unified kindergarten-primary work, 150
Irving, Edward, 1
Isaacs, Susan, 216, 232-33

Jackson, Thomas, 53
Jackson Street Kindergarten Association (San Francisco), 128
James, William, 184
Jenkins, Elizabeth, 208, 211
Jones, J.S., 159-60
Jones, Peter, 58, 59, 62

Kaestle, Carl, 26
Karger, Howard Jacob, 176
Kay-Shuttleworth, James, 32, 156
Kelsey, Lavinia, 138
Kelso, John Joseph, 10, 116
Kerikeri mission school (New Zealand), 69
Kilpatrick, William, 184, 190
Kindergarten Building Gifts with Hints on Program-Making (Harrison and Woodson), 244, 246
Kindergarten Collegiate Institute (Chicago), 247
Kindergarten Magazine, 208
Kindergarten Settlement Association of Winnipeg (KSAW): charitable and mission orientation, 176; child-welfare service, 191-92; critical report on kindergartens by Welfare Council, 198-99; curriculum and play themes, 194-95; educational and vocational role of kindergarten, 188; end of training program, 192; hiring of graduates of Winnipeg FKA Training School, 187; impact of start-up of public kindergartens, 197; influence of Montessori, 195; moral training for children, 188; no new initiatives after 1920, 192, 194; opening of Winnipeg Neighbourhood House, 198-99; professional development for teachers, 194; progressive ideas for kindergarten, 188-90; takeover by Community Chest, 198; trend to more independence, 196-97. *See also* Winnipeg Free Kindergarten Association (Winnipeg FKA)
Kindergarten Union of New South Wales (KUNSW): age requirements for admission, 209-10; changes with new directors, 247; curriculum and pedagogical approach under Buckey, 205-7; day nurseries associated with kindergartens, 209-10; education plus social welfare, 137, 205-7; founding, 115, 137; Gift work and circle time, 214, 239(i); kindergartens as crime-prevention programs, 169, 170, 200, 204, 207; manual education's value for children, 205-6, 242-43; Montessori and Montessori-Froebel kindergarten experiment, 213, 214(i); moral education, 201, 205; move to Woolloomooloo, 137, 200; nursery schools and training, 215-17; pedagogical status quo under Dumolo, 211-15; progressive and stricter approach of Newton, 208-9; progressive approach of Buckey, 201-3, 207; purpose-built kindergarten (Newtown Free Kindergarten), 137; settlement-oriented ideas regarding manual

327

education, 242-43; similarity to US kindergartens, 211-12; special needs children's programs, 206-7, 217; spread to South Australia, 210; study visits and introduction of change, 213, 217, 247-48; teacher training under Buckey, 203-4; teacher training under Newton, 207-9; teacher training under Dumolo, 211-12; training for kindergarteners by employer, 247; training of teachers in Chicago, 208, 211, 217, 246. *See also* Sydney Kindergarten Teachers College (SKTC) (Australia); Woolloomooloo kindergarten (Sydney, NSW)

Kindergarten Union of Victoria, 203, 215, 217, 247

Kindergarten Union of Western Australia (KUWA): "Dalton Plan" into sub-primary class, 228; formation, 168, 226; Montessori and Froebel in teacher-training program, 226, 227(t); Montessori preschool, 227-28; progressive reform, 226-28

kindergartens: as "appropriate" beginning of formal education, 5; bridge between home and school life, 153; circles as teaching method, 125, 214, 238-40; civilizing value of, 121-23; as deterrent to delinquent behaviour, 169-70, 180; "free" kindergartens and missionary tradition, 10; gateway to larger target community (parents), 10-11; in Germany, 103-6, 110; incorporation into state schooling, 235; for indigenous children, 123-24; initial lack of support in New South Wales, 85; international movement of people and ideas, 247-48; marching as a teaching strategy, 125, 126, 181, 183, 237-38; moral and social education, 110, 129, 130, 180, 182; organization of, 125-26; private kindergartens, 110, 125; "protection" from books and pressures of reading, 7; "race experience" of teacher, 5; similarity across countries, 3; structured, non-academic approach to early education, 102-3; unified kindergarten-primary work, 150, 151-54; vs infant schools, 125, 126. *See also* German kindergartens; *entries beginning with* free kindergartens; indigenous kindergartens; public kindergartens

King, Ann, 240
Kingsmill, Joseph, 114
Kitchen Garden program, 183, 192, 243
Kociumbas, Jan, 67
Kraus, John, 111
Kraus-Boelte, Maria, 111, 144-45

Laboratory School, University of Chicago, 150, 214
Lady Gowrie Child Centres (Australia), 217
Lancaster, Joseph, 15, 238
Lancasterian system: "emulation" as teaching method, 21; learning aids for mathematics and geometry, 30; monitorial system, 15, 17, 34, 131; punishment methods, 22, 34; use of circle for lessons, 238; use of galleries, 23, 31-32, 60
Lancet on wet-nursing, 97
Lawrence, Frances, 202-3
Le Fevre, Perry, 5
Ledyard, Mary, 5
Lee, Robert, 164-66
Leeds Mercury, 24-25
Levin-Froebel, Luise, 110
Leyland Stanford Jr. University, 128
Lindsay, Mabel, 187
London Foundling Hospital: admission restricted to children of poor single mothers, 88-89; admissions, 88-89; model for long-term

childcare institutions through Commonwealth, 88; monitorial system of schooling for older children, 88; mortality rates, 88; play and kindergarten for younger children, 87-88
London Missionary Society (LMS): creation of infant schools in Cape Colony, 51, 73, 74; indigenous infant schools in Australia, 65-66; infant schools in South Seas, 76-80; lack of support for infant schools, 77; missionary activity among indigenous peoples, 53, 75
London Society for the Prevention of Cruelty to Children, 98
Lothrop, Jeannie (née Barnett): advocate of Froebel kindergarten system, 179; character building the purpose of kindergarten, 184; on importance of marching exercises, 238; opinion of poor families, 175; teacher of kindergarten teacher-training course, 178; work with Winnipeg FKA, 177, 179
Louisa Street Public School (Toronto), 46
Lower Canada. See Quebec
Lyndall, Elizabeth, 73

Mackenzie, William Lyon, 60
Macnab, Henry, 15
Macquarie, Lachlan, Governor of Australia, 65
MacVannel, John, 251
Madras Military Male Orphan Asylum, 88
Male Orphan School in Sydney, 49
Maley, Lucie Calista, 8
Malting House School, 232-33
Manitoba: funding for public kindergartens, 143, 146, 173, 197-98. See also Winnipeg, Manitoba; Winnipeg Free Kindergarten Association (Winnipeg FKA)
Manitoba Daily Free Press, 146

Manual of Drill and Calisthenics (Hughes), 149
Maori Land Act (New Zealand, 1862), 72
Maori of New Zealand: assimilation policies after Land Wars (1860-67), 72; literacy rate, 71; population in 1820s, 44; support for mission schools, 69, 84
Maple Street Mission Kindergarten (Winnipeg), 177
Marean, Adaline Augusta, 145, 148
Marsden, Samuel, 55, 68-69
Marsden, W.E., 106, 149, 242
Marwedel, Emma, 128
Marylebone public nursery (crèche), 90-91
Marylebone Workhouse (London), 89-90
Mathien, Julie, 151
Maudsley, Henry, 130
May, Clara, 189
May, Helen, 51, 53, 122
Mayhew, Henry, 116
McCann, Phillip, 21, 51
McGill Normal School, 46, 143
McGrew, Charles, 129
McIntyre, Daniel, 191
McKenzie, N.R., 231
McLean, Helen: career after Winnipeg FKA, 192; director of Winnipeg FKA, 184; emphasis on child development in kindergarten, 189-90; graduate of Oberlin school, 187; influence on KSAW, 192, 194; introduction of "experiment method," 190; teaching at Oberlin school, 192, 250
Melbourne Kindergarten Training College, 215
Melbourne Teachers College, 157, 203
Memorial Kindergarten (Hawaii), 10
Methodist All People's Mission Kindergarten, 177, 178(i)
Methodist Church: Credit River Mission, 60; English immersion in

329

indigenous schools, 61; Grape Island Mission in Upper Canada, 57, 58-60; mission activity in Upper Canada, 58; Rice Lake Mission, 60
Michaelis, Emilie, 109-10
Middleton, Phyllis, 192, 194
Millet, Eugénie, 4, 37
Mills, Harriette Melissa, 240, 249
Milton Bradley Company, 142, 251
Miss Wheelock's Kindergarten Training School (Boston), 187
missionary schools: education as evangelizing strategy, 53; tradition of civilization and conversion ("salvation narrative"), 10. *See also* entries beginning with indigenous infant schools
missionary societies: attitude toward indigenous parents, 82-83; belief in ability to "remake" indigenous children into Europeans, 82; on conversion and civilization of indigenous peoples, 54-55; education as evangelizing strategy, 53; infant schools as component of mission work, 2; replicating life in England in missions, 69; Wesleyan Missionary Society, 62, 69. *See also* Church Missionary Society (CMS); London Missionary Society (LMS)
Mississauga (Ojibway) First Nations, 57-60
Mitchell, Elizabeth, 46
monitorial schools: in Cape Town, South Africa, 73; in foundling hospitals, 88; gallery instruction, 31-32; lesson posts, 31; in Sydney, Australia, 49; system suggested for kindergartens, 131; vs infant schools, 27-28. *See also* Lancasterian system
Montessori, Maria: children considered savage by nature, 4-5; on civilizing value of early childhood education, 122; goal of early education, 7; influence in Australia, 163, 212,

226-28; influence in New Zealand, 225-26; influence in Winnipeg, 189, 195; influence on Dalton Plan, 228-29; Montessori kindergartens in Australia, 213, 228; racial recapitulation theory, 4-5
Montreal Infant School Association, 47-48
Montreal Infant School Society, 47
Moore, H. Keatley, 109-10
Morley, Henry, 113
mortality rates of children: in childcare places in Canada, 94; in foundling hospitals, 88, 93, 94; with New World urbanization, 115; in urban centres in colonies, 135; in workhouses, 89-90
Moss, Peter, 3
Mother-Play (Froebel), 184, 185(t), 205
Mother's Association Day Nursery (Winnipeg), 175
Mount Cook Infants' School (Wellington, New Zealand), 164-66, 295n156
Mountain Street Infant School (Montreal), 47-48
Murdoch, Katherine, 10

Namibia kindergartens (Southwest Africa), 6
National College of Education (Chicago), 217. *See also* Cook County Normal School (Chicago)
National Froebel Union, 111
National Kindergarten and Elementary College (Chicago), 194
National Kindergarten Association, 119, 120
National Kindergarten College (Chicago), 247
Native Institution (Parramatta, Australia), 65-66, 84
Native School Act (New Zealand, 1867), 72
Native Schools Code (New Zealand, 1880), 72

Nawrotzki, Kristen, 111
Neagle, John, 62, 63(i)
New Education Fellowship Conference (Sydney), 216, 232
New Jerusalem Church (London), 22, 23
New Lanark (Britain), 16-17
New Lanark Infant School (Britain), 4, 12, 14-18, 29
New South Wales, Australia: compulsory school laws, 157. See also infant schools in New South Wales, Australia; Kindergarten Union of New South Wales (KUNSW)
New View of Society (Owen), 17
New York Association (free kindergarten), 136
New York Children's Aid Society, 117
New York Nursery for the Children of Poor Women, 95-96, 100
New York Times, 183
New Zealand: age of compulsory schooling, 42, 158; assimilation policies for Maori (after 1867), 72, 82; centres of European population, 134-35; day nursery development, 100-1; Dunedin Free Kindergarten Association, 137-38, 169, 171; European and Maori population, 44; foundling hospitals, 92-93; kindergarten teacher-training schools, 187; legislation to regulate fostering or boarding of infants, 99; Maori, 44, 69, 71-72, 84; population, immigration, and urbanization in late 1800s, 134-35; public kindergartens in New Zealand, 163-66; Treaty of Waitangi (1840), 54. See also free kindergartens in New Zealand; infant schools in New Zealand; Wellington Free Kindergarten Association (Wellington FKA)
New Zealand Company (NZC), 51-52, 134

New Zealand Company Ladies Committee, 52
New Zealand Council of Educational Research, 231
Newton, Frances, 207-11
Newtown Free Kindergarten (of KUNSW), 137
Ngataru, Mary, 70
North-West Territories, 139, 143-44
North-West Territories School Bill (1892), 143
Nova Scotia: combination of infant schools and childcare, 92; Halifax Infant School, 44, 45-46, 47, 92
nursery schools: as answer to many problems of childhood, 216; in Australia, 215; conversion of kindergartens during World War II, 233; introduction to New Zealand, 232; at KUNSW, 215-17; nursery school option at SKTC, 215-16; as pre-primary classes in New South Wales, 154-57; trends in United States, 215-16

Oberlin, Jean-Frédéric, 14, 104, 105
Oberlin Kindergarten Training School (Ohio), 178, 187, 189, 192, 193(t), 250
Observations Relative to Infant Schools (Pole), 34
O'Grady, Caroline, 237
On the Importance of Educating the Infant Children of the Poor (Wilderspin), 28, 104
Ontario: funding for public school kindergartens, 143; indigenous school, Grape Island Mission, 57, 58-62; indigenous school, Rice Lake Mission, 60-61; influx of settlers after American Revolution, 57-58; lack of trained teachers for infant schools, 46; school architecture, 43. See also public kindergartens in Toronto; Toronto, Ontario

Ontario Educational Association (OEA), 148
Ontario Public School Act (1885), 143
Organisation for Economic Co-operation and Development (OECD), 3
Otago Association, 134
Ottawa Normal School, 5, 142
Outline of the System of Education at New Lanark (R.D. Owen), 29
Owen, Robert: on civilizing value of early childhood education, 122; on corrupting influence of children's parents, 13; environmentalist view of child development, 236; infant school established at New Lanark, 4, 12, 14-18; on infant system, 26; influence of principles, 236; learning through play and activity, 105; sons' education at de Fellenberg's academy, 19
Owen, Robert Dale, 14

parallelepiped, 107
Parker, Francis Wayland, 169, 170, 201
Parkhurst, Helen, 228-29
Pastoret, Adelaide de, 4
Patty Smith Hill Blocks, 196, 214, 251
Peabody, Elizabeth: on annual reports of Golden Gate Association, 129-30; contact with Halifax free kindergartener, 136; founder of Temple School (kindergarten), 125; humanist philosophy for kindergarten, 167; on play as way to develop internal controls, 125; recruiter of kindergarten teachers, 128
Pendred, Gladys, 247
Perley, Moses Henry, 62-64
Perth Kindergarten Training college, 226
Pestalozzi, Johann: approach to teaching, 36, 259n63; "ideal women," 208; influence in Canada, 60, 81, 83; influence in New South Wales, 50-51, 154, 156; influence on British infant schools, 29, 36; influence on Froebel, 103, 104-5; influence on James Buchanan, 23; Institute of Education (Switzerland), 103; "synthetic method" for children's learning, 156
Pestalozzi-Froebel House (Berlin), 110, 207, 24
Pestalozzi-Froebel Kindergarten Training School (Chicago), 111, 188, 247
Petone Kindergarten, 233
Philadelphia Centennial Exhibition, 144, 145(i)
Philadelphia Normal School, 152, 153-54
Philip, John, 73, 74, 75
Piapot's Reserve school, 141
Pierce, Peter, 7
Pinchbeck, Ivy, 99
play: learning by amusements, 2, 12, 39, 81, 236; play principle, 202; purpose of playgrounds in infant schools, 32-33; as a teaching strategy, 188-89, 233; as way to develop internal controls, 125
Play and Activity Institute (Germany), 103
Poesche, Hermann, 106
Pole, Thomas, 31, 32, 34
Popkewitz, Thomas, 10
Poppenhusen, Conrad, 126
Poppenhusen Institute, 126-27
Postman, Neil, 122
pouponnières, 35
poverty: child rescue through migration schemes, 117-18; children viewed as victims, not vagrants, 119; Christian duty to give aid to the poor, 116; early childhood education as solution, 117-19; result of urban expansion due to immigration, 135. *See also* childcare for poor
Primary Teacher Association, Toronto, 153
Pritchard, George, 76-77

private kindergartens, 110, 125
Progressive Movement, 115-16
Prussian system for infant schools, 43
public kindergartens: bridge between home and school life, 153; Froebelian-Reconstructionist debate, 148-50; in New Zealand, 163-66; struggle between kindergarten and primary school teachers, 152-54; support tenuous, 131; unified kindergarten-primary school work, 150, 152-54. *See also other entries beginning with* public kindergartens
public kindergartens in Canada: impact on free kindergartens, 135-36; Ontario funding for, 143; in Quebec, 143; in Western Canada, 143-44, 146, 173, 197-98. *See also* public kindergartens in Toronto
public kindergartens in New South Wales, Australia: criticism, 160-61; Crown Street Public School experiment, 158-60; impact of compulsory school laws, 157; initial lack of support, 85, 156-57; integration of kindergarten work into infants' schools, 161-63; modified kindergartens, 154, 161-62; modified Montessori methods, 163; nursery schools as pre-primary classes, 154-57
public kindergartens in New Zealand, 163-66
public kindergartens in Toronto, Ontario: criticism regarding value, 150-51; Elizabeth Street School kindergarten, 148; expansion, 150; Froebelian pedagogy until 1930s, 148-50; idea of unified kindergarten-primary work, 151-54; introduction of kindergartens, 144-46; standardized training at Toronto Normal School, 147, 148
public kindergartens in United States: in St. Louis, Missouri, 127, 146, 147

Public Nursery, Infant Ragged School, and Laundry, 91
punishment: corporal, 22, 34; shaming, 22; Wilderspin's attitude toward, 19, 22, 34; Wilson's approach, 35
Puriri mission school (New Zealand), 69-70
Putnam, Alice, 201
Pye, Emmeline, 157

Quebec: age of compulsory schooling, 42; childcare in crèches, 95-96; Children's Protection Act (1944), 99; daycare (in *salles d'asile*), 95; infant schools in Quebec, 46, 47-48; public kindergartens, 143
Queensland, Australia, 157
Quinney, Amelia. *See* Crowley, Amelia (née Quinney)

"race experience," 5
racial recapitulation theories, 4, 121, 124
Ragged School Union, 113
ragged schools, 111-15
Read, Jane, 162
reading: in infant schools in Britain, 15, 27; "protection" from pressures of reading in kindergarten, 7
Reconstructionists' approach to kindergarten pedagogy, 148, 149-50
Reddall, Thomas, 49
reform schools, 19
Regina Industrial School (Canada), 142
religion and early childhood education: at Bristol Infant School, 23; Christian duty to give aid to the poor, 116; different opinions in infant school guide books, 26, 36; in ragged schools, 112
religious conversion, 10, 54-55, 56, 60
residential schools in Canada: Alderville Manual Labour School as first such school, 62; combination of industrial and mission schools, 83-84, 139-40; Crowstand Boarding School, 142; failure, 83-84;

favoured approach to Indian education after 1840, 64-65; incorporation of kindergartens, 139-42; indigenous parents as "obstacles" to assimilation of children, 83-84; industrial schools, 141-42; racialized and church-based schooling, 64-65
Reynolds, Rachel, 138, 219
Rice Lake Mission in Ontario, 60-61
Richmond, Mary, 167, 219-21, 225
Ridgway, R.B., 23, 27, 28, 36
Riis, Jacob, 116-17, 118
Riley, Nettie Birkenhead, 220-23, 225, 247
Robertson House Kindergarten (Winnipeg), 184
Robertson Memorial Presbyterian Church (Winnipeg), 184
Ronge, Bertha, 105, 111, 113
Ronge, Johannes, 105, 111, 113
Rooke, Patricia, 95
Ross, George W., 143
Rousseau, Jean-Jacques, 12
Routh, C.H.F., 97
Royal Commission on Employment of Children in Factories, 40-41
Runyan, Mary, 237, 249
Rupert's Land industrial school (Canada), 141-42
Russell, William, 34, 40

salles d'asile, 95
"salvation narrative," 10
Samoan infant schools, 76-79
Samuel Cohen Kindergarten for Deaf Children, 217
San Francisco: centre of free-kindergarten movement, 127; establishment of free kindergartens through philanthropy, 125, 128-31, 169, 204
San Francisco Produce Exchange, 129
Sanderson, Michael, 40
Saskatchewan kindergartens, 143
Savage, Michael, 232
Scheppler, Louise, 14, 28

Schissel, Bernard, 64-65
Schnell, R.L., 95
School Architecture (Barnard), 39
Schrader-Breymann, Henriette, 9, 110
Schwedler, Fanny, 126
Scientific Educational Institution for the Higher Social Classes, 19
Scott, Edna: director of Taranaki Street Nursery School, 233; studying nursery school methods in US, 232, 247; on use of Montessori materials in kindergarten, 225; on using Gifts at Wellington FKA, 225; work at Wellington FKA, 221-22, 233
Select Committee Investigating the Social Conditions of the Working Class, 114
Select Committee on Aborigines (Britain), 54, 82
Select Committee on Education (Britain), 34
Select Committee on the Education of People in England and Wales (Britain), 86
Select Committee on the Education of the Poorer Classes (Britain), 27
Select Committee on the Extinction of Slavery (Britain), 41
Selfe, Norma, 212-13
Selfe, Rhoda, 212-13
Selwyn, George, 71, 79
Sennett, Alfred, 91-92
settlement houses and kindergartens, 10, 128, 176, 242
Shahwahnekzhih (Henry Bird Steinhauer), 62, 63(i)
Shaw, Pauline Agassiz, 128
Shelley, Elizabeth, 65-66
Shelley, William, 65-66
short-time system, 41
Sifton, Clifford, 133
Silver Street Kindergarten (San Francisco), 128
Simon, Judith, 71

Simpson, Martha M., 162-63, 226
Slack, Ella, 215, 247
Smith, Adolphe, 116
Smith, Barbara Leigh, 22, 23-24
Smith, Benjamin Leigh, 23-24
Smith, John, 157
Smith, Linda Tuhiwai, 71
Smith, Meredith, 190
Smith, Nora Archibald, 107, 238-39, 241, 248-49
Smith, Olive, 187
Social Development in Young children (Isaacs), 233
Society for Ethical Culture, 126
Society for Family and Popular Education, 110
Society Islands (modern Tahiti) infant schools, 78-79
Society of Methodist Indians, 58
South African infant schools in Cape Town, 73-74
South Seas infant schools, 76-79
Southwest Africa kindergartens in Namibia, 6
Speyer School Kindergarten, 240
Spitalfields school (Britain), 20-22, 34
St. Andrew's Church (Dunedin, New Zealand), 138
St. James' Anglican Church (Sydney, Australia), 48
St. James' Infant School (Sydney), 48-49, 50
St. Louis, Missouri, kindergartens, 127, 146-47
St. Mary's Infant School (Walthamstow, Britain), 34
St. Michael's at Duck Lake, Saskatchewan, 140(i), 141
St. Phillip's Infant School (Sydney), 50
Stanford, Jane, 128, 131
Stanford, Leyland, 128
Stannard, David, 98
Starling, Ruby, 212-13
Stella Avenue Mission (Winnipeg), 175
Stockton, Betsey, 61-62
Stout, Anna, 137

Stout, Robert, 137
Stovall, Anna M., 129
Stow, David, 38-39
Sub-Dalton Plan, 228-29
Sunday, John, 59
Surry Hills kindergarten, 209
Suter, Andrew Burn, 137-38
Swedenborg, Emanuel, 23-24
Sydney Day Nursery Association, 210
Sydney Foundling Institution (SFI), 93, 115
Sydney Gazette, 49
Sydney Kindergarten Teachers College (SKTC) (Australia): centre of training in Australia, 168; changes in line with US-style nursery school education, 215; influence of Montessori on students, 212-13; nursery school option, 215-16; practical training under Dumolo, 211-12; reinforcement of bond with Britain, 8-9; students' travel to United States, 211
System of Education for the Young (Wilderspin), 28
System of Infants' Schools (Wilson), 34
systems for infant schools: Andrew Bell's system, 26; emulation, 21-22; gallery instruction, 20, 27, 30(i), 31-32, 35-36, 39, 42-43, 237; guide books or manuals, 26-27, 34, 36-38; learning aids for mathematics and geometry, 30-31; lesson posts, 29-30, 31, 39, 66-67; monitorial, 27-28, 31-32, 49, 88; New Lanark system, 14-15, 29; Pestalozzi system, 36, 50-51, 60, 259n63; picture lessons, 30, 36; punishment, 19, 22, 34; results of infant system, 39, 75; simultaneous instruction with child monitors, 31; standardization of methods and materials, 38-39; Wilderspin's "Infant System," 26, 28, 29-32, 37; Wilson's system, 34-36, 37. *See also* Froebelism; Lancasterian system

335

systems for kindergartens. *See* Froebel, Friedrich; Gifts (Froebelian)

Tahiti (*formerly* Society Islands) infant schools, 78-79
Taranaki Street Kindergarten, 220, 224
Taranaki Street Nursery School, 233
Tasmania (Van Diemen's Land), 44, 115, 158
Tate, Caroline, 139
Tate, Charles, 139
Taylor, Alan, 58
Teachers' Manual of Elementary Laundry Work (Calder), 243
Temple, Alice, 149, 150
Temple School (kindergarten), 125
Thematic Review of Early Childhood Education and Care (OECD), 3
Thompson, Florence, 5-6, 8
Thompson, Laura, 144
Thomson, John, 116
Tilke, Wilmott Huxtable (Ann), 51, 52
The Times (London), 1, 252n4
Tini (Maori woman), 69-70
Toronto, Ontario: childcare in foundling homes/daycare, 93-95; York Infant School, 44-45. *See also* public kindergartens in Toronto
Toronto Globe, 150-51
Toronto Kindergarten Association, 152-53
Toronto Lying-In Hospital, 96
Toronto Normal School, 147, 148, 177
Toronto Public Nursery, 95-96, 100
Trace, Margaret, 251
Treaty of Waitangi (New Zealand, 1840), 54
Truro Normal School (Nova Scotia), 136
Turner, D.A., 26, 27

United States: free kindergartens in San Francisco, 125, 127, 128-31, 169, 204; growth of day nurseries, 101; indigenous kindergartens, 124, 138-39; kindergarten teacher-training schools, 187; move away from Froebelian pedagogy, 150; nursery school trends, 215-16; private kindergartens, 125; public kindergartens in St. Louis, Missouri, 127, 146, 147; urbanization at end of 1800s, 132. *See also* free kindergartens in United States; Golden Gate Kindergarten Association
United States Bureau of Indian Affairs, 124
Upper Canada. *See* Ontario
Use of Kindergarten Gifts (Fulmer), 251

Van Die, Marguerite, 103
Van Diemen's Land. *See* Tasmania
Vicinus, Martha, 10
Victoria (Australia): baby farming, 99; first public school kindergarten, 157; infants' classes, 157; Melbourne Kindergarten Training College, 215; Melbourne Teachers College, 157, 203
Vincent Square Infant School, 20, 24-25
Von Marenholtz-Bülow, Bertha, 110, 111, 148-49

Waddell, Rutherford, 137-38
Waikato Mission, New Zealand, 70
Waimate mission school (New Zealand), 70-71, 72(i)
Waldorf Schools, 8, 254n29
Walker, George Washington, 74
Walker, Mary, 112, 136, 214, 218
Waters, Margaret, 99
Watson, William, 66-68, 74
Watts, Isaac, 48
Weber, Evelyn, 110, 149, 151
Webster, Thomas, 27
Welfare Council of Winnipeg, 198-99
Wellington, New Zealand, 135
Wellington Free Kindergarten Association (Wellington FKA): changes with new directors, 247; conversion of two kindergartens into nursery

schools during World War II, 233; crime-prevention role, 224-25; debate over value of kindergarten, 231-32; enrolment dependent on number of student-teachers, 221-22; facilities, 220; founding (1905), 167, 219-20; Froebel activities and curriculum, 225; grants and subsidies, 222, 231-32; introduction of nursery schools, 232; Montessori materials, 225; moral teaching, 223, 224, 225; new orientation and changes for kindergarten, 229-31; orientation toward Australia and England, 220-23, 226-29, 232-34, 246; parents' motivation for sending children to kindergarten, 223-24; primary class, 223; settlement-oriented ideas regarding manual education, 242-43; study visits and introduction of change, 232, 247; teacher-training changes under Wilson, 229-31; teacher training program under Riley, 221-23, 224(t); training for kindergarteners by employer, 247, 250(i); use of Gifts, 223(t), 225

Wellington Valley Mission for Wiradjuri people, Australia, 66-67

Wells Memorial House (Minneapolis), 178

Wertheimer, Joseph, 37, 104

Wesleyan Missionary Society, 62, 69

Western Australia, 158

Western Canada: diverse training for kindergarten teachers, 187-88; funding for public kindergartens, 143-44, 146, 173, 197-98

Western State Normal School, 184, 185(t)

Westminster Free Day Infant Asylum, 18, 25-26. *See also* Westminster Infant School

Westminster Infant School, 18, 20, 22, 24-25

Westminster Infant School Committee, 18-19, 20-21

wet nurses, 96-97

Wheelock, Lucy, 149-50

Wiebé, Edward, 104-5

Wiggin, Kate Douglas: on child's reaction to kindergarten activities, 241; circle time in kindergarten, 238-39; on Froebel's "Gifts," 107, 248-49; fundraising for kindergarten, 130; kindergarten teacher in San Francisco, 128; lectures on Froebelian pedagogy, 149

Wilderspin, Samuel: attitude toward punishment, 19, 22, 34, 237; claim to having originated infant school system, 25, 28; collection of rhymes, 22; on corrupting influence of children's parents, 13, 236-37; on crime reduction through infant schools, 13, 21; criticism of Buchanan and his school, 25, 86; criticism of Wilson's "folds," 35; description of infant system to House of Commons, 86; *Infant Education,* 28, 29-30, 33(i); infant system, 25, 26, 28, 29-32, 37; influence in Europe, 104; influence on colonial infant schools, 45, 48-49; on maintaining control in infant schools, 37; on moral agenda of infant schools, 13; organization of pupils in infant schools, 29-30, 32; promotion of infant system, 37-39; religious beliefs and influence of Swedenborg, 23, 28-29, 36; on teaching youngest children, 37; training by Buchanan at Spitalfields school, 20-21, 28; training of local teachers, 37, 38; on use of playgrounds, 32-33

Wildman, James Beckford, 41

Wilkins, William, 154-56, 158-60

Williams, Henry, 69-70

Williams, John, 75, 76

Williams, Talcott, 121, 122, 128

Wilson, Daniel, 74

Wilson, Enid Thelma: changes to teacher-training program at Wellington FKA, 229-31; introduction of "Dalton Plan" into sub-primary class, 228; introduction of nursery schools in New Zealand, 232; organizer of Montessori preschool in Perth, 227-28; principal of Wellington FKA, 229-33; study with Isaacs in London, 232, 247; training and work in Western Australia, 226, 246

Wilson, George S., 124

Wilson, Joseph, 20, 32, 34

Wilson, William: advocate of Bible-based approach to moral education, 36; founder of St. Mary's Infant School, 34; infant school system, 34-36, 37, 152; on maintaining control in infant schools, 37; "objects" of infant schools, 2

Wilson Industrial School's Kitchen Garden program, 183

Windeyer, Margaret, 115, 137

Windeyer, Mary, 115

Winnipeg, Manitoba: criticism of public schools (1948), 197-98; decision not to open public kindergartens (1892), 173; lack of funding of public kindergartens (1883), 146; public support for kindergartens, 197-98. *See also* Winnipeg Free Kindergarten Association (Winnipeg FKA)

Winnipeg Federation for Community Services, 191

Winnipeg Free Kindergarten Association (Winnipeg FKA) (*later* Kindergarten Settlement Association of Winnipeg): assimilation of ethnically diverse children, 180-81, 182; association with Methodist All People's Mission, 172; connection with Oberlin training school, 187, 195, 250; demographics of kindergarten children, 180-81, 191; educational and vocational role of kindergarten, 188; Ellen Street Kindergarten, 173, 175, 182, 240; emphasis on child development, 189; enrolment, 173, 174, 175, 181; expansion of services, 136, 174-77, 192; financial support, 191; founding, 136; Froebelian approach and Froebel School, 172, 174-75, 179, 184, 189-90; fundraising, 173-74; health care, 191-92; home visits and social work, 177, 192; impact of World War I, 183-84; on kindergarten as solution to civil and political unrest, 170; kindergarten structure and activities, 181-82; Kitchen Garden program for older children, 183, 192; Maple Street Mission Kindergarten, 177; Methodist All People's Mission Kindergarten, 177, 178(i); moral training for children, 182-83, 188; mothers' meetings, 176; perception of poor families, 175, 182-83, 186; progressive ideas in early 1900s, 184-86, 188-90; settlement work, 176-77; social-welfare and educational service, 136, 172-73; teacher training, 177-79, 186-88, 192, 247. *See also* Kindergarten Settlement Association of Winnipeg (KSAW)

Winnipeg Free Kindergarten Association Training School, 177-79, 186-88, 192, 247

Winnipeg Neighbourhood House, 198-99

Winterer, Caroline, 40

Wiradjuri people of Australia, 66-68

Woman's League of the German Colonial Society, 6

Woodfull, T.S., 166-67

Woodson, Belle, 239, 244, 246

Woolloomooloo kindergarten (Sydney, NSW): belief in malleability of young children, 9; changes to pedagogy, 214; first